Information Strategy Design and Practices

Sanjay Mohapatra · Ranjan Prasad Singh

Information Strategy Design and Practices

Sanjay Mohapatra
Xavier Institute of Management
Bhubaneswar, Orissa, India

Ranjan Prasad Singh
Enterprise System Solutions (P) Ltd
Bhubaneswar, Orissa, India

ISBN 978-1-4614-2427-7   e-ISBN 978-1-4614-2428-4
DOI 10.1007/978-1-4614-2428-4
Springer New York Dordrecht Heidelberg London

Library of Congress Control Number: 2011945851

© Springer Science+Business Media, LLC 2012
All rights reserved. This work may not be translated or copied in whole or in part without the written permission of the publisher (Springer Science+Business Media, LLC, 233 Spring Street, New York, NY 10013, USA), except for brief excerpts in connection with reviews or scholarly analysis. Use in connection with any form of information storage and retrieval, electronic adaptation, computer software, or by similar or dissimilar methodology now known or hereafter developed is forbidden.
The use in this publication of trade names, trademarks, service marks, and similar terms, even if they are not identified as such, is not to be taken as an expression of opinion as to whether or not they are subject to proprietary rights.

Printed on acid-free paper

Springer is part of Springer Science+Business Media (www.springer.com)

To
Our family members
Dr. Baishnab, Hrishikesh, Kanyakumari,
Bharati, Sanjana, and Shrestha
AND
N. K. Kanth Niraj, Suniti,
Priti, Astha, and Archit

Preface

The Reason for this Book

Information strategy has changed over a period of time. From being a tool for aiding business activities, it has become a business enabler and slowly has taken a strategic role in an organization. Strategy level decisions and directions are always a challenge to any management. These decisions guide functional and operational level managers. The information strategy domain has encompassed the strategic level and is increasing its presence in the boardroom as well. But the influence of technology has to be understood well so that the alignment with business remains.

The alignment of information strategy with business has several problems. However, these problems can be categorized into (1) issues related to rapid changes related to business strategy implementation, (2) need for human intervention for implementing and interpreting IS, and (3) awareness and knowledge on technology. In addition to this, there is always a need for revisiting information strategy from the perspective of business strategy and technology. The book addresses these issues through theoretical overview and implementable, practicable, and feasible approaches.

Over the years, IS has always been aiding functional and operational challenges. As a result, the true potential of IS has never been exploited. The book throws light on the role of IS at strategy level and partnering with business units to get the maximum business benefits. The approach for implementing IS, as explained in this book, is shown to be more people centric, involving all stakeholders and collaborating with business users. Key issues to implementing these strategies are discussed, and frameworks for designing the strategy as well as implementing have been presented.

The book is divided into two parts—the first part provides a detailed theoretical concepts required for understanding the role of IS at strategy level; it also provides frameworks for designing the IS for business benefits. It then discusses the need to involve stakeholders while designing the IS and the steps that need to be followed to achieve business alignment in a systematic and scientific way. The framework discussed here has been derived based on consulting assignments that the authors have carried out and hence are implementable and practicable. The book also provides case studies where the authors discuss the way IS can be designed and implemented. These case studies are from different industries and show how the framework can be used universally with customization as required.

Audience for the Book

The students who have background on basic strategic management and understand basic information systems will benefit the most. These students should have gone through different perspectives in strategic management courses, understanding the need for vision, mission, and business goals for an organization, how strategy is formulated using techniques such as SWOT, Balanced Scorecard, and Porter's five forces theory. It will be optional for these students to have been exposed to case studies in strategic management as these are dealt in this book prominently. In addition, the students should also have basic knowledge on information systems and their applications. For example, the students should have exposure to courses such as management information system or business information system or the like so that they would have footings on IS when they attend this subject. Typically, the book will find acceptance in master in business administration (MBA), postgraduate diploma in management (PGDM) programs. The students who would be specializing in information system and general management need this book, as it explains the frameworks from strategy designers' view.

The book will also be useful for consultants engaged in IT consulting and management consulting who advise business houses on strategy formulation and integration of information system. The consultants will find it handy, as they can use the proven frameworks with tweaks, if required, for their customers. They can also use it for providing training for designing and implementing information systems.

Senior executives and functional heads could use it for learning and applying the concepts in their organizations. They can align their business strategy with IS to meet their business goals. Corporate trainers could use the book for providing training on the role of IS, the need for IS, providing business alignment with IS.

Notes for Faculty

The book has the following pedagogical features:

- Learning objectives at the start of each chapter
- Summary at the end of each chapter
- Further readings for the concepts discussed in the chapter
- Review questions for the students to practice
- PowerPoint (.ppt) files for each chapter will be provided to the faculty; please contact local representatives from Springer

Bhubaneswar, Orissa, India   Sanjay Mohapatra
                                                                                                                    Ranjan Prasad Singh

Acknowledgments

The production of any book of this magnitude involves valued contributions from many persons. We would like to thank Amboy Matthew for providing us the editorial support and making this project a reality.

The book has been tested in class and we are thankful to the students from Xavier Institute of Management Bhubaneswar (India), Catholic University of Yaonde' (Cameroon, Africa) for their feedback in making it "class ready". In particular, we would like to thank Ankur Singh, Sumedh Kiran Vijayakar, Rupaj Das, Swarup Kumar Kar, Udaya Bhanu Satapathy, Zubair Jiwani, Abhinav Gupta, Gaurav Kayal, Rahul Nishit, Abhinav Mathur, Gaurav Mundra, Sourabh Choudhary, Ayan Dasgupta, Chandrasekhar Kartha, Mriganka sarkar, Pradeep Rajendran, Pradipta Acharya, Shakti Prasanna Mohapatra, Satya Suranjeet Behera, Siddharth Mohanty, Subhra Prakash Rath, Soumya Dash, Sumit Ranjan Das, Vivek Chandan Mohapatra, Snehasish Mahapatra, Sudeep Vaidya, Bandita Aruk, Anurag Pruthy, Ashwin Narayanan, and Dhanya K. for their contributions.

Our teachers, who have always encouraged me to learn by devloping conceptual ideas, experimentation and analysis. A special thanks to Late Medini Prasad Singh, my first teacher. They have helped me to orient to an attitude of aquiring knowledge and sharing with others, even though it is tiny piece of learning but useful to others. In this book I have just tried to do so.

Our friends and colleagues, who have been engaging into patient discussion and sharing their knowledge with me that helped to refine my understanding and approach to strategise and implement IT at clients' place. This has helped me to take wholistic view of IT, experiment with my ideas and evolve a practical and fruitful strategy.

Last but not the least, we would like to thank our family members who have been with us, shouldering many responsibilities while absolving us from many worldly activities.

Contents

1 **Understanding IT Strategy** 1
   1.1 Learning Objectives 1
   1.2 Introduction 1
   1.3 Historical View of IT Focus 2
   1.4 Roles of IT 4
   1.5 Strategic Intent 8
   1.6 Major Components of IT Strategy 10
      1.6.1 Business Purpose 11
      1.6.2 A New Strategic Mindset 12
      1.6.3 Holistic Approach 15
      1.6.4 Approach to Green IT 16
      1.6.5 Globalization 18
   1.7 Technology in Agriculture 19
      1.7.1 How it Works 19
      1.7.2 Remote Sensing 20
      1.7.3 GIS and Production Agriculture 20
      1.7.4 How it Works in Rural India 20
      1.7.5 Benefits 22
   1.8 Summary 22
   1.9 Glossary 23
   1.10 Review Questions 23
   1.11 Project Work 23
   Bibliography 24

2 **Getting Ready for IT Strategy** 25
   2.1 Learning Objectives 25
   2.2 Introduction 25
   2.3 Evolution of IT Strategy 26
   2.4 New Direction of IT Strategy 31
      2.4.1 Business Internal 31
      2.4.2 Business External 32

	2.5	Need for IT Alignment with Business	37
	2.6	Changing IT Strategy for Different Stages in Business Life Cycle	40
	2.7	A New Role for CIO	44
		2.7.1 Strategic Planning	44
		2.7.2 IT Alignment with Business	44
		2.7.3 Budget Formulation and Capital Planning and Investment Control	45
		2.7.4 E-Government and IT Implementation	45
		2.7.5 Programme Management and Performance	45
		2.7.6 Security and Privacy	45
		2.7.7 Salesperson	46
		2.7.8 Visionary and Business Focused	47
		2.7.9 Business Transformation and Change Agent	47
		2.7.10 Information Asset Promoter	48
		2.7.11 IT Manager (Organization Management)	51
		2.7.12 Creating a Culture of Performance and Value	53
	2.8	Planning for IT Strategy	54
		2.8.1 Collect Data Related to Business	55
		2.8.2 Prepare Management Team	55
		2.8.3 Initiate Collaboration Plan	56
		2.8.4 Create Mind Set for Process Re-engineering and Business Alignment	56
		2.8.5 Focus at Business Benefit and Investment	57
	2.9	Summary	58
	2.10	Glossary	58
	2.11	Review Questions	59
	2.12	Project Work	59
	Bibliography		59
3	**IT Strategy Framework**		**61**
	3.1	Learning Objectives	61
	3.2	Introduction	61
	3.3	Understanding of Existing Relation Between IT and Business	64
	3.4	Business Strategy and Drivers	69
	3.5	Stakeholders and Their Business Needs	73
	3.6	Process Strategy and Alignment	78
		3.6.1 Process Reengineering	79
		3.6.2 Functional Grouping and New Structure	84
		3.6.3 Opportunity Search	85
	3.7	Application and Integration Strategy	87
		3.7.1 Business Application Strategy	88
		3.7.2 Information and Data Architecture	94
		3.7.3 Infrastructure Application	96
		3.7.4 Application Portfolio: Physical Application Strategy	97
		3.7.5 Migration Strategy	98

	3.8	Technology Strategy (Including Convergence)	99
		3.8.1 Strategy for Technology Platform and Component	100
		3.8.2 Security Strategy	103
		3.8.3 Backup and Recovery Strategy	107
		3.8.4 Logical and Physical Architecture	108
	3.9	Summary	110
	3.10	Glossary	111
	3.11	Review Questions	112
	3.12	Project Work	112
	3.13	Annexure A	112
		3.13.1 CRUD Matrix	112
		3.13.2 Technologies Being Used for Security (Brightman and Buith 2009)	113
	References		113
4	**Strategy Implementation**	115
	4.1	Learning Objectives	115
	4.2	Introduction	115
	4.3	People Strategy	116
		4.3.1 Organization Design	118
		4.3.2 People Enablement	120
	4.4	IT Service Strategy	124
		4.4.1 Cost Centre or Profit Centre	133
		4.4.2 Cost Centre	134
		4.4.3 Profit Centre	134
		4.4.4 Vertical Organization or Matrix	135
		4.4.5 Make-it or Buy-it	135
		4.4.6 Recruit/Train or Hire	137
		4.4.7 Outsourcing or Co-Sourcing	138
		4.4.8 SaaS, BOOT or Own	141
		4.4.9 Open Source or Proprietary Platform	142
		4.4.10 Compliance	143
		4.4.11 Standards and Process Models	145
	4.5	Metrics and Measurement	149
		4.5.1 Risk Management	151
	4.6	EV and ROI	156
	4.7	Strategy Approval and Governances	161
	4.8	Summary	164
	4.9	Glossary	165
	4.10	Preview Questions	166
	4.11	Project Work	166
	4.12	Annexure A	167
		4.12.1 Cost heads	167
		4.12.2 Benefit heads	168

		4.13	Annexure 2	169
			4.13.1 IT Strategy and eStrategy	169
			4.13.2 Business Content Services	171
	Bibliography			173
5	**Learning Objectives**			**175**
	5.1	Introduction		176
	5.2	Industry Analysis		176
		5.2.1	Thermal Power	177
		5.2.2	About OPGC	177
		5.2.3	Vision and Mission	178
		5.2.4	Objectives	178
		5.2.5	Future Plans	178
		5.2.6	Stake Holders	179
		5.2.7	IT Department	179
		5.2.8	Growth of IT in the Organization	180
		5.2.9	Current IT Infrastructure	181
		5.2.10	Sample Process Overviews	182
		5.2.11	Business Capability Roadmap	183
	5.3	Research Framework		183
	5.4	Approaches for IT Strategy		184
		5.4.1	Key Business Drivers as Factors of ITS	186
	5.5	SWOT Analysis		186
		5.5.1	Strategic Map	187
		5.5.2	Balanced Scorecard	188
		5.5.3	Benchmarking	191
		5.5.4	Critical Success Factors	192
	5.6	Business Process Modelling and Recommendations		192
		5.6.1	Customer Management	193
		5.6.2	Knowledge Management	196
		5.6.3	Energy Management System	198
		5.6.4	Plant Management System	198
		5.6.5	Performance Monitoring System	199
		5.6.6	Energy Capital Management	200
		5.6.7	Availability Based Tariff	200
		5.6.8	Current ERP System: RAMCO	200
		5.6.9	Proposed ERP System: SAP	201
		5.6.10	Additional Systems	203
	5.7	Approach for Implementation of IT Strategy		204
		5.7.1	Implementation Plan	204
		5.7.2	Road Map	205
		5.7.3	Training	208
		5.7.4	Change Management	209
		5.7.5	Proposed IT Organization Structure Changes	212

5.8		Cost Benefit Analysis: ROI	218
5.9		Risk Analysis	221
	5.9.1	Probability Determination for Identified Risks	222
	5.9.2	Risk Mitigation	222
5.10		Practice Questions	223
5.11		Appendix	223
	5.11.1	Appendix 1: OPGC Financial Credentials	223
	5.11.2	Appendix 2: Questionnaire	223
	5.11.3	Appendix 3: Topology of the Earlier System (Source OPGC)	224
	5.11.4	Appendix 4: Sample Risk Management Form	225
	5.11.5	Appendix 5: OPGC Balance Sheet	226
	5.11.6	Appendix 6: OPGC Internal Target Operating Model	226

6 Case Study: IT Strategy for Mayfair ... 229

6.1		Learning Objectives	229
6.2		Executive Summary	229
6.3		Hospitality Industry	230
	6.3.1	Introduction	230
	6.3.2	Characteristics	231
	6.3.3	Issues and Challenges	232
	6.3.4	Major players	232
6.4		Mayfair	234
	6.4.1	About Mayfair	234
	6.4.2	Services offered	234
	6.4.3	Future Plans	236
6.5		Vision	236
6.6		Mission	236
6.7		Business Objectives	236
6.8		Corporate Strategy	237
	6.8.1	Balance Score Card	237
	6.8.2	SWOT Analysis	238
	6.8.3	Business Problem Statement	239
	6.8.4	What Is the Problem/Issue at Hand?	239
	6.8.5	Interrelationship of These Concepts: "Constructs"	240
	6.8.6	What Is/Are Fundamental in this Construct W.R.T. the Issue?	240
6.9		Benchmarking	242
	6.9.1	Scope of Benchmarking	242
	6.9.2	Benchmarking with Similar Hotels	242
6.10		Hotel Business Processes	244
	6.10.1	Key Business Processes to be Targeted	244
6.11		Evolution of IT Infrastructure at Mayfair	245
	6.11.1	Growth of IT	245
	6.11.2	Current IT Architecture	245

		6.11.3	Benefits of Current IT System	246
	6.12	Factors Affecting IT Strategy		246
		6.12.1	Industry Characteristics	247
		6.12.2	Organization	247
		6.12.3	Process Flow	247
	6.13	Alternatives		248
	6.14	Need for a CIO		249
		6.14.1	Job Advertisement	250
	6.15	Architecture		251
		6.15.1	Business Process Modelling	251
	6.16	Technology		256
		6.16.1	Modules Provided by SAP Business One	257
		6.16.2	Architecture of SAP Business One	257
	6.17	Organization Structure for Implementation		259
		6.17.1	Current Organization Structure	259
		6.17.2	Proposed Organization Structure	260
	6.18	Approach for Implementation		261
		6.18.1	Roadmap	261
		6.18.2	Implementation Plan	263
		6.18.3	Training	264
		6.18.4	Change Management	264
	6.19	Budget and ROI		265
		6.19.1	IT Strategy for Mayfair	265
	6.20	Benefits of IT Implementation at Mayfair		267
	6.21	Risks and Mitigation		268
	6.22	Practice Questions		269
	References			269
7	**IT Strategy for iSOFT Plc**			**271**
	7.1	Learning Objectives		271
	7.2	Executive Summary		272
	7.3	Introduction		272
	7.4	Overview of Healthcare Industry in the UK		272
		7.4.1	Value of the Market	273
		7.4.2	Factors Affecting the Industry	273
		7.4.3	Recent Developments	273
		7.4.4	Challenges	274
	7.5	iSOFT: The Company, an Overview		274
		7.5.1	About the Company	274
		7.5.2	Timeline	275
		7.5.3	Vision	275
		7.5.4	Mission	275
	7.6	LORENZO: Delivering the Future of Healthcare		275
		7.6.1	About the Product	275
		7.6.2	Uses	276
		7.6.3	Other Benefits of LORENZO	276

		7.6.4	Stakeholders	276
	7.7	Corporate Strategy		277
		7.7.1	Brainstorming	277
		7.7.2	Corporate Strategy	278
	7.8	Factors Affecting IT Strategy		278
	7.9	Risks for LORENZO		279
		7.9.1	IT Risks	280
		7.9.2	Non-IT Risks	280
		7.9.3	Risk Mitigation Techniques	280
	7.10	IT Security		281
		7.10.1	Firewall	281
		7.10.2	Data Encryption	282
		7.10.3	Information Security Management System (ISMS)	282
	7.11	IT Strategy for Innovation		283
	7.12	MIS		285
	7.13	Architecture		286
	7.14	Benchmarking		288
	7.15	Change Management		290
	7.16	IT Audit		291
	7.17	ROI Framework		292
		7.17.1	Benefits of Lorenzo	292
		7.17.2	Investments	293
	7.18	The Road Ahead		293
	7.19	Practice Questions		294
	7.20	Appendix 1: UK Central Government Spending		294
	7.21	Appendix 2: Timeline of iSOFT		296
	7.22	Appendix 3: Applications of LORENZO		297
	References			297
8	**IT Strategy for McDonald's**			**299**
	8.1	Learning Objectives		299
	8.2	Executive Summary		299
	8.3	Company Background		300
		8.3.1	McCafés	301
		8.3.2	Business Model	301
		8.3.3	Scale of Operations	302
	8.4	Industry Scenario (Fast Food and Quick-Service Restaurants)		302
		8.4.1	Industry Overview	302
	8.5	Key Points About Fast Food Industry		304
	8.6	McDonald's Vision Statement		305
	8.7	Mission Statement		306
	8.8	Corporate Strategy and IT Strategy		306
		8.8.1	Corporate Strategy and IT Strategy	306
		8.8.2	Corporate Strategy Focus Area I	306
		8.8.3	Corporate Strategy Focus Area II	307

		8.8.4	Corporate Strategy Focus Area III	308
		8.8.5	Corporate Strategy Focus Area IV	309
	8.9	Factors to Consider When Designing the IT Strategy		309
	8.10	SWOT Analysis		310
		8.10.1	Strengths	310
		8.10.2	Weakness	310
		8.10.3	Opportunities	310
		8.10.4	Threats	311
	8.11	McDonald's Operations and Where It Could Be Used		311
	8.12	Balanced Scorecard		312
	8.13	Change Management		313
	8.14	Management Information System		314
		8.14.1	Applications of MIS	315
		8.14.2	Data Processing	315
		8.14.3	Management by Objectives	315
		8.14.4	Benefits of MIS	316
		8.14.5	Core Competencies	316
		8.14.6	Enhance Supply Chain Management	316
		8.14.7	Quick Reflexes	316
	8.15	Return on Investment		317
	8.16	Conclusion		318
	8.17	Practice Questions		318
	Web Site			318
9	**Devising IT Strategy for a Non-Government Organization: CTRAN Consulting**			**319**
	9.1	Learning Objectives		319
	9.2	Executive Summary		319
	9.3	Introduction		320
	9.4	Mission		320
	9.5	Industry Background		321
	9.6	Company Background		321
		9.6.1	Partners	321
		9.6.2	The Competition	322
	9.7	Pricing Strategy		322
	9.8	Business Objectives		323
	9.9	Stakeholders		323
	9.10	Process Flow		323
	9.11	Balance Score Card		325
	9.12	Current Issues and Challenges		326
	9.13	IT Strategy		326
	9.14	Architecture Design		329
	9.15	Access Rights		330
	9.16	Implementation Strategy		330
		9.16.1	Rewards and Recognition	332

9.17	Risks and Mitigation	333
9.18	Return on Investment	334
9.19	Conclusion	336
9.20	Practice Questions	336
	References	337

Index 339

Chapter 1
Understanding IT Strategy

1.1 Learning Objectives

This chapter would

- Introduce and provide overall perspective of IT strategy
- Explain high level business and IT relationship
- Provide high level view of rising influence of IT in business
- Enumerate IT strategy components

1.2 Introduction

Information technology (IT) has travelled a long distance but quickly to reach to the stage where it is today. It started as a help to accountants (Chuck 1998), who used to do lot of number crunching and has reached to the place where it is helping a new business model to evolve. Over the past few decades, IT has evolved to become an important part of organization resources. The credit goes to those researchers and the corporate which made it possible. They kept supporting the innovators and visionaries with matching technology to expand the usage in number of domains. The possibilities are created so many that many new business domains evolved around IT only, such as online marketing by Dell, e-commerce portals for buying tickets for air travel, etc. The depth and breadth of this technology has affected all business domains and has infused new life to them.

The characteristics and possibilities created by this technology have given a new opportunity to business managers for managing and improving their business. We can not imagine managing shelf stocks of thousands of items at Walmart's store manually without stock outage and chaos in supply chain. Today, the information from shelf stock in USA to producers in China are so well connected that Christmas sell in USA is so smooth without an outage and over inventory. We notice that the technology has helped manufacturer to reduce cost of production, supply chain operators to reduce lead time, inventory and logistics cost and consumers to reduce cost of ownership, thus touching depth and breadth of business, its suppliers, customers, investors and regulators. A simple case of geographic information system (GIS) based mapping (see Sect. 1.7) has opened number of possibilities for business whereby optimization of usage of natural resources, improvement in citizen centric services, capability building in defence and betterment in other areas could happen.

It is obvious that as the world will make progress the importance of information will keep rising, whether it relates to our day-to-day life, governance or business. And that makes this technology play a vital role in managing business, governance or customer service. Even in developing countries the business and the government started making different consumer and public demographic analysis to improve quality of their service and resource utilization (Heeks 2002; Mohapatra 2009).

If a technology, a tool or a technique creates such an impact on business, can a business manager ignore while planning or managing a business. The simple answer is "No" (White and Bruton 2007). Now the trend is different explain with reference to research. People have started thinking on new IT-based business propositions to aid to their business. The IT-based sales channel has created new business entities like Amazon and eBay.

We can observe the way IT has touched human life from conceiving in mother's womb till final cremation. The contribution of IT for medical equipments, which helps in identifying the pregnancy as well as assisting doctors and nurses during birth, is well known. Similarly at the end of one's life it helps to maintain death and cremation records. And during the life time of ours it touches every walk of life. Chuck (1998) feels that the rapid exploitation of power of this technology is still growing exponentially and that is evident in the growth of power of Intel processors (4.77 MHz in early 1980s to 3.77 GHz processors working in parallel) as well as spread of applications (from DOS-based small applications to Internet and cloud computing with rich user interface as well as remote sensing). Therefore it is pertinent to understand the role of IT and use it wisely for our benefit in different areas such as business, environment, science, our eco-system, education, eradication of diseases and poverty.

Thus IT deserves to be part of the strategy of an organization. It can certainly add to achieve the organizational vision and objectives. It depends on our own creativeness how we exploit its power. And this is what translates to IT strategy.

1.3 Historical View of IT Focus

The focus of the IT has been changing over the period (Chuck 1998; Mohapatra 2009; Collin 2008). Earlier it used to be data crunching and reporting to collaboration and support to business across geographic and organizational boundaries. Dell exploited its power for reaching to large customer and enabling them to assemble their product and accordingly check the price before ordering, where as US

Table 1.1 The evolution of IT strategy

Time frame	Developed countries—focus	Developing countries—focus
1970s	Separate business and IT planning	Data automation planning
1980s	Strategic planning Alignment of business and IT	Application planning with eye on functional efficiency
1990s	Business infrastructure building Joint business and IT planning	IT planning with focus on business support
2000s	Integrated business and IT planning Adaptive organization IT oriented business models Mass participation	IT planning—business orientation with focus on functional enablement through technology Mass communication

Immigration Services exploited its power for qualification of applicant and keeping records online for use and information to stake holders. Walmart used the power of IT to reduce cost of its supply chain and US Securities and Exchange Commission used it for better regulation. Many a times we also believe that IT could have been exploited even more which could have given better mileage when we observe either in citizen centric services (Heeks 2002) or planning for disaster management in emerging countries (Nasscom 2008). Realization of true potential of IT could have helped to achieve business objectives (Martin 1998) as it depicts demand and improves chances of utilization.

When we talk of IT we can't forget the initial technological hiccups like scarcity of trained manpower and role of trade unions in the past that it has crossed. Today trade unions like INTUC and affiliated Tata Workers' Union at Tata Steel, AITUC (All India Trade Union Congress) affiliated to Communist Party of India, ILO (www.ilo.org) are using IT-based resources to manage their organization. http://www.unionlearn.org.uk/ict/learn-759-f0.cfm talks of many such business cases from western economy. IT has been job provider in India and other IT service providing countries. As per NASSCOM, trade body and the chamber of commerce of the IT-BPO industries in India, IT has become the largest job provider and crossed two million mark in direct employment by March 2009 in organized private sector. It has improved quality of life and has helped unions to save the jobs of their members by making the business more competitive. Now, more or less the strength behind objections has diminished.

Let us look at the changing focus of IT over decades in developed and developing countries (Table 1.1).

The table clearly shows that rising capability over decades has also given a boost to role of IT in Businesses and Governance. It has made many things feasible today which were unthinkable yesterday such as integrated Journey Planner for London Tube, Book ordering on Amazon, US from India. Today many part of business strategy like competitiveness, pricing, performance of investment, governance, integration of functions across organizations, employee enablement, reaching to distant customers, communication and service quality depend on the power of IT that has been exploited in the business. Everyday a new business model is evolving and we notice that underneath infrastructure has been provided by IT.

1.4 Roles of IT

It is not true that IT can only serve the business where number accountancy is required. IT has many facets and that make it fit to support different objectives. It is important to know the varying capabilities of IT and exploit them properly for business needs. Let us look at the some the characteristics of IT which can be useful for different scenario. With our experience on strategic usage for different business models, we observed that the following enhances the power of IT and attraction of business towards it.

Speed and distance: It can help business to cover distance. Today IT is helping messages to reach farther distance in no time. The network mesh laid around the globe is helping to connect people, businesses and gover\nments. It has made possible for any one to interact with any system, service or individual located on other side of the globe, instantly.

Data storage and manipulation, which have been its function since inception, has improved drastically and matured too. Applications related to functions, like weather forecasting, space navigation, astronomy, disaster forecasting and many others where large data are to be quickly analysed, have become possible because of IT only.

Warehouse management systems for Walmart integrates manufacturing in china to retailing in US. The plans are made in US and electronically communicated to all parties involved in supply chain, the manufacturer, the shipper, the logistic service provider, the import/export clearing agent, the shipping service providers, the transporters as well as third party providers to get organized and service. The bottleneck is at port clearing and physical distance covering, otherwise the inventory cost could have been still lower.

Communication: It can help in communication, with or without visibility. People are communicating freely, online as well offline, across globes and tomorrow they will across planets. The communication media and data transmission infrastructure have provided excellent infrastructure to IT to make it happen. Its integration with Telecom has further boosted this feature.

Logistics service providers to Walmart make sure that export/import documents reaches to the custom at US as soon as ships leaves China port. This has been made possible only because of IT.

Today Governments publish their concept papers for any act on Internet for organizations, academia and general public to comment and collects feedback within stipulated time. Earlier this process of public participation was almost absent due to lack of such mass communication facility.

Today delivering seminars and courses on web and remotely have become possible with IT.

Control and scalability: IT has helped in building good control systems. It has helped in streamlining business processes, controlling manual discretions, measuring the performance, generating alerts and alarms and ensuring consistency.

1.4 Roles of IT

Today it has reduced the need of auditing as once system auditors certify the system, they control changes and system behaves consistent with respect to controls built in. I heard one of the senior partners from a multinational audit company saying that IT systems had brought good discipline across the business and now it is easier to locate the issues too.

It has also supported scalability need of the business. This can be easily understood if we imagine the number of book shops to be operated to replace Amazon book shelf. Today stocks, sales and discounts of any retail chain spread across geography are being maintained centrally and accordingly discounts, production and dispatches are planned.

Application systems in western world were being audited since long. Even forward looking organizations in India like Tata Steel and Larsen & Toubro has moved in that direction during late 1980s and early 1990s. A separate system group of auditors called System Auditors is created, who used to audit the requirement and business applications and certify different compliance levels. They also used to institute the change management process so that changes can be qualified against statutory requirement and organization's specified controls.

Cost benefit: It has helped in controlling cost of manufacturing, sales, supply, delivery and services. Finance managers of all business establishments will agree that IT has helped them in data keeping, analysis and making cost related decisions. The facility of information storage, analysis and making decisions have become so easy. Analysis and understanding of cost performance over many variables have been made feasible by IT only. Every action and cost impact of the same can be tracked and reported so easily.

Cost sheet of such organizations having IT systems in place are getting reported within weeks in stead of months in manual system. Also the coverage and presentation used to be much less at manually operated organizations than the ones where it is supported by IT. While evaluating an IT need for an organization from Steel industry from SME segment, we heard from CMD that he never got cost of production in time. It was usually delayed by 6 months or so and by that time scenario had changed, so his most of the decision used to be based on his overall understanding of business.

Record keeping and analysis: Maintaining records, whether they are because of statutory requirements or business needs, have become easier than ever. Data mining and data warehousing based services have given different impetus to business. The information and record generation, processing, storage, retrieval and analysis on historical data have provided ample opportunity to manage business better.

I have seen the shrinking space need of the data and record storage in Tata Steel and Oracle, India. More and more IT penetrated the business functions the need for storage kept on reducing. Managers started using IT infrastructure for their records and analysis. Even their supporting staffs and secretaries became proficient and comfortable in using electronic data. Many a times the space marked for storage in senior manager's secretariat was reorganized and space was utilized for different purpose.

Multimedia and animation: The world of animation would have been very primitive and selective if IT would not have contributed. Use of IT-based animation in learning, gaming, movies and other applications are clearly visible.

Pictures and movies creation with rich features and supported by voice and animation have contributed a lot to learning and entertainment. Today people are creating eLearning exercises to enable employees and making them productive quickly. This technology is being used extensively to make worker productive, quickly, and bringing in efficiency to the work. Forward looking organization like Maersk Shipping uses this feature of IT extensively. Even in one of the Sponge Iron Plants at Orissa the business manager has identified this as good tool to improve in plant operations and maintenance. People are using eLearning to make employees familiar with their business processes and exception handling. Additional features like simulated behaviour and calls have been a good way to train Call centre service providers.

Research and simulation: Today almost all medicine researches are happening with the help of IT examples. When these researchers talk of millions of possibilities, it is only IT which can help in assimilating those data and bringing out the right ones. It has reduced the total time between concepts to market.

Similarly designing and operating of simulation models, whether it is based on mathematics or behavioural science, have become easier then ever. Research in the areas of atomic technology and others where human life would have been at risk are now being done in labs with the help of IT. These simulation models have expedited the knowledge generation and made smarter usage of resources possible. It has helped social scientist in understanding the demography and designing the stimulators.

Small research organizations like Dr. Reddy Lab, Biocon and the pharmaceutical giants like Merck, GlaxoSmithKline use IT for Drug discovery, record of clinical trials and molecule formulation as well as business management. There are specialized software companies like SAS (www.sas.com) which are selling IT products for the pharma industry, helping them in concept to market. They offer end-to-end solution to drive efficiencies throughout drug's lifecycle: from discovery, through development, commercialization and beyond and claim benefit like saving of time and cost to their users.

IT is extensively used in Bio-science research. Even a specialized discipline called Bioinformatics appeared. *New methodological breakthroughs in sequencing, genomics, proteomics, bioinformatics and imaging are producing vast amounts of information* and to use them productively, IT is being used. Today IT is participating in research of nanotechnology as well.

Integration and collaboration: Imagine the consolidation of accounts for the corporate operating through number of branches or subsidiaries across regions and countries without IT. We may not be sure how much time and effort it would have taken to reconcile and consolidate but we can definitely say that it could not have met the current regulatory requirements.

This has also helped in integrating functions and departments to produce right results and performance whether it is in business or government. All of us are very familiar with blogs, social sites and many such Internet-based applications which have facilitated connection, collaboration and participation across society, countries and continents.

There are multiple examples of use of software to integrate business across the globe. Dell has an integrated system, where all Internet orders, emerging from all corners of globe are locally serviced and centrally used for demand analysis. Toyota's IT systems are providing order, stock and production visibility and facilitating data interchange with its suppliers, online. This collaboration has become one of the techniques for achieving efficiency, for which Toyota is known for.

Regulatory compliance: Every progress in business capability, whether it is IT or knowledge enabled, brings in more regulations and the need for compliance. The governance rules are getting more and more comprehensive and tougher day by day. The introduction of Sarbanes Oxley act of 2002 threw new challenges to the industry. When Security and Exchange commission enforced the implementation, a good amount of changes were made to IT systems in US. The businesses needed to stick the auditing and reporting norms besides reporting certain information to the regulator, regularly. The auditors also verify whether the organizations have adhered to them. IT supported business in fulfilling those regulatory requirements. Wherever I am working with any business establishments, whether they are from private, public or government sector, for their IT strategy, they want special considerations for regulatory and statutory requirements.'

Knowledge management and learning: IT has brought breakthrough in knowledge generation, filtering and dissemination. The kind of knowledge available on Internet and the ease to locate them has changed the life of every person. This has created good infrastructure for every organization and professionals to generate, manage and exploit the knowledge for the benefit of their work and businesses. We have seen a small but effective initiative by Orissa Hydro Power Corporation (www.ohpcltd.com) to maintain list of failures and breakdowns in the plant, their analysis and learning system in power point. The user was very proudly said that he could not have met the target of plant uptime without this simple information system, which has helped his team in systematic analysis and initiating preventive actions. This helped them to improve on downtime for repair as well as mean time between failures. In a published success story, where Mercedes-Benz U.S. International Inc. implemented SAP® solution for efficiency improvement through better handling of maintenance order, it is clear that IT can contribute benefit to business in knowledge management.

IT has very effectively created the platform for computer-based learning system, Webinars (web-based telecasting of seminars), Call centre-based services and many such services, which we have just adopted in our day-to-day life without due credit to it.

The best thing is that the portfolio of IT and IT enabled business and services are still expanding. New ideas and business models are still evolving and emerging. Therefore, it is pertinent that while analysing business performance and casting a set of strategies, the capability of IT must be looked at. IT helps in breaking many of the thought barriers and makes them feasible so that the strategies are not defined under such constraints. Can we think of Banks' strategy to enable every customer to manage their own banking transactions without being dependent on bank branches and their local operation? IT has enabled that and let Bankers make customer strategy independent of branch operation and even inter-branch operations (Combe 2008).

1.5 Strategic Intent

Having understood the importance of IT and its contribution to any business, whether it is commercial or government establishment, let us focus on what "Strategy" is and why IT strategy is important.

If we summarize the definitions of strategy from Oxford dictionary and business consultants like Deloitte Inc., then it is defined as sum total of plans, policies and putting them into operations to achieve a particular purpose. Irrespective of domains, these components apply whenever a goal comes into picture and means are designed to achieve the same. This clearly identifies the intended goals, the commitment, organized approach and focused action. It is basically the road map of meeting organization's information requirement and services to meet business strategy.

For any progress every one including individuals, corporate and governments make strategy. All strategies focus on three basic principles

- Where you want to reach?
- Where you are?
- What takes you there?

In business strategy context, IT strategy adds answer to last question, i.e.

How IT can enhance the chance of success?: Thus while creating a strategy for a business, managers do think about organizing resources and enablers which can help them in framing better strategies, free from execution constraints and feasibility. IT is one of those strategic enablers, which help them in both, framing business strategies and successful execution and delivery. Its ability to support business is tremendous. I faced one of the senior business managers in India who wanted during early 1990s to allow their business customers directly interact with the systems and book and track orders, as part of the strategy to mitigate competition, create good experience and become transparent to the customers. And he had a hope that IT could only do it, unfortunately IT could not provide better solution at that time, but the expectation itself depicts the contribution of IT in defining business strategy.

Today many business managers invite CIO to strategic planning session to assist them in unconventional thinking. The idea is to leverage IT in the thinking process itself. I know one of the world's largest automobile companies, processing automotive parts data at different locations and countries and then through EDI they transfer to US before consolidation and analysis of orders and decide on dispatches. The whole process used to take 48 h, before any dispatch used to be planned. As part of customer service and inventory reduction strategy, they wanted it to happen as quickly as possible and it was made feasible by IT. This had created excellent effect

1.5 Strategic Intent

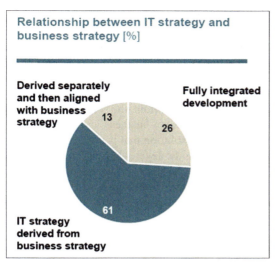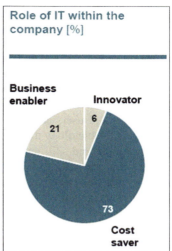

Fig. 1.1 Strategic intent

on their dealer network and release of money blocked under over inventory at each location. One of their senior managers thanked IT and IT team, and enumerated the benefit that IT had benefited to their business and made their strategy work. He wished if IT could have been involved earlier, they would not have postponed this strategy to this long this type of story might be better written up as vignette or mini-case example.

There are different strategies for IT needs more explanation. Many organizations start framing IT strategy along with business strategy, many plan it later but with a focus on business strategy and rarely IT strategy is made in isolation unless a serious localized pain point is to be eliminated by IT solution (www.cisco.com 2009). The first option is the best as IT strategy has natural alignment with business; next option needs full alignment effort where as last one may become bottleneck when expansion or growth is planned. But none is absolutely right or wrong. It depends on the situation and management thinking. There are pockets in developing countries where IT is still a support to accounting function and business managers are either not able to perceive the wide spectrum of options that IT is able to create or other constraints compel them to take bottom-up approach. In these situations, obviously they would start with third option. These are evident in large as well as small and medium organizations. Take an example of large Indian conglomerates; they were growing in fragmented mode till recent past. Their exposure to multinational competition and availability of technology have helped them to take up holistic approach, i.e. top-down approach, and now they are able to connect information from their field and shop floor to the corporate scorecards.

In one of the Internet-based articles "IT Value Management"[1] from Roland Berger, Strategy Consultants, Gerard Ritchter and Martin Bednaric also depicted similar results, as below (Fig. 1.1).

IT and IT strategy always has strategic business intent. It is leveraged for business advantage. It provides solutions to business problems. All those projects have gone bust where IT was not connected to business benefits. Those IT systems could never be assimilated in business and did not have longer life. A good IT project must focus at business benefits, users' enablement and support to business processes. People, who understand the complete gamut of IT solutions and factors improving IT usage, even quote that having latest technology is not that important, the solution and adaptability aspect of users are more important. I have seen business and IT managers agreeing to a technology that is not so new or the solution that is not even optimum as their people and skill level of users are not to the level where they absorb and benefit from newer technology. Thus "People" aspect is also important and an IT strategy must take care of them as well. Faulkner Consulting and Richard Ivey School of Business have presented three elements in business context of IT strategy. We find them quite relevant in our experience too. These three elements must grow together and remain in balance for a successful implementation of IT. We call them "3 Must" basic elements of IT strategy. (www.cioindex.com 2009) and they are

– Process
– People
– Technology

We have found IT managers as well as business managers talking on similar lines during our IT service selling process. They then talk of capability building in these business context elements. In some cases, we have observed that they have very balanced thinking when they talk of making good provision for people enablement when their people have to be enabled with IT-based system. Here a business manager focuses on contribution of IT.

1.6 Major Components of IT Strategy

Let us see the high level approach to IT strategy which goes in creating IT strategy, to understand the pillars and the components of it. No business strategy is left at a dream stage or like a wish list. Business managers do rigorous exercise to detail them in terms of critical success factors (CSF), roll out plan and implications to the organization/s (including communication and alignment of all stake holders), monitoring and mid term review, adjustment and many such items that ensures right implementation and success of strategy. Some business managers do call it strategy for making business strategy work. That's why, when you ask these managers, how are they sure that their strategy will work, you get a very high level analysis and feasibility response, explaining how different enablers will be exploited to make it work under existing scenario. Wherever I have observed the business managers meeting for drafting business strategy, I also could notice use of their high level understanding of enablers, such as assets, finance, process, people, technology or combination of those. They clearly state the strengths and weaknesses emerging from those blocks and how that will impact their business and strategy. Therefore,

1.6 Major Components of IT Strategy

Fig. 1.2 Components of IT strategy

they draft enabler strategies too either as part of main strategy or critical success factor, even though they are further detailed later. IT has become such an important enabler that it draws attention of these business managers there itself.

The following picture clearly depicts the top-down strategy building hierarchy and their interaction map.

The enablers build capabilities of the organization to achieve the business objective through the defined strategy.

Like any strategy, IT strategy should answer

- What we want to achieve
- Where are we
- How we want to achieve

It is recommended that third step additionally touches the following

- How to maximize benefit with optimum resource and investment
- How will we monitor and adjust while working on those plans

1.6.1 Business Purpose

The underneath thinking in IT strategy creation is depicted in the diagram below. This basically is outcome of structural thinking of business managers. They plan a business strategy and the business domain/functions that this strategy will encompass. Then they identify what exactly will make this strategy successful. These CSF are mapped on IT value chain, which help in identifying the IT characteristics that will support this CSF to happen. And complete IT infrastructure and associated enablers are developed and designed around the same.

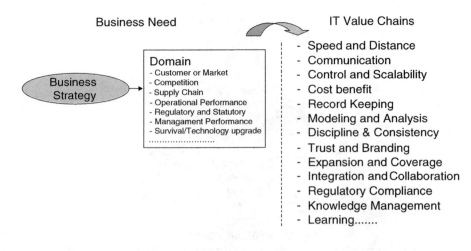

Thus we clearly see the first component is business purpose or the objective. It depends on the Business managers, supported by respective CIO, to help the organization in bridging this. At times when many strategies and plans become dependent on IT, business managers prioritize their strategies. This process too is like allocation of organization resources, where business managers allocate resources based on contribution to organization objective and strategic benefit. Now, in most of the cases expectations from IT are prioritized so that IT infrastructure is laid down keeping short-term and long-term goals and later scalability and expandability are achieved.

1.6.2 A New Strategic Mindset

Many people call it management commitment. The organization must realize that IT is not something which they are using just because many organizations have done it. It is common amongst top corporate when senior managers compare consultant's report and look for investment between 0.5 and 3% of turnover. Arriving at the investments in this way clearly presents the mindset of non-strategic thinking. The top management must take IT as a strategic value and drive with right perspective as their main business strategy or solution depends on its success. Even the investment in IT must be evaluated like any strategic investment. It depends on the nature of business, business need and investment capacity of the organization. The ratio of IT investment to revenue can't be same at Walmart, Morgan Stanley and CORUS or SAIL (Steel Authority of India). The reasons are simple. Critical Success factor for Walmart's business is based on Supply Chain where as for SAIL it is steel making and marketing. The business based on trading, retailing and supply chain needs relatively much more investment in infrastructure for data processing, information exchange and collaboration where as steel making business needs major investment in plant set-up and operations. The information need for per unit of items sold as well as per thousand dollar of revenue at Walmart is much more than any steel plant.

1.6 Major Components of IT Strategy

In one survey report published by IDC[#2] on IT status and trend in Western European countries, it presented that the government is moving slowly towards the usage of technology for governance and citizen centric services. In the same report it has come out that the familiarity with technology in government sector is reasonable and growing. But in developing countries IT in government sectors is still the laggard. Public sector units are better than the pure government establishments and offices. The success of railway ticket reservation and certain eGovernance systems in few progressive states are not enough to motivate and expedite local as well as central governments, in India. The hands-off approach to IT is quite common, especially, in government organizations. Many of government establishments providing vital services like health care, education, revenue services are yet to plan even. We can clearly observe lack of quality information in government offices, whether it relates to citizen, environment or health of government assets. Many a times land dispute while acquiring for industrialization happens because of no up-to-date records.

During run up to Indian budget for 2009–2010, the Chairman, NASSCOM Mr. Pramod Bhasin, Chairman, while representing IT industry, emphasized the need for more IT systems in India. He requested the finance manager to bring focus to IT adoption in government sectors, which have been far behind the private sector, especially the large capital corporate. He has been quite right. We too have observed while selling IT services in government sectors that the management wants to move forward and rapidly. But internal dynamics and constraints as well as inadequate understanding as how IT can scale and improve the services, make them apprehensive of quick decision and speedy implementation (www.cioindex.com 2009). Similar sentiment was sounded by IBM when it recommended that India should lead second wave of IT adoption.

There are very few progressive managers and organizations like The Dhamra Port Company Ltd, India, which started IT investment as early as start of the port construction. The CEO understood that foundation of IT must be laid along with the construction project if he wants to run a port of twenty-first century tomorrow and not of nineteenth century. When Maersk took over P&O Nedlloyd, the top management also thought about IT integration strategy to make merger smooth and successful This might be better written up as a mini-case example.

Demonstrating direct benefits because of IT is not an easy task. The business benefit does not come only because of IT or buying and installing modern technology and application. It comes by usage. And when we talk of usage, a complete eco-system comes into picture. This eco-system includes people, process and governance. Therefore, the benefit must be targeted with balanced growth in all the components of IT eco-system and not only in IT. Let us be clear that a modern IT infrastructure with costly applications in isolation will not yield benefit. It remains the toy in the hand of publicity makers. The users continue to follow their old practice and the business managers get disenchanted and blame IT. The effect of imbalances amongst these components are clearly visible in the government offices, where use of IT is still poor or out of focus. It is not being properly used for improving operational efficiency and quality of public services. To avoid this pitfall, one needs to drive with definite goal, develop all components of IT eco-system and monitor the benefit.

Another mind set change, which is desirable, is in the area of technology selection and infrastructure life. The preferences for technology or solution should be based on the suitability to the purpose, the support available and the vendor relationship. Most of the companies do not chase technology and big branded service providers. Thanks to the companies like Microsoft, Intel, AMD and other hardware vendors that the hardware are more or less standardized and their performances are comparable. It has made users' life simpler. But the rapid changes in technology and richness of software have made the life of infrastructure shorter. Unlike production manager of a factory, IT managers approach frequently to the business managers for investment to upgrade and changes in IT assets. Senior managers need to appreciate this phenomenon of this industry. Client-server-based technology existed till late 1990s and re-launched after dotcom burst. But the way dotcom and web-based systems returned with new features supporting remote access, facilitating collaboration across organizations and geographies and hardware architecture free applications, the infrastructure needed face change. Touch screen, Smart cards, RFID, Voice interface, Microsoft Surface technology and others have already started putting pressure for changes again in IT infrastructure and applications. IT enabled services have become new competitive tool to build new capability to reach to the customers, collaborate, improve financials and globalize their product and services. These changes have happened in a span of 10 years. Most of the business managers are unable to digest this phenomenon and don't allow modernization at right time which sometimes leaves them behind competitors.

Large organizations have flexibility to use different technologies for different functions. Even though that is part of their strategy, which could have been driven by cost saving or business needs, they have started thinking of integration. It has crossed the limit of information integration and reached to virtualization, i.e. common platform to improve manageability. They upgrade those areas first, which are on the priorities. Hence, one should apply own thoughts on investment and selection of right technology for the organization and it has to be based on rational need of the organization. Tata Steel has built its own IT strategy and based business function to certain application and line of technology. They have standardized these platforms purely based on manageability and coverage of business functions.

Generally upgrade of infrastructure depends on

- Where one wants his/her business to reach
- Whether there are compelling reasons from customers and competitors
- Whether it will negatively impact the current services
- Whether the requirements from regulators or government need changes, e.g. HDFC Bank's Disaster Recovery (DR) project was because of central bank (RBI) directive which recommended that Indian banks put in place a DR plan

Short life of these IT assets has been recognized by the government and that's why they also allow higher rate of depreciation. Even some organizations amortize software assets quickly. The idea is to choose your own option depending upon the need.

When we observe that the understanding and awareness of IT amongst senior managers would make IT adoption for business purpose better, we recommend CIO

1.6 Major Components of IT Strategy

and IT managers to take a pragmatic view and put an effort to educate and win the confidence (www.cioindex.com). It is but obvious that business managers will understand contribution of IT in terms of business benefits and money; and some successful CIO do adopt this approach. This helps the business managers to appreciate IT and connect IT-investments to their business. They get committed to leverage IT successfully.

1.6.3 Holistic Approach

We recommend the holistic approach to IT strategy similar to Gartner. They recommend three pronged approach for IT strategy, i.e. developing demand, control and supply side of strategy. They believe that the IT strategy must have Business objectives and capabilities needed under demand, governance and administration processes including financials, under control and under supply, it should address people, service and sourcing issues. From our experience, we have proposed in this book a slightly different approach and that is to design and develop strategies around there basic context, discussed above, while keeping the focus on business benefits. Though they are not fundamentally different to Gartner's approach, the assembly line appears to be different.

The components of all strategies must be developed and assembled in such a way that the expected goal is achieved. Therefore, it is important to depict these components clearly and vividly so that the executioners get good guidance and assemble them as perfectly as possible. At this stage policy wise decision could be a good idea, e.g. what should be the approach to technology selection, will we develop and implement in-house or through outsourcing. It should reflect good guidelines to executioners, a road map to all stake holders and expectations of top management with this investment.

Like any strategic plan, all IT strategies must present current scenario, future scenario and how the organization will reach there. And this must talk about the complete IT eco-system, so that holistic and balanced approach could be taken. Mention of high level action and measurements, which creates progress and directs to the right end, would be preferred content of an IT strategy. It should be like any investment proposal, where visibility on the following items should be provided.

- Current scenario
  - Process: Business effectiveness, business integration, business process, opportunity to improve
  - People: Capability and skill level of IT and business people, change management capability, design of services vis-à-vis employee involvement
  - IT: IT infrastructure, application portfolio, level of IT integration with business, stock of digital data, service and support
- IT management structure
- Business priorities and intended coverage

- Future scenario
  - Process: New orientation to process, change deployment, support needed from IT
  - People: Desired level of skill and capability, process for people enablement, change management
  - IT: Infrastructure and operations, new technology and application, implementation approach, service (outsourcing, technology upgrade, IT processes, etc.) and support
  - Approach to service delivery
  - IT and data security and business continuity strategy
  - Investments
  - Risks and mitigations
  - Benefits and success measurements

The approval from the top management can only be expected when they have good visibility and can analyse the benefit out of it. Since tangible benefits directly attributed to IT is little trickier, we suggest business managers to consider intangible benefits and enabler role of IT too for investment considerations. It is similar to education where tangible benefit to the society can not be arrived straight way.

It must be noted that the complete details on IT strategy are difficult to elaborate along with business planning. Hence, the preferred mode of IT strategy formulation breaks into two stages. At higher level, IT could be identified one of the strategic means to achieve business goals and next level the detail exercise or elaboration is done. The first level could have extra details if business people understand IT. I have also seen in couple of cases where IT becomes a key to survival or to maintain current level of operations, and hence, business people themselves elaborated many of the parameters. In one of the organizations, where obsolescence of IT has reached to service breakdown stage, business people wanted IT to be on high priority. They enumerated business risks, expected benefits and the way they would like the new system to expand wings supporting their other strategies on operational efficiency, cost reduction and customer responsiveness. This gave good picture to the concerned IT Manager how IT strategy should be driven and the assurances to extend good support in implementation.

More on these topics will be covered in coming chapters.

1.6.4 Approach to Green IT

The sensitivity to our environment and climate change has generated world-wide awareness. Many initiatives by the world bodies including communication from Commission of The European Communities to European Parliament, Kyoto Protocol and attempt by United Nations to arrive to an agreement amongst its members vide Climate Change Conference 2009 at Copenhagen (http://en.cop15.dk/) clearly show the concern in this direction. The world has become sensitive to Green house gas

1.6 Major Components of IT Strategy

emission norms. The world trade and business have not remained untouched with this movement. They are also expected to support this movement. This let an idea emerge that the industry and business must use resources optimally and reduce the green house gas emission, which is causing rising temperature of the planet. Thus recycling, use of bio-friendly materials, plantation and many such environment friendly steps were recommended.

IT can contribute to this movement by (www.symantec.com/greenit)

- *Green use*—reducing the energy consumption of computers and other information systems as well as using them in an environmentally sound manner
- *Green disposal*—refurbishing and reusing old computers and properly recycling unwanted computers and other electronic equipment
- *Green design*—designing energy-efficient and environmentally sound components, computers, servers, cooling equipment, and data centres
- *Green manufacturing*—manufacturing electronic components, computers, and other associated subsystems with minimal impact on the environment

The summit site (http://en.cop15.dk/) also suggests many ways to green computing.

We could see at least two areas in IT domain that visibly impacted by this campaign. The first is power consumption by the IT equipments and the cooling need, and the second is paper consumption. Reduction in usage of fossil fuels for power generation and mass reduction of paper consumption in business and offices are certainly a welcome contribution from IT. There are ample opportunities to save energy by choosing right hardware, right configuration and system design. Use of blade/rack servers instead of boxes, consolidation of systems and systems that are supporting online availability of data and information, use of LCD monitors instead of CRT monitors and use of solar panels for supplementing power need are also in support of this goal. Again the tendency of having more printed report for verification/analysis of data as well as records can easily be controlled by educating the users and providing matching features in the system. Recognizing electronic data instead of papers in government offices and government dealings with business will be another good step in this direction.

In one of the survey reports on green IT "Green IT Survey Results – May 2009" from Symantec it has been reported that "Ninety-six percent of companies are at least discussing a Green IT strategy. Fifty-two percent are in the discussion or trial stages, while 45 percent have already implemented a strategy. Additionally, 87 percent of companies said that it is somewhat/significantly important that their IT organization implement Green IT initiatives. Only two percent said it was somewhat/significantly unimportant". It also adds that Companies are willing to spend more today than in the past to implement green technology. Seventy-three percent of respondents predicted an increase in Green IT budgets over the next 12 months".

Today the international users/customers have become so sensitive to this fact that they ask for audit reports on energy consumptions and initiatives towards Green IT before outsourcing the IT business. *Martyn Hart, chairman of the National Outsourcing Association has quoted in his article dated 23rd Sept 2008, that* "UK government committed to ensuring its IT operations are carbon neutral by 2013".

The article also quotes, "The Brown-Wilson Group's 2007 Black Book of Outsourcing study indicates that more than 21 per cent of US and European companies that already outsource have added green policies and performance indictors to their outsourcing agreements". This number has been rising since then. Similar message is provided in the "2009 Green Outsourcing Survey" by TheBlackBookofOutsourcing.com.

One of the world's big logistics companies more detail needed which went under similar scrutiny by their big customer posed the same discipline to its vendors including IT vendors, and IT service providers from India too adopted these practices. Similarly while creating an IT strategy for a Hydro Power Generation company, which has policies for social responsibilities, the company wanted an exclusive consideration for Green IT in its IT strategy. This might make a good mini-case

This is new phenomenon and it will spread like epidemic soon. Therefore, it is important that any new IT strategy must evaluate an opportunity for this and adapt it. This not only provides an opportunity to be socially responsible organization but also saves cost, thus making good business sense.

1.6.5 Globalization

As per White and Bruton (2007), today IT has become a good tool to support the organizations' globalization plans. Big corporate of US from financial, trading and manufacturing industries have pioneered in globalization using IT. They extensively used the technology to integrate business across the globe and confirm the convenience and benefit from IT in achieving their objective. In an article on Itstrategyblog.com Raj Sheelvant highlighted how Coca Cola used IT effectively to make their global strategy of collaboration within different sets of employees, suppliers and customers were achieved. IT directly helped them to two of their vital business strategies, market Dominance and Defensive Strategy in supply chain. Like Coca Cola, many front runner organizations, which used IT extensively for their global ambitions, create new directions and opportunities of services for IT. Global strategy to reduce cost by outsourcing of IT and IT enabled services could be successful only because of IT. Currently, the industries, which are innovating new solutions based on global participation and collaboration, are influencing the new research and development in IT.

IT strategy must reflect the business strategy of globalization and plans to reach beyond geographical boundaries. This helps the planner to visualize the need of infrastructure and create strategy to support business till last mile. In context of having many differences including language, regulation, culture, demography, technology adaptation and business conditions across different markets it is better to indicate the expectations from IT as part of the business strategy. These must happen by design than on ad hoc basis.

Current infrastructure level and ever expanding the same have created good opportunities for business to integrate seamlessly across countries and continent boundaries. Even regulators have started collaborating and taking help of IT to globalize. This was evident when SEBI, The Indian Stock market regulator and SEC,

US agreed to share practices and data to monitor and regulate the stock exchanges and investments as well as investigations. The regulators cooperation again became important when US made Tax-heaven countries to declare the money and investments belonging to American citizens.

Many business establishments want to create new business models based on IT. This was evident when many new business models like remote tuition services through Internet, sell and auction services are provided by real estate builders, electronic payments for services, use and pay services for software came into being (Combe 2008). This means success and failure of business directly and holistically depends on IT. In such scenario IT becomes utmost important. There also business strategists provide certain performance and expectation guidelines which they think important for them to succeed. This dependence of business on IT makes business to develop their eStrategy and when this helps to globalize the business, it is called "eStrategy for Globalization" (Mohapatra 2009). This approach where complete business runs over IT, throws different type of demand on IT. This also demands that business managers have better understanding of IT thus helping in amalgamating IT with their thoughts.

1.7 Technology in Agriculture

A GIS, also known as a geographical information system, is an information system for capturing, storing, analysing, managing and presenting data which are spatially referenced (linked to location). GIS helps in integrating, storing, editing, analysing, sharing, and displaying geographically referenced information. These GIS applications are tools that allow users to search, create interactive queries (user created searches), collect data, use collected data for information, edit data, maps, and present the results of all these operations. This collection of data is done through GPS and remote sensing.

The GPS is a satellite-based navigation system made up of a network of satellites which are placed in orbits above the earth. Even though GPS was originally intended for military applications, but later on has been used for civil purposes as well as including that of agriculture. This was possible because in the 1980s, it was decided to make the system available for civilian use. Since the satellites are placed above the earth in the orbits, GPS is not affected by natural calamities and works in any weather conditions, anywhere in the world, 24 h a day.

1.7.1 How it Works

GPS satellites circle the earth twice a day in its defined orbits and capture and transmit signals as information to earth. At the ground stations, GPS receivers take this information and use applications, which have been designed and developed to calculate the user's exact location. The principle used for finding locations of a particular place is by comparing differences in response time. The GPS receiver compares the response time for a signal that was transmitted by a satellite with the response time for receiving it. The difference in response time tells the GPS receiver how far away the satellite is. This response time is then benchmarked against the data available with the receiver, by which the receiver can determine the user's position and display it on the unit's electronic map.

1.7.2 Remote Sensing

In the broadest sense, *remote sensing* is the small or large-scale acquisition of information of an object or phenomenon, by the use of either recording or real-time sensing device(s) that is not in physical or intimate contact with the object (such as by way of aircraft, spacecraft, satellite, buoy, or ship). In practice, remote sensing is the stand-off collection through the use of a variety of devices for gathering information on a given object or area. Thus, Earth observation or weather satellite collection platforms, ocean and atmospheric observing weather buoy platforms, monitoring of a pregnancy via ultrasound, magnetic resonance imaging (MRI), positron emission tomography (PET), and space probes are all examples of remote sensing. In modern usage, the term generally refers to the use of imaging sensor technologies including but not limited to the use of instruments aboard aircraft and spacecraft, and is distinct from other imaging-related fields such as medical imaging.

1.7.3 GIS and Production Agriculture

At a grassroots level, GIS offers farmers various opportunities to increase production, reduce input costs, and manage the land in their care more efficiently. From handheld computer mapping in the field to the scientific analysis of production data at the farm manager's office, geography plays a part. These examples of applications of GIS at the farm level are meant to provide users, both experienced and inexperienced, with some ideas for implementation.

1.7.4 How it Works in Rural India

The development and implementation of precision agriculture or site-specific farming has been made possible by combining the GPS and GIS. These technologies enable the coupling of real-time data collection with accurate position information, leading to the efficient manipulation and analysis of large amounts of geospatial data. GPS-based applications in precision farming are being used for farm planning, field mapping, soil sampling, tractor guidance, crop scouting, variable rate applications, and yield mapping. GPS allows farmers to work during low visibility field conditions such as rain, dust, fog, and darkness.

1.7 Technology in Agriculture

In the past, it was difficult for farmers to correlate production techniques and crop yields with land variability. This limited their ability to develop the most effective soil/plant treatment strategies that could have enhanced their production. Today, more precise application of pesticides, herbicides, and fertilizers, and better control of the dispersion of those chemicals are possible through precision agriculture, thus reducing expenses, producing a higher yield, and creating a more environmentally friendly farm.

Precision agriculture is now changing the way farmers and agribusinesses view the land from which they reap their profits. Precision agriculture is about collecting timely geospatial information on soil-plant-animal requirements and prescribing and applying site-specific treatments to increase agricultural production and protect the environment. Where farmers may have once treated their fields uniformly, they are now seeing benefits from micromanaging their fields. Precision agriculture is gaining in popularity largely due to the introduction of high technology tools into the agricultural community that are more accurate, cost effective, and user friendly. Many of the new innovations rely on the integration of on-board computers, data collection sensors, and GPS time and position reference systems.

Many believe that the benefits of precision agriculture can only be realized on large farms with huge capital investments and experience with information technologies. Such is not the case. There are inexpensive and easy-to-use methods and techniques that can be developed for use by all farmers. Through the use of GPS, GIS, and remote sensing, information needed for improving land and water use can be collected. Farmers can achieve additional benefits by combining better utilization of fertilizers and other soil amendments, determining the economic threshold for treating pest and weed infestations, and protecting the natural resources for future use.

GPS equipment manufacturers have developed several tools to help farmers and agribusinesses become more productive and efficient in their precision farming activities. Today, many farmers use GPS-derived products to enhance operations in their farming businesses. Location information is collected by GPS receivers for mapping field boundaries, roads, irrigation systems, and problem areas in crops such as weeds or disease. The accuracy of GPS allows farmers to create farm maps with precise acreage for field areas, road locations and distances between points of interest. GPS allows farmers to accurately navigate to specific locations in the field, year after year, to collect soil samples or monitor crop conditions.

Crop advisors use rugged data collection devices with GPS for accurate positioning to map pest, insect, and weed infestations in the field. Pest problem areas in crops can be pinpointed and mapped for future management decisions and input recommendations. The same field data can also be used by aircraft sprayers, enabling accurate swathing of fields without use of human "flaggers" to guide them. Crop dusters equipped with GPS are able to fly accurate swaths over the field, applying chemicals only where needed, minimizing chemical drift, reducing the amount of chemicals needed, thereby benefiting the environment. GPS also allows pilots to provide farmers with accurate maps.

Farmers and agriculture service providers can expect even further improvements as GPS continues to modernize. In addition to the current civilian service provided by GPS, the United States is committed to implementing a second and a third civil signal on GPS satellites. The first satellite with the second civilian signal was launched in 2005. The new signals will enhance both the quality and efficiency of agricultural operations in the future.

1.7.5 Benefits

- Precision soil sampling, data collection, and data analysis, enable localized variation of chemical applications and planting density to suit specific areas of the field.
- Accurate field navigation minimizes redundant applications and skipped areas, and enables maximum ground coverage in the shortest possible time.
- Ability to work through low visibility field conditions such as rain, dust, fog and darkness increases productivity.
- Accurately monitored yield data enables future site-specific field preparation.
- Elimination of the need for human "flaggers" increases spray efficiency and minimizes over-spray.

1.8 Summary

In this chapter, we started with journey that IT has taken since couple of decades back. We discussed that the journey have been full of events and hindrances, but the continued research and innovation have created respectable place for IT, today. It has found its place in the minds of top managers.

We also discussed different roles of IT and the upcoming benefits. It has expanded vertically as well as horizontally. One good element that enhanced its capability was to integrate with different infrastructure domains. It continued to connect business, people and governments and that made it special. It never tried to replace human minds rather it supported them to be more innovative and creative, e.g. IT has given a new dimension to painting; in a minute it draws a picture and shows effect of variety of colour and contrast combinations on a picture which was long desire of the artists. This could help them to give a shape to their imagination, so that they can make the world even more colourful and beautiful. It has contributed a lot to make newer generation more imaginative and innovative.

We also talked about the way IT has supported the strategic intent of any business including of governance. This has not only helped the business managers to capitalize its features to meet their business objectives, but also contributed in shaping the new business models and strategies. This has provided another major tool to them to solve many problems. The compelling reasons presented by its capabilities have made it to pass through hurly burly of business and reach to the top people in the organizations.

Finally we talked about different components of IT strategy, where we also touched upon the IT strategy creation at two stages, one at a very high level when business strategies, directions and policies are being finalized and next level where detailing of strategies specific to IT are created. Like one big manufacturing organizations in India planned to integrate the business of all its divisions and units spread across the country to improve manageability during downsizing the employee strength. Thus it created a high level map during business planning where it mentioned that the success of that level of downsizing would depend upon how the IT would integrate all units. Later in next phase, it was elaborated that the telecom network and redeployment of IT could achieve the same.

In subsequent chapters we will focus little more on alignment of IT with business before we embark on the approach to draft IT strategy and policies.

1.9 Glossary

CSF	Critical success factors for success in business
IT	Information technology
IT Infrastructure	Hardware, network and software used for IT
SAIL	Steel Authority of India, a public sector company
DR	Disaster recovery, a process for securing against data loss
RBI	Reserve Bank of India, the regulatory body in India
SEBI	Security and Exchange Board of India
SEC	Security and Exchange Commission, US

1.10 Review Questions

1. Discus evolution of IT strategy over different decades? How the role of IT has changed?
2. How can IT help at strategic level?
3. Explain how IT can help in aligning business goals?
4. What are the critical components of IT strategy?
5. Can IT help in greening environment? Please explain how can it do so?
6. What are the approaches related to strategy for Green IT?

1.11 Project Work

Develop a business strategy for a retail chain and discuss IT strategy for the same. The retail chain sells only through different outlets in different cities and has inventory for private brands as well as for reputed brands in apparels, books, toys and jewellery. Describe IT strategy can help in developing green strategy for this retail chain.

Bibliography

A preliminary viewpoint—the value of common framework thinking in IT, jointly published by Faulkner Consulting and Richard Ivey School of Business

Chuck M (1998) In net future: the 7 cyber-trends that will drive your business, create new wealth, and define your future. McGraw-Hill, New York

Collin C (2008) Introduction to e-business. Elsevier, New Delhi

Communication from Commission of European communities. http://www.euractiv.com/25/images/Draft_Communication_Copenhaguen.pdf

Copenhagen summit on climate change http://en.cop15.dk/

Green IT global survey report published in May 2009 by Symantec Corporation. www.symantec.com/greenit, an IDC survey

Heeks RB (2002) Information systems and developing countries: failure, success and local improvisations. Inform Soc 18(2):101–112

http://www.nasscom.com 2008

http://www.ohpcltd.com 2009

http://ecohub.sdn.sap.com/irj/ecohub/home?rid=/hub/uuid/f019b047-cd2c-2c10-52b6-aba90a3552d8: Mercedes-Benz using SAP

http://news.zdnet.co.uk/itmanagement/0,1000000308,39289055,00.htm

http://www.cioindex.com 2009

http://www.cisco.com/web/DE/pdfs/publicsector/idc_07_04.pdf, retrieved Oct 2009

http://www.encyclopedia.com

http://www.oracle.com/customers/index.html

http://www.pcguide.com/ref/cpu/fam/g3.htm

http://www.deloitte.com IT Strategy: The key to winning executive support by Dalibor Petrovic, PMP, I.S.P. Senior Manager, Deloitte

Mohapatra S (2009) Business process automation. PHI Learning, New Delhi

Use of IT by trade unions: http://www.unionlearn.org.uk/ict/learn-759-f0.cfmlibor

White MA, Bruton GD (2007) The management of technology and innovation. Cengage Learning, New Delhi

http://www.sas.com

www.TheBlackBookofOutsourcing.com

Chapter 2
Getting Ready for IT Strategy

2.1 Learning Objectives

This chapter would

- Identify evolution of IT strategy and the direction of the same
- Justify the need for IT alignment with business
- Introduce changing IT strategy for different stages of business life cycle
- Explain CIO role under changing business scenario
- Evolve preparation for IT strategy

2.2 Introduction

Corporate Board Member magazine (2007) in association with Deloitte reported a finding of a survey in "2007 Board and Information Technology Strategies Report: Maximizing Performance Through IT Strategy", published on CIOindex.com, which sums up the need of IT alignment with business very well. It says, "When boards are actively involved in IT, IT becomes more effective in supporting the business". The board has understood the value which IT can deliver for business; hence, they use it as any other valuable resource and exploit for business advantage. It quotes that the board was not so aware of strategic value earlier, but now 62–76% of boards approach IT as a board's issue. In financial organizations, where number and analytics play a vital role, the acceptance of strategic value is higher. Accordingly, participation of CIO in strategy formulation has gone up.

This rising participation of IT in business has been created by the unique value proposition that it offers. This has also increased the responsibility of CIOs and IT managers to understand the business imperatives and create more and more value for the business by using IT. They needed to create right plan and help business managers to visualize the upcoming values from IT without which the hesitant participation of board and its members in certain industries and sectors will continue.

2.3 Evolution of IT Strategy

The capability of IT has been expanding manifold and accordingly the contribution to the business. Till 1970s, IT strategy was focussing to installation of a set of hardware and few projects where data crunching was required. On hardware front purchase and installation of mainframe or mini computers with dumb terminals and on application side coverage of few functions such as accounting, purchase and inventory used to be part of any IT strategy. During those days, IS and IT were differentiated (Checkland (1981) and Holwell), as "IS" was used to point to applications and software and the "IT" referred to hardware and connectivity. However, later this differentiation became blurred and the term "IT" was simplified for customers and users. Now IT includes software, hardware, networking and services. These four branches and IT related services converged into one, i.e. "IT industry". The classification by stock exchanges and adoption of a new line of business, i.e. software development and services business by corporate such as IBM and HP, which were traditionally in hardware and networking, also contributed to this convergence. For our references too, IT includes hardware, software, networking and IT enabled services.

However, during those days, certain packaged software for statistical analysis and production planning used to be available, but they were neither very popular nor used to be part of IT strategy. IT strategy used to follow bottom-up approach. Speed of data processing and retrieval used to be the main consideration for IT participation in local business functions. Head of IT used to be third layer in the organization management and were not represented in top management directly. Even in progressive organizations this function used to be under a business functions mostly under finance and accounts, which used to be major users of IT. With rising capability and usage of IT across business functions, IT functions across organizations were consolidated and accordingly organization design for IT changed. By late 1970s, the representation of IT function was elevated whereby it started reporting to one of the top management members.

By late 1970s and early 1980s, role of IT started getting attention of business managers and they started considering it for solving business problems. IT started being considered for functional integration, but not contributor to complete business process efficiency. Use of EDI for data interchange started getting popular in 1980s. Slowly, the identification of opportunities for IT to contribute in business started happening in higher management too. The costly mainframe/mini computer era started fading, and hence, even organizations in SME sector, which could not have afforded IT set-up earlier, also started looking at this as an option. This phenomenon supported growth for IT, even though the strategy of new entrant too started with accounting and number crunching functions. The arrival of Personal Computer started impacting to different facets of usage of IT and IT strategy making process.

Till 1970s, the IT strategy used to be focussed primarily on hardware purchase, installation and applications. Organizations used to have their in-house IT function and they used to concentrate on data services. Some methodologies such as IBM's "Business System Planning" popularly known as BSP (supported by ISP—Information System Planning) used to be proprietary technique to create IT strategy.

Like IBM, everyone else also used them for their prime client without any emphasis on sharing with industry. In early 1980s IBM brought these to public domain. This mainly concentrated on requirement and process modelling and project portfolio creation. With a focus on evolving potential candidate for IT, it looked at process and data map. This could successfully connect data classes with business process and created consistency and integration map (Mclean and Turban 2005). During 1980s many academicians started coming up with their own concept and models that influenced approach to IT strategy itself.

During early 1980s, the principles of information engineering by Martin (1987) brought a new revolution. This approach based techniques helped CIOs better align IT with business by different modelling techniques. It captured business functions under data and process models and aligned them with each other with emphasis on the need for business process change and mapped them with IT. Business managers started understanding the need for holistic change for business benefits. This shifted IT industry from unstructured or semi-structured approach era to more structured approach.

Slowly, the business managers started using IT as one of the key enablers. They started finding merit in IT capabilities, and then, IT strategy started being driven by business purpose. Porter's theory related to competitive advantage and value chain helped managers to re-innovate IT for the business benefit. Managers started thinking of exploiting IT to manage five competitive forces that Porter postulated earlier in 1979. Evolution of IT strategy started becoming more structural and top-down. Business strategy started becoming the drivers for IT strategy.

During the decade of 1980s, cost-cutting and enabling users with personal computers started taking shape in big way. Most of the IT investments were being justified by cost benefit, whether it was through manpower reduction, lead time reduction, timely and structured presentation of information or improvement in fund utilization. This was the era of booming isolated systems caused by rising demand for IT systems and information from functional managers. IT strategy based on centralized systems could not serve the demand either because of high cost of central systems against small business benefits (perceived benefit) or due to limited capability and high lead time to development and deployment. This created the demand–supply gap which in turn supported the commercialization of Unix and Dos based systems. Functional users started managing their business and servicing information need from local systems using mix of small locally developed applications and certain packaged software. Low cost to development of such applications and packages created a boom in the availability of software in a different cost range.

All new IT projects have been transformational in nature, and to be successful it needed change in process as well as people capability. Till 1980s, technology interface to users was not disruptive, as they continued to work on papers and trained employees at data processing department used to take care of the rest. But more and more introduction of PC and other user end devices started putting more pressure on users and a holistic plan for user training and learning became essential component of the IT strategy. Similarly, earlier implementations were more related to data services and automation, whereas the new trend from late 1980s started whereby business re-engineering became a part of IT strategy. Business managers realized that they can reap better benefit if they revamp processes before automating them and that could yield bigger advantage to the business. This led to a complete plan on process, people and technology to become essential component of IT strategy.

This was the trend with which 1980s started. By then IT strategy and investment approval started happening based on cost–benefit analysis. The value in terms of financial saving or benefit to business became a standard practice. Even Hardware sellers used to work with CIOs to quantify the benefit to create a case for purchase. Some progressive companies in developing world too adopted this practice and made this a component of their capital investment proposals. Some direct benefits such as manpower reduction, space and facility rental saving, inventory reduction, fund realization, saving in working capital helped CIOs to justify new IT strategy and investment plan. But some intangible ones such as improvement and flexibility in decision-making capability and quality of information could not be realized by business managers till they went through the implemented projects. Slowly business managers started getting the confidence that IT can deliver and in-turn started encouraging newer technologies and ideas. During the period Y2K issue and ERP emerged as key IT issue and IT solution, respectively. They drew the attention of CIOs and business managers. The trade-off was between additional investments to increase the life of existing system and fresh investment for developing a new one. The cost and the risk of Y2K migration were difficult to estimate, and on the other hand, ERP products and Internet technology were just emerging. Many organizations adopted strategy of upgrading the existing systems, if they had one, to continue existing services, and opting for new system for new and additional business functions. They had two options for new system, custom development and ERP implementation. But none was a clear winner. Newer business started with emerging technology and in some case with new ideas and business model. This platform was later called ".Com".

The pressure of Y2K started taking the bigger place in the minds of CIOs and the business managers. The fear of Y2K problem took undue attention and managers started looking at alternatives. This made transition from current systems as major part of IT strategy. Alternatives to so-called COBOL era, was limited, even though new technology platform was upcoming. All large organizations around the globe needed to go through this transformation. CIOs and IT managers were so involved on Y2K during late 1980s that they found that the decade had passed while planning and organizing to come out of this issue. It was uphill task to get fund approval from the business managers for this kind of tasks, where no extra benefits to business can be shown. The justification for survival was not amusing to business managers. But even during this period certain organizations relied on Internet and created new business models based on it. The new business models, such as ticket delivery by Ryan International and American Airlines, account management by Meril Lynch, investment services by Charles Schwab, supply chain management by Walmart, started early and got benefited. These new ways to business also impacted organization design. Business started realizing power of collaboration. A distinct shift in business attitude from full control and complete ownership of business processes to

2.3 Evolution of IT Strategy

outsource, collaborate and customer experience started happening. IT was not only supporting this shift but influencing too. But it was the beginning. The industry and users realized later that it was early hype, only careful design based on good business model not only lasted long but also yielded business benefits.

In India large companies such as Tata Steel, SAIL and others planned a strategy to revamp IT infrastructure in entirety by redeveloping new systems to circumvent Y2K issue. Y2K issue made the western world first time realize that they do not have enough people to help them to fix this issue. They needed help of developing nations. The timely evolution of emerging Internet technology also came as a help to expand the team across geographies to manage this Y2K. And this created a new strategy and business model, popularly known as "outsourcing". Since then outsourcing became one of the essential components of IT strategy and that deserves due consideration, even now. Later, it expanded from application development outsourcing to complete software life cycle outsourcing. Slowly, it expanded to business process outsourcing, IT infrastructure and support and many other business and IT functions.

Just after when the world got a feel that Y2K issue had just passed through, managers and governments returned back to "business driven IT" principles. They found good merit in it and the world's big consultants too started attaching more importance to this approach. The concept of considering IT a business enabler, and evaluating the IT investment amongst other investment opportunities, started getting importance. IT in twenty-first century did not remain old IT, it became a good means for business growth. By then it changed from utility support function to business transformation enabler.

In the mean time Internet-based capability as well as its convergence with other technologies started maturing. People started making good business support infrastructure based on IT. This helped in reaching large number of people and facilitated direct participation of users, customers, suppliers and other external stakeholders directly. Business managers capitalized this phenomenon and started revamping their business models, processes and value chain. Rapid and large-scale benefits started coming to business. Even many used IT to create new business and service delivery channels and many used it to evolve new business model altogether.

By now IT strategy formulation had entered in board room. Many leading organizations started developing strategies based on IT capabilities to manage their business needs, competition and improvement drives. After realizing the potential of Internet-based channel, eCommerce and other new models started evolving. Developed countries took quantum leap in developing new business models based on IT, e.g. Dell's and Amazon's (launched in July 1995) Internet based order processing, Google's search engine, Walmart's supply chain integration, DHL's and FedEx's mail and material tracking. This in fact created a reverse theory that IT started influencing business strategies than business driving IT. The new era came out from the technology limitations and entered into idea limitations. Even in developing countries corporate started working out new channels, service models and business models based on IT. Initiatives such as Tata Steel's metaljunction.com Indian banks' Internet enabled services, eGovernment services in India and many

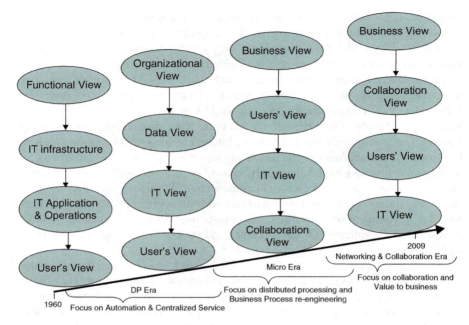

Fig. 2.1 Changing mind map of IT strategy

such business channels started taking shape besides infrastructure bottleneck. The telecom advancement and spread has made significant contribution to boost the capability of IT for business, government and people at large.

If we map the IT transformation, the map will look as Fig. 2.1 (Nolan 2000; Ward and Peppard 2002).

The above picture clearly depicts that IT has been transforming through three roles (Spitz and dePaschalis 2005). First, during early days, it played the role of support organization and performed the back office tasks. Second, it started with transitional role when it was contributing to goals of business process reengineering. And finally, it started focusing at business value, whether it comes within the organization or beyond. It facilitated collaboration and automation in big way.

This changed view of IT strategy formation was also reflected in one of the McKinsey's survey (Craig et al. (2007) McKinsey Quarterly), where it identifies that close cooperation between IT and business people are needed to form a good IT strategy. Amongst various practices the priorities are given to "collaboration of IT and business people", "IT alignment to business strategy" and "technology innovation", in that order. The same report has also highlighted the staged shift in IT focus from IT as supplier (service information on operational demand) to alignment and collaboration facilitator for business goals and finally to competitive differentiator, i.e. playing proactive role in building competitive landscape in shaping business strategy.

Recently a concept of "total cost of ownership (TCO)", which was dormant for sometime, re-emerged and took a centre stage in value evaluation. This forced the holistic approach to IT strategy, which covered capital and operational expenditure on IT infrastructure and services, for evaluating the cost and the benefit. With this CIO started defining their budget and controlling in entirety.

2.4 New Direction of IT Strategy

IT helps the organization in two ways, business internal and business external. During the early days, it used to be mainly business-internal focused. Its strategy used to be entirely organization-internal. This focus was so dominant that even internal cost reduction and efficiency improvement was never seen as business benefit in customer and competition domain. The new shift in IT strategy helped to bring this missing perspective too. Now the business started looking at internal performance improvement also in context to external factors. The new approach and mindset is to reduce cost of operations for improve competitiveness and responsiveness in the market. This integrated view of the business further helped IT to bring in larger perspective and show better benefits and returns. Even today, the business internal strategy mostly emerged based on traditional usage either for problem solving or for capitalizing opportunities in operational domain and the business external strategy has been influenced by customer need, technology capability, industry trend and competition.

2.4.1 Business Internal

IT for control and governance: This legacy perspective is more carried from management practices, where the management wanted to have visibility of operational data, standard processes, control on operations, and Information based management actions. Trade unions viewed it as management initiative to tilt the balance of power and control towards the management and hence, they opposed it. Better visibility to operations through data and information led to improved plans, actions and synergy amongst different functional areas.

IT for efficiency: The management started finding benefits from IT systems more than the expected goals of "control and governance". The sheer availability of information in right context gave them more insights in the business. Their actions started moving towards information based actions from the judgmental and personal understanding. They could see through gaps and opportunity to improve and used IT to cut inefficiency caused by delay in information availability for decision-making, process delays, poor understanding of resource availability and deployment, inadequate understanding of organization capability for new strategy and many others. Business managers started capitalizing it for innovating new practices and all-round business improvement. It also helped integrating different functions for common goals.

IT for performance: IT contributed to business performance at various levels. It could organize information aspect of business very well. Qualitative and quantitative improvements brought by IT slowly started seeping into business. Users from functional areas started looking at it as an enabler to improve their functional performance. Technology evolution and improved availability added fuel to this desire. Aligning business across functional areas became easier. Senior managers started defining measurements and reviewing through right set of data, made available from IT. Thus, it entered more into organizational domain than just in the functional area. For speed, integration, correctness, process and statutory compliance and many other functional performance, business managers started looking towards IT.

IT for management effectiveness: IT changed management style and refined management decision-making process. It could easily collect, collate and present the desired data for timely action. This was an additional help for business managers. Wherever, based on certain information a decision, guidance, an alert or an escalation was to be performed; it started doing so automatically without delay. And wherever more analysis and understanding were required for managers' intervention, it started presenting the trend and analysis to the managers. Thus, it started imbibing Business Intelligence and became a good aid to business managers.

IT for results with optimum resources: During early days of IT when the business were not so competitive and it used to make profit without much focus on cost of operation, investment in IT used to be cost heavy. The capital investment on IT infrastructure and operating expenditure on IT operations were not making business sense to managers. But as the time changed, business became more cost conscious and information hungry. Business managers wanted to produce more and more with same resource. IT emerged as good option for optimizing resources to achieve this goal. The investment gave competitive performance. It not only cut cost around inefficiencies and wastages but also improved by bringing change and better method to work.

Slowly IT reached to a stage where it deserved to be. When one thinks of efficiency, improved performance, good governance, cost cutting, optimization of resources and better management practices, IT is getting strong consideration.

2.4.2 Business External

Number of researchers and academicians used Porter's competitive forces framework and have shown that IT can bring competitive advantage to business. Other writers too such as Parsons (1983), Rockart and Scott Morton (1984), Ives and Learmonth had identified many competitive opportunities which IT can create to manage competition. Increasing customers' switching costs, Improving functional efficiency and effectiveness, Product and service innovation, using IT as a vehicle to inter-organizational synergy and customer collaboration, Substitution to labour and zatisfying customer with improved services have been amongst them.

2.4 New Direction of IT Strategy

Even Japanese strategy to excel in their operational efficiency and effectiveness to make competition difficult to beat, succeeded with the help of information network. The way they could integrate the complete supply chain with manufacturing, successful delivery with better quality at lower cost became evident. They integrated organizations and operated successfully for one goal and created win–win case for their own business as well as to their suppliers. This kind of business strategy worked based on integration amongst people, process and IT. The famous story of managing Accounts payable at Toyota by very few employees than large workforce for Ford at USA, presents the case for IT enabled business model.

Below are few examples of new horizons of IT strategy where IT could influence the business and helped them making their strategies work.

Building barrier for competition: It helps to take lead over competitors offering, in terms of improved service, lead time, overall customer experience. Self service option provided by airline reservation, Internet banking and similar customer direct services have created such a good experience to customers that today no competitor can plan a competitive business without these services. In India even local Cooperative banks and public sector banks are compelled to match this to retain their customers.

Customer management: It helped the retailers and other service providers to understand the customer and their purchase need better. Offerings based on customers' last purchases could easily be made with the help of IT. Even item placement strategy is being decided based on consumer (visiting and targeted) behaviour that are captured and analysed by IT. It helped the sellers and service providers to personalize products and services. Simple things such as volume based discounts and services loyalty points persuade customers to stay loyal and buy from the same channel or retailer. This helped in retaining customers and creating barriers to switch. In many case cost to switch as well as personal familiarization to process, people and IT enabled services make customers think to stay in relationship.

Cost cutting: Some of the IT enabled services have helped the industry to bring down the cost so much that it created big barrier to entry and competition. "Low price—No frills—Walk in" airline services could be enabled because of IT. Senior airlines found it tough to compete with these low price ones on price, efficiency and lead time. Similar barrier has been created by "Any time—Any where" banking, and "Online services" by Leisure and hospitality industry. Integration of suppliers with logistic service provider and customer systems led by Walmart and Toyota has created barriers for other suppliers. It has helped to bring the cost down and efficiency throughout the complete chain.

New business model: New and emerging business models based on online purchase, payments and delivery has created business barriers for others to scale and match the service. Amazon, UPS and FedEx are in the top list of these kinds of services. Most of the automations which integrate information from operations to supply and delivery come under this umbrella. Warehouse automation, GPS based routing and many such IT enabled services created new business models and processes which moved customers from one supplier or service providers to the early adopter. Direct delivery by GE on order booked by the customers on Dealers network improved the lead time to delivery which became benchmark for others. This gave continued leadership to GE.

The modern IT strategy is relatively matured. The good thing is that the IT strategy and the approach to draft it are keeping pace with evolving technology, transforming business and emerging concepts. This agility has made it contemporary in every era. The demand and expectations from business has also contributed to this evolution. During every period, CIOs collected good wisdom as what worked and what did not. This learning has helped in evolution of new approach. They remained focussed to make IT strategy work. Few important learnings are being listed below (John Ward and Peppard 2002), even though some are related to IT strategy and others relate to its execution.

- Apply structured approach
- Focus on contribution to business
- Involve business people and make strategy to develop and support them
- Provide composite solutions rather piece-meal approach
- Make system agile as far as possible as business will keep changing
- Re-engineer business processes for visible benefits
- Extend project management techniques to IT implementation
- Need support from organizational structure, process and policies
- Keep watch on emerging technology and the usage that can give edge over competitors
- Have holistic approach to manage IT

Their thoughts were also influenced by many factors including changing business scenario and practices, evolving technologies and services, emerging business opportunities and upcoming theories from academicians as well as experienced consultants. All these inputs went into to make new incarnation of IT strategy as it looks today.

Slowly the organizations realized that IT is not just the technology management, it is much beyond that. Now, the creation of IT strategy is much more matured approach than what it used to be earlier. It has seen many disruptive transformations and it will continue to do so till new technologies and innovative ideas to use the technology in holistic sense keep emerging. Many local as well as international events and policies such as WTO agreements, UN climate summit, Free trading partnerships, Sarbanes-Oxley Act, money laundering regulations in international business and Trade restrictions will influence the direction by posing new constraints as well as creating new opportunities. IT managers and CIOs are needed to keep abreast with these changes, especially if these are impacting the business for which they are managing IT.

Modern approach to IT strategy starts along with business strategy. Number of methodologies is used for developing business strategies and many of them lead to IT strategy too. Accordingly, consultants and literatures are available to guide.

2.4 New Direction of IT Strategy

Today IT strategy has the following business imperatives

- It must have business goal
- It must work in close collaboration with business
- Its growth must be planned in line with people and process
- It should be managed like any business investment
- It should be able to capitalize technology for organizations' capability
- It has to be integral part of business service delivery
- It must be sustainable in long term, i.e. grow with organization and technology
- It should provide flexibility to business

Finally it should depict a roadmap of technological transformation of any organization, such that the change remains manageable and achievable.

The Porter's theory on strategy in the 1980s, John Kay's (2002) "Distinctive Capabilities" (innovation, architecture and reputation) and Gary Hamel's and CK Prahalad's "Strategic Intent" and "Distinctive Competencies" influenced modern IT strategy and its approach a lot. Though their thoughts were centred on Business strategies, IT came into picture when the focus was taken to make business strategy work. Many of the authors even included IT strategy into business strategy.

The way IT grew and influenced business, it became synonymous to innovation and change. Business managers started expecting IT to bring positive changes and it has been certainly introducing visible and promising change. The struggle continued for many years as who is responsible for managing changes in the organization, especially on people and process front. But after many researches by academicians, consultants and business organizations themselves, it was established that the main reason for failure of managing changes and IT projects were because of passive participation of business and functional team, and poor integration of IT objective with business. Thus, they recommended holistic innovation and effective change management. Similar views were expressed by many including Stuart Crainer, in an interview with Costas Markides, published under "The innovation solution" under "News and Events" at London School of Business. He points out that the companies need to start thinking of holistic innovation without separating Product innovation with technological innovation, process innovation and business model innovation. He recommends that the managers must act upon with knowledge that they will be benefited more if they take all of them together and act upon.

Even during one of the presentation telecast (Forrester_BT), Forrester expressed that IT should be looked as Business Technology and CEO should directly be driving rather than CIO. The speaker further justified that CIO would have much smaller domain under his/her control than what IT could influence to. Today, IT has been able to contribute towards many facets of business; hence, it acquired an importance where it deserves management's and board's attention. All these must be reflected in IT strategy.

These concepts and theories presented integrated view of IT strategy with business strategy. These lines of thoughts further led to evolution of enterprise architecture (EA) approach to develop IT strategy. EA not only helped to integrate IT strategy with Business but also aligned IT strategy with business.

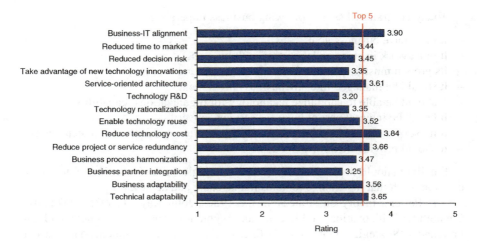

Fig. 2.2 Gartner report

Wikipedia defines EA as follows: "Enterprise Architecture (EA) is a management practice for aligning resources to improve business performance and help agencies better execute their core missions".

Architecture is generally referred as assembly of different components to make a complete structure, presenting unified value. Thus, architecture must reflect three elements, building blocks, their synergy and the emerging properties, e.g. The architecture of a software system (Wieringa 2004) has building blocks: software components, synergy: the way these components of the software are collaborating and unified value: functionality, services, behaviour, interfaces, reliability and usability. Similarly, if we look at Enterprises, we find that resources, people, assets, technologies and knowledge are bound together with common vision, mission, objectives, goals, strategies, structures and processes to produce value to customers, society and other stake holders. This representation of any organization is the base in creating IT strategy. The coherent and consistent view of IT across organization gives rise to common IT architecture and thus aligned IT strategy. That is why, under EA, IT gets self-aligned with business.

The FEAF (Federal Enterprise Architecture Framework—1998) and open group's EA definition (TOGAF—The Open Group Architecture Framework) covered four types of architecture: Business architecture, information architecture, application (system) architecture and IT infrastructure architecture. In this book we cover the last three under Enterprise IT architecture and IT strategy while referring to the first.

Gartner had published a survey, based on more than 200 EA programmes in March, 2007, depicting different drivers for EA and business-IT alignment has been the most important reason that the people adopted EA approach. The survey summary appeared as below in Fig. 2.2.

In the next chapter we will elaborate more on techniques to deliver IT strategy and that will include EA.

A very recent phenomenon which is becoming common now-a-days is assessment of Information assets during merger and acquisition. This is in line with takeover strategy that asset value of target organization is rightly assessed. Today it not only includes physical asset but also intellectual and information assets. During M&A, many companies have started evaluating IT Strategy and the potential costs and benefits of integrating IT systems besides workforces, facilities, processes and business functions. Some strategist and value assessor also derive the cost of transformation and alignment effort from current state of IT. A new approach is emerging through which better and quick assessment can be made with IT systems of target organization. Tata Steel, which has been acquiring companies since long, has always been evaluating this aspect. As a good practice, they do perform due diligence on this aspect and IT alignment as well. It has become priority item for them in making the merger successful. We also observe that IT not only represents the value of information asset but also presents the behavioural and attitude part of the management. Let organization behaviour specialist see through information base and they will foretell about the culture and the management practices.

On the other hand, many business organizations have made information as part of their product and services based on which their business runs. Well-known organizations such as Dun & Bradstreet and Standard & Poor base their business mainly on information assets. Today, many companies collect information, transform them to suit to their valued customers and sell. Interactive Prospect Targeting, UK, has been one of such companies which created complete business model based on information collection and services. Status of IT and Information base with companies such as Investment banking, Credit rating, Marketing and customer profiling and many others, present their intrinsic value.

Another area of strategy which has received prominence in IT strategy is use of convergence technology for business efficiency and smooth operation. This includes integration of data with voice, image, video, geographical maps, sensors and others. The trend to encompass all the aspects to make business process complete, automated and efficient with the help of convergence technology will continue to move up. And hence, IT strategy has to address this aspect to integrate data with this technology to make best out of information.

This topic just elaborated the expanding horizon of IT strategy, where it has retained its legacy in improved form and adopted many new areas. The current focus of business improvement and enablement has driven it to this stage and the same will take it even higher in future.

2.5 Need for IT Alignment with Business

The way IT has evolved from tactical role of supporting business to strategic, as key enabler, the perception of IT has changed in business context. This demanded IT being proactive and transformational in nature. Early role of just defining "as is" and creating application for business use changed to evolving "To Be" and enabling business functions. This required serious participation, collaboration and transformation.

The evolution of new way to business needed creativity with knowledge, will to be better, a roadmap to reach there and buy in of stake holders. These being the core management function, CIOs participate in business evolution and strategic planning process with different mind set than purely technological. CIOs bring similar perspective from information to what CFOs bring for financials. Realizing information being another valuable resource for business, CEOs and the board welcome inputs from CIOs.

While working through IT for such a long time, we observed that slowly business process knowledge gets embedded in IT. Sometimes IT people could explain and justify the current practices similar to, if not better than, the business people. This also happened because the IT people could see the organizational processes beyond functional and departmental boundaries. They have been more useful in evaluating and evolving business processes which could be more practical and acceptable to all the stake holders. (This observation is in no way to undermine the contribution of the functional teams, who can also contribute to what would make more sense to business in upcoming scenario.) The value in advice of IT managers and CIOs will depend on the relevance of their knowledge and inferences in context of the business, either existing practices or future processes. Therefore, when CIOs meet board or senior managers, the suggestions, recommendations and participation must have right alignment with business and then only their contribution will be appreciated.

The role of organization and senior managers are also important for effective contribution from IT and IT organization. They need to create right culture and opportunity for IT team to make useful contribution. Many of the researchers such as J. Yannis and Michael E. Tracy (1986), Ward and Peppard (2002) have traced certain reasons, which can improve the success rate of IT strategy and IT systems. And the cooperation and alignment have been amongst them. Even today, if we look deeply, we find the reasons are more or less the same, but they appear in different form which inhibits alignment of IT with business and IT playing right role in business. The lessons learnt have not been fully deployed across industries. These included inadequate understanding of IT and participation of senior management, misalignment of IT strategy and organization with business strategy, inability of organization to manage change and IT governance. We still find organizations creating IT strategies without considering above factors and then struggling in successful implementation.

The goal of IT team should be not to let the business people starve of information. The business people must get the information wherever, whenever and whatever form they need to execute their functions and play their roles, effectively. And to achieve the above goals of shaping IT for business and making information available in the hand of business managers, IT is aligned with business. Having business information, which fail to serve the purpose, will not only be wastage of effort and investment but also be loss of opportunity in the business sense. Today, every business is realizing that IT can give a new dimension to business and that is why the IT business has been growing all over the world. In an article "Better IT management for Banks", in "The McKinsey Quarterly" July 2007, reference to research performed by Ackermann et al. (2007), on "IT Operations of Banks in Europe, Asia and Latin America", the researchers clearly established the relations between various approach and status of IT in banking industry with the banks' performance.

They had indicated that banks' performance have been superior by not having superior technology or high spending, but effective and fruitful deployment of IT having reasonable technology. The banks reaped higher benefits, when they could integrate IT with business functions and managed it well. They well managed European banks have been able to manage IT better and that has reflected to their performance. They further analysed that some of the Indian private banks such as ICICI Bank, HDFC Bank have used IT strategically and innovated new products and services to build the strength of the business and attract new customers. These banks brought their service at par with what foreign leading banks could provide and thus succeeded in their customer strategy. The speed with which they have grown and grown successfully, IT had definite contribution to it. No wonder, ICICI (www.icici.com) CEO then, Mr. K.V. Kamath indicated in one of the interviews with McKinsey (with Lalit Puri, September 2007) that IT was so crucial for the success that he had started overseeing himself.

Business operations alignment to business strategy itself is a difficult process and need effort and strategy to achieve. Not only small organizations, which have limited resources and skill to quickly shift and align to new business goals and strategies, have problems but also the large organizations. In a recent SCTV telecast during November 2009, "New Ways of Working Together in the Consumer Goods-to-Retail Supply Chain", the speakers, Jim Falnney, Inez Blackburn and Mat Deeter (Falnney et al. 2009) shared their observations from assessment of organization alignment with organization goal at P&G. Large organizations are aware of this difficulty, and they take steps as well to improve organizational alignment with organizations strategy and goals because they know that they can reap benefit with alignment. The management must make the similar effort for IT alignment to reap benefit.

In an article, "What is Strategy", Porter (1996) suggested that organization must create sustainable strategic position. He elaborated that in a value delivery process chain all activities must fit and reinforce one another. Each activity must be strong in itself and complimentary to other links to yield competitive advantage. They should be consistent, reinforcing and optimizing effort. He explains with examples how the strengthening a series of activities, which produce competitive value, creates bigger barrier for competition. Finally he concludes that strategic fit amongst different activities is fundamental to competitive advantage and its sustainability. He calls it homogenization. IT is also viewed in same perspective, and hence, it is expected that it must be aligned to the business, reinforcing business processes and optimizing effort to produce better value for an organization; otherwise it works as negative force and turns out as retarding agent.

On IT Alignment with the Business Plan, Kearns and Lederer (2001), expressed five high level check points.

– The IS Plan reflects the business plan mission.
– The IS Plan reflects the business plan goals.
– The IS Plan supports the business strategies.
– The IS Plan recognizes external business environment forces.
– The IS Plan reflects the business plan resource constraints.

The authors could argue that CIOs' participation during evolution of business strategy improves IT alignment to business and quality of IT strategy, as they could understand the business perspectives and priorities better. They would align the effort and resources to achieve certain goals which they pick from the business strategy and business managers' perspective. We have seen the CIOs changing IT portfolio due to shift in new business strategies and priorities, rather sticking to what have already been initiated and held. This strategy works and helps to command respect and cooperations from business managers.

2.6 Changing IT Strategy for Different Stages in Business Life Cycle

There is neither one strategy which fits to all organizations nor one which works at each stage of the business. The same is true for the IT strategy too. Therefore, it is important to keep IT strategy aligning with changing business strategies and priorities of the organization as well as emerging technologies. In emerging countries where government policies, business scenario and customer demography are changing fast, IT strategy cannot be fixed for 5–10 years. But this does not mean that either an IT strategy cannot have a long-term perspective or it is stationary for life time.

If we see "The influence and Impact" model by John Ward and Joe Peppard, in a new context as below, it emerges clearly that the business environment is never static, and hence, the IT strategy has also to be as agile as the business is (Fig. 2.3).

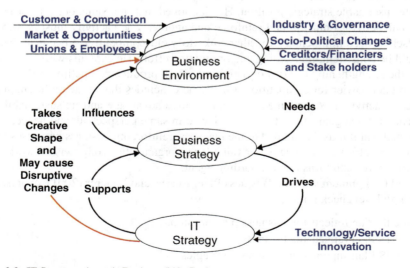

Fig. 2.3 IT Strategy vis-a-vis Business Life Cycle

2.6 Changing IT Strategy for Different Stages in Business Life Cycle

While business planning or strategy development, business managers take assumptions for certain business components to be static and others changing over a span of time. For example, rarely a business establishment takes product line or the factory location changing in short term, but market conditions could be changing quickly. This means that for certain components they plan on a long-term horizon and for others on a short-term horizon. The enterprise architecture and business strategy for infrastructure, product line, targeted customers are generally planned to be static over longer period but strategy for unskilled labour, intermediate stock level and price incentives are planned on shorter term. Same way, basic strategy for IT infrastructure, direction of IT services in the organization, line of technology platform, employee development and participation are made for long term, but user-end machines, resource deployment and H/W maintenance strategy could be of shorter duration. This division of what should be considered on a long-term horizon and what should be on a short-term horizon, depends on many factors, including business strategy, strategic intent of IT, time taken to build and stabilize, cost and organization preparedness to frequent changes, manageability and technological evolution. Market pressure and will to stay ahead are the other reasons which drive change. CIOs must consider the above factors and few more which are pertinent to their environment while preparing IT strategy.

We have experienced two very specific needs from business managers from both, the emerging economy as well as the developed ones. They have been information hungry. They always wanted more and more information, in line with their business needs, and secondly, they wanted it quickly. Most of the CIOs and the IT managers have the challenge to meet these expectations. By the time one system is ready and implemented, users return with some new requirements or the changes. Earlier, the system development and implementation used to take lot of time, long enough to change certain business needs. This happens more with the organizations which are relatively new to IT and evolving. This compelled IT industry and CIOs to change their strategies, including some good modelling techniques and tools which can give longer life to information infrastructure. This is what we discussed earlier that business users have been driving rather compelling IT industry to innovate and innovate on all dimensions. The IT industry has been coping with these phenomena with regular delivery of higher capability machines and user-friendly and industry specific software packages. Business process management (BPM), service oriented architecture (SOA), virtualization are few of them which support agility over stability while increasing life of IT infrastructure. CIOs too have to keep these in mind and exploit these offerings from industry to create additional value for the business, without getting into the jargons of IT. They need to manoeuvre as per the business users' preferences, i.e. evolving systems of shorter lifespan as well as stable and integrated system with reasonable life. CIOs need to understand this agility and create matching strategy.

This continuous evolution of IT does not let the IT department stabilize ever and yield the expected benefit. At the same time longer stability can leave it out dated and behind the industry. Therefore, a trade-off and a new strategy need to be adopted and that is careful balance and separation between evolution and stabilization.

Business managers too have to play a role in guiding IT team with necessary business need and direction. One need to plan with long-term strategy in mind while keeping eye on fundamental drivers and change agents which can give good guidance as what part needs more of research, trial and evolution and what needs stability. A constrained business strategy as well as implementation of new ideas will always be changing more frequently than core and main line of business. CIOs need to differentiate them as well as think of a mix that they can create to provide agile support to business. It is generally a good practice that a goal or an explicit expectation is created in the beginning itself. Continuous measurement and reviews must be held to keep the strategy and execution aligned. The achievements must be formally registered on every review. If IT strategy is on continuous change, matching the expectation of business for swift changes become difficult, it is recommended that a fresh start is made rather than creating too many work-around, which finally makes the strategy and the system brittle and vulnerable. It would be good idea to educate business managers with likely implication in this case.

McKinsey's "3 Horizon" framework for growth management is also applicable to IT (Coley 2009). It gives good understanding why a business has a mix of fast changing and stable business activities and why a CIO should also adopt both strategies at the same time. It indicates that the business starts working on "extending and defending core business" as first horizon, "building emerging businesses" as second and "creating viable options" as third. Depending on the current strength and strategy it focuses on one more than the rest two. In case business strategy is focussing more on internal efficiency and strengthening delivery capability, horizon one will get higher priority and accordingly IT should be aligned. But the other two horizons should continue to be on radar with an objective to quickly align IT strategy to new focus if the business strategy and focus shift. It is obvious that business scenario and the capability and maturity of the organization will keep changing and accordingly priorities and look-out of the business will change. What CIOs can do better that they do not let their eyes off from the other two dimensions. Thus, flexibility, scalability and upgradeability must be key features of IT strategy. McKinsey experts also suggest the same that Organization keep pursuing all three dimensions together, only the vigour to pursue some will be more than the other/s. Unconsciously or consciously, CIOs do work on similar strategy when they focus on delivering current need of business but continue to explore and work on emerging technologies and solutions for the future and upcoming business needs.

During 1990s, CIOs faced a dilemma of whether to spend on their existing systems to make Y2K compliant or to create new IT base for emerging business opportunities. Organizations which continued to keep their focus on all the three horizons came out in better shape after year 2000 to meet business requirement than those which just focussed only on Y2K compliance. The first category of organizations understood the opportunities offered by the Web technology and used the same to reach to their employees, customers and partners who are at distance while working on current systems. They helped the business to connect to their business partners and create value to business. On the contrary, the organizations of second category became laggard. In some cases, time being the essence of the business where early transformations provided lead to the business, the second category needed to do a lot to catch up. Quite often CIOs come across this kind of dilemma, which are posed by either business condition or the technology evolution. The IT infrastructure as well as capability mismatch are quite common constraints for IT organizations which does not allow swift changes to match the business expectations.

Similarly, business keeps changing their focus to different facets of their entire operations. Business strategy too moves around, based on their SWOT analysis. Sometimes it looks for strengthening their weak link in business and at others they want to exploit their strength. Its strategy is driven at one time by threats from competition and product substitution and at others by opportunities in the market. All business managers want their organization to move and shift swiftly as per their strategy, and IT is no exception. It depends upon the CIOs, how they tune IT strategy and align with business quickly.

Current state of IT in organization becomes one of the serious bottlenecks in this agility. CIOs work under constraints such that neither they can scrap existing strategy and infrastructure in one day nor they can be ready with new one next day. That is why McKinsey's "3 Horizon" model is important. This helps CIOs to respond to the changes quickly. They can keep the divide the team and be prepared to attend to static operational needs as well as transformational need of the organization. The business managers must encourage and support CIOs for maintaining preparedness on all the dimensions.

CIOs need to create different strategy for IT upgrade and service scope expansion especially for those corporate, which are already having some infrastructure in place and providing certain services to the stakeholders. This is called IT strategy for transition and expansion. We would recommend here as well to evaluate the transition from business perspective. CIOS need to evaluate the impact of continuing the current status and take the business manager in confidence for this transition. The case will be easier to justify when the likely impact is explained in terms of business. These could be collapse of service, trailing behind the business competitor, inability to service the growing business or increasing obsolescence and cost of operations. One can draft a strategy, which includes plans for service continuity, upgrade plan, transitioning people, process and systems, for the stake holders. In these cases well orchestrated move from one stage to the next stage is necessary, as transitioning stake holders from a stable phase is not an easy task. A proper risk assessment and controlled mitigation is necessary to have and demonstrate to the stakeholders. Stakeholders' needs at next stage such as integrated view of past and current must be taken care off. Some examples are like

- Easiest approach in transitioning the financial systems is to switch at the beginning of financial year with a strategy of getting past closed data in earlier system and new and live data in new system. This is most popular strategy where IT is taking quantum leap from small base.
- Post M&A, switch to the best system and practices at once with a conscious decision that there would be some hiccups for the other case which would be resolved with some or more effort but not what it would take for systematic and long drawn migration. This approach is followed when big organizations merge. Generally the bidder's systems and practices prevail.

2.7 A New Role for CIO

CIOs, who participate in business planning (F2), are more likely to understand business objectives and to link IT strategies closely with organizational strategies (Jones et al. 1995). CIO participation in organizational planning further improves the blending of technical knowledge with business and supports the goals of the business by creating alignment between IT and business strategies (Andreau and Ciborra 1996).

A CIO's role is influenced by many things including the business dependence on IT, CEO's game plan, stages of existing IT, growth and expansion plans, business focus and approach and attitude of business. The role has multifaceted dimension and that is why, the organizations have different expectations from IT.

In an article "Federal CIO Roadmap" published by Touchstone Consulting Group, Inc., a wholly owned subsidiary of Systems Research and Applications Corporation, a CIO is defined as critical role in any organization. This has summarized specific CIO responsibilities, as specified in law, regulation, and OMB (Office of Management and Budget, USA) circulars and guidance, and they are as follows. The expectations from CIOs in government governed organizations remain more or less same across governments.

2.7.1 Strategic Planning

It supports the idea that information is critical resource to organizations and the CIO is expected to play a strategic role for information resource management. This expects CIO to manage complimentary resources such as skilled IT workforce, technology and infrastructure, so that organization is benefited. But being biased to Federal organizations, it also expects to create strategies around budgets.

2.7.2 IT Alignment with Business

This mainly leads to IT alignment and IT modernization in line with government's agenda and scorecard. Even in government federation, it is important that IT is aligned to the structure and policies of the government. CIO uses different models including EA for IT alignment to business. She has to take initiative for performance improvement within IT and the business domain, create infrastructure which can be interoperable, secure, portable, scalable and cost-effective. The system integrates with other organizations in government and administration, as expected under government framework. US government promotes these practices in line with FEA (Federal Enterprise Architecture) reference model.

2.7.3 Budget Formulation and Capital Planning and Investment Control

CIO is expected to participate and guide the IT related investment and Control process. In government they may not have to do much of influencing or selling activities for investment proposal and approval, still they need to contribute initially to budget formulation and later to utilization. Generally CIO will be responsible to proper utilization and outcome of investments. They must take care of visible and justifiable usefulness of investment. Touchstone group indicates that under US federal structure CIO follows *select-evaluate-control* approach to monitor.

2.7.4 E-Government and IT Implementation

Every government takes help of IT for improving its business in governance, citizen centric services and efficient administration. It has become a good tool to communicate, listen and be transparent with citizens. Thus, a CIO's role becomes important in these initiatives and drives. CIOs need to develop strategy for eGovernance and promote such projects which align with government's objective and expectations of citizens, the customers of government. With limited resource but with wide scope, CIOs play key role in IT implementation. They need to keep in mind that they will get the budget in tranche and hence, the project should create its useful functionality in every sanction so that stoppage or late approval of further budgets does not waste investment.

2.7.5 Programme Management and Performance

This role is connected to planning and execution of programmes. A strategy to implement such a structure that funds are efficiently used, stakeholders are timely reported and benefits as well as connection to the governments' objectives and policies are measured and demonstrated. In consultation with the senior officials, a CIO must take due initiative in forming a suitable structure (Steering Committee) for programme governance. She should ensure that necessary policy and guidelines, standards, role definitions, monitoring and review practices are documented and followed.

2.7.6 Security and Privacy

This is vital function. Right strategy and implementation only can control and release information access. CIOs must create infrastructure, structure and policies to manage it, as lapses could lead to information leakage, misinterpretation, loss of confidence and some embarrassing moment for the government. There are many federal as well as local acts such as Federal Information Security Management Act (FISMA), The Privacy Act of 1974, E-Government Act of 2002, Health Insurance Portability and Accountability Act (HIPPA), Data Accountability and Trust Act (DATA)—HR 2221 in USA that are to be abided by. Every government has some what similar acts, which govern the data access and control practices. "RTI (Right to Information)", "Information Technology Act, 2000" from government of India and The "1998 Data Protection Act", "Census (Confidentiality) Act 1991", "Health and Social Care Act 2001—Section 60" from UK government are the examples of similar nature. CIO must ensure that relevant sections specifying the data accessibility and security vide different acts from respective governments are implemented and enforced in related IT systems.

At high level, a CIO's role in non-government business organization will be little different than that in government. Even though CIOs will do strategic thinking and participation in strategy formulation, budgeting, programme management and Information control as mentioned above, organization's perspective and more space to operate would make to play the role differently in business establishments.

Niloufer N Vazifdar, General Manager for Internal-audit and IT at Forbes and Company, expressed in an interview with "Searchcio Online" that soft skills are more important for CIO. He thinks, "The role of a CIO is not just limited to technology, but about management" (www.techtarget.in 2010). He quotes that the ability for Multi-tasking, Coordinating skills, Team building, Thinking at C-Level, Chemistry with boards, mental toughness, Right Balance makes CIO more effective player in the management. In our experience the following skills are must to play CIO role in any organization, effectively.

2.7.7 Salesperson

First and the foremost, a CIO must be a good sales person. Sensing and understanding business needs and selling solutions to business managers is key role of any CIO and IT managers. It is suggested (Austin et al. 2009) that CIOs should be playing a role of consultant and advisor to senior management which should give him close proximity to influence policy. And they have also demonstrated the business benefits. But first the CIOs themselves became passionate about making IT play significant role in business.

They need to understand it clearly that IT is for business purpose and more the value business manager perceive more the IT will become integral part of the business. This demands early and active participation of CIO in any business planning activity. Like any sales manager, she needs to understand the customer, customer's business and customer's industry, and then show a value map through IT. It is not an easy task, unless CIO understands business and speaks same language as the business people. The key function will be conceptualizing a strategic IT plan and selling and delivering firmly based on Business need.

2.7.8 Visionary and Business Focused

The basic responsibility to bring IT infrastructure and services to a level, where business finds IT as a valuable aid for growth and sustainability, lies with CIO and IT managers. Therefore, they need to be equally visionary if not more than the business managers. They need to understand upcoming need of the business and accordingly organize IT. Rather keeping IT ahead of business has become the need of the hours. Having this vision throws big demand on CIOs. They need to understand the business, business scenario including product/services, customers, market, competition, statutory need and many other key parameters and present a right technology solution for them. These solutions could be for managing current problems and issues or for the future. This creates goodwill amongst business managers and they start respecting this kind of CIO and IT managers.

This attributes also covers the responsibility of aligning the IT vision with Company's. Irrespective of the organizational strategic and tactical view, IT must play a vital role of supporting business (Weill and Ross 2009). IT is a critical resource and a CIO must make sure that this resource must be fruitfully utilized for business and that can only happen if IT is helping business to perform. It may work as planning tool, enabler to business process or tool to measure performance for analysis and corrective actions, but the goal and effort must remain in the same direction as of business. Even expectation of high investment in a small business, investing effort to implement non-priority systems while leaving strategic area out-of-focus, creating an application which cannot be absorbed by the business people or planning to outsource where support services are seriously constrained are cases of misaligned IT strategy. On the contrary, creating even a smaller system which can support vital and strategic need of the business while adapting to business constraints is a successful alignment. A small IT system (resulting from low investment) supporting maintenance requests, analysis of symptom and root cause, alerts and recommendation for preventive actions based on last reported solutions will classify as significant alignment to the business, than sophisticated system for payroll calculation for 200 employees. A CIO must restrict himself/herself from making decisions and adopting a strategy purely based on technology and personal likings, rather orienting all decisions to business will bring benefit to the business and buy-in from business people.

2.7.9 Business Transformation and Change Agent

CIO creates a roadmap and expands horizon for IT, based on business focus for today and tomorrow. A CIO is expected to not only create learning and performing organization within IT functional area but also proactively influence to whole organization. Supported by many innovations in technology and business practices, a CIO is expected to come up new and innovative ideas regularly (Smith 2006). I remember when I faced such expectations from a profit centre head and colleagues on my first assignment in this role. They always expected that I would come up with some better process and technology solution to a business problem and upcoming business practices. Later I became permanent member to business process innovation team. They not only expected that we will provide better solution but implement too. This threw a new dimension of our learning, i.e. understanding of business, the industry and the customers' business. For example, it helped me to understand why the customer wants standard mix of product variants in a lot than random mix at a time; and that influenced change in production planning process where dispatches were planned with respect to target customers. Again a business understanding of assembly process at client's factory helped to analyse and isolate cause of regular complain of component failure. A close association like this develops relationship and makes the IT team a partner and change agent. An IT strategy must create such opportunity for co-creation of value.

In an article in CIOCareer (www.ciocareer.com 2010), "The IT Organization of Future", the author summed it up this role very well. An IT organization needs to have 4Es (explore, engage, enable and evangelize) roles. It emphasizes that for a transformational role; exploration of suitable technology and solution, engaging all stake holders from inside and outside the organization, enabling business functions to make business strategy work and institutionalizing this change and mindset are necessary.

2.7.10 *Information Asset Promoter*

Information asset value creator and protector: The way CFO works continuously to ensure that the organization has the funds available for the business and the financial assets are in good health and of good quality, a CIO must constantly try for the same objective with information as asset. The quality and the value of information asset are ruled by its availability for operational and strategic purposes of the business. Other related assets such as Software and hardware come next. A business strategist would attach more value to HUL's IT asset in reference to its business than to what a coal mines have, and the reason being contribution and criticality of information for the business. A structured set of information and its integration and participation in business enablement increases its value. Therefore, a CIO must be on continuous watch to increase the valuation of this asset. Though the valuation of IT asset is not fully reported in published balance-sheets, the trend has started.

Protecting the value is equally important to value creation and addition. Theft, misuse and damage of information can erode the value and cause loss to the organization. The asset must be protected from falling in wrong hands such as pirate and competitors. There are many interested parties across the globe who indulges into this for personal and organizational benefit. Therefore, information must be secured from authorized users as well as unauthorized users, internal as well as external parties and through soft and physical mans. Framing good policies and practices and instituting them to protect these assets is responsibility of a CIO.

2.7 A New Role for CIO

Risk manager and whistle blower: In pursuit of increasing value of IT asset, a CIO has to play an entrepreneurial role. One cannot afford to take back seat as the role and function has inbuilt risk too. Most commonly risk happens around shift in business strategy and changing technology, which leads to obsolescence of this asset. Since both the risks are agile, IT cannot stand stationary. Thus, making long-term call on IT strategy and infrastructure would be difficult, but this, in no way, justifies no strategy and no plans. To mitigate the risk, some part of the strategy need to be developed with a long-term perspective and some for a short term. But regular review will be a good practice, as long term in reference to IT is not the same as in the case of setting up a manufacturing unit. As usual in every business, a risk is associated with reward; IT too appears having similar characteristics.

A CIO must take two calls, one what appears core static such as basic infrastructure, over a certain period of time, and another, what has short life. Accordingly, one needs to evaluate the benefit and necessity and plan for investment. An obsolete infrastructure, skill or legacy system would put more drag on business than becoming an enabler. The business people also need to be more open minded to consider cost of revitalizing IT as part of the cost of strategy implementation rather than taking it as overhead. Ignoring IT investment could become a costly proposition and risk to business. Knowing well the mind set of business managers, CIO must ensure that the business managers are aware of the risk as well as the benefit they will reap from the investment in IT. Selling IT in any organization is not an easy task except for few lucky CIOs whose counterparts in the business are enlightened with capabilities of IT. This too works on normal selling and buying principle, i.e. the value and the valuation. Therefore, a CIO must make sure that the balance between the value (usefulness) and the valuation (investment) are presented in favour of IT.

Sometimes, a CIO also needs to play a role of whistle blower. Organizations processes and disciplines are built into the IT system. The prevailing practices and health reflected by information is good indicator about the health of business and its practices in any organization. We support the idea that CIO should have her own scorecard which not only reflects the health of IT system but also the health of the business. A CIO can give a real analyst view as an outsider, as she is not part of day-to-day business operations. When the system and the practices in IT offer better value to business continuously, CIO has covered the occurrence as well as impact of the risk.

Programme manager: A business spends significant amount of fund from IT budget on new development, change transition and operations of IT systems. A CIO must manage it like any business manager, rather than a profit centre head, even though the organization considers it a cost centre. This is not because she would generate profit in real term but always be conscious about generating more value for business than the investment and the effort. More efficient and effectively a project is managed the benefit will be that much significant. This will also answer to some of the eye raising questions where business managers want to compare the investments between IT and other opportunities based on returns. This brings total shift in perspective and to make this happen she needs to be a good planner, organizer and implementer too. The value is generated all through the organizations in various forms, when IT helps in making good decision, achieving strategic goals, reducing cost, improving lead time and competitiveness and bringing efficiency and effectiveness in different business areas. As a business enabler strategy maker and committed to make this programme successful, a CIO must take the business people together. It would be good idea to inducing them to participate and develop ownership so that the success of the implementation is ensured.

Business managers and the CIO's peers look forward to the CIO for developing right IT strategy and implementing within the budget and stipulated time. This leadership requires a skill of good project manager, who can assemble different events and components in a right chain and ensure that they yield right result within given time and budget. This will need support from various agencies, colleagues and other stakeholders aligning to the main objective and working in tandem with the leader, the CIO. Thus, developing good relation and inter-dependence will help. Like any business, a good strategy and a matured plan create good foundation for execution, but effective and efficient execution along with the team is also necessary to reach to the destination, IT projects also need similar approach. This skill makes a CIO, a good programme manager. A successful IT strategy and IT project adds tremendous amount of value to the information asset.

Knowledge asset creator: Quite often, we hear that instead of having a good IT system users are not using it, rather they prefer their paper or self designed spread sheet for managing their business. The challenge remains for CIOs when they want to integrate these systems with each other. A business manager must understand that the value of information increases manifold when the information systems are integrated and are integral part of the value chain. Value gets added when users share common data and platform for their respective functional area in a complete value chain process. Again, the valuation of information asset moves up when it crosses boundaries of one specific function or user and become part of an organization and organizational process. More and more structured information participate and influence business, more the value it will have. Once information becomes essential component of business operation, improvement initiative and strategy formulation for various business functions, the information becomes knowledge and organization becomes knowledge driven. A CIO needs to address this facet of asset building at a priority.

The business goals, the strategies, the process, the performance and the measurements along with their linkages clearly depict the management approach and effectiveness. This set of information presenting the current status of any organization and its business performance, influence management actions and reactions, in future. That is why it is also termed as business knowledge. The key to knowledge is whether information helps in making inferences and learnings or not. A CIO must focus on the strategy to transform organization data into information and establish knowledge base while promoting its usage not only for regular operations but also for improvement drives and future strategies. This will help in transformation of business organization. A CIO must endeavour to achieve this goal, obviously with due support from CEO and the peers, as it needs cultural shift.

A smart plan for education and willing participation from users, managers and senior executives will help in this culture building. Under this plan information users and managers help to design the data and its source to make their role and effort more effective. Mostly the usage, inferences and direction for further refinement are pre-decided based on emerging data and trend. This work is led by functional subject matter expert. This helps the general users also to take a direction based on the information and initiate further exploration so that they can conclude the direction and initiate new set of actions to re-align with the goals and the strategies. The approach can be applied to any functional area including customer and competition management, operation, Sales and planning and others. A suitable policy and strategy for knowledge acquisition, storage, retention, distribution and usage must be part of IT strategy.

I saw a good example of this culture building, when I met a CIO who used to prepare proactively certain statistics and reports for even weekly coordination meeting based on the agenda of the meeting and importance of the business issues. He found that a good mechanism to facilitate useful discussion based on information, prioritization of issues and setting up new goals or alarms during reviews. This made IT an important organ of that organization.

2.7.11 IT Manager (Organization Management)

This is operation oriented role. Most of the people remain in this role without recognizing implied expectations and opportunities. Under this role one needs to manage a functional department of an organization as custodian of IT assets and expand/extend usage on demand. Incremental change and obsolescence management are business expectation. The focus is purely local where one tries to stay abreast of emerging technologies and propose new investment before it becomes critical. To make prudent use of infrastructure she organizes IT staff and other local logistics. She is also expected to assist organization in framing local policies, practices and standards pertaining to IT function. Even though it sounds like internal orientation and non-strategic in nature, from strategy execution point of view this operation is important. Keeping IT infrastructure ready to deliver information in time and in place is critical to IT as well as to business. This too demands Knowledge and understanding of IT along with business understanding. However, having sole responsibility of technology and technology direction, she must have good skill to understand the need and deploy the right technology, while protecting the organization from the bad effect of technology hype.

Most of the CIOs will agree that this role is obvious but hardly the organization realizes that the structure, reporting and support are necessary element for its effectiveness. We recommend that IT must be represented in the top management and during meetings for business strategy creation and review, not only for being aware of what emerges but also for active participation. And CIO must hold direct responsibility for this.

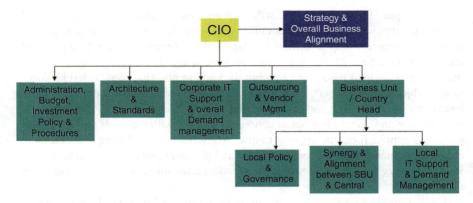

Fig. 2.4 Organization structure

A CIO is responsible to create right organization structure while keeping eye on the demand from business users and business priorities. A good governance practices must be put in place for effective operation and utilization. McKinsey's "3-Horizon" framework must be kept in mind. A federated organizational structure, as below (Fig. 2.4), is recommended for a CIO to manage IT function in any organization.

Some of the responsibilities related to the compliance with local and country rules and regulations also come under this role. They look for more information, transparency and evidence of compliance to the rules. They read and infer a lot about the organization practices through reported data. As McKinsey Quarterly indicated in the article "Five trends that will shape business technology in 2009", the government scrutiny and the regulatory expectations are on rise and CIO need to be vigilant about fulfilling these commitments on behalf of the organization. Rules and acts such as below have serious impacts and need to be adhered.

- Part 11—Electronic Records; Electronic Signatures (FDA, USA)
- Patients personal data protection (HIPPA—USA)
- Public company accounting and reporting (Sarbanes-Oxley—USA)
- Federal Information Security Management Act (FISMA—USA)

Many of these are not only the bindings on the businesses in and around the same country but also to the interfacing organizations from different countries. In India also ministry of company affairs started demanding more and frequent reporting, after Satyam's episode, to assess business health and identify if financial irregularities are creeping in. All these regulatory reporting originates from information and CIO is custodian of the same. Therefore, CIO must lead the practice in any organization to establish such systems, which meet government and regulatory mandates at manageable cost and minimal disruption.

2.7.12 Creating a Culture of Performance and Value

This is again strategic in nature. Every business head wants to have IT people who possess knowledge of IT and be business oriented while delivering innovative solution and value to business. These kinds of people are respected and are able to lead others too to make new things happen.

The good thing is that workforce in IT is still young, full of energy, interested in innovation and impatient to deliver. A CIO must channelize this energy and commitment for the business. No wonder HR managers think that motivating IT people is easier as well as difficult. With little encouragement and support from top managers, IT people will be able to influence respective business users and harness their skills and capability for the business. This is most prevailing practice in emerging countries and also seen in some cases in developed nations, where IT envisioning happens at the top and under the leadership of CIO the strategy is driven. Business people are not very willing partner to this transformation. This lets the organization put extra effort, investment and time to achieve the same goal what could have been easier otherwise. But time is changing, competition, efficiency and personal interests are bringing more and more business users into this initiative.

Knowing well that IT is a game of mind and people are greatest resource, a CIO must (IBM 2008)

– Create agile and committed team: Recruit, train and retain
– Nurture enterprise-wide collaboration within and across organizational boundaries, time zones and cultures
– Offer new challenges and portfolio of solutions
– Manage growth potential and expectations of employees
– Instil the confidence of fairness in reward, recognition, development, performance evaluation, nurturing innovation, supporting ideas and soliciting advices, exposing them to bigger role and offering opportunities.

Infosys Business Consulting team has presented the following chart depicting role of the IT organization, and CIO being the leader must make the organization to come up to that expectation. His biggest role would be to make the team perform up to the expectation of the stake holders (Fig. 2.5).

While writing about CIO's role or new incarnation of a CIO, we realized that CIO needs to be champion of soft as well as professional skills. Does it mean that he/she need to be from special breed and most ideal professional on this earth? The answer is yes as well as no. As discussed earlier, depending upon the business condition and road map to the destination, she will need better skill in one area than the others. On the other hand, the expectation remains the same from all professional managers and executives that they excel in multiple skills. The good point is that the technology has offered a big lever to the business and the benefit depends on how much it can be leveraged. Thus, achieving and demonstrating the business benefit is much easier than ever. All said and done, CIO also has limitations what she can do

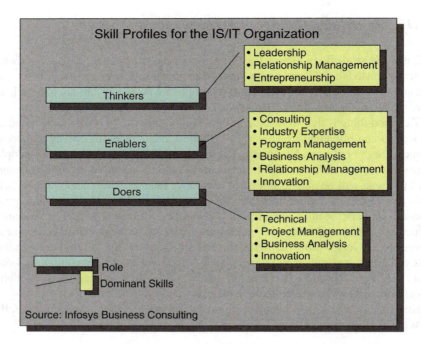

Fig. 2.5 Different facets of CIO (Source: Infosys Business Consulting published in CIOCareer)

herself and what would need cooperation and participation from others. It is up to the senior managers to see that the IT and the CIO are not choked in their organization. The outcome from IT still depends on business process transformation and collaboration, a CIO must learn to collaborate, lead and share the success. IT is just one out of three essential elements (people, process and technology) to successful transformation. A CIO, having good support from organization, can easily amalgamate technology with the other two to deliver best in the industry.

2.8 Planning for IT Strategy

Ideally the management initiate the task of IT strategy formulation after giving due guidance. Just in case it is not, CIO should initiate this task after taking CEO in confidence. Irrespective of the case, the tasks are the same, only this exercise becomes far easier, if it is driven by business strategy owners and key managers participate willingly.

2.8.1 Collect Data Related to Business

We discussed above that IT Strategy must be business oriented hence all preparation must start from the understanding of business. And a good point (Beveridge 2002) to start this is collecting information related to the following:

- What drives the business
  - Vision, mission and objective
  - Short- and long-term goals and strategy
- What business we are in
  - Industry and sector
  - Line of product and services
  - Key customers and competitors
  - Key market and market trends
  - Business model
  - Business drivers and transformation plan
  - Role and state of IT in the above
- How we are organized to deliver
  - Organization chart
  - Roles and responsibilities
  - Formal and Informal processes
  - Key measurements
  - Key suppliers
  - Pain areas
  - Role and state of IT in the above

Expectations of business from IT: These are basically to understand where the organization stands today. This step will also be helpful to identify opportunity for improvement. A good strategist should try to understand the behavioural aspect of the organization as well, as factors such as organization culture, inter-personal as well as inter-departmental dynamics, bureaucracy, management style (management by exception, management by objective), and power centres do influence IT strategy.

2.8.2 Prepare Management Team

It is important to take the important and influential stake holders of IT strategy in confidence and organize a briefing session to achieve their suggestions and concurrence. This briefing should contain the following:

- Why IT strategy is important
- How this supports to the management strategy
- Who all should be involved

- What will be the outcome and how the full journey will go
- Why their participation and guidance are important including what is expected from them to create a good strategy

Depending upon the organization culture and management's opinion about IT, the briefing should be organized and minute to be circulated. Sometimes, CIOs also hold one-to-one meeting with key managers before this briefing session. The success depends on how the benefits to the business in general and functional area of respective managers in particular are shown. It is sales process and CIOs prepare a lot for this session. The outcome of this meeting gives first glimpse of fate of IT strategy.

A CIO must get the management commitment to drive it like any Business Planning session and the approval for steering committee, suitable team structure and members with defined goals and timeline.

2.8.3 Initiate Collaboration Plan

CIO must identify key stake holders and manage relationship with them for support and guidance. As more and more organization culture becomes democratic even top person wants collaborative work and decision-making rather than taking hard decision and pushing it downwards. Though in a family-driven business as well as a business where top man is in a strong position, push works do not yield always a desired result. The resistance and the indifference derail this process and further execution.

I have seen couple of CIOs successfully getting the commitment from senior and powerful managers, not by delegation or through circulars and office orders from top person, but by attaching significant role and showing extra respect to them. One just need to keep in mind that the best strategy may not be the one that CIO thinks, but it would be the one that works and by which the organization is benefited. CIOs must control their ego and then facilitate collaboration. On items or agenda where stalemate is likely must be resolved separately before participants take egoistic stand and make it win–lose or lose–lose case. There could be a case where a CIO needs to take commitment and agreement on personal basis to move forward, but that should be avoided as far as possible.

2.8.4 Create Mind Set for Process Re-engineering and Business Alignment

There is always opportunity for improvement, especially in business domain. A CIO must take this opportunity for improvement and alignment. Process Re-engineering and Business alignment quite often gives good result. Therefore, it is worth influencing the respective business manager to think differently or out of box to identify such opportunities. A CIO should prepare and come out with ideas and thought provoking questions that can be placed before the team, working out IT strategy, such that the team explores possibilities with open mind. The examples could be like switching from centralized IT service stations to user driven self-service mode, introduction of information based preventive maintenance practices than break-down based or prioritizing sequence of inspection of incoming materials based on demand from stock manager and the past complains with respect to supplies from suppliers than first-in first-out.

The business priority must be central theme of IT strategy. SWOT analysis of the business might have indicated the high yield and focus area, and IT strategy must be in accordance to the same within certain parameters. It would be worth preparing to discuss demand from customers, suppliers, government, industry and other stake holders to set the tone for improvements. If current status is available a comparative statement would trigger good discussion and the outcome.

More the IT strategy is aligned, more the chance it will have for buy-in and over-all success. The CIO must get ready to control the expectation building too, as some managers may look forward to very optimistic change and the benefit. It could be based on their readings of success stories or the technology hype. A CIO must prepare to help them to elaborate and have realistic view with respect to their organization. At the same time, this would be right occasion to slowly set the expectation of upcoming changes in respective areas, so that all participants are getting mentally prepared for self change as well as influencing others in and around their domain.

2.8.5 Focus at Business Benefit and Investment

A CIO must keep in mind that selling of IT strategy will happen in accordance with the benefit that it can promise and achieve. Fortunately and unfortunately the benefit comes out from the business domain which is not under direct control of CIO. Therefore, this team must be persuaded in a way that they also identify the benefits clearly, whether they are tangible or intangible. At times, CIO may need to help them in this process. They need to evaluate the benefit in view of upcoming investment or effort. Fortunately, the willing participants apply their mind to innovate and come out with brighter ideas, having more benefits. Another way is to show them their current processes and value chain, and suggest some changes in process or introduction of IT that can improve benefits and help them to achieve the targeted goal from the strategy that they had formulated. A CIO must work with them to visualize such opportunities and reap the benefit. It will be worth considering the statutory compliances that organization needs to achieve and the cost of non-compliance. These benefits become good guidance for creating IT strategy as well as prioritizing the investment and actions.

These preparations followed by regular team meeting is the beginning of the good It strategy. In the next chapter we will discuss the technique at length.

2.9 Summary

In this chapter, we start with evolution of strategy, where we discuss the way it has been evolving over few decades. We discuss the changing focus and the approach from last few decades and the way emerging technology, business practices and business problems have influenced it. Learnings from successes and failures have also influenced the direction and the approach. Slowly, the whole IT and Business community converged to the idea that IT strategy must be aligned to Business strategy for its success and benefit to the organization. There are different approach and techniques to achieve the same but a top-down approach with Enterprise Architecture has been gaining more popularity. We also discuss that no strategy work for all the time and at all stages of business. Strategy for technology upgrade for sustenance and business improvements for managing competition will be different, as they have different focus but they can be combined together to be part of one common strategy.

Changing times demand change in roles and perspective. A CIO needs to be more business oriented and maintain balance between internal and external focus. A good understanding of business imperatives and collaborative approach always help to shine this role. Till a CIO understands the management perspective and appreciates the perspective of individual influential pockets, she can manoeuvre well and get buy-in from respective stake holders. She must be ready to create win–win situation and to keep focus on business benefit, which can make the job easier.

IT strategy process requires certain preparation. We call it "Strategy for IT Strategy" and it is recommended to every CIO that she pay attention to them. There could be few extra tricks too, but the main objective here should be to get the commitment and participation from all the stake holders.

2.10 Glossary

CIO	Chief information officer
CSF	Critical success factors for success in business
IT	Information technology
IT alignment	This term implies that output of technology investment should support business goals
Change management	This is defined as change that is required in an organization to achieve a new and desired state
Y2K	This refers to the problems that the business world suffered at the start of year 2000. During this time, because of programming logic problem, the world went through business turmoil

2.11 Review Questions

1. How IT strategy has evolved over years?
2. What is role of a CIO?
3. What are required qualifications of a CIO for a manufacturing organization?
4. What is outsourcing?
5. How collaboration ensures business integration?

2.12 Project Work

Please form a team of five members and visit a manufacturing organization which would have existed for last 10 years. Discuss with the head of IT department about the role of IT in achieving business objectives. Find out evolution of IT over years and the way the role of IT has changed in these years. Based on this discussion, draft a report on changing role of IT in a manufacturing organization.

Bibliography

Ackermann J, Yeung MA, van Bommel E (2007) Better IT management for banks. In: Extracts from the original article IT operations of bank in Asia, Europe and Latin America. The McKinsey Quarterly (by authors)

Austin RD, Nolan RL, O'Donnell S (2009) The adventures of an IT leader. Harvard Business School Press, London

Beveridge C (2002) Aligning IT with business strategy. In: Guidelines for IT management. National Computing Centre, Manchester

Business Technology (2008) www.forrester.com

Checkland P (1981) Systems thinking systems practice. Wiley, Chichester

Coley SC (2009) Enduring ideas: the three horizons of growth, Dec 2009. McKinsey Quarterly

Corporate Board Member magazine (2007) in association with Deloitte Touche Tohmatsu. 2007 Board and information technology strategies report: maximizing performance through it strategy. CIOindex.com

Craig D, Kanakamedala K, Tinaikar R (2007) The next frontier in IT strategy: a McKinsey survey, Spring 2007

Falnney J, Blackbur I, Deeter M (2009) New ways of working together in the consumer goods-to-retail supply chain. Telecast on Supply Chain TV, November 2009

Federal CIO roadmap. Touchstone Consulting Group, Inc. CIOindex.com

Hirnoven A (2007) Introduction to enterprise architecture. University of Jyväskylä, Jyväskylä and TietoEnator Corporation, Helsinki, 23 Aug 2007

http://www.opengroup.org/togaf

IBM (2008) Creating an adaptable workforce: important implication for CIO. The IBM Global Human Capital Study, March 2008

James M (1987) Information engineering (4 volumes). Savant Institute, Carnforth

Kearns GS, Lederer AL (2001) Strategic IT alignment: a model for competitive advantage. Twenty-second international conference on information systems, Charlotte, NC, 13–15 Dec 2001

McLean ER, Professor and Smith Chair in Information Systems. Business System Planning, Robinson College of Business, Georgia State University, Atlanta, GA

Mclean ER, Turban E (2005) Information technology for management, 5th edn. Wiley, New York

Nolan RL (2000) Information technology management 1960–2000. In: Chandler AD, Cortad JW (eds) A nation transformed by information. Oxford University Press, Oxford

Parsons GL (1983 Fall) Information technology: a new competitive weapon. Sloan Manage Rev 25(1):3–14

Porter ME (1996) What is strategy. Harvard Bus Rev Nov/Dec, 61–78

Rockart JF, Scott Morton MS (1984) Implications of changes in information technology for corporate strategy. Interfaces 14(1):84–95

Smith GS (2006) Straight to the top: becoming a world-class CIO. Wiley, Hoboken, NJ

Smith H, Fingar P (2003) Business process management: the third wave. Meghan Kiffer, Tampa, FL

Spitz JM, dePaschalis EG (2005) The "Quals" of the ideal CIO. Research report #15. The Systems Consulting Consortium, Inc., Orinda, CA

Stuart Crainer, in an interview with Costas Markides, published under "The innovation solution" under "News and Events" at London School of Business, http://www.london.edu/newsandevents/news/2009/11/The_Innovation_Solution_1045.html

Vazifdar NN, GM (internal Audits) at Forbes & Company. Searchcio.in http://searchcio.techtarget.in/news/article/0,289142,sid205_gci1376389,00.html?track=NL-1432&ad=740194&asrc=EM_NLN_10322749&uid=5632028, 2010

Ward J, Peppard J (2002) Strategic planning for information systems, 3rd edn (Chap. 1). Willey, Chichester

Weill P, Ross JW (2009) IT savvy: what top executives must know to go from pain to gain. Harvard Business School Press, London

Whittle R, Myrick C (2004) Enterprise business architecture: the formal link between strategy and results. CRC, Boca Raton, FL

Wieringa R (2004) Architecture is structure plus Synergy. http://graal.ewi.utwente.nl/WhitePapers/Architecture/architecture.htm

Wikipedia. Business system planning, http://en.wikipedia.org/wiki/Business_System_Planning

www.CIOCareer.com

www.CIOIndex.com

www.gartner.com

Yannis BJ, Treacy ME (1986) IT and corporate strategy: a research perspective. In coordination with Centre for Information System Research Sloan School of Management, Massachusetts Institute of Technology Cambridge, Cambridge, MA

Chapter 3
IT Strategy Framework

3.1 Learning Objectives

This chapter would:

- Elaborate the framework for IT strategy
- Help in identification of business drivers for IT strategy
- Assist in analysing stakeholders requirement
- Focus on process change for changing business needs
- Identify opportunity for IT in business
- Describe IT alignment with business
- Detail prioritization of key application area and integration
- Suggest the process for technology strategy

3.2 Introduction

Today, different frameworks are available to define IT strategy. The goal remained the same, i.e. IT for business purpose, but the scope and dimensions have changed. Slowly it shifted from business-internal centric to business centric. It started creating value within operations as well as beyond. It used to support service-provider in opportunity identification and justification to customer for IT usage in 1960s and 1970s, but later it shifted to assist customers to identify business improvement opportunities (in 1980s and 1990s). By the end of twentieth century, IT became fully Business-savvy. However, slowly its contribution in transforming business increased to the extent that it stepped into a new domain, what Dr Weill called IT-Savvy Businesses. This category of business has IT as its Strategic Asset and gets business insights and opportunity for innovation from IT. It exploits power of digital platform to have efficient processes and collaborate with its ecosystem of customers, suppliers and partners.

Over changing times, the priorities and focus for IT also change in a business organization. Its role changed from support to internal operation to business transformation. As presented in McKinsey survey (Roberts and Sikes 2009), during 2008, more business managers expected IT to contribute for improving business efficiency (39%) than that of cost cutting (27%). Even after financial meltdown, when "Cost Reduction" became buzz word, the scenario did not change much and in 2009 survey, 33% preferred cost reduction role of IT over 31% for business efficiency. This confirmed the consistency in expectation and long-term vision of business transformation role for IT. Now, many expect that IT will create new business and business models.

It is true that during mid 60s IT companies and consultants coined the word "Transformation" to revisit business practices for business benefit as well as to sell their products and services. But the meaning remained limited to mixing IT in selected business functions. Slowly the industries found merit in the approach, when they realized that this is good exercise to align business strategy with organization focus on one hand and operations on the other. IT just played its role effectively to make it happen. The meaning of transformation kept expanding and it means much more today. Every transformation has a goal and that is to improve business by bringing in the change. The change must be manageable and bring in enduring and sustaining benefit to the business, so that targeted goal of maintaining customers and winning over competitors continue. To monitor the journey and progress, defining Key Performance Indicators (KPI) and monitoring them on an ongoing basis have been a good technique.

According to Mike Morrison, "Business Transformation is a change management strategy, which has the aim to align People, Process, and Technology initiatives of a company more closely with its business strategy and vision. In turn, this helps to innovate and support new business strategies". Thus, transformation targets at the alignment of resources, people, process and technology in the direction of strategy and business goals to produce desired effect. This holistic approach to business where all these elements produce best effect, used to be called business transformation. Dr William Stratton has rightly pointed out while qualifying transformation that it could be small transformation for efficiency improvement, while large transformation can change business direction. Therefore, his wise advice to evaluate the need and quantum of transformation is essential before launching it, is very relevant (Sttraton et al. 2009).

Later a matching term Business reengineering was coined and gained credentials when Michael Hammer wrote an article in Harvard Business Review in 1990 and published a book with James Champy in 1993, and management thinkers such as Peter F. Drucker advocated this idea. Managers used to take this journey to build organization capability by changing in one or many areas. While keeping the proposed change in manageable limits, they used to be open to revisit strategies depending upon what they can achieve in each of the strategic component and overall. IT has always been in the focus of this strategy, as business people started finding IT a significant enabler, the capacity and capability is yet to be exhausted (Fig. 3.1). Looking at its usefulness in improving and transforming business, many started calling it business technology.

3.2 Introduction

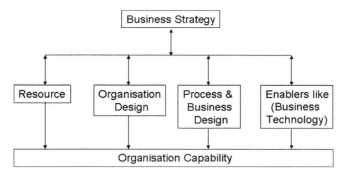

Fig. 3.1 IT as an enabler

This approach of alignment and creation of synergy amongst all the elements posed good amount of responsibility on IT to support the organization initiatives. It continued to be a disciplined player in this journey of value creation. Therefore, the CIOs plan IT transformation too to the limits that it remains in tune with other elements and do not create stress in the system by misalignment. They keep in mind that IT falls within the purview of organization's value chain analysis and making this link either stronger or weaker than other links does not create extra value to the organization. In one situation, it eats up the resource without good return and on the other it becomes a constraint to desired performance. A CIO also needs to trade-off amongst many variables, including investment, provision for future, time period and obsolescence. Business managers must understand this pressure and cooperate with CIO to make a right decision, which suits best to the organization.

- How much provision she should keep for future, which is rational investment and will earn right return for business without risking obsolescence during finite time period?
- What should be this "finite time" and whether business will be able to achieve the goal within it?
- How much she should move with current technology and how much she should provision for emerging technology?

Therefore, like any business manager, a CIO too look into objectively and analyse before making own decision and recommending to the organization. But she needs to keep IT in forefront of organization capability building initiative to achieve the business goal. In this process, when CIOs find that the collaboration with other organizations can help to build better capability or bring in better value in terms of skill, knowledge, expertise, investment and cost, they start thinking of partnering and outsourcing. Even then the focus must remain to the basic objective of how to achieve the strategic goal and goal of transformation. A CIO must help the organization in this journey too and the division of work must be intrinsic value based, like large organizations do. Most often they drive strategy, plans and critical business knowledge themselves and let the partner drive the area which are either commoditised or are of no business significance.

Phases / Stages of Strategies	Gather	Analyze to Align	Strategise & Design	Review/Finalise
Business Direction and Drives				
Business Needs				
Process & Organisation				
Applications				
Technology				
People and Motivation				
EV & ROI				
Options and Implementation				

Fig. 3.2 Approach for IT strategy

We recommend a step-by-step approach for IT strategy as below in Fig. 3.2. On phases from left to right, i.e. "Gather" to "Execute and Review", whereas for stages from top-down, i.e. "Business Direction" to "Investment and Benefits".

3.3 Understanding of Existing Relation Between IT and Business

This is an important phase where the CIO develops a high level understanding of current status of IT in the organization and its adaptability, before top managers. This is part of the precursor to business planning, so that the managers have somewhat realistic perspective of one of the important enabler during business strategy session. It would be right to form a high level team comprising business managers and the CIO being one of the members may be the managing secretariat of the high level committee.

It starts from home, where this team takes stock of state of IT internal and IT external factors, as below, while keeping eye on three means of business innovations (Fig. 3.3).

The following are looked into to understand the factors internal to IT:

– State of IT infrastructure and operations cost
  This provides information about status of existing IT infrastructure and whether the current support to business can be sustained and grown over a reasonable time. In case the infrastructure is moving towards obsolescence and causing additional operational and maintenance cost, it may cause interruption and risk to business continuity. It is right time to draw attention of the management about the health of IT infrastructure and justify for upgrade and change. The benefits that it can bring in terms of business and saving on overall operational cost must be highlighted. The alternatives in terms of buy or hire and own or outsource should wait till the team reaches to technology, implementation and service selection stage.

3.3 Understanding of Existing Relation Between IT and Business

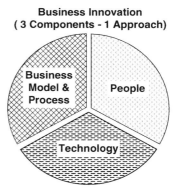

Fig. 3.3 Business innovations

Change one, two or all to create value and competitive edge.

- Skill Inventory for serving existing needs as well as futuristic need
  Many a time, the existing skill level of IT team goes below the level where it can sustain current services as well as implement new systems for future area. This can happen due to complacency, lack of opportunity, poor retention and skill upgrade policy as well as being out of focus on upcoming technology. This impacts whole IT function from the stage of guiding and supporting the management for right IT strategy to final service delivery. There must be right strategy to augment this capability which can save the business from losing a foresight on technology domain and its contribution to business.
- Pending needs of business
  When IT starts lagging to business and its other two innovation components, the biggest symptom appear is inability to fulfil the matching demand from business. The business people express their dissatisfaction over the quantity of the service if not the quality of the service from IT function. This includes time and effort dimension to serve as well, where time taken or effort spent is unduly high. Even though CIO organizes to create list and right business priorities, in absence of matching capabilities, she is unable to service them. It is good idea to revisit those pending requests once more before presenting the case for matching IT strategy. This list should include demands from all stakeholders from business operations and senior management.
- Issues in hand with IT organization
  This could be related to IT organization structure, overall capability of IT function, management approach to IT, integration of IT with other business functions, integrated service to business value chain and others. The objective here is to collect and define the issues that are causing hindrances in the performance as well as capitalization of full potential of IT. If IT assets are fragmented and integration can enhance the value, this aspect must be recorded in this list. This also includes the gap between new technology and state of IT in the organization, even though the value loss from the gap emerge later while working out Application and Technology strategy.

  And then a summary of state of external factors to IT function should be listed too.

Table 3.1

End user	User segment need	Opportunity for improvement	How IT can serve the need

- Gap between upcoming practices and trends and prevailing in the organization
  The team collects information from different sources about new trends in business models, practices and delivery, especially where IT has influenced. This is to basically create a feel to the management colleagues about the world and the industry trend, and what this organization needs to do if it wants to reach there. The benchmark and comparison do not limit to existing local competitor, but it expands to best-in-industry, best-in-class and international arena. This factor helps in opening up new ideas and new horizon.
- Emerging opportunities in business
  This relates to list of various opportunities around business functions that have passed through the eye-lens of the team. This relates to not only the explicit requirements for IT support that has reached to CIO, but also the observations of business and IT people as well as internal customers while working along with. In practice there are many areas which come on radar of CIO and business managers through feedback and suggestions from own employees as well as other stakeholders which emerge during various discussions, including management meetings and reviews. Sometimes this will include changes in business practice as well.
- Issues and demand from the external stakeholders
  This is to identify potential area where IT can contribute and create visible business benefit. Generally, the team meets the managers of organizational interfaces, such as Purchase & Stores for Suppliers, HR for employees and unions, Sales for customers, Finance for government, banks and auditors, and others. They collect demands from, issues with and wish lists of the stakeholders. These provide sense of direction to the team and CIOs and feedback to the management for prioritizing IT and its focus. Table 3.1 below can be handy for recording internal as well as external needs and analysis and prioritization during strategic considerations
- Business function distribution
  One organization, which has been operating units at different locations, wanted to stream line business process for quick consolidation of operations result and reduce lead time to decision, drastically. The IT team analysed the operational aspect and tried to understand the approach and impact before proposing IT strategy for the same. They came out with analysis as below (Table 3.2)

3.3 Understanding of Existing Relation Between IT and Business

Table 3.2 Business function distribution

SL	Functional area	Functional Integration between HO and units		
		High	Medium	Low
1	Power Generation and Sales			Local, One customer, Stable plan, Fixed price formula.
2	Procurement		Local as well as central purchase	
3	Stores			Local Store and function
4	HR and Payroll	Mixed & dependent HR/Payroll function		
5	Asset Maintenance			Plan and execution locally, major shutdown approval from HO
6	Budgeting & Costing	Integrated function for preparation to approval and pricing		
7	Payables		Budget and fund approval from HO	
8	Receivables and GL, Fund Mgmt	Sales, collection, depreciation and Main a/c Fund req and investment		
9	Docs/Records			Policies, goals, budgets, performance, reports
10	Approvals	Budget, special expenditure, HR plan, compensation, HR policies & others		
11	Statutory Reporting & Payments	Statutory & rehabilitation payments & reporting, PF, gratuity, taxes, audits etc.		
12	Projects		Plan, approval, monitoring, contracting, control	
13	Performance & Reporting		Performance reporting & review	
14	Security & Utilities			Local under unit mgmt

– Imbalances amongst three components of business innovation
  This is a structured approach to make right assessment about the gaps caused by imbalances amongst three components. As described earlier in this book, the three elements must balance amongst themselves to get the best benefit out. Over a period of time one or two elements move forward but the laggard impedes the progress and benefits of the other/s. Therefore, it is good approach to identify such a gap and present the case so that the business strategy also pays due attention to

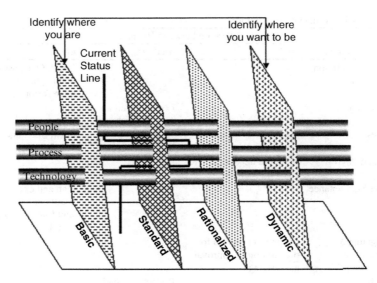

Fig. 3.4 Four stages of progress

this aspect before rolling out a visionary plan. Figure 3.4 below presents the status of these three elements over four stages of progresses, for a public sector organization.

"Basic" indicates whether they have the basics in place e.g. people have some processes and practices (even though they are not written) in place and they are using IT in some form for their work. This indicates that organization has some base and rest can be built after that.

"Standardized" indicates whether the system and process are standardized and being practiced as per the written procedures. People are aware of these and follow it more consistently. Written rules in government which are followed and enforced through audits come under this category. Achievement of this indicates that people are doing right things as per the defined practice. IT resources are available to help them achieve work completion. There still could be more opportunity for improvement.

"Rationalized" indicates that the processes and systems are optimized with respect to the objective of the business functions. Here the technology support is available to the business users for producing reasonable result. Here the opportunity for improvement is limited.

"Dynamic" is altogether a new state. It indicates the organization maturity too, whereby the system and practices are evolved by matured business users on regular basis while holding the business objectives and overall consistency in mind. This represents state of matured users, processes and systems with continuous improvement as the goal.

While understanding the above, the team can draw a line for an organization based on status. Like the one in the picture which indicates

- Overall grading of the organization as just better than Basic.
- Technology availability and usage too at just Basic stage.
- Process is standardized and being consistently followed and enforced.
- Employees and stakeholders are not very competent to use newer technology but more or less they are following the standardized process.

These are just the initial studies for creating business case for IT strategy. IT strategy is rolling practice, where between two major cycles, minor cycles must keep happening. This may need refinement if the business strategy has gone under major change or the expectation from IT has increased manifold.

3.4 Business Strategy and Drivers

At this stage the following items should be ready to enter into next stage:

- Business scenario
- Understanding of current Business and IT issues
- Existing capability in process, people and technology areas

Business strategy being the key to drive IT strategy, it must be clearly defined. As far as IT strategy is concern, its transformation has reached to third stage. At first stage, IT used to just provide operational support to business. It has been automating some part of business functions and the focus remained to that silo of the business operation. At the second stage, it started contributing to business transformation, but it used to be IT centred business process reengineering. As Thomas Oestreich, discussed in his article on Business Innovation, the business followed the many approaches including Taylor's (F.W. Taylor, author of Principles of Scientific Management, 1911) approach to systematically optimize business processes and IT helped to automate it as well as improve quality of information. The integrated business functions and standardized practices homogenized the business information semantics. IT could add value to business processes and established its capability beyond IT domain. But the rapidly changing business wanted more and it brought IT in third stage i.e. IT needed to transform and participate into business transformation being done for business purposes. Even IT led transformation such as IT-based business models started happening for a business purpose. This business centric holistic approach wanted IT not only to be agile and enabling business processes but also to assist in business innovation. Unlike early days when IT used to be automating utmost reengineered processes, today it is able to challenge many assumptions and limitations built into the new processes. Now it is able to take strategy to its basic purpose and create new options, to make strategy better and implementation easier. That's why IT participation in business strategy becoming important day by day. Integration of complete supply chain from raw material provider till finished product retailer, cutting across multiple parties, countries, currencies have been only possible because of IT. IT has been able to show new horizons and possibilities which were capitalized by these business strategist.

This kind of contribution is better capitalized when IT has exposure to company fundamentals too. That's why business managers provide the opportunity to CIOs to think wide open by involving them into business planning sessions. Business drivers such as Mission, Vision and Strategies are the first ones in that series. It is wise to start thinking of IT laden strategy from very beginning. If an organization has a vision to be the cheapest producer of a base material or a product, let the strategist also come out how IT can contribute to this vision. This is also true that if any organization has achieved such a vision without much of IT contribution, they can achieve even better results and create further edge over competitors and barriers to new entrants, if they make IT an integral part of the whole business chain.

Over a period of time the vision do change, rather become bigger and bigger. As organization grows its vision becomes more global and moves up in value chain. A steel roller can grow from "Preferred supplier to Auto ancillary" to "Preferred steel supplier to Auto industry" when adds flat products, casting and other facilities especially for auto specialities and then further to "Preferred steel supplier to global large steel users" when it starts multi location integrated steel plants with good rolling and service facilities. A horizontal expansion can also happen when diversification, mergers and acquisitions are done in related or unrelated business. Similarly, Mission and Values are enhanced and strengthened and go under some changes, even though they are small when business perspective changes. For example, Green energy and carbon emission control is becoming part of this change now when the world is becoming more sensitive to the environment. These changes are visible with small growing companies more regularly than large and big conglomerate. We do not see any harm in it till they give a consistency and sense of direction on a long term; and whenever diversion is being taken it is in line with overall direction of the business and as per local statutory and social norms. When ITC, (BAT's Indian subsidiary) diversified its business from cigarette and tobacco to hospitality, paper, food and retail, the vision and mission have gone under some revision. A CIO must keep watch of these long-term perspectives and plans, and accordingly tune IT strategy and its execution with respect to a long-term view. Senior managers too expect and approve such changes and agility.

These documented Mission, Vision, Values and Strategy are revisited again and again during business life. It is in the interest of IT strategy, that they are reviewed and confirmed if they exist already, or documented afresh if do not exist. They help in deriving business drivers, business process requirements and measurements, which are essential prerequisite for right technology strategy and architecture.

Business innovation happens in many ways including new products or services, creating new and breakthrough business processes and business models. The end goal remains creating value for customer as well as the business, preferably more than what competitors, industry and existing processes are offering. This innovation can be by imbedding, automating, enabling and integrating IT with business.

3.4 Business Strategy and Drivers

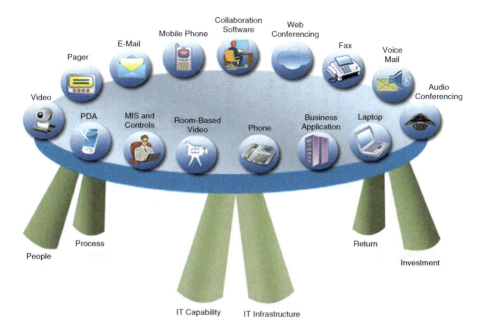

Fig. 3.5 IT enabled planning

Today, the mind set of managers need to be searching whether we can use the technology and options created by IT to do a better business, than how to use the same for a defined process. An understanding of new options and possibilities obviously helps in thinking process. It would be a good idea to share a thought on IT and IT enabled options when managers go through series of presentations during strategic planning session to understand the opportunities and innovations in theirs and related industry. Just as a sample, the picture below can be used to convey the message on possibility of IT-based integration of different business tools. The picture also presents six ingredients to make this happens. Similarly, different examples from emerging technology usage, such as application of IT integrated voice to improve the functions of warehouse, IT-enabled video-based joint planning and performance reviews across different production, service and sales centres, IT enabled video for employee training and behaviour simulation could incite managers to start exploiting technology at strategy building phase itself. Again success stories and IT enabled business models should be presented, so that business managers can think of new and innovative options for business strategy, we call it "IT Enabled Strategic Planning" (Fig. 3.5).

A sample list of business strategy, which is reoriented to stakeholders for action and monitoring, may look as below (Table 3.3). This can be used for further elaboration and evolution of IT strategy.

Table 3.3 Evolution of IT strategy

Stakeholders	Critical success factors	Key performance indicators (KPI)	Strategy	KPI current state	KPI desired state	Business activities and process
CEO	Stakeholders' value	EPS reward to stakeholder	Expand to more profitable market	INR 6/share	INR 8/share	
			Increase reward to shareholders	20%	30%	
		Compliance level	Introduce system to alert, alarm and report	80%	95%	Compliance identification and monitoring
COO	Business operation value	Cost per unit	Drive productivity initiative	65%	75%	Planning to production, HR and maintenance management
			Increase availability of machines and equipment	75%	85%	
		Order fulfilment rate	Increase planning efficiency and flexibility in manufacturing	75%	85%	Order fulfilment
CFO	Cost of finance	Interest rate per million $ of fund	Be financier friendly	11%	9.75%	Fund fulfilment
			Improve brand in financial market (Domestic as well as International)			Financial health management Relationship management
CMO	Marketing value	Margin per unit of production capacity	Be customer friendly	Mktg cost = 15% Net Mktg margin = 8.9%	Mktg cost = 14% Net Mktg margin = 10.25%	Sales and marketing, Post sales service
			Create brand in terms of customer value			
		Market share	Expand in existing as well as upcoming market	23.50%	25%	Sales and Marketing, Post
CIO	IT value	Cost of Service delivery per unit of production value	Build credible and cost-effective delivery mechanism	1.30%	1.20%	IT project development and service
			Enable users			

Template source: www.microsoft.com

3.5 Stakeholders and Their Business Needs

At this stage the following items should be ready to enter into this stage:

- Vision, Mission and key objectives
- CSF, Business Strategies, KPIs and Priorities
- Other Business Drivers
- Guidelines for IT

In McKinsey Quarterly, January 2010 edition, Jörg H. Mayer and Marcus Schaper discussed a case of large global multibillion-dollar logistic company, having tough time with their Executive Information System. It says the system was able to track transportation of material across globe, but was having difficulty in providing uniform view of data and intelligence to executives for analysis and decision-making Mayer and Schaper (2010). This caused loss of confidence on the system. The management was unable to hold single view point. A senior level team, including people from business as well as IT quickly identified the reason. It was because of the mismatch of definitions and expectations from executives at different levels, spread across HQ, BU and IT. The semantics and interpretation of data was different too. Therefore, aggregation and consolidation used to provide unreliable data. Comprising with conflicting KPIs and other business parameters could not reflect true picture of the organization. When these business requirements were aligned with common definition and understanding, the system started producing useful data satisfying all stakeholders.

The above story clearly indicates the consequences if business process, data semantics and stakeholders' expectations are not aligned. Many a time, the symptom will appear in IT domain but the route cause lies in business domain. That's why the functional alignment is important step for success of IT strategy. This process standardizes the data and semantics, aligns expectations across functional areas and creates common KPI based on which IT strategy is created.

Similarly, managing IT like Free-Market economy, where IT products and services are created and made available to the business units to buy or pass, will not work with all the businesses. It needs matured organization with professional IT team having good understanding of business needs to design and develop right solution with competitive cost. Without due diligence, the risk of investment is higher, like any new product. It is always a better bet to have stakeholders involved to guide IT with known as well as perceived requirement. This helps CIO to understand what is to be done and in which direction one should be going.

Traditionally, changing business requirement has been forcing the IT system and IT strategy change more frequently than technology evolution itself. Therefore, it is important for a reasonable life of IT strategy and stability in IT systems that at this stage the business needs are properly analysed and understood, some provisions based on upcoming changes in business scenario, industry trend and company vision and mission are provided. The way Indian business scenario has been rapidly changing since 1991, most of the IT system could not match with business need. Any IT strategy prepared for 5 years without much envisioning of the upcoming changes quickly needed a change. Same is the story with the IT systems. Some industries such as consumer products manufacturer, retail, telecom and few others have been swiftly changing. Strategies and system designed for high stability based on trends prior to 1990s could not change themselves as the business wanted. Some IT strategists just adopted the IT systems of the West, assuming that India is moving in that direction and any system that worked in Western world would work for Indian companies as well. They thought this will provide flexibility and scalability with agility. In our opinion this has not been fully right and it got further vitiated when the business could not tune with those strategies and system, leading to heavy customization of the strategy and solution to suit the current. Some good organizations first vetted their own organization's capability and introduced changes in business practices too before adopting such an imported idea.

This happens even in the developed world, maybe the source for necessitating changes is different, such as growth of booming economics of 2006–2008, and has made the business grow, diversify and change rapidly. Even though on the name of best practices, many components in the process chain have been standardized especially in large capital segment, the changes could not be stopped. The way new business models and technology have been evolving that keeping pace with the technology and the competition have put lot of pressure on IT strategy and IT systems. IT was always expected to match pace of change as efficiency and good customer experience strategy always evolved around IT. During one of the SCTV show where success story of Dal-Tile, USA was being discussed, Dal-Tile manager Rick Odoriko discussed that IT system was constrained when they started expanding business from selling to large consumers to whole-sellers for retailing. Merging some of new businesses, integrating systems with customers' and changing business processes such as capturing a variety of orders for delivery to different locations under single order, drop shipment and integrating their sourcing which used to be 30% of their capacity, just could not work. Rick's comment that in this market even though one may not have the growth but necessarily has the pressure to change, and change for business and the customer, speaks the need to be agile. And this necessitated change. Along with that they also adopted some good business practices such as dashboard at different levels in user organization, and improved user interfaces. He agreed that along with the new system, change in business practices and upgrade of people skill were also made to reap the benefit. The mix of meeting current requirement, introduction of some best practices as well as futuristic business needs with agility and good user interface brought wholesome benefit to business functions and created better customer experience.

Here, it is important to understand the value for the organization and the respective stakeholders. On the name of value, it cannot be a dream and a casual statement; rather, they must be very well defined and measurable in context of the business. All stakeholders must agree why this element is important to the business, how they would try to achieve this and how that is linked to their high-level business goals.

The IT needs of different business stakeholders may differ. Sometimes they are misaligned and also appear to be in conflict. This resolution is management responsibility, but CIO must bring this to the stakeholders' notice and escalate if

3.5 Stakeholders and Their Business Needs

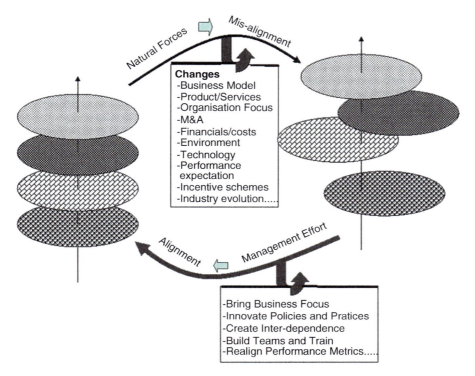

Fig. 3.6 Stakeholders participation

they continue to be unresolved, as moving with this state is high risk. Many times different business activities misalign because of normal business actions as depicted in the picture below (Fig. 3.6). It is worth to get them aligned before creating necessary IT strategy and solutions.

IT provides good opportunity to support alignment of different components of a business organization towards the business strategy. But first the organization strategy and approach to market and competition needs to be understood. Treacy and Wiersma (1995) presented their model in 1995 for creating market leadership. They indicated that Customer intimacy, Operational Excellence and Product leadership are mainly three ways to approach to this leadership. Thus, it is important for any organization to evaluate themselves and their own position in the market while pursuing one, two or all the three. Generally, an organization takes one of these to differentiate from competition and other two to catch up to reduce the gaps with its competitors. And this strategy is important for IT function too to focus and supplement.

Having knowledge of what to achieve, the solution and the path must be searched for. The solution could lie in one or combination of various areas such as Process, People and Organisation, Applications and Data, and Technology. The solution must show the path to bring the organization to a desired state and achieve the strategic goals.

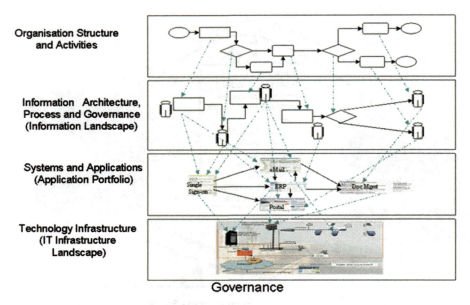

Fig. 3.7 Business alignment with IT strategy. Source: Jaap Shackkerman model, Institute for EA development, 2005

Developing Enterprise Architecture under any framework is a structured process. This presents the view of an organization which helps to understand what they want to achieve, how their systems work, how their people collaborate, how they are aligned for a common objective. It has been shifting from internal view to holistic view which contained its interaction with external stakeholders too especially the way the organization has created value for itself and for those stakeholders.

The Institution of Enterprise Architecture Developments (Ref: EA model developed by Jaap Schekkerman, Fig. 3.7) defines Enterprise Architecture as, "a collection of related architectures that model an existing or future enterprise. An Enterprise Architecture is intended to provide core content for architectures associated with individual elements within the enterprise". It further explains as Enterprise Architecture is about understanding all of the different elements that go to make up the enterprise and how those elements inter-relate. In this context, the elements such as strategies, business drivers, principles, stakeholders, units, locations, budgets, domains, functions, processes, services, information, communications, applications, systems, infrastructure and others, span over people, process, business and technology. By this process the structured view of the organization emerges and that gives complete picture of the organization. Depending upon the stage the business is in and the outcome that they want to achieve, the inputs are collected from previous stage and the elements are defined, gathered, analysed, designed and baselined at this stage; e.g. if an organization just want to identify Application and Technology, they can enter into system and application stage with information (business drivers, processes priorities and governance) available from Organisation and Information architecture stage. This happens when the business managers escape their participation and CIO need to drive from a given business scenario. In this process the organization carries a risk of poor outcome at Application and Technology architecture stages. The business managers must understand that well engineered, aligned and prioritised organization structure and processes only can lead to good data architecture and in turn strategic goal oriented applications and technology. Just selecting any application and technology will not yield right result.

Business Architecture specifies an organization's high level picture of an organization. This provides external as well as internal view of business with information such as Vision, Mission, Strategies, CSF, KPIs/Goals. These finally turn into business drivers and play great roles to align business sub-organizations and processes. This helps in identifying key processes and their links to each of business strategies and KPIs.

Process and Information architecture is derived from these business drivers. They guide to the business operations and answer how the business is organized and operate to make these strategies work and achieve these goals.

Application and system architecture involves application portfolio and deals with business data. This maps organizations structure and processes with IT applications. Here IT comes into the picture as enabler and key resource. This not only assists to the business operations to be efficient and effective but also helps in innovation. It facilitates collaboration within and across organizational boundaries and facilitates effective business administration.

The technology architecture describes the technology to be deployed which can provide right infrastructure for all the above to happen. This is to make coherent organization design to facilitate right information to right person to act on any-time from any-where.

Zachman framework for EA also suggests top-down planning and construction. The model is defined in a matrix where each stage or the business context (Business & process model, System Model, Technology Model) is constructed on six dimensions (What representing Data, How representing Functions, Where representing Network, Who representing People, When representing Time and Why representing Motivation). When each dimension is applied on each context in sequence it creates well structured blocs with well defined context and information about the business. The outcome of the each bloc leads to the next for the similar work.

TOGAF (The Open Group Architecture Framework) was developed by Open Group as framework and method for designing and describing an architecture. Each organization following TOGAF uses it in its own unique context, in terms of the practices and status it currently has and the practices that it intends to follow for architecture development, business planning, and enterprise integration. Both of these models have matching objective to create right architecture and framework to IT-enable the business. Therefore, their focus has been more on data, application and technology/infrastructure architecture.

Business architecture represents the business purpose, its mission, vision, strategy and goals. For this different techniques such as Business Scenario, are used where by relevant information and their inter-relationship are developed. The business alignment starts from here. This is achieved through overall interaction of organization structures with business services or processes, while keeping the overall business objective in mind. This depicts Operational view of the organization. The architectural view of the organization is developed in new perspective and the gaps are identified with the existing.

Next step is to develop Information and application architecture. Since information architecture is combination of process and data, the architectural view should represent both. From better understanding and smoother implementation perspective, we recommend starting with process and taking up data architecture next. The both, combined together, help to generate right application architecture and portfolio. This represents Systems view of the organization.

Technical architecture is defined after application architecture, when application portfolio is ready. This contains platform and platform applications which provide the infrastructure for application and system parts interface and their interdependence. This should depict how technology will be deployed to support entire set of application and information need, and how they will stand in tandem. The technology architecture must represent an integrated view for simplified function, control and overall management of technology. This represents technical view of the organization.

We are presenting the summary of these approaches. We have also mixed our experience, in support of practical approach. These present development of architecture for different elements and connecting them to develop right IT strategy, without deviating from basic EA principles. The process and outcomes from each of these stages are presented below.

3.6 Process Strategy and Alignment

At this stage the following items should be ready to enter into this stage:

- Business drivers and direction
- Stakeholders
- Team to move ahead with business re-engineering and automation
- Sub-domains and Business critical processes and benefits expected, if the exercise do not cover whole business

This is the process of comprehending the business and the strategy, and creating right processes to achieve the goal. However, from IT strategy perspective, one may even start from the understanding of the process areas where the opportunities have been identified by the business. The natural alignment of processes with business strategy and CSF can be achieved by this process. Otherwise, some CIOs and IT managers also use alignment check-back process, where the opportunities from IT perspective are identified and then it's validated with business, while searching the handshake line. The analogy is whether to create product and services for identified customer and opportunities or look for customers and opportunities for existing product and service. But the technique of finding and selling with the most compelling reason to create alignment without falsifying the fact is required in both the cases. The first process has natural advantage where the effort and time, both, are saved and stakeholders support is obvious as they understand clearly that IT is trying to help them to achieve their goals. The top-down linkage also helps in managing changes when there is any change in strategy, KPIs or priorities, which increases risk to IT strategy.

The obvious goals at this stage are to simplify and have lean, manageable and sustainable processes and structure to support the key strategies. The processes in new incarnation must cut waste from the value chain and adopt high contributing activities. In case of difficulties in comprehending the large scope, a modular approach is adopted. Each comprehensible part is worked out under defined sub-goals while keeping common goal in mind and at the end they are again evaluated in consolidated shape for the final goal.

These strategies and KPIs as depicted earlier in this chapter must have linkage and alignment from top to down, e.g. if CEO is looking for increasing EPS, the next level must have KPI for expanding margins, reducing cost, performing tasks more effectively and efficiently. This alignment helps creating IT strategy which helps at operational level and the benefit is reflected at the highest.

There are situations when IT may not be able to start the work in all the identified areas at once. Therefore, CIO must take her top colleagues into confidence and their help to ascertain priority areas based on collective understanding of high yield and high business impact. Some CIOs facilitate multiple functional areas initially so that the overall progress reaches to a stage where visibility of feasibility and capability is better to make such consultations. At this stage, the process innovation and a rough investment picture for people and system changes are ready which makes the consultation more useful and the decision more realistic. We advise that one must keep in mind that a visible benefit must emerge out of the selected areas for going forward, otherwise, business people soon lose sight and confidence and IT strategy is declared a failure.

3.6.1 Process Reengineering

Process reengineering provides good opportunity for value chain integration and this opportunity must be capitalized to align the business as well. In context to process and technology, the BCG used a term called "Digitized Process Platform". They define it as a coherent set of processes, having supporting technology, application and data. This one term defines the complete relationship between business processes and how they are enabled by digital technology.

People use processes to produce results. These processes also presents the mindset of the organization and approach to customer, competition and business as a whole. If the outcome of these processes does not meet the organization's objective, the processes need revisit. Here, applying Michael Porter's value chain analysis technique could be useful to identify core processes that

- Would give best results as far as business strategy is concerned
- Can be done better than many
- Are critical to our business

These business processes are potential candidate for reengineering to create better business value. The idea of process reengineering remains as transforming business processes and restructuring the supporting entities so that they are simple, sustainable and continue to generate value for the organization for finite time period.

A process map for each of the strategy and stated requirements are identified. One need to be careful here that stated strategy and priorities must be in line with the organizations' business objective. We have seen that even though business strategy talks of operational performance and capability as prime driver, people start putting over-emphasis to customer and technology assimilation. Although customer is the centre point of business, it will not be a good idea to rerun the business strategy development process again if business people have come out with operations centric strategy for the time being. The idea is not to leave customer on back burner, but over-emphasis may pull the complete process in different direction and emerging priorities and changes will not match with business needs. Similarly, if the strategy is to improve customer experience, starting with operational process may not be the right way to start with, even though both of them will finally converge. Only note of caution is one does not become short sighted while focusing intensely on what is stated in the strategy. Hence, at this stage the end purpose must remain aligned with the main goal of process engineering.

To understand the process and functional distribution two sorts of maps are developed. One provides location distribution and another provides organizational distribution. The first confirms the way different locations such as HQ, Production Units, Sales Offices, Warehouses and Country subsidiaries work on one set of processes to make them complete in business sense or create value in customer sense. The sample in Table 3.4 below is for an energy company having multiple units.

This is providing a business integration view and the functions that spread across. The second provides visibility of departments and functional units that are interacting on any process chain. These maps start from existing practices and are evaluated whether any organizational change or change of functional responsibility would create better value (Table 3.5).

One needs to understand the difference between improvement programmes and seeking ways to improve end-to-end processes. The first has short scope, may be local and provides small leap, whereas under the second, the review and change is for strategic advantage that are deeper and sustainable in nature. Process is guided by strategy, business model and the organization structure. Since organization structure runs in parallel to process, there is no harm in investigating it for a suitable change, if newly designed process provides added advantage under new structure. Shifting reporting structure, empowerment, changing collaboration rules, defining new measurements and other such changes are part of process design.

3.6 Process Strategy and Alignment

Table 3.4 Functional integration of HO and units

SL	Functional area	Functional integration between HO and units		
		High	Medium	Low
1	Power Generation and Sales			Local, one customer, stable plan, fixed price formula
2	Procurement		Local as well as central purchase	
3	Stores			Local store and function
4	HR and Payroll	Mixed & dependent HR/Payroll function		
5	Asset Maintenance			Plan and execution locally, major shutdown approval from HO
6	Budgeting & Costing	Integrated function for preparation to approval and pricing		
7	Payables		Budget and fund approval from HO	
8	Receivables and GL, Fund Mgmt	Sales, collection, depreciation and main a/c fund req and investment		
9	Docs/Records			Policies, goals, budgets, performance, reports
10	Approvals	Budget, special expenditure, HR plan, compensation, HR policies & others		
11	Statutory Reporting & Payments	Statutory & rehabilitation payments & reporting, PF, gratuity, taxes, audits etc.		
12	Projects		Plan, approval, monitoring, contracting, control	
13	Performance & Reporting		Performance reporting & review	
14	Security & Utilities			Local under unit mgmt

In association with stakeholders of CSF and KPIs, business processes are defined and analysed. Sometimes, it is difficult to define a new set of processes and activities that need to be performed to achieve the desired result; one can start with existing ones. Only note of caution here is to look beyond for innovation and complete transformation without remaining biased to existing practices. It is good practice that these process flows are developed in reverse sequence i.e. from CSF & KPIs to finer activities which helps in eliminating non-value added processes and creating

Table 3.5 Mapping of goal with customer focus in a manufacturing unit

A Discreet Manufacturing Unit

SL	Process	Goal	Suppliers[a]	Customers[a]	Service providers[a]	Sales	Production Planning	Manufacturing	Maintenance	Project	Purchase	Stores	Quality	Finance
1	Procure to pay *Requisition-Enquiry-Quototion-Order-Carrier-Supplies-Receceipt-Inspection-Deliver/Stock-Bill-Pay-Account*	Purchase cost Reduction = 5% Inventory reduction = 3%	Quot Supp		Carr		Requ	Requ Rece	Requ Rece	Requ Rece	Enq Order	Requ Rece Stock	Insp	Bill Recp Pay, Acc
2	Plan/order to produce *Order-Plan-Requirement-Schedule-Production-Stock-Sell-Dispotch-Carrier-Deliver-Invoice-Collect-Account*	Customer fulfilment = 90%		Order	Carr	Order Sale Deliv	Plan Requ Schd	Prod				Stock		Inv Coll Acc
3														

[a]Organization external

3.6 Process Strategy and Alignment

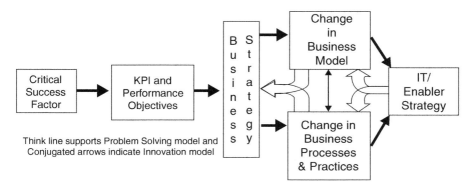

Fig. 3.8 Critical success factors alignment with IT strategy

alignment. To identify each of the predecessors, a questioning technique could be useful, where one needs to ask for what is required to do to achieve the goal or value at this stage and whether that falls within the scope of the business model. Some people also record those processes, which are beyond to assess whether there exists a better model outside. After all, new business models like switching from manufacturing and supplying in distant market to purchasing from local market and servicing after value add emerge from this technique only. At this stage, understanding of IT becomes handy, as it opens up the horizon of possibilities. Once the sequence is ready, it is also run forward to check continuity, completeness and feasibility (Fig. 3.8).

Different techniques such as flow charts, Process dependency network, cause and effect diagrams, affinity diagrams, fishbone graphics, and sequence diagram can be used to elaborate and analyse the processes. Again some kind of representation indicating importance based on value contribution, lead time, total volume and exceptions on each process/activities helps in exploration and decision to improve, eliminate or retain. Based on the time and the expertise available, the degree of approximation as well as elaboration and detailing with field data are done. Those processes which are contributing to the CSF are identified and a marking is done based on the size of contribution and the criticality to the CSF. Sometimes an analysis of investment in terms of ratio of effort and cost of activity/process to value addition is also done to make trade-off between alternatives and feasibility. Similarly, those processes where gaps are higher with respect to existing practices, or serious business transformational need exists, are identified. This helps in change planning and risk management.

Lean technique (Toyota—Since 1970s) is useful to cut waste and no-value activities. This also supports similar concept. The value stream is mapped, altered and redesigned to maximize the value and identify and cut those activities which are either not adding value or working as impediments. Basically processes are evaluated on three criteria (Frampton and Jones 2009)

- Value Add: Those processes which help to transform material, product, services, or information and for which the customer is ready to pay or differentiate with competitors. To analyse the same, one need to understand internal processes and

customer's purpose. Even small items such as needing invoice data in electronic form to integrate bills payable could be value for supplier as well as customer, if it expedites the process (efficiency) and saves manpower for manual processing (cost saving) at customers' end. The benefit to supplier may appear as direct benefit when customer shares the saving and indirect benefit or when cost of integration and manpower is not loaded on the contract value.
- Value Enabling: The processes which are essential to maintain business but are not of any value to a customer, for example tax filing, upkeep of the factory, managing employee morale and machine maintenance.
- Non-Value Add: The processes and activities which consume resources but do not contribute to product and services that customer would buy for. It is like offering an additional product or services free which holds no value or serves no purpose for the customer. It is waste to all the stakeholders including buyer, supplier and organization itself. They must be trimmed off the value chain.

Some of the basic principles such as Process simplification, reduction of hands-off, holistic knowledge of the chain, time to market, enabling and empowering the employees, boundary-less operations are applied to make effective process. The technique of answering "what-are-the-right-processes" is performed first, and then "how-to-do-them-right" is applied. Once the right processes are ready, the search for opportunities starts. In an article "Using IT to enable a lean transformation", published by McKinsey Quarterly, February-2010, Nicklas Ilebrand, Tor Mesøy, and Remco Vlemmix quoted a case of a large European bank, "The bank could save €4 million just by improving Account-opening process, 20% by process improvement and 25% by involving IT. This also gave confidence to the bank to take up more areas to apply lean technique and improve the business. This just shows the potential of improvement that an organization can have by business-IT collaboration" (Ilebrand et al. 2010).

3.6.2 Functional Grouping and New Structure

At times, individual process and activity is not able to show the value or may not even appear meaningful. Our suggestion would be not to hesitate to merge or sum up with the neighbouring processes so that the value clearly emerges and the team can decide on its fate. We have also observed that merging of some processes cutting across functional areas and departments creates better value. The emergence of Logistics function in a manufacturing plant is the result of the same. This may happen because of different reasons such as the following:

- Different functional groups which are stakeholders to different links of the value chain are not able to synergize amongst themselves to generate a better value for the organization as a whole. It could be because of poor alignment of performance objectives.

- The integration amongst all the links in the value chain is not properly defined, sequenced or balanced.
- The organization structure and inter-group relationship are causing stress and inefficiency in the system and the value chain.

Neither all the above issues can be taken up and resolved at this stage nor IT led strategy development can address all of them. Utmost CIO may confidentially report to CEO, offer her suggestions and seek his advice. But cases such as process integration definition, synchronization of processes across functional areas and such issues must be taken up and resolved here. We suggest that these symptoms rather must be evaluated at all the interfaces and confirmed.

Sometimes restructuring roles and responsibilities too can bring the desired effect. Therefore, this must be considered while looking at the processes and creating structure around it. The process owners are assigned with defined objectives. Generally the clubbing of functions and processes are done based on their close affinity and logical proximity, with an idea to achieve better focus and performance. But sometimes it also happens based on individuals in mind, especially when the person concerned is in a position to lead the team and the improvement and the integration drives, better, and that is the need of the hour for the organization. These people are generally strong and influential who can drive the function and those links in the value chain better. Even though it is not an ideal way to reorganize the processes and the value chain, keeping in mind the practicality and feasibility the CIO must take this call and be ready to reshuffle when normalcy returns. We call it risk mitigation, as it is better to create some flexibility and keep the organization going than bring the work to a halt or let the IT strategy collapse.

In all these process respective stakeholders must participate and commit to the changes and reshuffling. The big change or creation of new organization structure which involve and impact many, must happen only with approval from senior management. It would be ideal if they only lead this transition identification and drive it. People in all organizations are very sensitive to it and take positions quickly on this subject. Even the gossips can spoil the purpose. Therefore, all such discussions, whether it is a small or big, even for evaluating as alternative, must happen in controlled and conducive environment and with due care for confidentiality and right communication.

3.6.3 *Opportunity Search*

This step is exploring the opportunities for leveraging process automation to make processes efficient and effective at reasonable cost. The opportunity for IT use, to increase the value being delivered, is identified either by supplementing or substituting the identified activities. J. Peppard and J. Ward classified these identified opportunities into two categories, Problem-based (the opportunity for resolution for known problem) and Innovation-based (new ways for conducting business i.e. end-driven). Therefore, the approach too will be different. The first approach is to remove irritant and known impediments, therefore, it works more like business process automation, whereas the second applies to all through new thoughts and new solutions. In the latter case, the focus is to do something new, which could be different, while involving IT and allied elements such as processes and people. But the focus remains on organization and business improvements that may be significant.

At this stage the value chain which IT can create are matched and applied through different processes and their performance expectations. The value proposition from IT could be in many ways, including

- Covering distance and creating Speed of work
- Facilitating communication
- Scaling and enforcing Control
- Cost reduction
- Record keeping
- Modelling and analysis
- Forecasting
- Enforcing discipline & consistency
- Building trust and brand
- Expanding scope of coverage
- Integrating business functions within and beyond organization boundary
- Setting up collaboration
- Complying with regulatory norms
- Managing knowledge and expertise
- Learning and training etc.

For example, if the business of a retailer needs to process the stock status on large number of items and confirm the dispatch to warehouse during business hours so that the supplier can plan immediately and deliver them next morning before opening, it can achieve through use of IT only. Without IT, it could be difficult to meet the time line goal even after investing large man-power. If the business managers can quantify the benefit from this in terms of direct as well as indirect, irrespective of its form (tangible or intangible), it would help in decision-making. So here, they capitalized on speed, collaboration, communication and integration characteristics of IT. Similarly, the needs of different processes in the whole process chain are identified where IT can help them to achieve the performance goals. When all identified opportunities are summed up, IT need in terms of application and technology emerges. The context, scope and objectives of these opportunities must be documented, which will be used to create road map for well managed transition and success measurement after implementation.

For multinational and multi-location operations, the processes must be validated for situations prevailing in different countries and business locations. The processes and practices, the statutory needs, the business environment and many other factors may influence the decision of alignment. Some organizations such as Oracle found conducive business conditions to align and adopt common business practices and succeeded in rolling them out, thus claiming Billion Dollar saving. But all may not be as lucky as Oracle has been. The effort must be made to align them even if they cannot adopt common business practices. The benefit of this alignment and consistency is reaped when IT systems are developed and information is consolidated across units for business managers. It is also true that business needs flexibility and the definition of this varies from country to country and location to location in some cases. But a trade-off between commonality and alignment on the one hand and flexibility and variability on the other must be a well thought off decision.

We suggest that process reengineering team must not try and lead the organization for the best reengineered processes unless the organization is ready to digest. The whole process is like any change management and organization should be able to adapt. Therefore, the feasibility of implementation of reengineered processes must receive due consideration. If the organization fails to adopt the change, it causes bigger harm. On the one hand, the half way to change causes instability of the system with a sense of failure in the organization, and on the other the failure on misdirected IT causes loss of investment too. The difference between the business practices and the IT systems causes misalignment and utter frustration to business as well as IT team. We have observed that this kind of misalignment has been one of the most important reasons for failure of IT strategy.

It is good idea to benchmark the new processes at the end of this stage with the best in the industry or with the best in any industry. This benchmark reveals whether there exist more opportunity for reengineering. It is good to accept the gap with respect to the best with knowledge, even though it was because of various considerations such as higher risk and so on, than accepting them with an idea that it is the best. The industry association, data-consulting organizations such as Aberdeen Group, Dun & Bradstreet and some of the academic institutions could be of help in this regard.

3.7 Application and Integration Strategy

At this stage the following items are generally ready:

- New business process maps and process goals
- Stakeholders commitment for changes
- Catalogue of process and policy changes
- Processes/activities vis-à-vis Opportunity for IT
- Roles, responsibility and structure

A technology enabler can be a product, a feature, a set of products, or a custom business application. The support from the experts, having knowledge of current as well as emerging technologies, solutions and risks involved, help to create an application architecture which is helpful in integration of information, delivery of services and management. These experts could be from IT organization, supplier of technology solutions or external consultants.

Table 3.6 Deriving solution for business goals

	Business goal	Functional area	Goal for the solution
1	Operational cost reduction	Inventory management	Inventory reduction
2	Improvement in sales margin	Sales management	Sales force automation
			Sales cost reduction
3			

3.7.1 Business Application Strategy

There are three approaches to create application strategy

3.7.1.1 Business Focus

This approach works better when there is search of solution to improve the business and business process. More a less the bottleneck, the improvement and the area where innovation is required, is known. The identified opportunities at the previous stage are the starting point for this stage. For each of these opportunities, specific IT initiative or solution is identified. An example is enumerated in Table 3.6.

The solutions can solve specific business need or group of business needs. The process is called solution through digital platform. Dr Peter Weill (2009) mentioned the importance and the benefit of digital platform to a business. He emphasized that IT helps not only in cost reduction for running existing business processes but also improves the quality and the speed of innovation. He thinks that the companies that have optimized and standardized processes and enabled them on digital platform, they make all round gain including improvement in revenue, speed to market and agility in business; and hence, the business transformation.

IT helps in generating ideas and building capabilities for transformation, but to reap the benefit the transformation process must be carried through. This must be

- Complete
- Robust
- Scalable
- Faster
- Efficient and effective
- Secured and reliable
- Responsive
- Agile

These will ensure that the effect is encouraging and visible.

3.7.1.2 Technology Focus

IT and its integration with other technologies are opening innovative applications regularly and rapidly. Many-a-times technology appears on horizon before the business wanted a solution of that nature. It could be said that the need was either dormant or people were yet to realize the potential of the technology. In this case, the application of technology reaches to business with new ideas and thoughts to improve the business and business processes. There are many such examples of this nature which helped transformation of business. I remember during 1990s these technologists use to talk about a small chip tracking material and people movement as well as connecting to mobile workmen. To help business-users and implementers realize the potential and possibilities, they used to create likely stories of its application. But today when RFID is here more useful applications such as stock-keeping at warehouse, jewellery retail showroom, theft prevention and vehicle management in a factory premises become reality. The early adopters such as Walmart have created an edge over the competitors in logistics area.

Another new technology, named as Surface technology, is coming up now. Another round of revolution is expected in coming time. If we ask business team today the way this technology could be useful in business area, very few ideas will emerge as possible application in the business. They will not be ready to use the same because of no business case rather big cost. Slowly the technology will mature and it will certainly start creating competitive edge, thus improving its application and justification. These are called disruptive technology, which enter in business forcefully, as they help business organization to differentiate with others.

3.7.1.3 Mixed Approach

The first approach sometimes is inhibited by localized approach and the demand. In case the business people are unable to visualize greater opportunity, they remain limited by many constraints and choke innovation. Their limitations are aberration of "Necessity is mother of invention". And they drive IT too in that tunnelled approach. On the other hand becoming fully technology driven and search for application in each instance of business is tedious, unjustifiable and never settling affair for many organizations. Therefore, we suggest a middle path where the business demand and technology & applications are matched somewhere in the middle. Both of them influence each-other and necessitate change in the approach and the strategy. This is best driven when the goals and KPIs are also set in a range of most optimistic and minimum acceptable. Therefore, the hunger of achieving more stays with managers and they continue to watch and explore the opportunities without working on evolution process indefinitely. The progress is treated ready-to-move-forward, when targeted achievement is in the range of the goals without unduly delaying the process beyond reasonable limits.

Just to explain this "Mid-point meeting" strategy, we take an example of Banking industry and Surface technology. The strategy and the process obviously start with bank's strategy. Let us assume that a bank XYZ is in Retail Banking, some call it Consumer banking as well. Its functions are characterized

- By offering multiple products such as deposits, loans, credit-cards and insurance
- Through multiple channels such as branches, call centres, Internet and mobile banking
- To customers and customer groups such as individual consumers and business corporate

Since, this line of business provides good margin and spread, the customer management and customer experience take the central place to this line of business. While understanding the importance of these consumers, the bank set a goal, "To improve customer satisfaction by 8–10%". This is for maintaining customer-friendly image and to attract more such consumers. The delivery of service and overall customer engagement management processes are the main contributor to this KPI. This could be for all or more interactions during deposit & withdrawal, loans approval, credit limit approval, cards issue and settlement, investment advice and creation, insurance selling and settlement, payments, online services, wealth management and request management. At this stage the technology and application comes into the picture. Instead of solely focusing on how to address the process and structure in perspective of existing and proven technology to manage interaction with customers, the focus could be on finding a even better technology and solution, which has been or would be enriching individual's experience. These technologies could be under use by front runners in the banking industry, other industries or even from emerging technology fold.

Two things certainly create an impact in this direction. One is empowerment, whereby someone can do himself/herself and another is ease of operation, i.e. user-friendliness and at consumer's convenient time. Like the way ATM and Internet banking have created an impact, surface technology would also create at least similar impact if not better. This has capability to interact in terms of pictures, sound, video, animation and many other ways. Again the technology can react to the commonly practiced gestures; hence, it can be used to communicate and respond in a very user-friendly manner. It does not need IT literacy either. A consumer can interact through this technology-based solution and get answers and service without needing banking staffs for interaction. He/She can even complete many formalities and submit documents for processing. The transparency and the governance too improve. Thus, it has a high potential to create an enriched experience for consumers. This also eliminates the bad customer handling caused by attitudes and exhaustion of customer facing individuals. This marks a good match of technology with the business need. There could be even better solution to whole value chain, when the business processes are accordingly created to integrate with these new technology solutions. This finally gives birth to an innovative business model and if properly implemented it could be in breakthrough category. Therefore, we recommend the bank to take this approach of match making between the goals and the technology which can unlock the value while creating new options.

The above approach points to fundamental thinking. Now-a-days, many application solution providers embed new technology and offer an optimized and industry specific solutions. They bring specialized packages for a specific functional chain as well as versatile such as popular ERP to cover many with generic solutions. In case the organization is trying to catch up with the industry, picking up from offered basket could help, but the organizations, which have created specialized business model containing business specific knowledge, which gives them industry leadership and business excellence, prefer to create their own applications. After all, most of the readymade IT applications are the outcome of learning of business from the user

3.7 Application and Integration Strategy

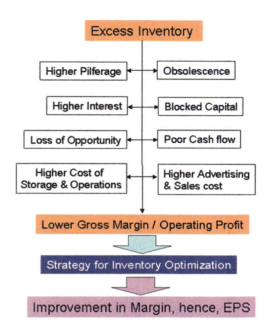

Fig. 3.9 Business functions and alignment with applications

industry and they have proven and known ideas. But some packaged application sellers are innovative in the sense that their packages have agility to apply new processes to an extent but they have successfully embedded newer technologies to create extra value for their customers. Therefore, the application and integration strategy for the leaders and the ones which are catching up are different. The first category looks for newer ideas and creates new benchmark. They are the ones who are the path finders and use the strategy mentioned above, whereas the organizations in the second category look for proven solutions. The organizations in the first category also do not apply the same strategy for all their business functions. They work out high yield core business processes and apply "new technology—new application" strategy there, even though there is a higher risk, whereas for others they take the common approach. They remain quite confident to experiment with and benefit from the mix of applications and their integration. They know that IT and IT-based technologies are expanding faster than their business and newer business models can evolve around these technologies which can take away their leadership and business opportunities. Therefore, they do have periodic technology review programmes to evaluate emerging technologies and applications that can create opportunities for their business. No wonder why Walmart became first commercial user of RFID. The standard and proven solutions and packages are also not free from challenges, but they are of different nature. We will discuss later in course of explaining the application selection and implementation.

The map below (Fig. 3.9) could be useful for mapping business functions and connect them to a category of applications. This mapping can give a direction to the team for exploring the opportunities to match the business need with applications.

One can start at the identified opportunities after process reengineering and then proceed. The team must keep the bigger map in mind to have holistic view. In our experience, proceeding with value chain based full set of processes and their performance goals is better than trying to look at the processes at micro level and find matching applications to each of them. The pull for micro level processes and their solutions would be strong under an organization structural of departments and functional divisions, as each of them may have different perspective and priorities. For example, searching for an opportunity to improve Procure-to-Service process chain is better way to look at than Purchase, Quality control, Inventory and Manufacturing function, individually.

The identification of application portfolio emerges from the analysis of KPIs and the impact of related business functions on them. If we see a diagram below, one can notice the correlation between problem of Excess Inventory with the Margin and EPS. Now whether one has started analysing from the pain-point of excess inventory and check the impact on EPS, or sees the opportunity to improve EPS and how the excess inventory is impacting it, the outcome is the same. During Process re-engineering the team quantifies the impact on KPI. It comes out with the changes required in the process by which the inventory can be optimized and the way IT would create a platform to achieve the goal of Inventory optimization. If the impact is higher or the opportunity is bigger, the Inventory Management application is registered higher in the priority list with a connection to the CEO's KPI i.e. EPS.

From IT application perspective, just to identify the application area is not sufficient, it is worth further investigating the way the application will support to build business knowledge and intelligence to have continuous improvement. Those features, which help in improving and sustaining the business performance and the management capability, also need to be identified. A list of applications available in respective business areas are identified from detail study of solutions available in the market and catalogue of technology solution providers. Once the list of applications is ready, an application map, as presented in Sect. 3.7.4, is created. The team should try to quantify the benefit that each functional area will get and overall the impact it will make on respective KPIs, if the application is successfully implemented along with the new processes. And this drives the interest of the organization.

Another technique to identify business applications is "Entrepreneurial View". This helps to look at any finite business function with an idea of business cycle. They (ref: TOGAF 9e)

- Business acquisition and service
  This covers Marketing to Order, and Customer relationship management.
- Capability and infrastructure building
  This covers functions such as Asset and Infrastructure development, Product engineering and Quality control
- Supply chain and logistics
  This covers Supplier management, Procurement, Stock & Service, Dispatches and Delivery

- Manufacturing
  This covers Planning to Production including manufacturing asset maintenance
- Human resources
  This includes all employee related functions such as Recruitment, Training, Assignments, Progression, Appraisal, Payroll, Reward & recognition, Unions and interfaces, Separation, etc.
- Finance
  This covers all financial and statutory matters including payments, accounting, receipts, finances and banking
- IT and business process
  This covers complete Information asset and service, business process improvements, integration and business initiatives.
- Management functions
  This covers complete business management practices including Policies, Strategies, Reviews, coordination, Stakeholders management, Compliance etc.

There could be some more, depending upon the business and its scope.

Integration of Application and data are required to collate and present information in integrated manner for the business users. A new concept of Service Oriented Architecture (SOA) has been proposed for developing new application architecture and the industry believes that it helps in building agility in the organization and improves application maintainability. The concept is based on the concept of function-based organization where roles and responsibilities are divided in such a way that a functional group serves a specific functional need to all in the unit rather each have their own sub-group to serve the same need. It is centralization of service groups based on their functional role. To complete their business process or value chain, all other groups also take the service from the common group. This lets the organization to achieve scalability, critical mass for the function and performance. This also eliminates redundancy and allows capitalization of business knowledge built around the function for the benefit of the organization. A best example could be purchasing function. The group entertains purchasing requests from whole organization irrespective of whether it is for projects, production or maintenance, and serves to all of them. Thus, while designing respective processes by others, they just refer the purchasing function and then consider the link completed. Utmost, for performance reasons one can define the SLA in context of internal customer reference. Similarly, SOA provides the framework for architecting IT infrastructure to eliminate redundancy and accelerate IT project deliveries via consolidation and reuse of services. Thus, SOA rules out the idea of embedding the business rules and infrastructure for common functionalities in each functional flows and application chain. This architecture aligns IT applications with business besides achieving agility. The concept is similar to "Build-once-Use-many", where by the services are independently built while providing interface for service request and response. Thus, the changes are isolated and service is leveraged across multiple functions. However, in pursuit to achieve modularity to the finest level, it should not become unmanageable. Since many application packages and new development platforms support this architecture, one can easily look for this architecture for new applications.

SOA framework can be even built over existing monolithic applications infrastructure, but that may not be as efficient and effective as the freshly built. The effort to build over existing one must be justifiable with business benefits.

3.7.2 Information and Data Architecture

Along with Process model, organizing a high level data model, gives pretty good picture of IT Application dimension of an organization. Although principles are more or less like the system development approach, it is at much higher level while providing reasonable insight into business data.

The information architecture must have single goal to make right information available to right people and role/s at right time to facilitate improved decision and working performance. It has been a challenging task Mayer and Schaper (2010) worldwide to make right information available to facilitate sound decisions. These information are lost in organization silos, organization of data, semantic interpretation, presentation formatting and corporate dynamics. Since organization data and information play a significant role in business performance, CIO must pay balanced attention to all segments of the organization. Therefore, evolving right information architecture with integrated data hierarchy and common semantics is good contribution of IT to the business.

TOGAF defines the objective of Data Architecture as "to define the major types and sources of data necessary to support the business, in a way that is Understandable by stakeholders, Complete, Consistent and Stable". It says that the data entity linkages can be developed to understand the value that the data delivers.

Identification of business data and model them with processes is the first step in this direction. One of the approaches that was practiced is BSP-ISP model of IBM. This was called CRUD matrix, a process and data entity mapping. This maps the processes and their interaction with those data sets (sub-sets of a data entity having value to business in collective form) by marking their interface with creation (C), use (R), update/transformation (U) and deletion/archival (D) that are being performed by those processes. The same is represented under TOGAF data architecture as how they are created, distributed, migrated, secured, and archived. At this stage, data is classified and sub-classified to depict high level information about the entities in the organizations. The entities are those things in business reference about which business is interested in having information and use them for business purposes. Employees, Items & Products, Locations, Assets, Partners are the few examples of it. These entities independently as well as when connected together, produce meaningful set of information and business purposes. Each of them has one or multiple distinct instances, like each employee is an instance of employee entity. There are two techniques which are used to identify more meaningful state of these entities. One is called "Life cycle Mapping of Entities" and another is called "Entity Relationship Model". Under Life cycle mapping, the four states of the data instances are mapped. They represent "Generation", "Storage", "Update" and "Archive". When data advances from generation state to storage and update, many new information sets are added. For example, employee's career, salary and performance are different sets which come along when that instance passes through those states over time. Accordingly the value map also goes up. However, over a period of time the business relevance of each instance reduces to a level where carrying the related information is costlier, when it is archived. The Entity Relationship represents value of data when they are independent as well as when they relate to each other. This again involves high level entity modelling which can give clear understanding of important datasets.

A third technique is known as "Creation of data building blocks". This uses top-down as well as bottom-up approach to evolve data structure and hierarchy

- First, the data need of an organization is defined for higher functional level processes and then for related operational level.
- Again the operational data are collated and integrated to service data need of higher levels. This is connected up to business scorecards and KPI.

The mix of the three approaches creates right view of business data (Data Entity/Data sets and Component Catalogue) and depicts their relation amongst themselves as well as with business processes and organization structure and roles. This helps in visibility of corporate performance from the perspective of core areas: financial accounting, management accounting, compliance, and operations management. It also improves down ward visibility of performance data their connection up to operational level and understanding as how operational level data roll up to achievements at organizational level. This model helps in business alignment and creating visibility, at each level, the way their work and performance impacts organization goals. This exercise could be done in more detail before and during application design and development, but at this stage it must provide fairly good idea of data architecture, hierarchy and flows (horizontal as well as vertical) in the organization, besides the gap in availability of right data in right hand.

The business values strengthen the idea of information by data collation and integration. Accordingly, application integration is also driven by the data representation requirement and the business need. There could be many factors that drive the business need for integration and there also exist many ways to manage and present them to right users. The main focus remains on simplification and business goals. At times the duo (simplification and information collation) may come in conflict where on the one hand the organization finds value in clustering of processes and data, and on the other, clustering may make the process complicated and difficult to manage. A trade-off is required to maximize for the business benefit.

The business need could be for

- Process integration to create better business value
- Operational and service efficiency
- Effective organization structure
- Better controls, governance and risk management
- Collaboration need to meet demand of business and customers
- Effective management and empowerment

And they could be serviced by different integration strategies (as below) as well

- Change in organization structure and responsibilities
- Process change, reorganization and automation
- Data clustering and interchange (IDE)
- Application integration based on Service Oriented Architecture etc.

The data clustering appearing from CRUD matrix would help to identify the high density regions, where more processes are interacting with a common set of data and having more inter-dependence for better performance. During early days this used to qualify for integrated architecture and common platform. However, as the technology progressed and solutions for separating presentation, application and data service layers become feasible, the consideration for single platform and common database started fading out. This made integration need more driven by business needs and the way the application strategy evolves to service this information. Even in this situation, we used CRUD matrix successfully to evolve clustering and inter-dependence need of business processes and applications for creating better business value. But the technology strategy and feasibility were used to decide whether they need to be under monolithic structure or be spread out while serving each other on SOA (Service Oriented Architecture) model. A high level sample CRUD matrix is given in Annexure A. This could be even in more detail, which can depict more data-sets and sub-processes in this mapping.

The integration framework must answer the following (Ref: Zachman Framework Associates on EA)

- Why: Why the integration is required, i.e. what is the motivation?
- What: What data will be integrated?
- How: How the integration of functions will happen to fulfil the integration objective?
- Where: Where they will be integrated in reference to business location and business connection?
- Who: Who and which role will be ensuring integration services as well as using the same for business work?
- When: When the integration will be used in terms of business cycle and business chain, especially on time and event dimension?

This framework will not only hold the integration focus to business but also help in developing right strategy at technology level to achieve business oriented scalability.

3.7.3 Infrastructure Application

TOGAF (Technical Reference Model) identifies all such applications under this category "which are commercial off-the-shelf (COTS) available and that are considered sufficiently ubiquitous, interoperable, and general-purpose within the enterprise". This category is in between business application and technology platform services. Earlier they were qualified as applications having no direct linkage with business processes, but certainly supporting to manage business activities efficiently. However, number of software products, which serve common business functions such as payment and collection services, workflow and approval services, email for communication have blurred the divider. Again standard packages/web-services connecting organizations and facilitating inter-organization business processes are invading the boundaries.

A simple rule would be to include such generalized commercial off-the-shelf applications in overall strategy, even if they have not emerged as business need during business application strategy development process. The consideration must be on whether they would facilitate or contribute to business process performance.

3.7.4 Application Portfolio: Physical Application Strategy

Application portfolio includes the complete list of business application as well as infrastructure applications. A logical assessment of their compatibility, integration, co-existence and collaboration must be done. Similarly, redundancy must be eliminated. The overlapping features need to be evaluated if one can be dropped or at least features can be deactivated in one of the applications. This may not be an easy task, like what we found in one of the client's place that they used document management feature of a standard ERP product, but at the end it could not serve the purpose of full set of users. One of the user groups that wanted a specialized application to manage their requirements could not be serviced from standard solution provided from ERP. This opened a new set of issues where other users too came out that ERP-based system is cumbersome to use. Now the EA team is working along with the IT team to evaluate the business requirement again and finalize which application should be part of their application strategy and how they need to integrate and roll-out. Therefore, careful assessment in the beginning itself, is required in selection of such applications to address the business needs. In case selection is temporary or for selective set of business requirement, the CIO needs to make decision accordingly, while keeping in mind the future need for change and integration vis-à-vis cost. A consolidated map of category of requirement and application could be drawn as below (Fig. 3.10) to have high level view and for management reviews.

While identifying the application portfolio, generally all processes get included as they are visible, but some of the management processes which are not so visible or may not be practiced are left out. These processes also contribute value for the organization as well as the customers. Business Intelligence is one of such areas. Most of the analysis to identify bottleneck and reasons for poor performance come from this process, which helps in making meaningful reviews and designing new action plan. Another branch of it is predictive analytics, which helps in predictions, forecasting and generating alerts, are very meaningful for managing business. Applications, of those kinds of business processes, must get due importance and place in the application strategy.

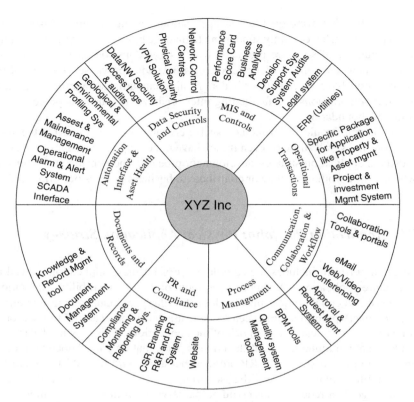

Fig. 3.10 Consolidated application map for a utility company having a single customer

3.7.5 Migration Strategy

All companies including new ones need the application and data migration whenever they plan any upgrade or new systems. Minimum they need account opening balances, business partners and certain business transactions, which are live and still relevant, onto new system. Therefore, all changes in IT a migration need and the strategy for migration must be evaluated and planned for. There are different techniques to identify them and sort out the minimum need based on their applicability and usefulness in future, but answers of some few simple questions, as below, will also help to understand the business need and criticality, and right strategy to migrate them.

- What are the business areas impacted with new change?
- What are the processes that are owned by those businesses?
- What data and application those functional owners use for their processes?
- Which set of data and application still has useful life and would contribute to business performance and continuity when taken forward?

- Why migration of those data and applications are necessary, and could it be referred in their current form without impacting overall manageability and information serviceability?
- Whether those data and application can be taken forward in a different form such as summarized, abstract or any other?
- When these data and application need to be migrated?
- How these data are integrated and related?
- Whether they can be taken in isolation or they are cascading to other areas, if so how cascading effect will be managed?
- What form and state of those data are, do they need qualification, repair and correction to make them complete before migration?
- What should be the sequence of their migration?
- How will they be validated for their correct migration?

Timing aspect is important as the business does not hold for this exercise to complete. The preparation for data and application migration is incomplete if the user readiness is not there. At the end not only the IT system needs to be ready but also their user and interfacing applications and business partners; hence, the strategy must be holistic.

3.8 Technology Strategy (Including Convergence)

The technology strategy is not just buying and setting up certain set of server, PCs and Laptops in a network. It is host of technology solutions, which are IT enabled and provides much better result in consonance with business. They could be Radio Frequency Identification (RFID), Voice solution at warehouses, Global Positioning System (GPS), Sensors and Signals or Robotics. The idea is to capitalize the power of these technologies and solutions and provide better solution to business problem while integrating them with IT. These devices help to enhance performance by collecting information, informing and guiding systems at work and/or creating enhanced functionalities by collaborating with man and/or machine. IT as a back engine helps them to achieve the collaboration. Again the focus is on value creation for the business.

This provides opportunity to select right technology, considering the following

- Manageability and governance
- Cost of I/O (integration and operations)
- License management
- Maintainability
- SLA
- Technology architecture (Cloud computing, virtualization)
- Risk of obsolescence
- Network and data security

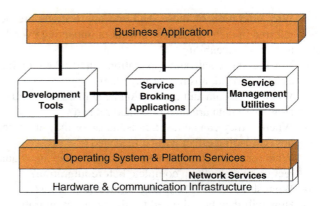

Fig. 3.11 Framework for technology strategy

3.8.1 Strategy for Technology Platform and Component

A simplified framework for technology strategy (Ref: TOGAF Technical Reference Model V9, 2009) could be as below (Fig. 3.11).

This clearly depicts linkage and top-down approach of technology model, and accordingly strategy formulation. The Business application is major driver.

TOGAF guidance on the above model is quite practical. The layers will remain the same however different services mentioned in the three middle boxes could differ from one set of requirements to the other.

The technology components have been getting complicated over period of IT innovation. During seventies it used to be the Machine, Operating system and the Database. The operating system used to include wholly family of services such as I/O to its peripherals controller, database and file system management, printing, etc. As technology and inter-operability concept developed, these services started becoming independent. Today, printer drivers are coming more along with printers than OS. Databases have their own management systems. User interfaces have changed from OS driven terminal to independent, intelligent and external to server domains. Fortunately, many such service components are standardized based on worldwide accepted standards such as IEEE, but still there are more which follow their proprietary standards. Therefore, selection of right technology has one more rider and that is the selected components and technologies must be compatible and stay compatible in future. Examples are many, such as Microsoft browser (IE) may not be compatible to Linux operated platform, even all browsers in the market give different results unless common compatible syntax are used for Internet enabled applications. SQLServer database is not compatible with UNIX-based open systems as well as it gives different results if Oracle database-based SQL applications are used. If CIO and her team has good understanding of technologies, their future direction and compatibility, they can refer TOGAF for the list of platform services under chapter 43.4 and 43.5 (Version 9) and choose the best COTS for them from market. For others, it is better to focus on main technology areas such as OS, DB and Applications Server and involve technology partner/s to evolve the rest based on business need and organization policies.

Sometimes the Technology solution is overdone in anticipation of availability, integration and security needs. If these needs are assumed beyond threshold limits, the solution complexity and the cost go up dramatically. The resources will not be optimally utilized and the return to business will be poor. This over-investment can also happen in cases where IT investment is ones in a blue moon kind of phenomenon or CIO looks into distant future and plans for the investment serving in long future. The financial viability becomes a risk. These kinds of investment also cause assets to remain non-productive for long and lead to wastage of resource by obsolescence. We suggest that a CIO should be little more transparent to the top management and create a case where by further investment is linked to certain business needs and benefits. The management would be agreeing more easily for such solution and would not expect that extra bit if the investment is not approved.

There are basically two lines of technology platform, Open Source and Proprietary. However, currently neither one proprietary platform provider offer complete technology solution for full range of business requirement nor stable and architecture level integrated software are available to service all business needs. Some such as Microsoft offer major set from proprietary portfolio and Oracle is buying business as well as platform-based software companies to match, but still the portfolio is yet to reach to the stage to service all the business needs, hence, the organization needs to pick from the mix not only from these two vendors but also from others, including open source, to fulfil the needs. For specialized needs the options to select are still many more. The good thing is hardware and server platforms are more or less standardized. Even the strength of each of these vendors, software set and their features are different. Because of integration, compatibility, licensing, features and many others, an organization may land up into a mix of technology set. Sometimes, the licensing cost and specialized applications also drive organization to have mix of technologies. This causes fragmentation of data centres and its manageability issue. The virtualization technology is trying to address few of these issues. Although the attempt is still timid, a good beginning has started. The organizations are rapidly evaluating and implementing virtualization as they look to further consolidate and reduce the hardware footprint in their IT environment. Under this the hardware and platform services are consolidated as far as possible without changing application and its basic Operating System services. This is likely to create following benefits:

- Simplified management
- Lower server, software and support cost
- Improved resource utilization and data protection
- Easier revision control
- More flexibility, still better control on data protection and security

The benefits depend on type and extent of virtualization solution implemented. The server virtualization, which certainly improve the usage of hardware capacity and goal of power and space saving. But one needs to evaluate the cost in totality. Currently license requirement and capability required to manage are complex issue

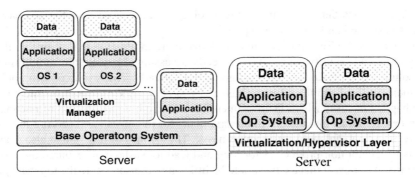

Fig. 3.12 Server side virtualization

and it may cost higher. The basic concept of server side virtualization is as presented in Fig. 3.12 (Rose and Perry 2009)

CIOs should even look at options of virtualization at users' end, i.e. Hosted Desktops which not only helps in reducing price at user end, but also overall management and backup complexity. In this case, based on user profile the access and functions are mapped and a virtual desktop is created on server which a user gets when logs in. All data management function is done on the server. The virtualization manager virtualises all hardware resources governed directly by base OS for OS1 and OS2 as if they belong to them. It seems the technology is moving towards interoperability across platform technology, similar to what JVM (java Virtual Machine) has provided in its limited sense. Like this many such technologies and solutions will keep emerging which will change the landscape of technology architecture and options. They will provide their own share of technological as well as business benefits. Neither one should wait till it loses its competitive edge nor keep chasing and thus keeping the organization on continuous roll. One needs to pick and choose from different models and options depending upon the best fit for the organization, while remembering that every option and architecture will have its own challenges.

Besides cost factor the technology platform selection (Ref: TOGAF v9) is also influenced by the need of the following

- Availability: the degree to which IT infrastructure is supposed to be available
- Manageability: the ease to manage the technology, in other words, ability to gather information about the state of something and to control it
- Serviceability: the ability to identify problems and take corrective actions to repair or upgrade a component in a running system
- Performance: the ability of a component to perform its tasks in an appropriate time
- Reliability: resistance to failure
- Recoverability: the ability to restore a system to a working state after an interruption
- Locatability: the ability of a system and service component to be found when needed
- Security: protection of information from unauthorized access (also discussed in next section)

- Integrity: assurance that data will remain consistent and has not been corrupted
- Credibility: the level of trust in the integrity of the system and its data
- Usability: the ease-of-operation by users and IT Staff
- Internationalization: multi-lingual and multi-cultural abilities
- Adaptability: the degree of flexibility to make system changes as per business needs
- Interoperability: the flexibility to operate with different environment whether within or outside the organization, the Boundary-less Organisation
- Scalability: the ability of a component to grow or shrink its performance or capacity appropriately to the demands of the environment in which it operates
- Portability: the compatibility of data, people, applications, and components to different platform
- Extensibility: the ability to accept new functionality and access across technology domain

We also recommend that while selecting technology a long-term perspective must be kept in mind with respect to life of technology and its future besides architecture to scale. There have been many technology providers, including some big ones, which could not survive for long. This could be because of poor economics or merger and acquisition that they die down. No one thought during eighties and nineties that Database and ERP technology providers from top five lists will be out of business within a decade or two. Similarly, many hardware and networking technology companies went out of market sooner than later as they were acquired and that line of technology was withdrawn by the acquirer. On the above, the Murphy law of technology growth is still applicable and hence, obsolescence is much faster in IT than any other industry. Therefore, it is pertinent to make a strategy around a technology that can give longer life. Still be ready to face these facts and risks, which may not be because of CIO's decision about technology and the provider, but the market forces, where no one has control.

IT technology is integrating and expanding into other service domains such as telecommunication, multimedia and animation, education and learning. It is expanding horizons as well as changing landscape of the business. The new technology is bringing compelling reasons and distinct business benefits, which sometimes impacts the competitive edge of existing business models negatively, if not making it obsolete. Therefore, it must be part of Technology strategy to review and upgrade them regularly. There is no other way to protect the investment as well as grow except keep pace with technology. Only note of caution would be, not to chase the newer technology unless there is business reason and organization is ready to build capacity to digest the change.

3.8.2 Security Strategy

IT facilitates more collaboration and reach to users, customers and partners. More we reach to people and more we promote "any-where—any-time" information, more we need security. As businesses are capitalizing Internet and collaboration across organizational boundaries for mission-critical communications and business operations, serious security risks are proliferating. The information network grows porous and need structured approach to manage security risk. The technology and its components have not only increased features for improved business services but also made the security management more complex. In today's context Security has become even more relevant because of the following, which have increased vulnerability.

- Business data may be hosted out of premises
- Business systems are being developed and implemented by external parties
- System access and connectivity is required to and from outside
- System administration are being performed remotely
- Disaster data backup or fall-back sites are out locations
- Working environment and miniaturized data storages have increased chances of data leakage
- Presence of malware such as VIRUS, Phishing, Trojan, SPAM
- Motivated hackers

Security breaches do not happen always from external interface and external parties. Many a time, the threat is generated inside, when the business internal people leak and sell the information. Earlier, the disposal of printed reports and documents also used to be hazardous practice. Applying security with these authorized users is more difficult than the outsiders. The explosion of information network, messaging systems such as email, Blogs and IM, and wireless networking, usage of common equipment such as laptop and mobiles inside organization and outside, and USB storage devices have made the protection of critical enterprise data even more difficult. Many organizations are struggling to maintain information security under these conditions. Some have started working at disabling many devices in office equipment and logging of messaging and file copies at OS level for audit. The review of log creates a sense of fear for malpractice and hesitation amongst users. Although it is not fully fool proof, with a mix of good policy, awareness and audit practices it would provide better control and reduce the incident to a very reasonable level.

Just to get an idea of threat from only one source, we look at the report from Aberdeen Group. It reported, "at least 75% of all email traversing the Internet is spam and 38% of organizations reported that malware had infiltrated the corporate network through email during the 12-month period ended April 2009. And more than 60% of organizations believe that the IT department holds the majority of the responsibility for communications security and compliance, but fewer than 20% feel they are well equipped to handle it". And our understanding is that the ignorance including limited capability of selected technology & solution, cost, organization priority and resource allocation are the major causes.

A survey by Deloitte in 2009 shows grim picture on IT security in TMT (Technology-Media-Telecommunication) industry. Only 22% of survey participants, mostly CXX class of managers, find security effective, the rest finds either somewhat effective or not at all. It is o more concern when 50% plus observes that the requisite fund has been made available. This depicts the complexity of technicalities involved, thus need for growing skill, management attention and fund availability.

Security does not mean hiding information from every one, rather it means access to authorized person, process and business entities only. The entity covers person, process and other inter and intra-business actors such as web-services and soft connections which take out information with no further control. To achieve security objective, the entity looking for access must be identified and authenticated to be true to its introduction and then as per the organization policy its authorization and entitlement are enforced. No resource should be accessible beyond the authorized limit. This requires well defined security policy, which must categorize the entities likely to access the resource and accordingly the policy is defined and implemented. Since entities represent at individual level, group level, class and category level; and each can have varying access permission, a security policy could have layered structure with clear guidance on order of precedence. Even permissions for an entity can differ based on time, location, assignments, access mode and other dimensions, the policy guidance must address different possibilities and respective authorizations.

The strategy for security need to be designed at the following three levels

- Network and Communication
- Application and Data centre
- Administrator and Users

and they must be made compatible and complimenting each other. These must be validated with respect to information at rest, in use, in motion and in archive.

Regularly new threats are emerging and the organizations need to catch up to mitigate the risk. Generally different technologies are being applied at different points. The CIOs are vetting the threats and the effectiveness of the deployed technologies regularly to safeguard the interest of the business. Solutions such as firewalls, intrusion prevention systems, network scanning solutions, antivirus, SPAM detection and quarantine, and many more are used. The challenge is that one technology or a solution does not provide complete coverage, hence, a suite of such technologies need to be deployed, which are coming from different providers. Therefore, it must be ensured that they are covering complete need in integrated manner. Since the cost of such an elaborate coverage is pretty high, organizations apply a "Probability-Impact-Priority" technique. The threats and the vulnerability are assessed and the impact is visualized. Giving the effect of the probability of occurrence quantifies the total impact. Higher the impact, the higher priority it takes for readdressal. The creeping vulnerability, which either spreads and takes shape of epidemic or opens gate for other attacks, is also classified as high priority. Even the rest is not just left, but they are covered through "Log and Audit" approach, where such cases and complaints are logged and analysed in due course for their occurrence and impact. When organization finds any of them to be big irritant or creating significant impact, necessary technology is deployed to control.

The security solution cannot be just by technology. The security framework has multi-layered approach. The layered approach to address security need is applied to information, application and technology components. One must consider people, process and technology to have comprehensive and cost-effective security. The prevailing principles of grading information to design matching security solutions and operating cost also applies in IT environment. The classified and confidential information may need different strategy than normal operational data that are published in public domain. The sensitive data needs special mechanism to handle security. A university needs higher security on examination, evaluation and certification data than course curriculum. The business process, organization structure and data access structure are also reviewed and redefined to implement security of information. One can create balance between policy driven discipline and automated tools to manage vulnerability at reduced cost.

Setting up a right framework which gives scalability and operational simplification is important for enduring security. The best practices are as follows:

- Create Information security policy comprehensively that includes leakage, theft, damage and spoilage
- Create security and verification organization
- Classify assets and define controls (Security objectives & measurement, Assumptions, Constraints and a practical as well as appropriate Approach)
- Define security at role and personnel level who are having access to such sensitive data
- Train and Sensitise authorized users, make them accountable
- Organize physical and environmental security
- Secure identity and devices
- Control access, not only at the server point but also at the user end
- Manage security at development, maintenance and migration stage too
- Plan and provision for business continuity
- Define and ensure compliance
- Watch industry news of pilferage and attacks and accordingly prepare
- Focus on identifying intended and unintended attempts and be ready to implement fitting solution if the threat rises to a threshold

Large organizations, having distributed IT installations and users, follow very rigid process to change or introduce new elements. They do conduct periodic security audits with the help of experts and if required, policies are changed or new processes are set in. Some of the good strategies that reduces chances of leakage or pilferages drastically are

- Maintaining good physical security
- Auditing of service providers' processes, practices and installations
- Keeping record of all the accesses to vital information and tracking the privileged users such as server, system and database administrators
- Tracking mass data transfers and attempts to unauthorized commands
- Disabling local copy devices in user machines
- Implementing and enforcing regular update of malware control application in network and on such machines and devices entrusted for such malefic access

This demands good policy, information classification, setting right infrastructure, having intelligent workflow for discovery, monitoring, reviewing & auditing, reporting and demonstrating severe punishments to culprits. Therefore, security strategy influences technology, bill of material and overall technology architecture, hence, need attention of the organization as well as CIO. This must be considered as part of business security. It is like insurance where vulnerability and likelihood of occurrence exist.

We think that international community must collaborate to discourage information pilferage through harsh policies and legal framework. Even if they work seriously on all such matters, excluding diplomatic and government supported pilferages, the situation will be much better for individuals, society, the business at large and the Internet world. Many acts and directives such as US federal Sarbanes-Oxley and Gramm-Leach-Bliley Acts, California's pace-setting Security Breach Information Act (SB-1386), HIPAA, the European Union's Data Protection Directive demand strict discipline to maintain confidentiality of customer information from service providers only. During the era of boundary less operations, there has to be international laws to deal with intruders and intended offenders across countries. More the prosecution happens, less such incident would happen and hence, the cost to maintain security will be lower. Still the need for precautionary measures will remain.

3.8.3 *Backup and Recovery Strategy*

Today, many of the hardware components have been standardized and their failure rate has reduced drastically. For normal use one can consider any server and use most of the network boxes to connect users with the data centres. But rising need of online and real-time business applications have been demanding high availability from network as well as data servers. The connectivity of data centres with users, spread across Internet and the world as such, has posed higher risks and vulnerability. Therefore, the need for secured connection and data security has gone up. On the other hand, the skill required to integrate different components and equipment having modular and specialized features have gone up. The optimization of performance in integrated form has become a necessity today. Hence, the consideration of availability, security and manageability has become real differentiator between good equipment and ordinary ones. Prices also vary accordingly. Right selection of technology and solution which can serve the purpose is becoming the job of specialized skills and that too, a CIO need many such technology specialists to create right solution. Technology consideration to manage Backup and Recovery strategy is one of those decision influencing aspects.

We again advised CIOs to consider the business need and drive accordingly; otherwise, investment may go waste as well as operations will become a costly proposal. F5 Networks have quoted a picture from Network World below, which is very helpful to arrive at the right strategy and investment for an organization.

It is true that if the availability need is not extremely high, such as supporting retail sale for a large store or controlling the metal production, having synchronous replication and real-time backup system is a costly choice. Many applications such as back-office operation and applications where time is not critical, backup on media such as tape or disk could be acceptable. In this case, data recoverability and protection are only criteria and the availability is not business critical. It is also true that one solution is not the one fit for all backup-recovery need of an organization. Therefore, a backup and recovery policy with classification of data and right SLA must be defined before selecting the right backup technology. Once the policy is in place, the right selection criteria are drafted and accordingly the "Failure Point Analysis" is done before opting for a technology and a solution. Under this analysis, each and every possible failure point is considered and accordingly the solution is verified for providing alternative route and solution within stipulated cost and time. The backup of failure points are also considered at different levels, for a server (Processor, Power supply, Disk and Storage devices, Network port) to the business users (Network, Application component, Internet) as their turn-around time and switching without feel and interruptions are different. Just remember not all applications and users need 100% fault-tolerant system. Today most of the equipment and cables do come with alternatives available, which are constantly monitored and verified by software components and as soon as one fails the second one takes over. It may not be possible to test and verify each substitute at each level, but having due information and understanding from the supplier, as well as simulated testing is desirable, before confirming the preparedness to meet policy objectives.

For a need at high end of availability and high volume of data, it is pertinent to select right technology for managing storage solution which can support the backup-recovery policy better. The complete solution addresses the all three dimensions, availability, security and manageability (in isolation as well as in integrated infrastructure environment). And to combine business continuity plan, one may need live backup environment running concurrently and being updated to switch the operation from backup site. Sometimes, business critical data and application, such as 24×7 online banking, need more than one concurrent station to support multi-point failure even. Just storage and the servers are not the only part of this strategy, but also need holistic solution to provide uninterrupted service to users. On lower end, automated disk replication and archival & recovery could be reasonable solution and accordingly the strategy need to be put in place.

3.8.4 Logical and Physical Architecture

The IT technology has been on continuous evolution. It has also been impacting accordingly the technology architecture. Earlier it used to be single tier (Mainframe, Central Server with dumb terminals), then it evolved to two tier (Client-Server) and now it reached to n-tier architecture. As technology advanced, different components which were facilitating communication and services became more intelligent, independent and started working in collaborative and peer mode than master-slave.

3.8 Technology Strategy (Including Convergence)

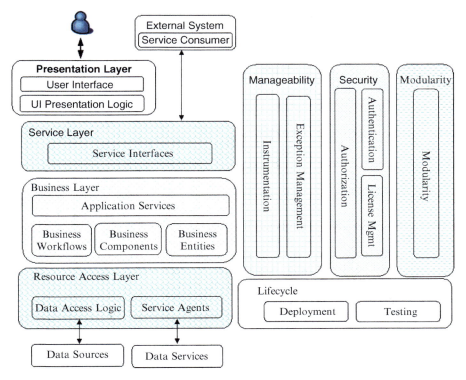

Fig. 3.13 Logical view of a typical architecture with service components—Source Microsoft

This provides a logical architectural diagram representing different components of servers at data centre. This typical MVC (Model-View-Controller) architecture (Fig. 3.13) today may look as above, but as service components become more independent and quantum of services rise along with interface and collaboration capabilities, the generalized architecture will also evolve. The Fig. 3.14 below is physical view of the same.

In this architecture, the users are browser-based. The firewall and the web server, together, validate the users and user requests that are emerging from outside network, handle exceptions and provide only authorized entry. The web server authenticates and routes the request to application server for authorization permission checking and request response generation. The application server accesses database or hooks to other service agents to fetch data from other sources to create response. Communication between two stages works after due introduction and identification. This communication may be even in encrypted form to ensure no intruder is masking and accessing. For security reasons even data by design could be encrypted so that direct access or backup copy too will not be misused. A unified communication controller integrates data network to voice and video facilitating application to voice and media devices.

To enhance the capacity and still have manageable unit, not only the number of servers and service units are required, but also group or service controllers are

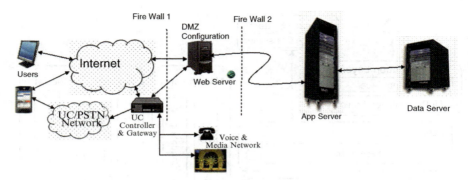

Fig. 3.14 Physical view of a typical architecture

needed. These controllers control and direct the traffic, keep unauthorized checks in control and balance the load amongst many. On database server side number of other technologies is being used to manage terabytes of data. Similarly, when the installation becomes large, independent servers for each service are deployed. Even the technique to provide such services and their interfaces change. All these elements together influence the technical architecture to service the business need. More complex it grows, higher the skill it requires and in turn involvement of technology providers.

Technology selection, Consolidation, different trade-offs such as in-house and outsourcing, buy or hire and others are discussed in the next chapter under Service models.

3.9 Summary

This chapter has provided good guidance on approach to IT strategy. It has described the IT framework and presented a simplified and crisp description of ways to create good strategy. As the business aligned IT maximizes benefit and minimizes risk, we always recommended including business perspective for each component. Hence, starting with identifying business drivers and strategy is good practice, still taking stock of current status and demand pattern gives quick idea of direction. A good team of corporate stakeholders is must to start this work. We have seen chances of success for such a model is much more than CIO led team. There are clear examples in Western world where some progressive organizations have involved their premium customers in direction setting for their business. The senior managers of these customer organizations not only provide candid feedback to set directions but also walk along, for arriving business drivers and KPIs. And then the business managers sail through. The business-managers led cross functional team always keep IT aligned to business and makes implementation easier. Also selling the IT and IT-related investment to the organization becomes an easy task for a CIO, who can contribute by facilitating to the team creativeness and amicable environment for them to work. Obviously inputs from technology perspective will still be expected from CIO.

We suggested the approach to go through stage by stage, from business strategy to economic value identification of IT strategy via process strategy, application and technology strategy, people strategy and IT service strategy. During the process business alignment and identification of opportunities for IT must remain in focus. We also recommended that all the identified opportunities must be prioritised in perspective of business benefits and business strategy before starting action, however, part implementation will also remain within the big picture. The team may require subject matter specialists and it would be worth to supplement them even though it requires hiring outside skills. At times, CIOs make decisions based on advice of product and service providers; and that is perfectly all right. One must realize that the technology and application options have grown so much that very few CIOs and installations can have full idea themselves.

Business Process Management tools are in the market, which helps users to define the flows and create process model. Some extends it to application generation within their set framework. SAP and Oracle are of those kinds. Even though their products have some limitations that the platform and technology base is proprietary the granularity to the extent an innovative organization would like to have is yet to be achieved, their customization model takes care of for the time being. In case an organization has decided about application technology in advance this could be a better tool to depict business processes and link them to applications. But it seems step in right direction.

Further detailing on other components of IT strategy (after the stage of technology strategy) is done in next chapter. Just that one keep in mind that IT strategy formulation is not one cycle approach, but it may require revisits based on many considerations such as investment approval and organization capability to digest. But it is always better, if all components are in tune with each other, before investment and strategy start being rolled out.

3.10 Glossary

BU	Business Unit
CEO	Chief Executive Officer
CFO	Chief Financial Officer
CIO	Chief Information Officer
CMO	Chief Marketing Officer
COO	Chief Operation Officer
CSF	Critical Success Factor
EV	Economic Value
HQ	Head Quarter
HR	Human Resource (function)
IT	Information Technology
KPI	Key Performance Indicator
ROI	Return on Investment
SOA	Service Oriented Architecture
TOGAF	The Open Group Architecture Framework

3.11 Review Questions

1. What is the need for business alignment with IT Strategy? How do you achieve this alignment?
2. What are benefits of IT and business alignment?
3. What are steps involved in designing an IT Strategy?
4. What is process reengineering and how does it help in business alignment?
5. What is he role of application integration in IT strategy?
6. What is the need for security strategy? Please give examples with respect to intranet and extranet.
7. What is the difference between Logical and Physical Architecture?

3.12 Project Work

Please visit the web site of a vehicle manufacturing organization (example—Toyota). Through secondary research, find out different applications that are used in the organization. Design IT Strategy for Toyota using logical and physical architecture.

3.13 Annexure A

3.13.1 CRUD Matrix

Entities / Process	Customer	Order	Invoice	Vendor	PO	Check	Warehouse	Shipment	Shipper	Employee	Plant
Customer Management	CRUD	R	R				R				
Order Entry	CRU	CRUD	R								
Invoicing	R	R	CRUD								
Purchasing				RU	CRUD	R					
Vendr Management				CRUD	R	R					
Accounts Payables				RU	RU	CRUD	R				
Warehouse Management							CRUD	R		R	R
Inventory management							CRUD				R
Shipment Tracking	R		R				R	CRUD	R		
Production Management							R	R		R	CRUD

(Politano 2001)

3.13.2 Technologies Being Used for Security
(Brightman and Buith 2009)

- Antivirus
- Firewalls
- Spam filtering solutions
- Virtual Private Network
- Web content filtering/monitoring
- Wireless security solutions
- Intrusion Detection Systems (IDS)
- Antispyware software
- Vulnerability management systems
- E-mail encryption
- Intrusion Prevention Systems (IPS)
- Web access management systems
- Security log and event management system
- Incident management workflow tools
- Antiphishing solutions
- Web-services security
- Data at rest security/encryption (e.g. Tape, database and SAN encryption)
- Data leakage technology (for Insider Threat Detection)
- Security compliance tools
- Enterprise Single Sign On
- Biometrics
- Encrypted storage devices
- Network behaviour analysis
- Network access control
- Active threat management system

References

Brightman I, Buith, Jacques (2009) 2009 TMT Global Security Survey Full report. Deloitte Inc.
Frampton, Janice and Jones, Duane (2009) Lean beyond manufacturing. Jean Cunningham Consulting, US
http://online.wsj.com/article/SB10001424052748704431804574541640953856278.html
http://www.opengroup.org/architecture/togaf/
Ilebrand, Nicklas, Mesøy, Tor and Vlemmix, Remco (2010) Using IT to enable a lean transformation. Mckinsey Quarterly
Mayer JH, Schaper M (2010) Business Technology: Supporting Top Management with Next generation Executive Information System. McKinsey Quarterly, Jan-2010
Mayer JH, Schaper M (2010) Data to dollars: supporting top management with next generation executive information systems. Mckinsey on Business Technology
Microsoft application architecture guide, 2nd edn.

Morrison M (2008) Business transformation—a change strategy. RapidBI Limited, London. http://rapidbi.com/created/businesstransformation.html

Oestreich T (2009) Business innovation: the CIO perspective. J Manage Excellence: Business Transform, Issue 7, An Oracle Publication

Politano AL (2001) Salvaging information engineering techniques in the data warehouse environment

Rico DF A framework for measuring the ROI of enterprise architecture

Roberts R, Sikes, Johnson (2009) IT in the new normal. McKinsey Quarterly

Rose M, Perry, R (2009) Quantifying the Business Value of VMware View. White Paper by IDC and VMware

Ross JW, Woerne SL, Scantlebury S, Cynthia (2009) IT advantage—the IT organisation of the future. www.bcg.com

Schekkerman J, Verdonck Klooster & Associates Institute for Enterprise Architecture Development. http://www.enterprise-architecture.info/Images/Presentaties/MS%20Roundtable%20EA%20Optimization.pdf

Security Strategy Development—Building an Information Security Management Program, An ISS White Paper—2010

Sttraton W et al (2009) Can value chain analysis lead to business transformation? Journal of Management Excellence: Business Transformation, Issue 7, An Oracle Publication

Treacy M, Wiersma F (1995) The discipline of market leaders: choose your customers, narrow your focus, dominate your market. HarperCollins, London

Trend Micro Inc (2010) Leveraging data loss prevention technology to secure corporate assets

Peter W (2009) Interview with MIT Sloan Management Review's senior editor Martha E. Mangelsdorf for Business Insight. The Wall Street Journal, November 30, 2009

www.BPMInstitute.com

www.cio.com

www.iso.org

www.sctvchannel.com, "Best Practices in Order Capture/Dal-Tile Case Study", an interview of Rick Odorico from Dal-Tile and Richard Douglass from Sterling System with Dan Gilmore, Dec 2009 http://www.sctvchannel.com/webinars/Videocast3.php?cid=2862&ctype=content&CntID=MTc3NDc4fDEyNjQxNTk0NzI=

www.searchcio.com

Chapter 4
Strategy Implementation

4.1 Learning Objectives

This chapter would

- Define the approach to people strategy and creating suitable organization
- Elaborate strategy for IT services
- Identify ways to manage risks
- Define and create focus on IT alignment and benefit measurement
- Describe the benefit evaluation framework
- Introduce IT strategy governance model and practices

4.2 Introduction

The managing strategy implementation is as important as strategy formulation. It involves guiding, organizing, driving, leading and adjusting. The principles to implement other business strategies and IT strategy are the same. The IT strategy roll-out is not the job of CIO alone, but it is also the organization's responsibility. The top management team must own it and support.

It has three steps:

- Endorsement and participation by the management
- Development of core strategy (as depicted in Chap. 3)
- Roll-out carefully (as below)

The roll-out of IT strategy is like effecting any organizational change. It needs good planning and careful steps. Enabling people and putting organization structure in place is the first step in implementation. Knowing well the behaviour of people that they resist the changes being proposed by others, whereas demand for change to break monotony and make progress, managers must create a strategy of people driven change. And this is achieved through their participation in decision-making as well as taking care of their needs in terms of "Maslow's Hierarchy of Needs". Sometimes their group behaviour dynamics including unions also need to be managed. In our experience, getting a scenario where the business need, people need and the presence of supporting elements may not be aligned and balanced. The management team including CIO must plan to face certain unfavourable situations while implementation. This can impact IT service strategy as well. We have observed the cases where the debate of in-house vs. outsourcing decisions is being finally decided by these factors than actual merit.

The promulgation of government rulings or incentives and disincentives too impact service strategy, whether it connects to outsourcing, technology, taxation, business obligations, applications or Internet. These statutory policies and incentive packages need careful study before they are embedded in the strategy.

Every strategy implementation has its inherent risks, which can surprise, at times, and impact strategy-elements. They can be from the area of business, business drivers and priorities, people including skills, technology and implementation approach and infrastructure. Sometimes they are so severe that they change the direction itself. Merger and acquisition, financial crisis such as the one in 2008, invasive and compelling technologies such as remote IT services and outsourcing after Internet technology maturity are the few examples. No one had thought about financial meltdown in 2008, which impacted most of the strategies and changed the direction altogether for many. Therefore, a risk management strategy must go hand-in-hand with implementation, whereby they are regularly watched and actions to mitigate are initiated in a timely manner.

IT strategy is for certain purpose. It is in the interest of the organization that they identify the goals in measurable form for different stage/phase and time blocs. This provides a sense of direction, helps in identifying deviation, and maintains alignment. Some could be IT internal, which CIO can review but some are external to IT functional area, where business managers must be involved. This also includes economic value and ROI from IT.

4.3 People Strategy

The people are the most important factor to make strategy work within an enterprise context. And to realize the strategic value from this factor, the organization must put in place appropriate organization structures, processes, roles, responsibilities and skills. Putting all these elements and the motivation in sync with the business strategy is all about the people strategy. The people strategy framework is as shown in the figure below.

The Fig. 4.1 below clearly depicts the people enablement through building their capability, knowledge and providing right environment and infrastructure to use the same to produce results. The business strategy and the technology infrastructure create right platform, the training, the knowledge and the process develop their skill and expertise, the motivation orients them and make them committed to deliver

4.3 People Strategy

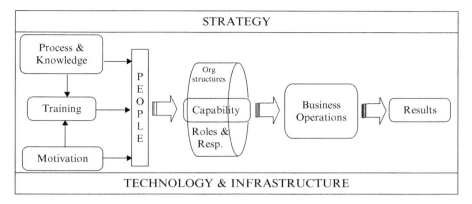

Fig. 4.1 People enablement

results, the organization structure and the role and responsibility make them focused, IT provides right tools; and finally when they apply their skill into business under the supporting framework, they produce excellence.

People strategy is not only important in developed economies as organizations find definite merit in people enablement and alignment, but also in developing economies where the gaps between people skill and the technologies are generally wider. The approach may be different, but the objective remains the same, and this is to make the work force and the managers competent, effective and willing partners. This is true in case of all change management whether it is for disruptive and invasive or non-disruptive change. This touches large functional area of HR and industrial relationship management. Though it is true that CIOs, being the part of the management, are also exposed to trade unions, but without going into the nitty-gritty of managing trade unions and collective bargaining process, CIOs must understand the importance and relationship of IT strategy with people and handle it strategically. In our experience people do cover more mileage even with second rug technology than from front running technologies, if employees are committed and motivated.

Today many IT systems are unable to see light of the day because of this issue, where either willing or unwilling employees are not able to use IT for their business functions. Unlike the West, most of the developing countries wasted lot of energy and resources to cross the barrier of labour union mind set, where these unions saw IT with wrong eye. But that has been things of past, now most of the countries and industries have come out of that era, by proving that IT is good for employment and survival of business. Thanks to outsourcing and globalization that today, IT has become major employer all across these developing economies including China. Still, the management needs to consider the genuine difficulties of people involved, and create win–win situation for all stake holders, such as any change management process needs.

If one watches certain organizational behaviour and practices, she can gauge the people aspect and understand what needs to be done and how they need to be approached. There are certain symptoms and measurements as below, which clearly depicts weaknesses to people aspect of the organization especially for the IT

- IT compass: The gap between IT Skills requirement and the availability, is large
- Information flow: Managers and their staffs are more comfortable with paper based information collation and reporting than using IT systems for the same
- Informal network: Managers apply more discretion than defined rules and the work happens more through informal network
- Performance review: Neither the measurement yardsticks are well defined nor the quality information is available for performance review, thus indicating weaker management practices, KPIs and measurements
- IT resource: IT enabled systems and devices are not under optimum use or the infrastructure is ready to be obsolete
- Demand for file cabinets: The demand for file cabinets, stationeries and storages are regularly increasing
- Signatures and seals: The culture of seals and signature are more prevalent and prominent
- Transaction posting: Data entry assistants are interfacing system on behalf of managers and business people

Some of the symptoms also appear in Western countries, but that is not because of people capability but they are more because of system capability, which may be starving of right strategy and investment. This is clear case where management does not perceive the value by switching to new technology and creating enhanced platform for collaboration, unless the organization is seriously fund starved.

It is widely observed that high performing organizations have much better work practices which contribute to their performance. Department of Trade and Industry, UK also shared their findings during a study in 2004, that the following practices are much better in such organizations

- High employee involvement practices
- Human resource processes that included employee life cycle
- Reward and commitment practices

The people perform when they get right opportunity to work, have skills and motivation, and supporting tools and Infrastructure. For example, people on mobile such as sales and field service need to have enabled infrastructure to remain connected with their colleagues and the IT systems. Technology such as GPS, mobile applications and other matching infrastructure are of great help to their performance. But organization design and its alignment in right perspective is major contributor to the people and organization performance and that deserve careful design and considerations.

4.3.1 Organization Design

Even though poor organization design causes lot of stress in drafting IT strategy and execution, the overall organization design is out of scope of IT strategy. It is part of corporate strategy and involves large-scale exercise, as full organization design is a fundamental process and not a patch work. Depending upon the industry and business set-up, organization structure, suitable to the business, will be different. Even in same organization, the organization design can vary from region to region and country to country. It depends on whether the organization has product, market, operations, customers or process value chain focus. Sometimes they do have a hybrid model. Under premise of IT strategy, small shift or changes in responsibilities and functional distribution could be acceptable to the organization but not a large restructuring, unless the top management combines the purpose. We have observed the organizations, having complex structure, usually create more constraints to efficiency and performance than simple and flexible ones. organization design is also an alignment process Stanford (2009) in context of business, whereby various elements of an organization such as people, structure, systems, culture, processes and performance measures, are aligned to transform business and achieve higher results. Therefore, during IT strategy formulation too, the opportunity for alignment or gaps may appear. The team involved in defining IT strategy may find that the existing organization is posing constraints to optimally utilize business processes and IT systems to generate expected business value. This could happen even when the team senses a better organization structure or new management practices can make significant contribution to the business performance. The change, whether small or big, must follow five rules Stanford (2009)

- Design when there is compelling reason
- Develop options before deciding a design
- Choose right time to design
- Look for clues that things are out of alignment
- Stay alert to the future

Some simple processes, as follows, could help to create better options. The strategy starts with stakeholder identification, managing their expectations and organizing their participation so that they have clarity and motivation to achieve the performance expected. The process clubbing based on their alignment in the value chain and measurable performance objectives as well as data clustering is the technique to group processes together and create functional groups around that. Sometimes, time or function based performance objective, inter-related subjects and need for close coordination are also considered for clubbing. These bring in information and KPI linked hierarchy into figure. Now the volume and variety analysis for current and future scenario are done to look at scalability and personnel need. With the help of HR organization and concerned senior managers from related areas, the roles are tagged with each unit of functions. To validate whether the match between the organizational structure and demand from respective business functions and processes are balanced, a simple charting under five pillars of function management on the Table 4.1 below is performed for each functional area.

This depicts what to do, who should be doing that, what processes they will follow to do those work and when they will do or take action, under each column head. And each column head depicts planning, execution, measurement and review functions under control and facilitation by the management.

Table 4.1 Planning process

	Planning	Overall management (operational + interface)	Work execution	Measurement	Review
What to do?					
Who should do?					
How should be done?					
When should be done?					

If the team is not very comfortable in validating through the above table, it can breakdown the processes role-wise and create one for each process and later consolidate to have a summarized view. They can follow hybrid model of BPR and industrial engineering principles to create roles and hierarchy, and attach responsibilities. The objective is to achieve clarity of expectations for each role and full coverage of all the processes, at the same time. The stakeholders can follow the document and would be able to connect the organization role and structure with the processes and the work.

Another decision which impacts organization design, though in small way, is the decision on self-service or shared-services. Many organizations adopt practice of self service in the areas of business knowledge and managing IT enabled processes. Thus, concerned functional areas and group of stake holders make provision for their own IT interfaced work and related services such as training, business rules definition, local configuration, service request management, internal coordination. Central IT group is involved only in policy decision, IT strategy or architectural change, vendor selection, standardization and such work which impacts other functional groups and external processes and stakeholders as well. This can happen by design or compulsion of spread location.

But this is right occasion to re-look at the organization design for IT strategy.

4.3.2 People Enablement

IT brings change, hence, preparing stake holders to accept and adapt to changes must be part of IT strategy. This part of the strategy is to enable individual stakeholders who can make use of infrastructure and the information systems for their business, effectively. In a strategic term, the goal is to make human capital a competitive differentiator. The following are the three steps to achieve this, once the business alignment issues are resolved

- Make employee capable and empower them
- Equip them with right tools and information
- Motivate them to use their capability, information and tools to deliver results

A good CIO takes care of all the three parameters in close coordination with the peers as well as the management board. We suggest creating special strategy for business managers and business partners too, otherwise driving process adherence and system usage will be very difficult. In absence of their usage, the organization returns back to earlier stage quickly.

The capability comes from the learning and skill. A good strategy not only creates change awareness programme but also works out the way the stake holders feel confident to face the business challenges caused by change initiative. It is good idea to prepare such strategy along with HR management and respective line managers; may be along with behavioural and learning facilitators, and opinion makers. For learning too, a blended approach (Woodall 2004) should be taken which suggests mix and match different approaches such as technology-based learning (such as eLearning, virtual class-rooms and collaboration), combination of pedagogical approaches (such as behavioural and constructivism), instructional technology (face-to-face and Internet) and mix of instructional technology with on-the-job. The best delivery and learning for each category of stakeholders will be different. Hence, offering a mix takes care of them as a group and also as an individual. Most of the time only workers dealing with transactional and operational levels are covered under this, which is not complete and it should cover all concerned.

Making them equipped with tools and right information in-time and in-need, encourages them to make decision and take informed actions. And the strategy for this is to reach to the users, under which they are not only skilled to operate IT facilities but also proficient in deriving right information. Earlier customized reports used to play this role, when even plant managers and field officers used to hold the report at their work place and make decisions. Having large-scale integration with variety of mobile equipment and devices can service the information to the team in field. We have seen migrating work force in a steel plant from reports to on-line terminals and now to mobile devices such as mobile phones and laptops. This kind of interaction serves right information to right person at right location, in time. And that delivers value to the business.

Next is motivation, which addresses the interest and internal drive of the stakeholders. Many people work out incentives and other reward and recognition scheme to motivate. But in our experience, the conducive work environment and sense of achievement work most of the time and far better than any monetary and positional incentives. Transitioning the process to the newly adopted system will have hiccups but a set of motivated stakeholders make it successful, as if the change was simple and it could have been done lot earlier. Even if the organization needed to offer incentives, there is nothing wrong, after all it's a normal human behaviour to search and find what is in it for them. But these incentives need to be designed carefully and there must be graded performance and time factor. In one of the cases, we have seen that the organization designed an incentive scheme for a set of users when they switched from post event data posting to online scheme of things. The overall process and system performance started improving. The innovative ideas of this set of users made them achieve 200% performance. Few line managers were not comfortable approving such a high incentive even though they cut the manpower in numbers which gave them greater advantage. The innovation was not the outcome of the monetary benefit, but to meet the challenges of the occasion and commitment to make this system successful. That's why even after not receiving higher incentives the gains were sustained. In another case the organization changed the qualification of certain set of users and recruited fresh graduates. These youngsters along with some existing employees were deployed in the business. The mix pulled up the performance of the set and set new benchmarks in customer management and service quality. The older employees too started taking responsibilities and performing. Even though they were promoted, but the main improvement was driven by the youngsters in pursuit to recognition and self motivation. The idea here is that the money or just recognition may not work always and may not be fit for all categories in all the situations. One needs to design different strategies to make the stakeholders to see right reasoning for change and take pride of. They should feel like collaborating and co-delivering the result.

Every person is different and in organization context they show a mix behaviour emerging from their personality, their role and organization culture. Even though the organization makes a most acceptable common enablement model to approach this need, we recommend a CIO to make special strategy to deal with each of the senior stakeholders and opinion makers. In our experience, approach through "Maslow's Hierarchy of Needs" is good approach to understand the motivational need for operational level staff. Since most of them may be showing common group behaviour, a common platform and approach may work. But IT strategy involves senior managers too as critical stakeholders and they mostly behave in individual capacity. It is important to understand their behavioural style to communicate with them, solicit their ideas and support. It is important to get them involved for the cause of good IT strategy being rolled out in the organization and show them the way their teams are getting benefited. It could be efficiency, productivity or overall performance; we have observed that the strategy works. These managers have one of the four dominating behavioural styles, analytical, driving, amiable and expressive (www.Tracom.com). A CIO need to understand the individual's style and the corporate dynamics around him/her to design a suitable approach to reach to them and solicit their positive contribution. For example, an analytical style person needs reasoning and data, but the same approach with driving or amiable style will not work. Similarly, expecting quick decisions, especially from the area which may be sensitive and being headed by a manager having amiable style, will not be appropriate, whereas for persons with driving style it will work.

Learning is first step of transition. Most of the people hesitate to participate in transition process due to fear of learning and starting from first step, whereas they may have reached to higher steps and become proficient in existing practices. A CIO must realize their paradigm and appreciate why they hesitate and do not wish to change, which appears as resistance to change. In cases of IT strategy roll-out, the organization too needs to understand the dilemma and hence, create smooth transitioning of people, irrespective of their cadre. It could be through mix of education, persuasion, regulation and incentive. Even the willing stakeholders sometime find difficult to transition and for them one need to apply IDC's 5A's model of corporate learning (Anderson 2003)

- Information Available on convenience
- Create Appropriate information for each role in business context

4.3 People Strategy

- Make those information *A*ccessible from defined source
- People are able comprehend and *A*bsorb
- They should be able to *A*pply and taste success.

A provision for facilitating learning must be done all stake holders including suppliers, partners and some times customers too. A good technique to manage change such as steps below, help these people to transition successfully

- Let them know why organization is making this journey of transition
- Let them understand what they need to do to make it successful
- Let them know what arrangement for their learning and transition has been done and how they can take advantage of
- Facilitate patiently and sympathetically
- Make leaders (natural or through organizational process) who can take leadership role to propagate learning and change
- Let them know the progress in the journey of transition
- Let them know when journey is completed and the achievements
- Felicitate the success for all to cherish the achievement

But every people enablement must follow retention and motivation strategy. Today, in the era of knowledge economy, the skilled people are becoming greatest asset of any organization. A CIO must draw attention to the business managers towards this. Business people having IT skill are in demand and will remain in demand. Therefore, a good HR strategy (driven by HR and personnel wing) must be in place in the organization by the time their transition to new scenario which is in line with IT strategy is activated. Once, my manager said, "Let us face separation of trained employees in pursuit to their career than retention of those, having obsolete skills, as the latter will be more harmful for our organization, whereas the first one will benefit the society". If the organization has option to recruit for the job, we recommend framing right policy and performance framework, which shall include recruitment, training, assessment, reward, progression and finally superannuation. This will guide all HR functions for a common goal and keep them in sync with business objectives.

A CIO must think for HR policy for IT function too. The strategy will be little different for people in IT team. This is because of fast change in technology and churn out of people. Therefore, a CIO does have sometimes a short-term view for IT people strategy. Even though we find that a person cannot achieve professional excellence without experience in implementation and support, preference is tilted towards development. On the one hand the organization needs knowledge of new and emerging technology and on the other hand to reap the benefit of the system it needs stability for longer period. Since there are lot of opportunities for IT people at this stage, they always prefer development stream from market perspective. This keeps them updated and provides regular exposure to new domain and technology. Therefore, a CIO must make a strategy to offer equitable opportunity for all and motivate professionals to draw balance between the two stages. Another issue which CIOs from developing countries face is large salary difference between user industry and IT industry. This has made them a learning ground for professionals who cannot launch themselves directly in IT industry. Now it has become contagious and spread to business users too. Many large industries have managed to cover the salary and employment benefits gap to large extent for retention. They also make up for the skill gap with hiring, but SMEs face serious issue and quickly land up either with professionals having not so good skill on newer technology or fresh graduates. One of the methods which created more relief is "key resource" approach to manage. This worked in user industry as well as IT industry. The organization must identify key people having key skills and knowledge who are fast learner, good driver and capable of taking work out of average performers too. The spurt of demand could be fulfilled by hired resources. The key people provide continuity and help to modulate the demand and switch between project and operations, effectively. The organization must focus on retain those few and keep them motivated and skilled. Monetary benefit is great motivator, but not the only one. There are other techniques too to retain. While observing the skill and exposure gap between developed and developing countries as well as the opportunities around, we do see reasons that this issue will remain there for some more times. We suggest the organizations to have plan B also ready. Some organizations do have the strategy of good processes and user participation for functional and operational roles to alleviate this problem, at least partly. No one strategy gives full benefit, it has to be a mix with each giving part but the sum is significant.

Knowing well that most of IT professionals are having analytical mind and they need more functional and soft skills, CIO must have right strategy to support her team which will make them more effective at the work in an internal team and with business users and customers. We have observed many senior managers, working to develop soft skills of these professionals for better ideas and speedy implementation. On the other hand, these professionals may have good technology understanding but little direct experience or influence in leading a business-wide change programme. And these skills make difference. CIOs want to leverage the intelligence and radical ideas of IT professionals but their lacking understanding and appreciation of business functions are supplemented by inviting business users in the team. The skill to bridge the gap between business and technology make big difference to success of projects and services, and that's why developing such skills deserve greater attention and special strategy.

4.4 IT Service Strategy

Like any strategy, IT service strategy too has certain goals and objectives. The key to this strategy is identification of service requirements, which emerges from business process design and service them effectively. Whenever such organizational processes change or reorient, the stakeholders need adjustment too. These could be related to strategy, roles or operational practices. The service strategy revolves around these requirements and become link between business and IT services.

IT service in an organization is means for delivering value to users through IT by supporting the cause for which the users are striving in business context. IT service strategy supports putting IT facilities in place, maintaining them in good health and productively utilizing to produce strategic results. The value from service comes when information is delivered to business people, who need it, when they need it, and how they need it. The quality of service is also measured in same perspective. The purpose of service and the service delivery are seen in two perspectives

- Utility of service: In IT terms it is value of information and support to complete the business process in the value chain, such as reduction in inventory, improvement in product mix, cost improvement in product/service delivery cost and customer's realization of value.
- Service attributes: This defines the characteristics of service and its produce (information) such as cost of service, risk involved, security of information, timeliness of delivery, ease of availability, reliability of service and the information, continuity of service, interpretability and presentation of information.

These are in tune with the concepts of five principles (ITSMF, An Introductory Overview of ITIL V3) of ITIL, service strategy, service design, service transition, service operation and continual service management. These five principles are also represented as five stages of service life cycle.

ITIL is promoted by the Office of Government Commerce (OGC), UK. Being a framework based on the best practices standard for IT services. It tries to define guidelines to help the business and IT service management as the service-customers and the service-providers respectively with an idea to align IT with business and resolve many issues in service arena. ITIL focused on certain business goals such as increasing user satisfaction, improving service availability and quality, increasing financial benefits to the users as well as the providers by improving productivity and utilization, business competitiveness and decision-making, and optimizing risk. The ITIL model from ITSMF, shows clearly the service strategy as core, wrapped with service design, transition and operation. To keep the model agile, the opportunity for service improvement is continuously explored and applied. The continual improvement receives feedback from all stages and influences changes to any of them with an objective to keep the services agile and in tune with the business need and the expected performance. A simplified version is being presented below which also shows the flow (Fig. 4.2).

ITIL has five staged approach that covers 20 plus processes (ITIL V3, www.itil.org) and related activities. The five stages are published in a set of five books, each covering one stage. And then there are many complementary publications covering the same from different dimensions, such as introduction, executive edition, case studies, governance methods, etc. Below is the summary of five staged framework and related processes. Even though the framework also touches upon role and responsibilities, key functions and common activities besides processes, we are deliberating the processes as the process definition and design will cover them.

- *Service strategy*: This covers service goals, service values, business case, approach, assets and market based options and selections. The focus remains on customer's perceived value and the way it can be delivered.

    This answers issues such as what services should be offered, who are the service recipients, who are the potential providers (internal/external), how will they

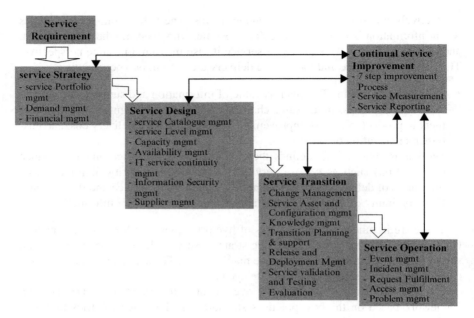

Fig. 4.2 ITIL flow

take up the work, how the service providers will be selected, how the cost will be optimized, how values and the performance will be measured, etc. The three processes it covers are as below:

- Service Portfolio Management (SPM)
  This is living process, under which the organization defines, analyzes, approves and charters the services. The process must provide the guidelines as how the organization identifies and creates service inventory, maximizes values, aligns and balances demand and supply, prioritizes services and finalizes resources.

- Demand Management (SDM)
  Any organization goes through different phases of service demands. Sometimes it nurtures to generate demand and at others it needs to contain when demand is exceeding the supply. Generally, the management likes demands surpassing the supply, as it helps them to maximize the benefit by prioritization and makes IT implementation easier as there is pull from user community. Under this process the organization describes the service demand generation, provisioning and capacity improvement strategy. Maintaining and improving service level while moderating service demand without curtailing buoyancy is the key goal.

- Financial Management
  This covers functions and processes of budgeting for IT services and includes attaching monetary value to IT services. This should help the organization to analyze the financial benefits under existing mode of service and amongst

4.4 IT Service Strategy

available options. Many organizations define detail accounting and reporting structures for cost reporting, budget control and benefit reporting.

- *Service design*: ITSMF describes this, "The design of appropriate and innovative IT services, including their architectures, processes, policies and documentation, to meet current and future agreed business requirements". This covers the processes and interactions amongst different service components as well as its ecosystem to make the strategy work under overall organizational framework.

  During this stage, the organization designs and develops services to meet business results, means to mitigate risks, secured IT infrastructure and environment for service delivery. The design must help in enhancement of skills, capability and capacity to meet service objectives consistently, definition of methods to execute and metrics to measure and improve. People, products, processes and partners are in the focus. ITIL recommends the following processes

  - Service Catalogue Management (SCM)
    Service catalogue is collection of IT and related services that the service provider organization is authorized to provide to the business. This is extract from service portfolio and includes active as well as ready to offer service lists. The process defines how this catalogue will be maintained and the items are added/deleted, who all authorized to access what all services and how.

    This is especially important for large organizations where units need clarity on scope and services being offered by IT and other internal or external organizations. We have observed that in absence of this, a large organization really struggled to streamline and standardize the services and the providers. Finally they made a bureaucratic circular that no fund allocation for IT purchase and vendor registration can happen without approval from IT organization and tried to enforce through purchase, accounts and projects organizations.

  - Service Level Management (SLM)
    This process supports service quality management through definition of service levels and monitoring them whether they are delivered as per the expectations. This covers standard operational services as well as discreet service requests. This helps IT operational and field staff, including IT service partners, to plan and deliver services against defined goals and service Levels. The metrics and the measurement always help in improving performance and without which service level do not serve any purpose.

    Most of the time the service level expectations (SLA) are defined based on business needs, such as payroll by second of every month and monthly financial closing and reporting to the management by seventh of every month, but at times it may also include other operational characteristics, as below

    – System availability such as 14 h 6 days a week or 99.99%
    – Reliability and consistency such as 100%
    – On-line transaction response such as 3 s
    – Data recoverability such as till last day or last hour
    – Service continuity such as critical functions restored in 3 h, etc.

IT strategist design systems as well as infrastructures and processes in a way that they can meet the service levels. Sometimes they also tag penalty clause for failure, which can have staged service-levels, to the service provider organizations. At the same time, one needs to keep in mind that stiffer the service level expectation, higher is the cost of infrastructure as well as services. Therefore, service levels expectations must be optimized to better cost–benefit performance. They need to be designed in a way that they support the business needs and encourage service providers to stretch to meet as well as exceed the service needs of the business.

- Capacity Management
  This process must provide guidelines to balance IT capability and capacity to meet business needs during whole service life cycle. IT organization must get full support from its ecosystem to be capable of meeting service demands of business. Many organizations also check the rationality in the business needs, before approving the investment in building the matching capacity. We have observed that organizations perform due diligence to ensure reasonable demand and prioritize them before approving capacity building initiatives, which could be in various form such as people, skill, infrastructure and others.

- Availability Management
  It defines the IT service (including system and application access), availability for business functions. The process guides for defining availability in measurable terms, planning and creating right infrastructure, proactively, to make sure that expectations are met, performance are quantitatively measured and actions for improvement are initiated. Generally, the availability is defined as ratio of time period when the service was ready and fit for use to total expected, during the agreed time period. This also forms part of SLA. Some organizations define it in a staged form so that the service provider keeps improving the performance. At occasions, this also includes the infrastructure and facility upgrade to achieve next milestones, such as improving availability from 12×5 to 24×7, it would require whole lot of change in data centre and network facilities, people and process.

- IT Service Continuity Management (ITSCM)
  The purpose of this process is to maintain IT services to support business continuity under different risk situations.

  Interruption in IT services also adds to business risk. The process must help in identifying such possible scenario of interruptions, understanding the impact on business, drawing risk/impact reduction strategy and planning to mitigate the same, on regular basis. The service continuity must be aligned to overall business risk management plan.

  Refer risk management detail in next section.

- Information Security Management (ISM)
  The importance of IT security and options are discussed in previous chapter. However, from ISM perspective, IT security must be dealt like business security

4.4 IT Service Strategy

and it must be effectively managed during services. This must be part of overall business security and dealt on priority accordingly. The control and audit policies must be put in place so that leakages and damages are quickly traced and repaired.

- Supplier Management
  Supplier integration with service, delegation of goals and accountability are covered here. The process must guide for the full supplier life cycle management in accordance with the service goals. This must include contract administration as well. We recommend that supplier must be considered as extended arm while providing the service to the business, hence, their integration, motivation, reward, recognition and administration is as important as to own employees. A motivated supplier and its employees not only provide the service as per the contract but also bring industry knowledge and experience to add value to the business. Maintaining the service quality and relationship as well as exceeding the service objectives are the key to supplier management process.

- *Service transition*: This covers the transitioning designed services for business into practice. Hence, it relates to service life cycle as well as service transitioning processes. At this stage the designed services are subjected to different scenario and tested for its smooth functioning even in exceptional situation. The chances of failures and errors in service components could be reduced by design, testing and piloting. The focus is on understanding of services and their utilities, change management and flexibility, supporting knowledge and innovation. The key processes are

  - Change Management
    Agility is an important aspect of service delivery to support innovation and keep them relevant. This process should cover implied as well as externally forced changes in services. This may be caused by strategic, tactical and operational shifts. This should guide how the changes that includes addition, modification and removal of services, will be executed. The idea is to introduce the changes in controlled manner and the impact of the changes is minimized as far as possible. Generally, the changes may impact process, people, knowledge repositories, infrastructure, and service delivery practices. This process helps in identification of impact and the way they re-synchronized for smooth transitioning.

  - Service Asset and Configuration Management (SACM)
    Changes disturb alignment amongst service assets that includes information, documentation, tools and techniques as well. It is important that the alignment amongst different service assets is maintained for controlled environment and delivery processes. The purpose of this process is thus to identify, control and account for service assets. General practice is to mark these assets as configurable items and on every change, conduct an impact analysis with respect to all interdependent and related configurable items. And if required the changes to those configurable items are made. Thus, a configuration control system is obvious requirement for this process.

- Knowledge Management
  The purpose of this process is to enable and equip the people engaged in service delivery with information and intelligence. The process should target to develop intelligence so that the overall value including efficiency, quality, cost to service, improves for customers as well as for providers. Every service has the value which relates to the time, content, recipient enablement and mode of delivery dimensions. The process must enhance them under transformation model, "Data-Information-Knowledge-Wisdom".

  Capturing data and converting them into wisdom has two important factors, the first is provisioning and the second is motivation to transform. A good service organization focuses on both and they give them a handsome return when their customers take pride from their service. These organizations manage knowledge so well that this becomes their business advantage over competition.

- Transition Planning and Support
  As discussed earlier transitioning designed services into practice is important for making service strategy work, this process exactly work for that goal. This focuses on mobilizing resources and effort towards service goals. As a good practice to make a plan or system work, the support systems and the structure must be actively supporting them, especially when failure or disruption happens. And this process must handle the same. We have observed that the extra authority vested in IT organization in cases of new service roll-outs and exigencies work well. The organization clearly defines such situations and the power vested in service providers. That spreads across organizational functions such as procurement, payment, service deployment, mock drills, invoking emergency services, escalation, etc.

- Release and Deployment Management
  This relates to roll-out of new and modified services at optimized speed, cost and risk. This involves planning and assembling different elements to successful roll-outs through early life support, when it goes through teething problems. Since the new/modified services go through issues of credibility at early stage, it is always advisable to have careful release with calculated risk and controls. This process must address this aspect of service roll-outs.

- Service Validation and Testing
  Like any product, service roll-outs must go through proper validation process to ensure its success when in production. This process describes the validation and testing steps before putting the service in production. This holds good for services from both sources, in-house as well as outsourced ones. The designed service must be tried and tested to meet its service goals before final roll-outs. The functionality, feasibility, availability, consistency and security are amongst the areas through which the designed service must pass through.

  We know that all organization run through different processes and procedures. Some time they cross each other and create conflicts. Like a case which we observed when a supplier started providing desktop support services in an organization, a process to access vital installation restricts any outsider but employees using desktops at the installation needed support for maintenance. There are many such cases and they must be addressed either by design or field testing and piloting. Another case was without having proper clearance to allow female workers in the night shift, 24×7 support was rolled out with mix of female staff, whereas Indian law under "The Factories Act 1948" restricted their presence in factory premises in the night shift.

- Evaluation
  This focuses of keeping the service relevant and aligned to the business needs. Therefore, the service must have goals, evaluation criteria, and measurement and evaluation process to confirm and initiate adjustments. On the other hand it shall also show reflection of other service processes such as validation and testing, release and deployment, and others. The idea is to confirm whether the processes are still relevant and meeting their expectations. This is important as at times, organizations become more process compliance centric than the purpose and benefit centric.

- *Service operation*: The service value is delivered under this phase. This is actually service delivery and benefit actualization phase. At this stage the services become part and parcel of business activities. Service operation or service delivery staffs keep their asset and infrastructure in good health and use them to deliver the services to meet their service objective and service level expectations. This covers the following processes which are important to maintain good service and prevent from deterioration.

  - Event Management
    Event is a significant activity that needs to happen periodically or occasionally from IT service and configurable items perspective. This process is to ensure normal activity happens and on failure detection, incidents are raised to restore normalcy.

  - Incident Management
    An incident is unplanned interruption to IT services, resulting into likely loss or actual loss of quality of service. This process is to manage such incidents so that normalcy is restored with minimum impact. This requires formal mechanism for incident reporting tracking, assigning for resolution, testing and implementing the solution in controlled environment, closing with consent from the users who have been affected. The process includes escalation and reporting procedure too. The process also helps in analyzing incident trends and initiating proactive action to prevent. Some organization uses the data for predicting an incident too to achieve zero-incident goal.

  - Request Fulfilment
    IT services are categorized under planned and periodic and on-demand service. This process takes care of on-demand services as well as changing the service attributes such as category, status, recipients and their rights. The procedures to service such needs are defined and concerned stakeholders are informed about the way they can call for such services. These requests are

logged, tracked assigned, coordinated and on rendering the service they are closed, if the requester is satisfied. In case the organization finds a need for proper evaluation, approval and prioritization before initiating the fulfilment activity, the process must address that process too. Example of this could be the requests that have wide impact or involves financial expenses.

- Access Management
  Today data and system access is controlled not only for preventing tempering but also the leakage and misuse. Most of the organizations have defined process and controlled facility to keep hackers, thieves and wrong hands away without disturbing the authorized users. These control definition become active since the conceptualization of IT infrastructure and continues during the operations and even after that, i.e. archiving and release. Thus they handle confidentiality, availability and integrity together. The process covers definition, design, logging and prevention.

- Problem Management
  When the same or similar incidents are reported, an incident needs detail investigation or invasive resolution, they become problem. The process must guide on conducting investigation, ascertaining the route cause as well as preventive solution or workarounds, tracking for repetition and closure of the problem. A problem may require time, effort and financial investment. It should have preventive approach as well as priority and impact based investments. One must understand that repeating minor irritants can also detract users and spoil the party; and hence, they too must not be ignored.

- *Continual service improvement*: Under this, the IT service strategy to delivery is continuously improved for better results and alignment with changing organizational needs and strategy.

  - 7-Step Improvement Process
    This process covers improvement process across various process areas. This focuses on the following:

    - Business and operational goals
    - What data should be measured and what is feasible
    - Collection of data from what, who, when and semantics and integrity perspective
    - Data processing and generating information, trends and intelligence
    - Designing corrective and preventive actions
    - Implementing action plans
    - This is similar to six-sigma approach to make improvement

  - Service Measurement
    This could be strategic as well as tactical process, depending upon the end purpose for measurement. The metrics could be for different components of IT services that contribute to success and quality. Even though the ITIL model

suggests technology and process metrics at component level before arriving at service metrics at summary level. We recommend including People metrics too as this impacts service metrics heavily.

The metrics and the measurement must be so practical and connected to service process that they are collected and measured in natural service delivery process, rather needing separate effort to record, track and measure. Again they must not lose their meaningful information when collated or summarized. SLA provides good clue to have right metrics and measurement.

- Service Reporting
  It is not enough to define metrics and collect data to measure them. It must have good reporting structure and process in place, so that they reach to right stakeholders for their inferences and improvement drives. A good practice also involves letting those stakeholders know the measured values first who may be asked to take action or whose performance has reflection in the data.

  Defining these processes takes time and involves lot of thinking. This also needs service users' agreement, hence, it is good practice to design in consultation with them and seek approval from wide spectrum of user groups. The practices that we find in matured organizations have not been developed at once; it came up in stages and phases. We recommend the same approach for every one while making sure that the direction is right. This gives birth to IT service model for the organization.

  The creation of professional IT service set-up needs decision and selection amongst many trade-offs, as below, which are required at service strategy and service design stage. Today, the service innovation has created many options for each of its building blocs and processes, thus selecting right options and mixing them with right organization structure can make difference to IT service strategy and the outcome.

4.4.1 Cost Centre or Profit Centre

IT services are generally represented as centralized service organization in a business. Most of them prefer to have it under management services functions such as finance and treat it as purely cost centre, but some provision it under each business unit. This distributed provisioning practice is most common in large organizations, which have number of business units. These business units may have been based on line of product or service, functional role, geography and other business reasons and the organization wants to have proper budget and expense management practices in place. But all of them need IT services. Varying capacity to bear the cost makes the model still complex. Even small units in a large organization demand more IT services than what an independent same size of business would call for. This inheritance, sometimes need higher provisioning than what they can afford to. Hence, the organization needs to design the best structure for themselves, out of the categories below

4.4.2 Cost Centre

- Centralized services: All the cost of IT organization and services are provisioned in a central pool. IT cost is treated as overheads and allocated on different heads as per the organization practices. The model is very useful for SMEs and organizations having strong centralized controls. The cost to service may be favourable in some instance and may not be in others, as overheads are applied uniformly to all, irrespective of which functions receives service and how much.

Earlier some of the technology based constraints separated geographically separated units and needed separate installations. But Web enabled applications and modern networking facilities overcame this and made one data centre for geographically scattered units too, a possibility. This is categorized at centralized cost centre.

- Centralized infrastructure: Centralized infrastructure is created from central pool, mostly through capital expenditure, but the services are charged to each unit as expenses. The allocation happens based on the distribution of defined service and consumption of service quantity. This is more suitable where organization wants to make units accountable for their service consumptions, benefits and priorities. In most of the cases this is transition phase from centralized to distributed or shared services. However, this makes the system fairly complex when question of service allocation at unit level of services are to be done. ITIL categorize this model as Shared services.
- Unit funded: Irrespective of whether data centre and IT services are managed in centralized or distributed form, the cost (capital and revenue expense) is distributed and charged out to each unit. This is more suitable when organization wants to do costing for each line of product and services or units are more or less behaving like profit centres. ITIL categorizes it under managed services provisioning.

There is another variant of this which happens in cases of on-demand services, where the capital cost is built into the service utilization charges by the service providers. The user like each unit pays for their service consumption. ITIL marks this model under utility category.

4.4.3 Profit Centre

Under this model, the IT organization is run like a profit centre. A basic funding or set of assets is provided from central organization such as start-up or VC funding, but later it has to run like an independent unit. The business user communities pay as per use basis, like utility category.

It sounds good, but it has some inherent risks, such as misalignment of business objectives, rising cost, focus on opportunities outside, loss of IT skills and scalability in many senses. The user community and the IT organization start behaving like independent units. The user community may dry up the projects and the opportunities, and force IT organization to compete with other IT vendors; at the same time IT organization starts looking outside opportunities to scale and survive. This is like managing any business hence, cost of IT services may go up. Some organizations also use this as transition phase to hive out their IT organization for selling.

4.4.4 Vertical Organization or Matrix

IT being a management function, most of the managers prefer that this function too gets aligned with business objectives. They prefer this to get organized and structured in such a way that it makes significant contribution to business strategy. However, being a specialized line especially for knowledge and capability building aspect, it demands different considerations. And these factors make IT organization evolve into different functional and reporting structure. But at the same time, it cannot create its impact alone and needs to work with business functions to make business sense. Therefore, some organizations create clear interdependence between the two verticals, IT and other functional organizations.

The size and the spread of the business too need different type of IT organization structure to synergise overall demand and keep IT aligned in organizational framework. Over a period of time the IT organization evolved and have been changing the shape and structure, we are depicting below in Fig. 4.3 a set of structures, which may suite different size of organizations. An organization needs to adopt one of them or a mix depending upon their size, business operations practices and overall culture. However, we recommend that the third structure (a matrix organization) should be adopted, which takes care of modern need and proven practices. This binds business and IT together and ploughs IT best for business benefit. Only the scale will be small for SMEs.

4.4.5 Make-it or Buy-it

Unlike early years, when only feasible option was to have own data centres, employ professionals, develop own applications and maintain them, today many options are available. Considering the capital investment and the gestation period, business managers and CIOs look for "quick to production" options. Depending upon various criteria such as what they need, what capability they have or interested in building, how much risk that they can take, what investment they want to make and how quickly they want, they make decision for "buy or make". Large organizations have greater capacity to make, hence, they have many options to create a mix of "buy" and "make", but SMEs depend more on what is available in the market.

Hardly there exist an organization, which can make all the components of IT infrastructure, applications and services of its own. And it does not make any sense

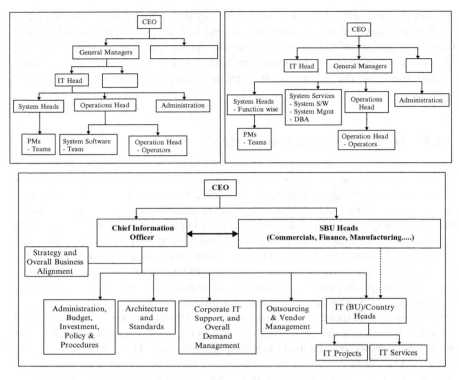

Fig. 4.3 Organization structure

either in this world of specialization and availability. At the same time, a business organization may develop capability to source different components from different partners and architect the infrastructure and services for its IT need under own leadership. Today when "Box" concept is getting popular and provides good alternatives and solutions to make the asset productive quickly, most businesses start sourcing building blocks to fit into a matured architecture. This could be done by the organization itself or in association with selected technology and service partners. However, certain custom solution will still be made to fulfil specialized functional and integration. The challenge with generic product is that they do not have depth and require time and specialization to configure, whereas specialized ones are yet to achieve breadth and coexistence. Thus selecting right solutions and integrating them to work in tandem and seamlessly amongst themselves as well as with some custom solutions is a challenging task and requires decision and trade-off between many items including pricing. IP restrictions, licensing cost, scalability constraints and maintenance cost too sometimes influence "buy" and "make" decision. A CIO must make right choice in pretext to her organization's policy direction, capability and commitment going forward.

Table 4.2 IT life cycle elements

SL.	Components	Life (years)
1.	IT strategy	3–10
2.	IT infrastructure	3–7
3.	Applications	
	Projects (development)	<3
	Usage (operations)	3–10/15
4.	Technology	3–7
5.	Technical skill	3–5

4.4.6 Recruit/Train or Hire

In IT life cycle different elements have different life; hence, they need review, refurbishments and upgrade to increase their life for continuity in value delivery. We have observed that even with adjustments the life has limits, as below, and after which it needs serious revamping. Change in business needs and technology evolution are the major source to limit the life (Table 4.2).

Currently, technology and technical skill has much shorter life than any other components. IT being people intensive, people strategy must be carefully drafted and practiced. Today, every CIO has dilemma of having full in-house team and keep them abreast or hire from outside to manage spikes in the requirement. For example, if a 5,000 person-days project requires around 25 persons working on project at one point of time within a delivery period of 1 year, whereas to support after implementation it may need 4–6 on going basis. Now, the challenge is what skill set and how many people the IT organization employ to serve the need for development and service. If many projects are lined up, perhaps recruiting and pooling may make sense, but in absence of this recruiting 25 plus IT resource for this project is not recommended. Hence, hiring on temporary basis helps. Hiring also helps when a CIO wants internal resources to address business critical functions including process, people and system transitioning and hired ones to manage the peripheral work including outgoing applications and daily operations. This work division also can happen on motivating work and not-so-motivating work based on employees' perception and internal retention policy. The table below (DIR 1998) differentiates the strategic advantages and disadvantages between employing a resource and hiring (Table 4.3).

Hiring, especially where foreign nationals are involved, has become employment sensitive issue for some. Many organizations develop a complete policy in accordance with local government policies and regulations. US government enacted a bill on hiring and subcontracting, Senate Bill 365 of the 75th Legislature, giving guidelines for cost–benefit analysis between using in-house and sub-contracting resources to all state agencies, including universities. This helped in evaluating need and creating a business case for the both. Since hiring has such a compelling business reason, one must make cost–benefit analysis before making any other decision.

Table 4.3 Advantages and disadvantages of permanent vs. hired employees

Employee		Hired	
Pro's	Con's	Pro's	Con's
Better ownership and control	Time to mature and cost of Retention	Time to be productive	Not sure of quality, till tried out
Knowledge retention and continuity to some extent	Ongoing technical upgrade	Flexibility to augment and change people and skill set as per business need	Knowledge retention and contract administration
Internal practices are challenged for the good of the organization	Not much of flexibility for deployment	May have exposure of industries and different ideas	Practices are not challenged unless provider's interest is hurt
Team work and cultural match	Limited exposure	No risk for retention and in separation	Cultural mismatch and partner's ability to retain resource

Cost of hired resource appears to be higher on face value, but it could work out cheaper when cost of employee along with overheads and cost of retention is considered for equitable performance. In cases where the utilization period is large, employee may have cost advantage, especially for customers from developing countries. In case hired resource is working from offshore (such as India and the Philippines) for North American, European and Australian customers, more or less it is certain that hired resource will provide cost advantage in short term as well as for long-term deployment

4.4.7 Outsourcing or Co-Sourcing

Hiring is the process to augment staff/skill in own team for a service, whereas if a defined service is contracted, it is generally termed as outsourcing. Hiring started in 1980s when mainframe staffs were augmenting the IT resource need, whereas outsourcing came into being later.

Therefore, outsourcing is about deciding what component of IT strategy will be delivered by IT organization directly to one or more business units and what it will deliver along with valued partners. Outsourcing must be in line with the organization structure and policies. During the era of partners and business process outsourcing (BPO) to complete the value chain for customers as well as to own business, the decision has become more complex. The general outsourcing principles are as below and that applies to IT too.

- To identify the unit set of business processes (IT or functional domain). The unit set is one or combination of processes which works as unit.
- To identify the business critical or core processes amongst them, which make the business sense to retain and perform internally. The experts define them as the processes where the organization can deliver higher value cost-effectively or which relates to IP and USP.
- To identify and involve right partner which can take care of those processes and deliver similar or better results at lower cost.
- To integrate the partners' objective, processes and people to deliver better result.

4.4 IT Service Strategy

IT outsourcing is an option which is utilized for the following business values:

- Cost advantage
- Competitiveness
- Speed to implementation and transition to new technologies
- Scalability in skill and services
- Access to specialized products, services, knowledge and industry practices
- Management of demand fluctuation and growth
- Risk sharing and scalability
- Location advantage such as proximity to user centres
- Access to new market and data centre, etc.

and they can be achieved by one or mix of following components of IT services:

- IT service strategy
- Infrastructure and platforms
- Development and implementation
- Verification and validation
- Operations
- Skill
- Training
- Support

Today, there are many success stories around the both, in-house as well as outsourced IT services. However, in view of specialized hardware and network related services and standardized and proven application products, it is sensible to outsource some services. We advise all the CIOs to assess outsourcing options and feasibility like any strategic activity before deciding the scope. They can follow the advice of McKinsey, "Outsourcing isn't an end in itself but rather a strategic tool for enhancing overall performance". Hence, the focus must remain on business benefit than outsourcing advantages. Any bias and soft consideration towards scope and the partner may compromise the outsourcing goal and business benefit.

The outsourcing scope is not that easy to decide. Generally, it is based on the mix of capability available, suitability to business, service requirement, organizations' comfort and cost. We recommend the model as below (Fig. 4.4) for making a choice as what to outsource and what services must be done in-house. Generally it is preferred to manage all business critical and proprietary activities in-house, where better controls and agility is maintained. However, a committed and capable partner can substitute there too.

In one of the articles published by McKinsey Quarterly, the author quoted Dun & Bradstreet reports that 20–25% of all outsourcing relationships including IT fail within 2 years and that 50% fail within 5. Even though poor definition of requirement and goals as well as poor contract management have been identified as major reasons, outsourcing management needs overall good processes, as below (Equaterra 2010), and a structure to manage to succeed.

- Scope and contract definition
- Service quality and performance management

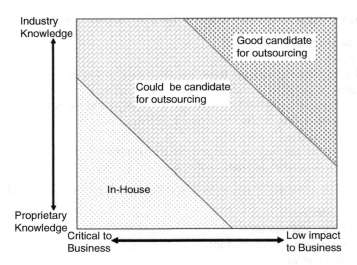

Fig. 4.4 Outsource model

- Partner selection and contract management including audit, measurements and controls
- Transition and knowledge management
- Demand/change management
- Risk and compliance management
- Financial management and
- Relationship management and alignment

Service level agreement (SLA) is critical to manage outsourcing. A fair and equitable SLA must be defined along with the partner. Managing without SLA, especially with multiple service providers, becomes very challenging. If their boundaries are not well defined and they are not bound by SLAs and aligned accordingly, the cost to manage the contract and services shoots. Hence, we advise to

- Establish the service baseline, so that partner/s knows what is expected out of it while leaving scope for innovation and improvement.
- Ensure accountability of the programme so that the success and failure could be rightly attributed, and the responsibility to improve clearly emerges.
- Identify the service to be measured so that it is evident to all what they are striving for and measure to know their performance themselves. These measurements are not only defined for the partner but also the service consumers.
- Identify a measurement method, so that all parties know and understand the measurement points and process, and interpret the result in the same way.

We have observed that CIOs get more than the expected values when they provide clarity, and guide and nurture relationship with partners, the service providers too, commit and stretch themselves to provide extra mileage beyond written contract.

Once the contract is awarded, a transition plan must be made and rolled out in accordance to service continuity. This kind of transition plan holds good at entry, exit, enhancement as well as curtailment of scope of service. The service consumers must be communicated and taken in confidence for the transition.

4.4.8 SaaS, BOOT or Own

This is emerging concept as the user industry was finding licence and subsequently maintenance cost high for the products. Although the software product vendors started selling the licences on per user basis, the initial capital cost and fixed cost for maintaining the system in good health are still higher. High bandwidth connectivity across the globe and network connection up to the last user created an option to reduce use cost. The vendors or even third party started hosting such software at their data centre and provide connection to the business users for usage, while charging them per user per period or pay on use basis. The users can connect to the centre and use the software. This facility has come up for services beyond packaged applications and includes infrastructure (IaaS), platform services (PaaS) for development and testing, custom business applications, full data centre and many other services. These service or data centres scaled for multiple customers to make it a viable business model. It depends on the scope of service in such models that the service provider provides the complete services by itself or allows a mix of customer and customer hired third parties to complete the value chain. Many such services are being offered and many others are still being innovated. When few more parameters such as flexible and scalable IT resources, automated provisioning, pay as you use, location and network independent access are added, it becomes cloud computing. Cloud computing in current form provides excellent match for growing business. Today, large organizations are centralizing their business application and data centres, as it makes sense for them. The cost to manage such private cloud comes down along with benefit of centralization. They are going for their private clouds, which provides similar infrastructure concept with internal resources managing the centre. The key to success to all public cloud or SaaS service providers lies with standardization of product features and service provider's capability, business ethics, neutrality and customer oriented contract.

The customers must have complete clarity on scope, SLA, response and responsibilities to manage conflict or issues in future. Since international legal framework to manage issues and disputes across international borders is yet to mature, it is always wise to have such contract with service provider's local arm. The security of all business information and core processes, and data recoverability especially at the end of the contract must be taken care off.

Currently, SAP qualifies best fit customers for this model on the following criteria

- Do they have limited capital budget, limited IT support, or no desire to invest in building a large in-house IT backbone?

- Do they need an immediate fix for a particular area but cannot risk a disruption to their business, all at once?
- Are they using manual processes, spreadsheets, or basic off-the-shelf applications and do not want to invest in expensive custom applications or systems?
- Do they want core process automation and best practices but do not require deep, customized functionality?
- Does they company typically embrace outsourcing as a business principle?
- Do they need better control and more predictable costs associated with managing and maintaining applications over the long term?

If the answer is "yes", it is considered as a right candidate. When one looks at the cloud computing or services beyond packaged applications all of the criteria apply except third item. SaaS generally targets the following benefits:

- Time to value: Quicker to be productive
- Affordability: Does not need large capital investment
- Cost reduction
- Simplified management: No need to hire high skilled personnel for maintenance support
- Integration and security

Another model, which has not been so popular, is BOOT. Here an organization looking for large implementation or data centre set-up, hire a group of professionals or a specialist organization to build the data centre and implement key application/s. The provider operates for some time and once the system stabilizes it transitions and moves out. The cost calculation and equitable payment terms are little difficult to arrive, but it provides very reasonable deal for both the parties; unlike the case of hired for implementation, which is more tilted towards implementer. The customer's healthy participation, timely response and change control along with provider's capability to deliver are keys to success here.

4.4.9 Open Source or Proprietary Platform

Open Source, in its current form in reference to IT was coined first in 1998 when Y2K was on its peak. User community was not happy either with traditional set of technologies which was not able to support Internet applications or Internet enabled platforms which involved high licence and usage cost. That is why the concept of free software for wide use attracted attention. The community worked with the philosophy of distributed development and improvement by sharing, use and contributing to developed codes. During initial period, the monopoly of platform technology providers such as Microsoft appeared as a threat to many IT industry bellwethers and they also joined the movement. The initial discussion started with Windows vs. Linux, but later it caught momentum when the community expanded and started working on business applications and databases too. Offering Java as an open source platform by Sun Microsystems poured fuel into this. The contribution of founders and senior community members to define standards and practices, and making sure that community flourishes with original principles, made it to stand with proprietary platform providers. The model offers free source code from members with a binding to the users to contribute enhancements and attached developments. The commercial model for members is based on fees for services, implementation and by packaging their products. Large vendor organizations created a good mix of software from there own sources as well as open source and offered more packaged solution to customers. Overall open source helped the user community to control prices and offered more options. Once this start providing good quality and wide range of products for business and matching services, it will pose real challenge to proprietary software providers, unless they innovate and come out new value additions.

Open source is working on three basic principles *no licence fees, openness and interoperability, and standard compliance*. Today it has variety of software ranging from platform software to business applications, including integration, conversion, migration, analytics tools. Even though it offers more on server side, but client side applications are also on rise. Slowly it is moving in the direction of packaging of entire suite of software to meet business needs. The proprietary platform providers such as Microsoft, Oracle, SAP and others are charging for perpetual user licences, even though they started offering their products to work in tandem with open source systems. They enjoy the advantage of tradition and backing of large organization, which is missing in case of open source. Thus for an user, proprietary platform providers appear to be more organized to service, having more muscle to attend to customers and more proactive in selling and offering extended features. These providers have more organized approach to commercialization, whereas OSG focused more on building the community and product offering. The usage of open source applications has started but user industry still prefers proprietary applications for their business critical functions.

A CIO needs to make a trade off between cost and software maturity in terms of functionality, suitability, security and maintainability. There is no harm in creating a mix of the two if the business integration and business information are not risked as well as providing IT services as per SLA is not compromised.

4.4.10 Compliance

IT strategy and services must be compliant to regulatory norms and help business too to be compliant. This includes reporting, statutory payments, auditing, social and environmental responsibility, and Industry standards and guidelines (from governing bodies, industry association, WTO and customer countries). Although compliance appears to be burden to the organization, but IT can enable compliance as an opportunity to create an image of trusted and quality service organization. It can support brand image as well as brand building exercises. IT has the potential and can help in demonstrating such a leadership image of socially and nationally responsible organization. The usage of IT as part of corporate social responsibility (CSR) varies from analysis of social demography and reaching for help to the needy in cases of disasters to tracking and reducing the carbon foot print in a business.

This can touch many facets of our life and contribute to improve quality of life, products, services, environment, arts and sciences. This has demonstrated its capability and contribution in all those areas as well. Some of the recent and direct contributions have been the potential to improve carbon footprint by heavy reduction of paper consumption in any organization through online information services and the opportunities of virtual office to reduce need to travel to offices. It automated information collation and reporting in such a way that all information filing to the regulatory bodies and the government are happening in time and with correct information. Adherence to compliance needs such as reporting retail sales and tax data and tax deposits through banks within hrs of becoming due in Western countries, collecting and reporting fertilizer sale in the remote villages on daily basis to the central secretariat in Delhi are good examples of IT contribution to compliance. It showed clearly that we run short of ideas but not the capability. Even if we imagine the paper consumption for the eMails going around the world, it would scare any environmentalist. Reduction in coal and energy consumption of per ton of metal production have been modelled and achieved with IT. IT is with business on every opportunity of direct reduction in production of greenhouse gases and consumption of natural resources.

Like any regulatory compliance audit, the carbon audit and installation/premise certification is catching up. A CIO has such a privileged technology in hand and hence, must take special initiative to discover above kinds of opportunities which will demonstrate that her organization is socially responsible and regulatory compliant. This could be by cutting consumptions in IT organization or facilitating the saving in user organizations through systems and information. The optimization systems have improved coke and water consumption in metal industry all over the world. Many such ideas could be generated if a critical analysis of business activities is done to understand the potential opportunities to improve compliance and performance. Potentially good ideas must be included in IT strategy and its execution. In coming days this brand image will not only save the cost and help in sustenance but also create competitive edge.

It may be an option today whether a CIO plans to make IT a serious contributor or just adhere to the mandatory and explicit requirements of users, but tomorrow it will be mandatory and then IT organization will be constrained. Obviously flexibility and compliance built by choice is far better than being forced and mandated.

The other part of compliance is storage of business records for its defined life. Regulators of different countries as well as business policies demand business records to be available for certain period of time. This also must be part of IT service strategy, as to how the IT will keep those records for defined period and make them available when demanded by business or the regulator. For example a large organization in India defined the following life period (Table 4.4) for their financial data based on the statutory as well as business needs and IT needed to preserve them.

The challenge happens when the technology and infrastructure changes during the period. We have observed migration of systems in a large Indian organization where the migration of records was as tedious and time taking as the development. Many a time, failure of backup media demanded reconstruction. Even though the period is

4.4 IT Service Strategy

Table 4.4 Life period for archiving records

SL.	Record category	Content	Life
1.	*Main accounts*	GL (capital/revenue ledgers)	16 years
		P&L, BS	
		Foreign ledgers	
		Main journal books	
		Sub-ledgers (suppliers/customers)	
		Cash books	
		Fixed assets	
2.	*Subsidiary books of account*	10 Years	10 Years
		All tax registers, acknowledgements and certificates	
		Petty cash	
		Personal ledgers	
		Insurance register	
		Clearance register	
		Travel expense	
		Interest paid register	
3.	*Costing and inventory records*	Cost sheets	10 Years
		Stock ledgers	
		Journal vouchers	

shorter but wage revisions and arrears quite often need large payroll data from past years. This being sensitive issue to labour unions and the governments, preservation and maintaining compatibility needs strategy and sometimes investment.

Large organizations have audit functions working as a management eye. Like normal business audits, they also have system audit wing, which keeps eye on requirements, processes, system implementation and compliance. Depending upon the size and the need, a CIO may propose for this function to endorse and enforce policy and procedure adherence through IT systems. This is different than the quality function in IT, which basically governs the process definition, adherence and quality production during system development within IT department. The system audit function also becomes handy to CIO to manage aberrations, if any, on the business interface and provides greater comfort to business managers that systems and practices are compliant.

4.4.11 Standards and Process Models

IT is no exception when business processes are discussed in holistic sense. We have observed that well defined processes helps IT organization to achieve its goals including project goals and meet even internal customer expectations. The common services such as administration, HR and other processes are in line with rest of the organization, but its business has two distinct parts, projects and operations. Both the parts are aligned with processes of project functions and support functions, respectively. However, flavour of technology and role of dominant enabler make the processes more proactive, leading and knowledge oriented.

To make IT strategy work, its all components, as described above, must work in close synchronization. It always helps to follow standard practices and processes to evolve each of those components, so that they are interdependent, aligned and integrated. There is no single framework supported by one set of universally accepted standards and practices which can be clearly adopted by an IT organization. Even the market and vendors offer different standards and practices, which may not be fully compatible within themselves. Enterprise architecture framework for evolving IT strategy, ITIL for IT services and "SEI-CMMi for Development and Services" from Carnegie Mellon University (CMU) for software engineering, project management and IT services have been used in this book to explain the concepts. But many best practices framework and governance guidelines such as the ones listed below are available in the market which comes from different sources.

- SWEBOK from IEEE Computer Society for software development practices
- Project Management Institute (PMI) supported PMBOK and PRINCE2 from UK for project management
- ISO standards for equipment and development of projects (ISO/IEC JTC 001)
- ISO 9000 standards for quality management systems
- BS 7799 and ISO/SEC 27000 family standards for information security management
- ISO/IEC 20000 for IT service management
- COBIT, ISO 17799 for IT governance
- BS 7988 and ISO/IEC 23988:2006 for IT in delivery of assessment
- ISO/IEC 38500:2008 Corporate Governance of IT and ISO 14001:2004 for environment management
- Six sigma for product and service improvement
- Malcolm Baldrige overall organization governance.

Even CMU has published different practice models suiting to different scenario such as eSCM for outsourcing-client and the service-providers to manage IT projects and services. Some of them have elaborated more and presented new dimensions. They have overlaps as well. One can appreciate the difference amongst three IT service related framework from the quote of Dave Greenfield (2007), published in InformationWeek Global CIO, December 8, 2007, "COBIT tells you what to monitor and control. ITIL describes how to go about implementing the processes for doing that. ISO/IEC 17799:2000 lays out a process for securing those services and addressing legal requirements". Therefore, it will be always a challenge for a CIO, which one to pick that will work and create cohesive framework for developing IT strategy and executing them successfully.

The CMMi framework has been traditionally for IT and covers most of the functions related to IT project development and implementation in an organization. CMMi model (v 1.2) for development, as depicted below (Fig. 4.5), categorizes its processes into four groups.

4.4 IT Service Strategy

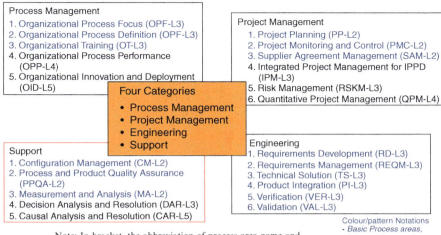

Fig. 4.5 CMMI process areas

They basically cover full Project life cycle. As the name indicates, Engineering relates to technical tasks of the projects, project management covers the overall project management practices, process management and support cover the overall capability building, monitoring and effectiveness improvement processes. From day-to-day practice point of view engineering and project management are the core practices which are visible, but their performance and effectiveness too depend upon the other two. The structure is also simple, three layers, process area, goals and practices. Each process areas under above categories have specific goals and generic goals. Specific goals have specific practices and generic goals have generic practices. The process goals must be aligned with IT organization goals and in turn the business goals. The idea is to adopt practices which contribute to organization goals. When they are adopted in structured form in organization context, a quality system comes into birth.

As an alternative to ITIL, for IT service operations too, "CMMi for Services" model can be adopted. The advantage is most of the processes are common to CMMi for Projects except the following which need to be added. The organizations, which can afford to have best of the lot, can adopt "CMMI for Development" and ITIL for Services.

Under Project management

- Requirement management (REQM-L2): Specific to IT services
- Capacity and availability management (CAM-L3)
- Service continuity (SCON-L3)

A new category service establishment and delivery is added

- Incident resolution and prevention (IRP-L3)
- Service delivery (SD-L2)
- Service system development (SSD-L3)

- Service system transition (SST-L3)
- Strategic service management (STSM-L3)

The measurement and maturity are also well structured and defined under CMMi maturity model. A CIO can make decision to adopt all 22 processes for development of service system (projects in IT case), at once or basic process areas first and advance process areas next, depending upon the need and capability. In fact CMMi also sub-categorizes each process areas for different maturity levels. Hence, under staged approach a CIO can proceed with processes with respective maturity levels and keep maturing and move up in the level. In our experience, different process areas shows different type and different degree of benefits, but Level 5 having all processes in place provide distinct and visible advantages. The maturity levels are as below:

- *Level 1*: Known as performed or initial: Where organization is just performing those defined tasks which are necessary for the goals but the processes are not institutionalized and no prediction for consistency and outcome quality can be made. The processes are diluted over time and during tough times.
- *Level 2*: Known as managed: The processes have basic infrastructure and resources in place, and are being executed in accordance with the policy and goals. Monitoring and review processes are in place. But better results come mostly because of individuals than processes.
- *Level 3*: Known as defined: The process assets are well defined and tailored from the standard practices in the organization to suit specific need to meet the goals. Major deviations from Level 2 to Level 3 are processes are tailored, even defined at micro level, focus on goals, predictability in overall result, consistency in practices and still opportunity for innovation and deviation. The outcome is more driven by processes than individuals.
- *Level 4*: Known as quantitatively managed: Management by information and analytics is more dominant here. The control, review and decision-making practices are based on facts and statistical analysis.
- *Level 5*: Known as optimized: When Level 4 processes are continuously being optimized and improved on incremental or breakthrough basis, Level 5 is achieved.

Fortunately, the above five level maturity model is in process of acceptance by all, only their specific explanation differs in different context. This gives staged level of maturity unlike other certifying groups, which goes in binary, certified or not-certified.

We recommend that IT organizations draft one set of standards and practices after a study and consultation. They need to have cohesive and seamless flow for each set of activities. Although it requires skill and expertise, one can create a hybrid model for standards, practices and methodology to cover all aspect of IT Strategy and its execution in her organization. Another option could be to adopt few connecting standards and practices in Toto and provide the bridge and guidelines to make smooth hopping and transition. Since most of them are generic in nature, one will still need to provide specific explanation, interpretation and applicability in own organization's context while providing references to the original. In any case the organization must offer a simplified scalable and stable model to achieve consistency, sense of direction and a platform to standardize infrastructure and practices within the organization. Otherwise there will be utter confusion and the practices will be driven by individuals and influential vendors causing loss of control, direction and execution problems.

4.5 Metrics and Measurement

The importance of metrics and measurement is summarized in two common sayings, "If it can be measured, it will be done" and "The value proposition is weakened significantly, if it cannot be quantified and measured".

Defining metrics again follows normal business goals tree structure. IT as enabler participates with different branches and helps each of them to achieve their business goals. IT also defines certain metrics for itself, so that it can rise to the occasion and be able to contribute, as desired. These two principles help to design metrics.

It has been observed that organizations not only face resistance to change but also they drift towards their original position (Chakravorty 2010). He rightly pointed out that the organization goes through two phases (stretching and yielding) and then to falling, if not controlled. These principles apply to any change and transition. Stretching is the phase when the organization is learning new ways of doing things, as well as new rules, new processes and procedures, which are under implementation. Organizations need to nurture, guide, promote and make visible support to have this transition successful. During this phase, the resources including people are at stretch. But it does not end here. Like any metal, the change must cross the limit of elasticity to create a new form. The transition must enter in next phase to have sustained and durable change. This phase is called yielding phase. The system and people crosses their limit of elasticity and enter into new phase. The biggest challenge here is when the people and/or the system breaks either by too much of stress or wrong direction of force and motivation. The system either moves towards betterment or starts deteriorating. This is phase of instability. Smart managers understand this phenomenon and they continue to be involved during this phase too so that the system does not enter into falling phase or retreating towards the old. And for this they define smart metrics or change the context itself, which not only gives the organization a sense of direction but also generates signals when the change starts drifting back. One such smart move we noticed when we implemented ERP system in a port company, which had very minimal IT system, the CEO wanted all interactions (including proposal, approval and reporting) with him to happen through system. Though he also spent time to learn to manage his work and interaction through system, but his simple metrics (100% business transaction oriented interaction through system) forced whole organization to become system savvy. The organization also changed the SLA of supporting services accordingly, so that people do not have reasons to excuse and revert to paper. The adaptability and transition was smooth.

This gives three clear learnings, the first, to define right metrics which has definite business purpose and the second, to provide right support to the people and the system which will reduce reasons to revert or discard new system and the third, to monitor regularly and resist the retreat.

Every stage of this transitioning needs to be monitored for their sustained achievements. Irrespective of whether it is process and strategy change or IT technology upgrade, the transitioning must move in controlled environment and in right direction, and for that metrics and measurement is important. Smart metrics have following symptoms

- All stakeholders understand and interpret the metrics in the same way. The managers, who are setting the goals for the organization, understand the metrics, its measurements and the process to derive the value clearly and draw same interpretation when there is variance.
- The symptoms for success as well as failure are vivid and clearly visible, which makes it easier to monitor, such as the one in the above case. If any one would have come with paper based report or request for approval, the CEO would have clearly understood that the adaptability is a problem.

The organization can use defining metrics and measurement as an opportunity to business alignment. It is true that while creating components of various KPIs for different functional groups, sometimes, conflicting goals or a trade-off is required to create balance amongst goals of different departments, which need to cooperate. IT organization is no exception to it. At times, a CIO while driving for IT Strategy roll-out may feel that business managers have different priorities and hence, the IT roll-out will starve for attention. Therefore, the CIO must be cautious of this kind of goal setting phenomenon, and work with senior management to sort them out. Therefore, the metrics and the measurement must be means to reaffirm the priorities and create balance amongst all stake-holders, business managers as well as the CIO. If they have common set of metrics to work with, it is ideal. All the stakeholders also need to agree on "How" part of measurement, and finally the inferences. This will also save time, effort and provide consistency while aggregation.

Some of the metrics, which could be relevant and practical to measure the IT strategy progress and achievements, could be as below. However the CIO needs to select relevant ones for her environment and agree with the CEO and the management team. Regular review will help the IT strategy implementation, IT alignment with business and management participation.

- Customer and Business

    - Contribution to CSF or business benefits
    Worth of delivered value
    Expected value vis-à-vis delivered
    - Users' (business managers) satisfaction score
    - IT service-SLA fulfilment score (response quality, timeliness, quality of information)

- Budget distribution ratio over new projects and operations
- Actual system availability as percentage of promised availability
- Life-expectancy of IT components vis-à-vis actually delivered
- Risk occurrence and mitigated: They are calculated in terms of absolute numbers and the ratio of numbers as well as value to agreed risks.
- Number of T security lapses and value loss.

- Financial
  - Net present value (NPV): NPV of benefits >NPV of investment
  - Internal rate of return (IRR): The IRR is the rate of return that would make present value of future cash flows and final market value of an investment equal to current market price of the investment
  - Return on investment (ROI): ROI=(benefit−cost)/cost, or ROI in n year is (future value of all receivables by nth year−future value of all expenses in those years) as percentage of cost
  - Payback period of investment is number of months/years when net cash flow becomes equal to Investment
  - Return on assets (ROA)=yearly profit/asset (gross block)
  - Earnings per share (EPS)=(earnings+projected benefit)/(outstanding no. of shares)−current EPS

- Projects and IT internal
  - Project percentage delivered within budget and on schedule
  - Deviation on effort and schedule
  - Project percentage achieved intended goals
  - Attrition rate
  - Per resource, technical and non-technical training days and cost
  - Cost of poor quality including project failure, risks mitigation, verification and validation, rework, knowledge transition
  - In-house to contract labour ratio in different skill category
  - Supplier performance and failure rate
  - Development productivity (HRs/FP)
  - Service SLAs (availability, reliability, recoverability, response time and request resolution time for different severity category)
  - Coordination and user enablement effort vis-à-vis project and service budget

4.5.1 Risk Management

Risks are blocks and impediments which can retard, deviate or derail the plans and progress. Every strategy and every plan has its own risk. Managers trade off between risks and gains. They maximize gains to the limits where risks are manageable. This optimization exercise is done for IT strategy as well. In business certain risks are

Table 4.5 Risk assessment

Market	Operations	Reputation
Customer	Revenue/cost	Brand
Product and services	Logistics and supply chain	Privacy
Competitiveness	Quality	Statutory compliance
Channel and demand	HR relations	Business continuity
Price and margin	Productivity	
Business model	Health of assets	
Exchange rate		

necessary to grow and benefit. The same rule applies with IT; hence, the strategy should be more for risk management and not for risk avoidance. This is also valid as there is no way where all the risks can be avoided and still optimized results can be achieved.

Risks are of various types and could be caused by many reasons, including poor connection of IT with business, change in management thought or shift in business strategy, ambitious plan, midcourse downslide of business, loss of critical resource. Therefore, there must be due provision for such risks in IT strategy and the risks must be on radar and watched continuously by CIOs.

Normal risk management practices are applicable here as well. Some of the management techniques could be as below (Thiel et al. 2009):

A. Identify opportunities and business areas on risk and analyze why this is risk and what are the implications
B. Analyze business and predict risk by understanding likely shift in business strategies in the areas as below (Table 4.5) and management perspective to IT on different front
C. Apply scenario based strategy development and develop hypotheses for different areas which can help in mitigation

- IT cost reduction in projects as well as operations
- Optimization of investment and reshuffling project portfolio and priorities
- Change of focus from long-term business benefits to short or medium term
- Enablement of people either on business side or IT side or both
- Balancing weight-ages between external and internal focus, as well as amongst business transformation, enablement and operational performance
- Transformation of IT organization, service delivery model and participation of IT in business

D. Communicate, move swiftly and start implementation in consonance with stake holders.
E. Get ready with Plan B.

The risk could be of various categories (Microsoft.com), and all of them deserve due evaluation, before identifying the ones, needing mitigation.

4.5 Metrics and Measurement

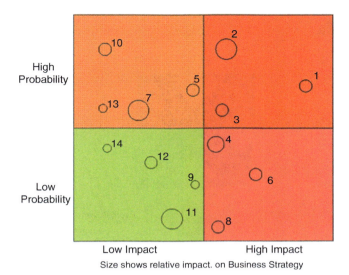

Fig. 4.6 Risk mapping

- *Strategy and alignment*: Risks caused by insufficient guidance on strategy and goals. This also includes alignment issues between business and functions as well as business and IT.
- *Expectation*: Risks caused by mismatch and over expectation from IT.
- *Solution*: Risks caused by the proposed approach and solution. This includes solution complexity, silo coverage and incompleteness of solution. Non-availability of right skills to create right solution with respect to goals and capability is also covered here.
- *Financial, branding and statutory*: Risks impacting investment, benefits, brand value, compliance goals and information security are categorized here.
- *Project*: Risks impacting project timeline, budget and project objectives are classified here.
- *Organization and change management*: Risks caused by poor preparedness of organization either by capability or by culture are covered here. The unwilling and non-participation of stakeholders, in adequate capability to manage the change and the transitions also generate risks of this category.
- *Technology and operations*: Risks caused by imbalance in adaptability and assimilation of technology, insufficient skill and resources for continuity and operations management are covered under this category.

A proactive initiative is always appreciated. During communication, the assumptions are also validated and business people also take call on perceived risks; thus, it becomes a collective decision. The risk map as presented in the Fig. 4.6 is very basic way to start. The risks are presented on the map between impact of the risk on

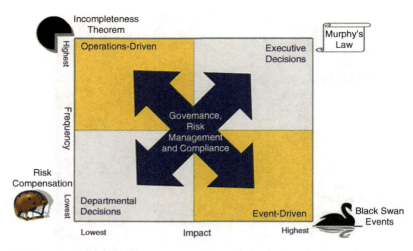

Fig. 4.7 Four quadrant model source: Aberdeen Group, January 2010 (Reprinted with permission)

strategy and business, and probability of occurrence. Since IT strategy and plans are for business, the map view is prepared as risk to business and business strategy than to IT strategy and plan. This is to bind business managers with benefit optimization and risk mitigation strategy. The size of the circle represents relative quantum of impact and the position represents intensity of impact, this means bigger the size more wide spread impact it will have and similarly right on the position will create more intense impact. Similarly, higher the probability of occurrence, it will be placed above the others on y axis. Once they are prioritized by the organization, a relative number is also marked, indicating order of attention.

In one of the Aberdeen Group's reports on IT security it further elaborated on the four quadrant model, as in Fig. 4.7, and presented a different view of likely source of the risks.

The knowledge of source helps in taking precaution and working out the mitigation. The Incompleteness Theorem proves the existence of exception, which may cause risk in an organizational operative set-up. Black swan are those which can happen mostly outside the organization and can have serious impact on the business scenario of an organization. Risk compensation relates to very local and may have caused by over-confidence and complacency. The most vital ones are those which are caused by executive decisions where the outcomes and reactions are mostly unpredictable.

It is important that a CIO must not hold biased view from IT and own position while identifying risks, qualifying them and making plans to mitigate. I have worked in an environment where I could see the positive effect when a CIO works selflessly and shared the power, growth and ownership for successes with teams and business managers. And it had worked splendidly for risk management. In such cases, the whole organization appreciates and endorses the mitigation plan as well as encourages for extra risk to make extra gain. This also mitigates a major risk of business managers' indifference to IT strategy. In this process the ownership of risks are shared, prioritized as shown by the numbers on the map and accordingly the mitigation strategy is worked out and acted upon. If the risks need contingency provisions, they are to be provided for, as well.

Approach to risk taking and management of the same varies organization to organization. As in a study report, Derek Brink from Aberdeen Group classified risks broadly under two types. One, he calls "Unrewarded", which refers to threats vulnerability and regulatory compliance. But the second one "Rewarded", which matters the most, help in creating value, competitive edge to business and growth. The first one is for protecting value, minimizing downside and defensive in nature, whereas the second one is for maximizing upside and enablement. The first one calls for attention and action, whereas the second one is by choice. In the research paper the Group also found that "Best in Class" organizations are able to show maturity in risk management and hence they are able to perform better and reduce cost of risk management. According to them, the best show disciplined approach to manage risk:

- Effective identification
- Clarity and timeliness in communication to key stake holders
- Status and impact visibility to the management
- Translation into actionable recommendations
- Speedy decision-making to mitigate with lower cost and in time

Many corporate have appointed risk manager to manage the risks in holistic manner. This function must be invited to participate and lead the team on practices and standards for risk identification and management. ISO:31000, which is a process-oriented risk-management framework, could be useful at this stage.

A category of set pattern of risks such as theft and network security is more understandable and manageable than the ones which are just emerging on the horizon and could take any shape. Green IT and environment protection is one of those. The shape and impact is yet to be fully known. Therefore, not only one needs to be cautious and watchful of its trend and impact but also initiates work in that direction. The areas, that are open, are the following:

- Impact of legislation, regulation an international accords
- Impact of public and customer motivation
- Indirect consequences of regulation or business trends
- Impacts of actual climate change

In case business organizations need to report the risk or carbon generation in the business, IT will be on the corporate radar for the bad as well as good reasons. On the one hand it will be expected to reduce carbon emission by reducing power consumption, paper consumption and other internal activities; on the other it is expected to help others by servicing information on existing carbon foot print, tracking the progress and the impact.

4.6 EV and ROI

Traditionally the mindset in business organization has been to "IT—a cost centre". The reason used to be the value perception of the senior managers, CIO's position in the organization and her inability to communicate about the business value that IT has been creating. That's why, the CIOs were also stuck discussing budgets and investments. Recent phenomenon of rapid growth of business with IT has marked change in this thought, when these managers observed value creation by IT around the industry and business establishments. The same change has also been seen in government organizations across the world, when country leaders such as the US president, the British prime minister and the Indian prime minister call for IT enabled citizen centric service delivery mechanism for cost benefit and effectiveness.

CIOs need to look at the IT investment proposal in business perspective, as there could be many projects vying for the same fund. Arriving at the economic value of IT is good way to justify its claim for the fund against many parallel proposals. This is not an easy task, unless the likely benefits from IT to the business are identified and quantified. This approach binds IT and business while helping business managers to appreciate the contribution of IT. This helps in informed decision-making today and stops eye-raising on investment and decision process tomorrow, besides setting a direction and goal for this business activity. A good practice would be to define these before implementation, monitor during the implementation and finally evaluate and conclude at the end. This practice must address the following questions that could be in the minds of business managers, irrespective of the type of organizations, whether it is commercial or governmental:

- What benefits it will bring to the organization
- How realistic the investment plan and likely benefits are
- How much it will cost to the organization for these benefits
- When the benefits will start and how long will they sustain
- Whether there exists a better investment opportunity for this capital.

There could be different techniques to do so. Smart business managers apply their own tricks too to understand the value, like what I observed of an executive director of large Indian company doing. While explaining the economic value of IT investment, he asked the director of accounts what he would need for completing the payroll of all employees in time and how much interest he was earning through short-term investment on surplus after looking at the expenditure forecast. The guess was 200 more people would be required for payroll and couple of million of INR are earned on short-term interest. And the ED answered that IT had generated so much value for him in just these two instances.

There could be more structured and elaborate way to arrive at the EV generated by IT and accordingly the ROI. For this, the CIO must understand the way financial decisions are made in the organization and key information which are required to facilitate this decision. The organization and the business managers need to appreciate that the location of benefit is within the business and not the IT. As Robert McDowell also expressed in his book In Search of Business Value,

4.6 EV and ROI

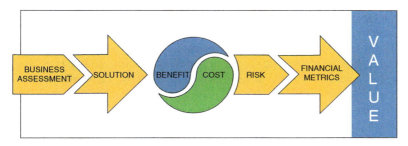

Fig. 4.8 Rapid economic justification model

"Technology provides no benefits of its own; it is the application of technology to business opportunities that produces ROI". Therefore, all effort for financial justification will be revolving around the business. Some organizations structure a team of all stake holders including financial and value engineering specialists for this purpose and manage this activity too like a project. In case organization follows a budget or scheme formulation standards, templates and practices, the team must review in IT perspective and tailor it for the use during this process.

The rapid economic justification (REJ) model defined by Microsoft is good way to achieve this. This defines a complete framework to arrive at IT contribution and the cost for this purpose.

It is six stepped process:

Step 1: Business assessment: It starts with assessment of business needs, which include CSFs, strategies, KPIs, related processes and means and ways to achieve the goals to make those strategies work.

Step 2: Solutions: At solution stage, gaps in performance and opportunities for IT are identified. At conceptual level the IT infrastructure and service needs are recorded to arrive at the cost later.

Step 3: Benefits: Accordingly the improvements that it can bring in the processes and strategy as a whole are identified. It could be good idea to record current level of performance, which can be measured later on to determine the improvements and benefits. These value propositions from IT are further refined when detail plan and execution of IT strategy starts. These identified contributions become the goals for IT, in case matching investments are approved.

Step 4: Costs: By now the benefit areas and improvements are known along with changes required in IT and the business areas. The cost of change is estimated.

Step 5: Risks: For each line of approach risks are identified so that business managers can weigh the investment and the benefits vis-à-vis risks involved.

Step 6: Financial metrics: Now the exercise begins to assign a value to each benefit and cost to changes in business and IT, presenting the number for economic value expected from the specified investment and total cost of ownership (TCO). Thus EV and ROI are arrived.

The strategy framework, above, will be of help. We discussed the process re-engineering for business improvement, identification of areas for IT to create value, IT for business continuity and sustenance and many other points which mark the benefits. Similarly, we made strategy for applications, technology, people enablement and IT services which can help to identify the cost. Generally two to three options in terms of investment and return are created so that business managers can deliberate and based on their understanding of priority areas, likely benefits and resources at command, they can decide what strategy and approach IT should take.

Though it sounds very correct approach, but it is not without challenges. The first challenge would be to get the business managers in collaboration mode; the second one would be to identify and quantify the changes and the benefits; while the third would be to assign realistic value to benefits. Similarly, there could be some for estimating costs. These challenges are managed differently in different organizations.

For the first, generally top management aligns local managers for this exercise. They set strategic goals and expect the team to come out of possible ways and means through which they can achieve. Once these managers see IT as one of the routes, they not only participate but also start driving. Another way could be forging stronger relationship and trust, so that the business managers listen the CIO's point-of-view and agree to work together to achieve common goal. The idea is to make them feel that this is in the interest of business and their organization. Lacking commitment from business managers become serious risk to whole IT strategy.

For the second, the team of business managers and CIO work with IT team, HR managers and other stakeholders who can help in identification and quantification of benefits. In case IT is likely to be funded by different business-units or line-of-business, representatives of all those should be involved. They run through various ideas to improve the business through people, process and technology. In the process they identify opportunities and benefits.

There would be many intangible benefits identified for which the team will have initial difficulty in quantifying and attaching a value. And for this challenge, the help of experts from financial and investment valuation can be taken. One such example could be revamping the outdated and troubling IT infrastructure to continue IT support. This must be taken as if manufacturing assets are being replaced after its life, where loss of production is considered as value for justification of new investment. Similarly, the loss of service-value must be taken as intended benefit for replacing and upgrading IT infrastructure. Similar approach and analogy helps to a large extent when IT related benefit valuation is being arrived at. Robert S. Kaplan also quoted in Harvard Business Review on "Business Value of IT", "Although intangible benefits may be difficult to quantify, there is no reason to value them at zero in a capital expenditure analysis. Zero is after all, no less arbitrary than any other number. Conservative accountants who assign zero values to many intangible benefits prefer being precisely wrong to being vaguely right". There is no harm in seeking help of experts in the organization or outside to help in arriving at the value of benefit or cost. Even though at this stage the numbers need not be so accurate, they must be realistic enough to trust and move.

Well selected and enabled processes can produce result and help in realization of benefit. The organizations can look for IT enablement for full value process chain.

In this case the benefit realization can be derived in a consolidated manner. But for the cases where IT enablement is in discreet manner and for part of the process, the benefit calculation and realization too would be stage wise only. This can happen because of phased approach, investment constraints, stepped growth and implementation or time spread investments. A benefits dependency networks (BDN) approach to identify benefits from IT, as mentioned in the research paper by Joe Peppard and John Ward, could be useful.

"Value One" and "Real Option Theory" (Microsoft.com) are good techniques to quantify future value. The first one suggests that stakeholders must agree to quantify the benefits while making unit improvement in CSF. And then quantity of improvements (in terms of units) required to reach to new target value of CSF is arrived. This quantity multiplied by the value per unit gives rise to total benefit. For example, if 1% profit margin gives X amount benefit, the business improvements contributing to 2% margin will be worth two times. The team must keep in mind that the stakeholder from benefit arising area must have reasonable comfort to achieve. This will be administratively easier task to manage as the quantitative management of KPIs will continue to happen under organization management practices as well. Only catch is to stand guarded when a new factor also influences the KPI and in reverse direction, such as the one happened in 2008, when many organizations could not meet their revenue growth and margin because of world wide financial trouble.

The second approach is based on different scenario and their chances of occurrence. This works on the basis of what benefits/savings would happen if that scenario occurs. A realistic chance lies between most optimistic and most pessimistic scenario and that probability is applied on the quantified benefits. This can be individually applied and the benefits (economic value) are summed or applied on a cluster of process if the end benefit is quantified based on the effect of each sub-processes and event within it.

Arriving at the cost is not that difficult as arriving at the benefit and getting the stakeholders committed. This step involves identification of investment area, solutions and components and making cost estimate through experience, data available in the organization and the quotation from the technology and service providers. These are budgetary quotes. Just for an idea, an indicative list of cost heads and likely benefit heads are given in Annexure A. These cost heads may need little more elaboration before assigning a cost.

A cost–benefit summary can be recorded in a format like in Table 4.6 for further progress and monitoring. Since the cost and the benefits both will be spread over time, presenting them over years will help the stake holders to have right picture and the investment accountant to calculate for financial metrics. The tangible benefits can be specified whether they are one-time or recurring periodically. Refer Annexure for an idea on cost heads. One needs to remember here that the process of arriving at these costs and benefits need not be accurate and very precise, which could be very resource intensive, but it must give the right feel to decision makers.

Based on the chart above, value to financial metrics may be arrived at. Just to note that the making a decision purely on these numbers while ignoring other signals and symptoms of business and its plans, which could not be quantified, may not be a good idea. In today's economy the financial metrics indicating poor return with

Table 4.6 Template for cost–benefit analysis

Benefit area (functional and process)	Year–month	Benefit/value		Cost estimate/allocation				Risks
		Tangible	Intangible	Non-IT	People	IT-capital	IT-revenue	

IT should not happen and it would deserve revisit. To say "no-go", the organization must make sure that they have done due diligence on benefits, priorities and the impact on the future before making such decision. Business managers must apply their business acumen too along with financial metrics to decide on go/no-go. The right advice in such cases where the financial metrics is not in favour of IT even after due considerations, would be to split investments in logical group and invest without compromising the targeted benefits, instead of starting with large investments at once. These metrics along with due business considerations help in ranking project and IT portfolio in terms of investments and starting priority.

Forrester has developed total economic value impact (TEI) methodology to take holistic view on a company's technology decision-making processes and assists vendors in communicating the value proposition of their products and services to clients. TEI systematically looks at the potential effects of technology investments across four dimensions: Cost, benefits, flexibility and risk. The advantage of this methodology is that it considers the opportunity value being created for the organization as well as the risks involved in totality.

Costs represent the investment necessary to capture the value, or benefits, of the proposed project. These may be in the form of fully-burdened labour, subcontractors, or materials. Costs consider all the investment and expenses necessary to deliver the value proposed. In addition, the cost category within TEI captures any incremental costs over the existing environment for the solution. All costs must be tied to the benefits that are created.

Benefits represent the value delivered to the user organization by the proposed product or project. The TEI methodology and resulting financial model places equal weight of the measure of benefits to that of costs, allowing for a full examination of the impact of the technology on the entire organization. The methodology suggests that the calculation of benefits estimate must be done in agreement with user organization and in accordance that financial model places equal weight of the measure of benefits to that of costs.

Flexibility generally represents the value that can be obtained as new options and opportunities to improve the efficiency, collaboration and performance in future. Forrester believes that organizations should be able to measure that too as the strategic value of an investment. For instance, an initial investment in an enterprise-wide upgrade of an office productivity suite can increase standardization (to increase efficiency) and reduce licensing costs.

4.7 Strategy Approval and Governances

Risk is the fourth component of the TEI methodology. It is a measurement of the uncertainty of benefit and cost estimates that are contained within the investment. Uncertainty is measured in two ways: (1) the likelihood that the cost and benefit estimates will meet the original projections, and (2) the likelihood that the estimates will be measured and tracked over time.

Net benefit = (benefit − cost + flexibility value)(1 − uncertainty due to risk)

Per period net benefit is derived and ROI is calculated.

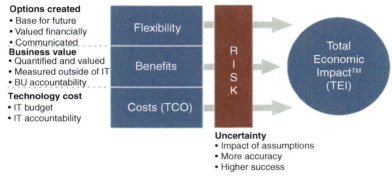

(TEI's Value Delivery Process - Source Forrester)

4.7 Strategy Approval and Governances

Developing an IT strategy is as important as its implementation and governance. Then there are many factors which influence the strategy over a period of time, which calls for proper adjustments. Sometimes they may be so vital that they create major impact on the strategy and a mid-course correction is required. One of them is synchronization of different strategies on regular basis as the life and the maturity period of each strategic component are different. And on change of one, the others also require some shift and adjustments. This not only impacts in top-down manner but also creates bottom-up effect. For example, a change in business drivers certainly needs review of processes, priorities, application and technology. Similarly, a change in technology may also create ripples to business strategy. That's why the architecture is important, so that modularization, integration, interdependence with plug-in and plug-out feature can be achieved.

A CIO needs to identify all such factors which can create impact on IT strategy and requires adjustment while going forward. Some could be of risk category which can cause serious dent and others could be of opportunity nature, which need to be picked while going forward. She has to be on constant vigilance to keep these elements aligned, strategically. A large deviation can cause stress to system and

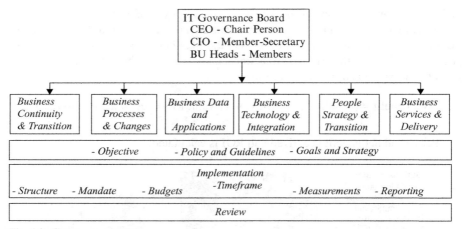

Fig. 4.9 Governance model

organization, loss of trust of business people and wastage of resource. All these need a governance structure which can provide direction, extend supports and exercise controls to keep the IT strategy relevant and ticking. ITIL defines governance as, "Corporate governance is the set of responsibilities and practices exercised by the board and executive management with the goal of providing strategic direction, ensuring that the objectives are achieved, ascertaining that the risks are being managed appropriately, and verifying that the enterprise's resources are used effectively". All the characteristics of governance hold good in IT strategy case too.

A good governance strategy always goes along (TOGAF v9)

- Cross-functional or cross-organizational board
- A comprehensive set of policies and principles
- Compliance structure

We recommend the model below (Fig. 4.9) for good governance at organization level. At the highest level there is Governing Board or Steering Committee, chaired by the highest authority. Different unit heads are the members and CIO is member-secretary. They overall oversee the six areas. They define the objectives, goals and overall strategy. To have successful implementation, they mark overall structure and composition of the team/group, assign goals, delegate authority, allocate initial budget and resources for delivery, and define reporting, review and measurement practices for each of those areas. In case they mark the responsibility to a person or role, the person concerned invite members from related domains to form the team and take due approval for the same. They can define financial and business change approval limits depending on certain scope, so that the team do not run to the governing board for each item. The board meets at a certain frequency, such as monthly, to take stock and issue fresh guidance. The CIO must make sure that the board members meet regularly and review effectively; otherwise the team below is quite sensitive and catches the signal for lower priority and of complacency, fast.

IT strategy is multi-staged approach and at times different stage misses complete linkages. It can happen while working through various strategies for process, people

4.7 Strategy Approval and Governances

and technology, and evolving risk and mitigation as well as economic benefits. Even certain instances such as consideration of viability since beginning, developing different components of strategy by different teams, prejudice and preconceived solutions create tunnelled view and restrict the team to achieve the best possible results. Irrespective of whether inconsistency is found or not, one should be prepared to go through few iterations to evolve a better strategy in pursuit of a better and aligned proposition. Once the cycle is complete, the team can claim consolidation and overall connections amongst all the elements. At this point of time, the team must get present its findings to the stakeholders including the management and/or the board members to seek approval and guidance to move forward.

A presentation should contain the summary of the initiative, approach and value proposition while seeking guidance and approval. This meeting works like any business planning and review session. The CIO and the leading stakeholders must prepare well for this meeting. The team should also prepare the participants and decision makers for fruitful participation during the meeting. Basic protocols such as agenda, briefing, expectations and many others must be taken care of, such that the outcome of poor organization of this meeting does not reflect on the objective and the basic goal of the meeting. Different aspects of the presentation must be presented in balanced and professional way so that the decision makers do not get more influenced by emotions and undue emphasis of a subject. Even though this is an internal selling activity after such an involved exercise, there is no harm to tune the preparation and the presentation to suit the collective style of decision-making, which may be prevailing in the organization. It is always a good idea to help the decision maker debate and agree on the benefit rather than the cost. Once they agree on probable benefits, the cost will be evaluated in that perspective, otherwise, they become apprehensive of cost and that reduces chance of approval and improvements.

The presentation should address

- *Why this exercise*: This should set the tone of the presentation and report while providing justification of this exercise. This should cover the business goals, current state of affairs and KPIs and the gaps. Preferably very senior executive or the sponsor of this initiative should present.
- *What business benefits* are expected: Respective stakeholders from the team should present the business benefits and their KPIs which they would target to meet the organization level KPIs. This also links organization level goals with functional level, and demonstrate the alignments.
- *What options* were considered and the business changes being proposed over time: Again the respective stakeholders present the options and solutions they considered and how they come out with one solution that will help them and the organization to achieve the organization goal.
- *What technology and projects* are being proposed: CIO should present the case for IT, which should show linkage of IT with business and the way IT is envisioned to participate and support respective area stakeholders to meet the business goals.
- *What the investment need* is over period of time: The lead stakeholder should present the recommendations and investment needed to achieve them. The investment case must have different financial metrics and the risks as well as means to mitigate the same.

– *When the benefits will start* accruing: Stakeholders should present the value map and their accrual over span of time subject to approval of investment and overall approach plan.

CIO and the lead stakeholder should be ready to address different queries and what-if situation, like what happens in any such meeting, to get it concluded and the guidance for going forward. The "Way Forward" must emerge from here.

The CIO must document and publish the complete work (refer Chap. 1 for content title) and baseline. An execution team must be formed which can start executing it. The team should be empowered to make suitable adjustments depending upon the emerging scenario and feasibility. Hence, the full life cycle (design-execution-review and adjustments-realization) of any strategy must be walked through for the benefit realization.

4.8 Summary

This chapter worked around soft part of any strategy. It started with people development and team structuring. We discussed the people strategy for business as well as IT organization. We firmly believe that organizations having good people and people strategy can have consistent growth and take any competition. They are the strategy makers, executioners and success achievers. Right people having right skill can produce best results when subjected to right environment with right guidance. And that should be the goal of people strategy. Sometimes it appears to be encroaching into HR development domain, but it is all right as far as it serves business purpose. We advise that the team and the CIO must get HR organization involved to define right strategy and execute them. Some people also believe that success of IT strategy is not in integrated system but in integrated team and integrated business for value to customer, and we agree with them.

We also discussed the service delivery as part of the IT strategy. This strategy includes back office operations, keeping up the IT infrastructure in good health and support to the business users. Today, the IT industry offers many alternatives and options to choose. None is absolutely right and none is absolutely wrong. The organization must pick those ones which they think that matches with their culture, suits to their needs and can deliver as per the envisaged plan.

Managers make strategies based on their knowledge and perceptions at a specific point of time. However, all internal and external events do not happen the way they were planned and that causes a risk. As a good practice, a CIO must be aware of this phenomenon and must have a risk management practice to assist her in early sensing and mitigation.

The whole strategy is for certain business goals and they deserve a central place on the organization's performance radar. Since they can not be achieved at once as well as in short duration, those goals are divided into sub-goals over time and investment dimensions. This division and mapping provides good guidance and direction to control and keep the IT strategy and its execution aligned towards the business goal.

The organization must design these milestones and review mechanism to exercise proper controls. Since the business best understands the financial aspects of the benefits, the best practices are to judge the benefits in financial terms as well. This helps in making business decision about investments and strategy as a whole.

Finally, some wise words from Alan Matula, Executive VP and Group CIO, Shell (having 25 business portfolios and operations across more than 100 nations), which he shared with McKinsey during Spring 2010. He suggested four steps to make IT successful:

Step 1: Stabilize IT Operations through right discipline in projects, IT assets, cost, people, IT practices and services. This puts own house in order and control, while providing right platform to launch.

Step 2: Demonstrate efficiency and simplification through IT and help business to achieve their goals. Here IT alignment with business is in focus.

Step 3: Collaborate with business units for benefit delivery through organized processes and practices. This collaboration is to get their support in maintaining accountability, monitoring progress and delivering distinct benefits to the organization. This helps in standardization, transparency, accountability and working together for a common cause.

Step 4: Build work pool of talented people through careful recruitment and learning programmes in association with business people. Learning and innovating together builds and strengthens trust between IT and business, which is important for sustained transformation.

4.9 Glossary

Acronym	Abbreviation
BOOT	Build own operate and transfer
BPO	Business process outsourcing
BU	Business unit
CEO	Chief executive officer
CFO	Chief financial officer
CIO	Chief information officer
CMMI	Capability maturity model integration
CMO	Chief marketing officer
COBIT	Control objectives for information and related technology. A set of best practices defined by information systems audit and control association (ISACA), and IT governance Institute (ITGI) in 1996 for IT management
COO	Chief operation officer
CSF	Critical success factor

eSCM	eSourcing capability model
	    For service providers
	    For clients

(continued)

Acronym	Abbreviation
EV	Economic value
HQ	Headquarters
HR	Human resource (function)
IaaS	Infrastructure as a service
IEC	International electrotechnical commission
ISO	International organization for standardization
IT	Information technology
ITIL	IT infrastructure library. A public framework that describes best practices in IT service management
ITSMF	IT service management framework
KPI	Key performance indicator
NIST	National Institute of Standards and Technology. Develops standard under Section 5131 of the Information Technology Management Reform Act of 1996 and the Federal Information Security Management Act of 2002 (Public Law 107-347), US
PaaS	Platform as a service
PMBOK	Project management body of knowledge
PMI	Project management institute
PRINCE2	Project in controlled environment
ROI	Return on Investment
SLA	Service level agreement
SOA	Service oriented architecture
TOGAF	The open group architecture framework

4.10 Preview Questions

1. What is meant by IT strategy?
2. What is the difference between IT strategy and strategy?
3. Why people management is important in IT strategy implementation?
4. How do you assess risk?
5. How is alignment of business with IT strategy ensured?
6. What are the different practices in IT governance?
7. How ITIL can be beneficiary to an organization?

4.11 Project Work

Form a group of five persons. Visit a manufacturing organization which has factory which manufactures automobile parts. Understand the strategy after discussion with senior executives. Find the issues and challenges faced by the management team while implementing these issues. Based on your understanding of these issues and challenges, design an implementation strategy that can have following objectives—implementation should ensure that interests of all employees are taken care of, business objectives of the organization are met after effective implementation. What are the risks that can impact this implementation and how do you plan to mitigate them?

4.12 Annexure A

4.12.1 Cost heads

Indicative list of cost heads are as below:

Cost heads		Total cost	Year 1	Year 2	Year 3
1	Functional				
1.1	Planning				
1.2	Communication and consulting				
1.3	Organization				
1.4	Documentation				
1.5	New/augmented resource				
1.6	Transition and facilitation				
2	People				
2.1	Planning				
2.2	Communication and agreement				
2.3	Organizing reorientation				
2.4	Training				
2.5	Incentive				
2.6	Stabilizing performance				
2.7	Users time and productivity loss				
3	IT				
3.1	Hardware and networking				
3.1.1	New equipment and devices				
3.1.2	Upgrade of existing equipment				
3.1.2	Installation, configurations, service and utilities				
3.1.3	Spares				
3.1.4	Space				
3.2	Software and service				
3.2.1	Operating system				
3.2.2	Software tools				
3.2.3	Licence				
3.2.4	Solution mapping and configuration				
	Development and testing				
3.2.5	Consulting and implementation				
3.2.6	Project management				
3.2.7	IT team Reorientation				
3.3	Operations				
3.3.1	Support and trouble shooting				
3.3.2	IT operations (labour and material)				
3.3.3	System administration				
3.3.4	Outsourcing				

(continued)

Cost heads		Total cost	Year 1	Year 2	Year 3
3.3.5	AMC/spares/supplies				
3.3.6	Renovation and upgrades				
3.3.7	Utilities and consumptions				
3.4	Cost of capital				
3.5	Purchasing and vendor management				
3.6	Consumables				
3.7	Cost of continuity				

4.12.2 Benefit heads

Indicative list of benefit area, where IT and IT enabled process can benefit.

Direct benefit heads		Total cost	Year 1	Year 2	Year 3
1	Cost saving				
1.1	Manpower				
1.2	Process efficiency and effectiveness				
1.3	Lead time improvement				
1.4	Information storage and availability				
1.5	Cost of fund and capital				
1.6	Cost of purchase and purchased material and services				
1.7	Wastage control—blocked capital, material deterioration, over-consumption, over-inventory, etc.				
1.8	Cost to partner management				
1.9	Cost to order fulfilment and service				
1.1	Cost of poor quality				
2	Revenue, market and margin				
2.1	Improved customer satisfaction				
2.2	Cost of business with customers				
2.3	Revenue and margin improvement				
2.4	Effectiveness in competition management				
2.5	New sales channel and effective management of others				
2.6	Improved performance in logistics				
2.7	Increase in brand value				
2.8	Opportunity to sell new knowledge and practices				
2.9	Product and service value				
2.1	Organization flexibility and free resources				
3	Governance and compliance				
3.1	Improvement in statutory compliance—saving penalties and loss of credit				
3.2	Cost of compliance fulfilment				

(continued)

Direct benefit heads		Total cost	Year 1	Year 2	Year 3
3.3	Conformance with customer practices				
3.4	Cost to manage and management effectiveness				
3.5	Data security				
3.6	Cost to quality system management				
3.7	Lower business risk				

4.13 Annexure 2

4.13.1 IT Strategy and eStrategy

IT strategy is holistic strategy for IT enablement, whereas eStrategy is part of IT strategy. The objective of eStrategy is generally to create conducive and online environment for customers, partners, employees and others to make business with the organization. It is enabling business processes through use of Internet/Intranet and brings efficiency and cost saving to business process by use of IT. The example includes eCommerce, eService for customer, supplier and employees, eRecruitment, eProcurement, eStock-trading and eMarketing. This helps in integrating business processes across organizations to provide complete service and single view to the customers. Many see it as another channel for sales and service, but it has more potential than this. eStrategy offers variety of benefits including new business models, innovative products and services at low cost, and this has made it popular. The very possibility of integrated service to a customer promoted co-creation, whereby organizations, even sometimes competitors, join hands to offer better options to customer and hence, create win-win situation for all. An integration of airline and railway reservation with payment gateway facilitator such as banks and credit card service providers are good example of it. But this as well needs justification in light of overall business strategy and goals, like any enabler, before initiation. Then for making it work one must have right approach to integrate, implement and sustain. Most of the time, business managers make industry and market assessment and benchmark before they set goals for eStrategy. IT could be to match competition (problem or market driven) as well as to beat competition (strategy/opportunity driven), and accordingly gets driven. This helps in managing risk as well, as this strategy can create not only risk to the investments but also loss to the business credibility and the opportunities. Since it increases the speed and reach to internal staff as well as external parties such as customers, some may not like opening of this channel, like what Levi Strauss faced when it was pressurized by retailer to stop online selling. The performance expectation also goes up from all stakeholders, end-users and the beneficiaries from eStrategy enabled services.

The Aberdeen Group reported in its report "Retail E-Commerce Analytics", published during Feb 2010 that gross margin of "Best-in-Class" group improved to 30% and the conversion rate improved by 21% over last year with eCommerce solutions. This clearly shows the pull that eCommerce is creating. They also identified that improving the "online customers' experience" and "data availability to affect online commerce decisions" are two top goals to achieve to make eCommerce successful. Their survey response indicated that sub-optimal online customer experience has most adversely impacted. Hence, the organizations introduced solutions to track customers and their profile along with their behavioural and Web usage pattern to get more insight to do better business. For eCommerce and other eStrategy enabled services, it makes more sense to have analytics engine to analyze behaviour and use data for business purposes.

Recently, a new trend of social networking has emerged, which compelled the business entities to evolve a strategy to take benefit from and manage as well as protect brand image through networking sites. There are different forums and informal networks such as twitter, facebook, linkedin, badmouth and blogs where the customers, suppliers, business analysts, stock brokers and many such entities in individual as well as organizational capacity have started connecting and communicating. The business organizations do not have any control on what these people are sharing. Many customers use this to collect the information about best price, product and service performance, their impressions and experience. These are shaping the opinion of the market and potential customers. In an article, "A new way to measure word-of-mouth marketing", on McKinsey Quarterly, Bughin et al. (2010) described rising influence of "word-of-mouth" on product sales. Internet enabled social network is becoming most important and dominating of all means of spreading word of mouth. They observed that the market share of Mobile sales can go up by 10% and down by 20% over a period of 2 years with all things equal, because of this. They quote, "With so few companies actively managing word of mouth—the most powerful form of marketing—the potential upside is exponentially great". They described three forms of this as experiential (based on experience with product and service), consequential (based on exposure to marketing technique, messages and the brands) and intentional (based on motivated reasons and endorsement by celebrities). The impact too goes in the same order, after all the intensity of trust and persuasion also depends upon what is said, who says it, and where it is said. They also observed, "understanding which dimensions is most important to the product, the business and the brand: the who, the what, or the where, and using them appropriately for the business benefit evolves right strategy". We observed one more dimension that adds to the influence, is mood and mode of recipient, i.e. whether the message is received when one was looking for it, "pull mode", or when it was presented just on the way, "push mode".

Similarly, people from other communities such as suppliers and stock brokers share and collect information on these networking sites. The marketing people use it to assess the market and marketing tricks that will work. This has forced business managers, especially brand managers, to create a strategy and approach to what is being shared in these forums so that the company as well as the product brand is not disturbed if not enhanced. Smart stakeholders not only collect impressions and field data from here, but they also make virtual marketing and create pre-launch hype and demand. In fact this has opened a new era of connecting people and its application and usage is still exploding. The full potential is still to realize. This can be used for good as well as bad purposes; hence, a CIO must make the management conscious about this new trend and potential of it. She must guide the business to use them for the business benefit.

We suggest that the following steps may help to develop and create a supporting Internet community. Even then, the poor performers run a risk, as dissatisfied customers will deface it fast.

- Understand the Internet community behaviour
- Understand own industry and create a community like "fan club" matching with the community needs
- Build a site which provides valuable information to the community
- Invest to develop trust such that the community relies for information and opinion formation
- Collect online feedback from them and share with the community
- Improve content and offers to attract more visitors and members

A recent example of it has been the case of parents of babies in USA who started complaining about the new diapers. They used diapers where "Dry Max" technology from P&G was used and they caused rashes. The parents started sharing the problems on the facebook and other social networking sites. P&G took immediate notice and tried to rope in its Fan-Club that held the trust since long, to defend the brand. In the mean time as a responsible organization it also started re-looking into the product and the technology.

Today the social networks are called Web 2.0 technology and tomorrow a new name or acronym may appear, but this has brought a new dimension to business and its branding. Whether it is used for brand building or brand defending, a conscious effort to identify such intrusive technologies and their usage must be watched and taken care off.

4.13.2 Business Content Services

Web sites have been good means to publish corporate information which people wanted to share with the world. But it had multiple handicaps including

- Keeping the information updated
- Facilitating interaction between the content readers as well as providers
- Providing single place for internal, confidential and public information

This led to search for better solution. Portal technology, which came up well to address those and provided more. Portal provides platform for concise presentation of enterprise information as well as facilitates interaction and collaboration from all stake holders.

Forrester's survey indicates that content publishing, compliance management, cost effective search of enterprise information and automation of business processes are top four reasons to use this technology platform. This also evolved over a period of time and struggled through lacking interface with sources of information and performance issues. Today's Portal (also called as Enterprise Content Management Tool) is able to present consolidated view of different types of contents, data, communications, alerts, content centric applications, interface to business applications and people interface platform together in a secured manner. The platform has been able to support content integration, emerging from different platforms and sources. Its capability to integrate and transform information from different sources on fly and present them in the personalized format to the content consumer, made it popular. It facilitated system and information interface to the stake holders while providing single window information services to them. It has been used as collaboration platform, facilitating interaction and exchange of ideas within and across organizations. The two pictures below from Oracle Corporation present true picture of the scope of services integrated under ECM tools as on today. The tool's integration with identity management and Business Intelligence applications enhanced its purpose and value for a business organization. Even its design and configuration process has been simplified for creating personalized pages. We recommend that every CIO must evaluate this technology as a solution component for collaboration, content management, workflow and approval management, collaboration management, work and assignment/delegation management, record search, publishing information and security needs within and beyond organization.

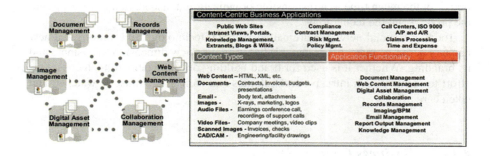

Source: Oracle Corporation

The picture on the left depict six main functionalities being serviced through Portal; and that on the right side, shows how the various types of contents and application functionalities are combined to make business applications. And the list is just indicative.

In an article on digital marketing, David C. Edelman has drawn difference between digital marketing and traditional approach. The customer approach as well as the approach to market any product and services has changed. The reach of a customer to seek advice and opinion has gone beyond friends and family. The research on feedback from users and consumers as well as pricing became easier. He observed that attracting Internet customers, engaging them, qualifying them and building their loyalty have been four staged marketing approach. The idea is to create good experience so that they not only buy products but also bring in new business ideas and participate in innovation. And this kind of technology helps to keep them engage with the corporations.

The spending towards marketing shifted towards influencing consumers through

- Ease of locating the product and related content (by improving performance of its own search engine as well as Internet search ranking)
- Facilitating conclusive evaluation with requisite information
- Increasing presence in stores and online
- Presenting consistent contents on all sales channel and
- Cultivating recommendations from important online influencers, such as twitters and bloggers

He recognized that most of the companies have become publishers and whole world as consumer of the published content. It can help business in creating good value through published content by cost reduction in content creation, by optimization, reuse, consistency and reach of the content, and finally by improving the customer experience in B2C as well as B2B scenario. We agree to his observation that a tightly disciplined, personalized digital publishing saves cost over traditional advertising and reaching to customers. Digital publishing makes a great advantage in customer tracking to collect data in passive as well as active manner, which also helps to understand their behaviour. Before digital interaction, it was so difficult to get the feel and preferences of customers, partners and employees. Today some of the companies are building intelligence on what are customers seeing, how and what are they searching, and what are they saying from their portal. This helps in design and development of right approach and attractive content for potential customers. That day is not far off when these data will emerge as a new business opportunity in itself.

The trick is selection of right product which can meet the following need and allow easy creation, personalization and administration with full security.

- Coverage of content types
- Interface with other products and platforms
- Tools available to configure information and the page
- Availability of comprehensive search
- Feature for dynamic update of content
- Ease to configure and publish
- Performance and
- Cost for licences, implementation and management

And then continuous evolution and improvement makes the difference.

Bibliography

Anderson C (2003) At the speed of business: 5 A's of the corporate learning chain. An IDC White Paper, Skillsoft.com

Belkin G (2010) Retail E-commerce analytics: cornerstone of the complete customer profile. Aberdeen Group, February 2010

Brink D (2010) IT security: balancing enterprise risk and reward, January 2010, Aberdeen Group http://www.opengroup.org/architecture/togaf/

Bughin J, Doogan J, Vetvik OJ (2010) A new way to measure word-of-mouth marketing. McKinsey Quarterly, April-2010

Casadesus-Masanell R, Ghemawat P (2005) Microsoft vs. open source: who will win? June 2005. http://hbswk.hbs.edu/item/4834.html

Chakravorty SS (2010) Where process improvement projects go wrong. MIT Sloan Management review, January 22, 2010 edition http://sloanreview.mit.edu/business-insight/articles/2010/1/5214/where-process-improvement-projects-go-wrong/

Managing IT transformation on a global scale: an interview with shell CIO Alan Matula. McKinsey Quarterly, Spring 2010

CMU CMMI-SVC V1.2. Technical report: CMMI for services—Version 1.2. www.sei.cmu.edu/publications/

Department of Information Resources (1998) Outsourcing strategies: guidelines for evaluating internal and external resources for major information technology projects. DIR, The State of Texas, June 1998

Edelman DC (2010) Four ways to get more value from digital marketing. McKinsey Quarterly, Mar 2010

Forrester's October 2009 Global enterprise content management online survey, www.forrester.com

Greenfield D (2007) Standards for IT governance. Information Week Global CIO, December 2007. http://www.informationweek.com/news/global-cio/showArticle.jhtml?articleID=204701897

Harvard Business review on the business value of IT (compilation) www.hbr.com

http://www.iso.org/iso/iso_catalogue.htm

http://www.opensource.org/about

https://www.sme.sap.com/irj/sme/solution/whybusinessbydesign/saasredefined

IBM. E-strategy, Internet communities and global EC. CIOindex.com

McCafferty M (2010) Global technology solution group, Avanade and IDG Enterprise on CIO. com; http://event.on24.com/eventRegistration/EventLobbyServlet?target=lobby.jsp&eventid=193340&sessionid=1&partnerref=cioale_app031710&key=CB58BDFB60DC9D958D7C99126A4AAADC&eventuserid=34177051

Microsoft Inc. A step-by-step guide to optimizing IT investments that forge alliances between IT and business. Rapid economic justification methodology www.microsoft.com/value

Oracle fusion middleware: Oracle content management, 2010. www.Oracle.com

Peppard J, Ward J (2007) Managing the realization of business benefits from IT investments, March 2007, MIS Quarterly Executive, UK

SaaS Realities (2009) Business benefits for small and mid-sized enterprises. Saugutack Technology Inc., Research paper funded by SAP

Stanford N (2007) Guide to organisation design. The Economist

Thiel W et al (2009) (Blumstengel, Astril, Colsman, Tatjana, David, Stephen, Gubitz, Benjamin, Molenkamp, Heinz and Ramchandran, Sukand). Putting information technology at the core of the business for Boston Consulting Group publication. IT Advantage

Thompson W, Stolovitsky N (2010) Seeing the big picture: a corporate guide to better decision through IT. Technology evaluation centers. www.bitpipe.com

Woodall D (2004) Blended learning strategies. Skillsoft Corporation

www.cio.com

www.CIOindex.com

www.iso.org

www.searchcio.com

Chapter 5
Learning Objectives

The case illustrates how OPGC plays a catalyst role for industrial and economic development of Orissa, a state in India. The case also shows how OPGC has been able to promote and assist in rapid and orderly establishment and organization of industries, trade and commerce in the State while being able to develop and manage its production capacity, available resources and political factors in the State. OPGC has been able to achieve this by using information system for assisting its business strategy to become a strong force in utilities sector. The case shows how IS has been effective in monitoring the development and growth of different departments in the organization. This has been achieved through a systematic approach by defining detailed process flow and then automating to the extent required. The extent of automation has been decided through ROI calculation, and these aspects have been highlighted in the case. Data have been collected through primary survey by interviewing executives at different managerial levels and information available in public domain.

The case can be taught in financial management, IS courses as well as in management development programmes (where senior officials from government would be the target audience), workshops held for government officials involved in utilities and energy sectors at state as well as federal government levels. The chapter objectives are as follows:

- To explain how IS is essential for the survival and growth of an enterprise while executing complex business processes in a regulated environment.
- To understand how to draw information flow at different levels and use that for designing information strategy.
- To decide how to integrate information system with business strategy for getting maximum benefits for all stakeholders.
- How to implement information strategy in a public sector enterprise?

5.1 Introduction

IT as a means of productivity enhancer is not only limited to service and new economy organizations. It is also a source of competitive and operative advantage in the era of globalization. Orissa Power Generation Corporation is a government owned energy company having its footprint over dispersed locations in Orissa. It has its own IT needs which have been addressed in bits and pieces till now. There is no unified IT strategy in place for the organization nor do they have a CIO to lead the IT division that is in place. With the increase in its revenues the need for IT will be huge. To take care of the IT needs, the team has recommended a number of measures with broad timelines as part of the IT strategy for OPGC. Notable of those strategies is the change of the present ERP system called RAMCO to a SAP ERP system, appointment of CIO and strategic role of the IT division, energy management system and power management systems among others. The IT strategy has been defined over a long time period spanning 5 years and an implementation roadmap of 37 months. The strategy also looks into critical aspects such as training, change management and risks, which often do not get the importance. The systems in place have a payback period of less than 2 years even with a conservative discount rate. The measures recommended will not only increase the efficiency and productivity of OPGC but also be a source of cost saving and therefore increase profitability for OPGC.

5.2 Industry Analysis

India is the world's sixth largest energy consumer, accounting for 3.4% of global energy consumption. Due to India's economic rise, the demand for energy has grown at an average of 3.6% per annum over the past 30 years. More than 50% of India's commercial energy demand is met through the country's vast coal reserves. About 76% of the electricity consumed in India is generated by thermal power plants, 21% by hydroelectric power plants and 4% by nuclear power plants. The country has also invested heavily in recent years on renewable sources of energy such as wind energy.

In March 2009, the installed power generation capacity of India stood at 147,000 MW, while the per capita power consumption stood at 612 kWh. The country's annual power production increased from about 190 billion kWH in 1986 to more than 680 billion kWh in 2006. The Indian government has set an ambitious target to add approximately 78,000 MW of installed generation capacity by 2012. The total demand for electricity in India is expected to cross 950,000 MW by 2030.

Electricity losses in India during transmission and distribution are extremely high and vary between 30 and 45%. In 2004–2005, electricity demand outstripped supply by 7–11%. Due to shortage of electricity, power cuts are common throughout India, and this has adversely effected the country's economic growth. Theft of electricity, common in most parts of urban India, amounts to 1.5% of India's GDP.

5.2 Industry Analysis

5.2.1 Thermal Power

Current installed capacity of Thermal Power is 93,392.64 MW which is 63.3% of total installed capacity.

- Current installed base of coal based thermal power is 77,458.88 MW which comes to 53.3% of total installed base.
- Current installed base of Gas Based Thermal Power is 14,734.01 MW which is 10.5% of total installed base.
- Current installed base of Oil Based Thermal Power is 1,199.75 MW which is 0.9% of total installed base.

5.2.1.1 Environmental Issues in Orissa

The thermal power generation of the State is 5.5 thousand megawatt and with the existing capacity Talcher-Angul is declared as Critical Problem Areas by CPCB for a long time. For every megawatt of electricity produced, around 7 tonnes of waste is generated every day and for 32,000 MW of power project the waste will be 2.24 lakh tonnes per day and 81.7 million tonnes per year that will require around 810 ha of land for every year for disposal of solid waste.

Thermal power plants are the major sources of green house emission and contribute in climate change and global warming. In a thermal power plant about one third of the heat energy gets converted to electricity and remaining two third goes back to the environment, resulting in temperature rise in the vicinity causing a heat island. Thus, the ambient temperature in this region is likely to be at least 2–3°C higher than its neighbouring areas.

5.2.2 About OPGC

Orissa Power Generation Corporation Ltd. (OPGC) is the only thermal power generating company of Govt. of Orissa. OPGC was incorporated under the Companies Act 1956 on 14th November 1984. It has a set-up of two 210 MW capacity power plants at IB Thermal Power Station, Banaharpali of Jharsuguda district in the State of Orissa.

These plants enjoy a major locational advantage, as they are located within close proximity of the Hirakund dam reservoir, which has allowed them to have a dedicated intake channel connected to the reservoir. OPGC also enjoys an assured income due to the presence of a payment security mechanism which comprises an escrow account and a revolving letter of credit with Gridco. The plants' basic raw material, coal, is purchased by OPGC from Coal India Ltd., more specifically from Mahanadi Coalfields Ltd. The coal that is supplied is of F and G types which have an ash content of approximately 45%. The consumption of coal is around 8,000 metric tonnes per day. The coal costs OPGC Rs. 800 per tonne. The coal is delivered to the plant using the MGR (Merry Go Round) system.

Through a disinvestment process under the power sector reforms initiated in 1997, AES Corporation of USA was selected as the Strategic Investor in 1998. AES was entrusted with day to day management to bring in operational and financial efficiency in OPGC. They have a long-term Power Purchase Agreement (PPA) with Gridco, which buys 100% of their power. Hence, marketing of power is not an issue. The rate at which OPGC sells power to Gridco is Rs. 1.30 per unit. OPGC, which has been generating the power successfully with an average plant load factor of 80% since last 12 years, is a profit making and dividend paying company of Orissa.

5.2.3 Vision and Mission

- To be one of the best and reliable power utilities of India.
- To make every work place a safe work place.
- To keep the environment clean.
- To be socially responsible for employees and society.

5.2.4 Objectives

- To acquire, establish, operate, maintain, renovate, modernize in the State of Orissa and elsewhere hydroelectric generating stations and thermal electric generating stations and any other electric generating stations based on any non-conventional sources of energy.
- To be into power trading business outside the PPA with Grid Corporation of Orissa.
- Expand its business to multiple locations across India.

5.2.5 Future Plans

OPGC originally planned to open four new plants of 600 MW capacities each. This planned capacity figure has now gone up to 660 MW. These new plants are estimated to cost OPGC to the tune of Rs. 600 Crores. For these new plants, OPGC is entering a tie-up with MCL for setting up a coal washing plant, which will reduce the ash content of the coal.

The new plants mean that there will be a lot of new workers. These workers would need cheap and affordable housing nearby so that they can easily get to work. This will require a new colony to be set up which means an investment of around Rs. 30 Crores.

At the plants themselves, many provisions for modern amenities will have to be made. An ERP system will need to be put in place which means an investment of Rs. 15 Crore. Also, an automated security system (ITPS) is on the cards, which would cost around Rs. 12–15 Crores. In addition to these, others amenities such as electric fencing, watch towers, CCTV monitoring system, infrared cameras. Keltron has been identified as the supplier of an office attendance system, which would be gradually replaced by a biometric system. This would implement access control to sensitive areas in the plant using boom barrier and RFID tags.

Currently, OPGC employs 500 workers and has contracted 1,000 more. Each year, an annual overhauling exercise is carried out for which 500 temporary workers are hired for the duration of the exercise. This overhauling exercise generally lasts for a period of 1 month. The new plant is expected to employ 7,000 more workers which would also require a monitoring system. The original plants (Units 1 and 2) would have to be enclosed because of the development of the new plants. This is necessary in order to avoid interference in the normal functioning of Units 1 and 2 due to the construction of the new units as also to enhance security.

OPGC is in the process of entering into mining development activities for its own captive use in the expansion project. For the purpose, OPGC has been applied and allotted got two blocks of coal mines at Manoharpur and the dip site of Manoharpur which has a capacity 531.68 million tonnes from the Ministry of Coal, GOI through Govt. Dispensation Route.

5.2.6 Stake Holders

- Management
- AES
- Employees
- Customers—GRIDCO
- Suppliers
- Vendors
- Environment and society

5.2.7 IT Department

OPGC IT department is primarily managed with one person with two supporting staffs serving 200+ users both at ITPS and Head Office for their IT and communication needs. There is no formal IT organization and clear definition of roles and responsibilities. The IT department is operating from IBTPS. The IT department at OPGC is structured as shown below.

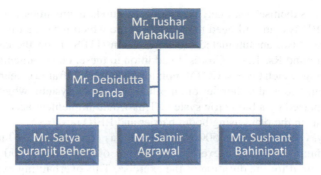

The entire IT set-up is not stand alone, but comes under the Maintenance and Planning division. All decisions regarding IT strategy have to be passed by the Director Operations and the MD.

5.2.8 Growth of IT in the Organization

Before 1999, there was no formal IT set-up at OPGC except some stand alone system which was having applications running in FOX Pro to cater to the need of Efficiency Department, Ware house & Purchase Department. The user departments had been using diverse software for diverse functions supplied by different vendors, the software specifications and workflows were disparate. Manual procedures were followed in various maintenance activities and planning. There was no system for inventory tracking.

After 1999, OPGC moved towards an IT set-up for computerized resource planning and utilizing the computerized network in all fields for optimum utilization of resource and material, for cost economy with minimum time. As a result, IB Thermal Power Station had installed local area network based on Fast Ethernet Fibre-Optic Backbone and Structured Cabling System to interlink various areas such as operations and maintenance, MIS, administration, finance, central store, coal handling plant, workshop, water treatment plant and switchyard for information exchange. The installation and maintenance of LAN was under the purview of Control and Instrumentation department (C&I). Within a year they went back to the manual ledger as they found using LAN cumbersome.

In 1999, AES bought 49% stake in the organization and that brought a renewed stress on IT in the organization. The choice was between implementing of structured or unstructured LAN network. In order to take the decision, OPGC conducted a benchmarking study in various plants of NTPC such as Dadri and the Delhi corporate office. The ideal strategy was found in NTPC corporate office where structured LAN in mesh network was used along with fibre optics as its backbone. NTPC had good inventory planning and database and it was decided to implement a similar system with star network at OPGC. This was in year 2000 and the work of implementation was under a General Manager in Control and Instrumentation department and the technical team comprised four people. It was decided that OPGC would focus on implementing hardware first and on a strong hardware platform it would go for software implementation. In 1999 OPGC issued NIT (Notice Inviting Tender) for software implementation. After a long scanning process which included criteria such as familiarization to OPGC processes, a combination of two companies was selected.

At the corporate office, Bhubaneswar, local area network is established to interconnect all the users. Currently around 250 PCs and Laptops are there in all the departments. ITPS have its own 64 kbps VSAT connection and 1 Mbps terrestrial line to access the Internet. OPGC corporate office is also having broadband connection for Internet. OPGC has its official web site which has all information regarding the location, monthly/yearly performance, achievements, tender notices, financial information, etc. The web site is actively used for Tender (Work/Purchase) publication. The mailing facility is extended to the users through the use of Microsoft Exchange Server & Linux Send mail. Executives were provided with Blackberry facility for easy and fast communication.

5.2.9 Current IT Infrastructure

At IB Thermal Power Station three modules (Maintenance, Purchase and Inventory) of RAMCO e-application was implemented during 2003 and has been used for the Maintenance, Inventory and Purchase functions. Finance and HR are using legacy system for their day to day operations.

All employees were now quite aware of the requirement of computer and communication usages for the organization. All departments are highly dependent on the computers, application software for the required functions and the communication means (mailing/Internet, etc.).

Important processes such as RFQ handling, quotation management, tender management, procurement, etc. are manually managed. Since these processes are not automated, there is no workflow system in place. Hence, a lot of data replication also takes place. For example, if one employee enters an order for H_2SO_4 and another employee places an order for H_2SO_4, the existing system takes these as two separate items and treats them as such. This results in a lot of operational and logistical issues. Accounting is also affected significantly, as it becomes difficult to justify purchase of two items viz. H_2SO_4 and H_2SO_2. This certainly does not contribute towards the company's efficiency. Another glaring issue is that the staff is not fully trained and competent enough to use even the existing systems.

Plant level automation has been taken care of by ABB DCS system which is take care of by Control & Instrumentation (C&I) department. Currently they are in the process of implementing latest technology plant automation system, i.e. MAXDNA by BHEL. Generation of MIS report, fuel management system, HR activities, payroll processing are the processes which can be automated in the future. This will result in Manpower reduction, effective man-hour utilization and easy availability of information for quick decision-making.

5.2.10 Sample Process Overviews

For the purpose of demonstration, an existing process of purchase processing is shown below.

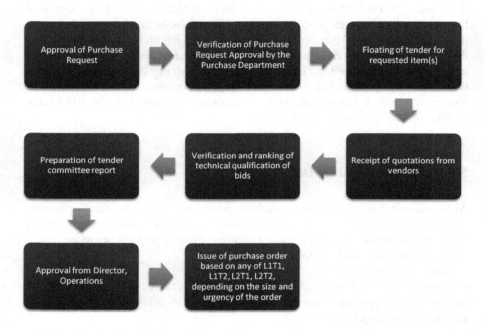

As is clearly visible from the above process, the organization is in dire need of an automated system which will ensure that the correct process is followed through efficient workflow management. Also, the system needs to ensure that the right document/proposal reaches the right person so that there is no delay in taking the process forward, at the same time, ensuring data security by preventing non-authorized users from gaining access to the data.

5.2.11 Business Capability Roadmap

Degree of Competence	Aware	Capable	Mature	World Class
Timeline	Days	Weeks	Months	Many Months
People				
Process				
Technology				
Data				
Applications				

OPGC is in the growth phase right now. Hence, the technology being used will be dynamic in nature. Most of the employees will be unaware about the latest technologies being implemented. Hence, the degree of competence for employees will be evolving from a lack of awareness to world-class knowledge. Similarly, the degree of competence when it comes to processes is capable at the moment, technology unaware, data mature and applications capable right now. The objective is to reach world-class competency in the medium term to long term.

5.3 Research Framework

Management dilemma

- Improve reliability, operational efficiency and manpower management without having any adverse effect on the environment.

Management objectives

- To improve reliability and efficiency to meet international standards and guidelines
- Reduce cost of generation and transmission to drive profitability
- To have a comprehensive safety management policy and a safety management system
- To fulfil the environmental commitment of the company by developing and implementing a environment management policy

Research objective

- To develop IT strategy which are best aligned with the management objectives and provide a strategic edge to OPGC

Concept

- Cost
- Process
- Safety
- Environment

Construct

- Efficiency
- Reliability
- Cost reduction
- Reduction in accidents/safety failures
- Environment impact

Research methodology—qualitative study

- Secondary data collection
- Non participant observation
- Structured interview
  - Senior executives
  - Middle level manager

Data analysis

- Qualitative interpretation technique

5.4 Approaches for IT Strategy

The following steps were followed in the formulation of the IT strategy

1. Analysing the prevailing processes, practices and organization of OPGC
2. Study the paradigms of IT strategy implementation across similar organizations which can be followed at OPGC
3. Breaking down of vision, mission and business objectives into short-term and long-term IT related objectives
4. Formulate an IT strategy to achieve the IT related objectives in a time based manner with due consideration to ROI
5. Create feedback mechanisms, metrics and a framework to measure and enhance the degree of success in the implementation of IT strategy

   IT strategy formulation framework

5.4 Approaches for IT Strategy

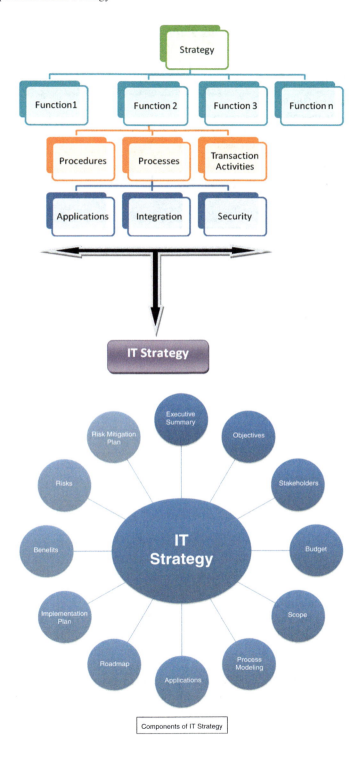

Components of IT Strategy

5.4.1 Key Business Drivers as Factors of ITS

State of the Industry
- Current status of the industry
- Regulatory framework for the industry
- Industry dominated by state owned or privately owned companies
- Competitive environment in the sector

Merger and Acquisition
- Threat or opportunity of Merger or Acquisition

Revenue Protection
- Checks and balances to protect revenue inlets
- Scope of IT in the revenue growth.

Productivity
- Productivity of Labour
- Productivity of Capital Employed

Production and Energy Supply
- Cost efficiency in the procurement process
- Process efficiency for electricity generation

5.5 SWOT Analysis

Strengths

1. Cheap availability of coal in the vicinity (within 20 km), and access to captive mines
2. Availability of cheap labour (the area is not very industrialized, unemployment rate is high)
3. Collaboration with AES provides latest technological knowhow
4. Predictable cash flows owing to demand side certainty

Opportunities

1. Demand far outstripping supply
2. Huge increase in power requirement expected in the next few years
3. Liberalization from the Government
4. Potentially, one of the largest power markets in the world
5. Large pool of highly skilled technical personnel
6. Implementation of central grid makes it possible to distribute the power produces all across India and hence very less chance of overcapacity and demand side related issues

5.5 SWOT Analysis

Weakness

1. Huge transmission and distribution losses lead to low price realizations
2. High carbon footprint due to dependence on coal based energy
3. Fixed price model is in place and hence cannot pass on the cost fluctuations to the immediate customer

Threats

1. Selling of power possible only through PPA with Gridco. No scope for price fixation
2. Nuclear energy might be taken up in a big way in the near future when the technology is stable enough. This might hinder the growth of thermal energy

5.5.1 Strategic Map

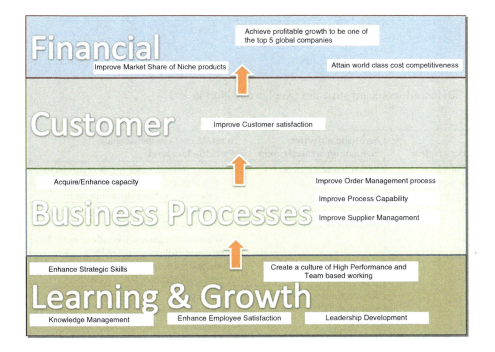

5.5.2 Balanced Scorecard

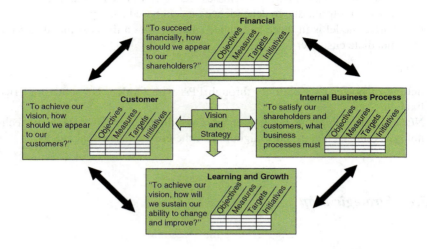

Balanced scorecard structure (Kaplan and Norton 1992)

Perspective	Strategic objective/ element on strategic map	To attain cost competitiveness of world-class levels
Financial perspective	Definition of element	To remove redundancies and bottlenecks to ensure a high quality of production to keep the costs and overheads to a minimum
	Key performance questions (KPQ)	A. What are the current bottlenecks in the processes followed by OHPC? B. What are the current redundancies in the processes followed by OHPC? C. Are the costs and overheads in our units in sync with industry benchmarks?
	Key performance indicators (KPI)	A. Cycle time B. Cost of production C. Energy efficiency D. Overheads E. Inventory holding costs

(continued)

5.5 SWOT Analysis

Perspective	Strategic objective/element on strategic map	To continue with profitable growth in future
Financial perspective	Definition of element	To carry on the profitable business of purchasing, selling, importing, exporting, producing, trading, manufacturing or otherwise dealing in hydroelectric power, thermal and nuclear electric power based on any non-conventional sources of energy
	Key performance questions (KPQ)	A. What percentage of profits is reinvested? B. What are the different balance sheet ratios?
	Key performance indicators (KPI)	A. Profit per unit of electricity B. Profit per employee C. Share price D. Return on capital employed E. PBIDT/sales
Perspective	**Strategic objective/element on strategic map**	**Improve customer satisfaction on identified critical attributes**
Customer perspective	Definition of element	To provide incremental levels of satisfaction to the customer
	Key performance questions (KPQ)	A. Which of the performance measures are related to customer satisfaction? B. How to measure customer satisfaction?
	Key performance indicators (KPI)	A. Load factor B. Customer feedback C. Service level on new projects
Perspective	**Strategic objective/element on strategic map**	**Help in the setting up of new projects across Orissa**
Customer perspective	Definition of element	To study, investigate, collect information and data, review operations, plan, research, design, prepare feasibility reports, prepare project reports, diagnose operational difficulties and weaknesses and advise on the remedial measures to improve and modernize existing stations and facilitate and to undertake for and on behalf of others the setting up of hydroelectric power plants, thermal and nuclear electric power plants and any other power plants based on any non-conventional source of energy
	Key performance questions (KPQ)	A. What best practices of OPGC can be replicated in other projects? B. Are the current resources and infrastructure capable of taking care of external projects?
	Key performance indicators (KPI)	A. Break even period B. Return on investment C. Conception to Implementation lead time

(continued)

Perspective	Strategic objective/element on strategic map	Improve cost-effectiveness by enhancing efficiency and optimize resource utilization
Business process perspective	Definition of element	Time based process improvement to enhance efficiency and efficient management of resources
	Key performance questions (KPQ)	A. What is the process capability of different processes? B. Are the processes at par in quality with respect to industry benchmarks
	Key performance indicators (KPI)	A. Wage bill as % of value addition B. Cost of quality C. % reduction in overheads
Perspective	Strategic objective/element on strategic map	Improve cost-effectiveness by enhancing efficiency and optimize resource utilization
Business process perspective	Definition of element	Time based process improvement to enhance efficiency and efficient management of resources
	Key performance questions (KPQ)	A. What is the process capability of different processes? B. Are the processes at par in quality with respect to industry benchmarks
	Key performance indicators (KPI)	A. Wage bill as % of value addition B. Cost of quality C. % reduction in overheads
Perspective	Strategic objective/element on strategic map	Automation of business processes
Business process perspective	Definition of element	Automation of repetitive and non-value-adding business processes through business process modelling to enable the workforce to focus on more productive activities
	Key performance questions (KPQ)	A. What are the processes which need automation? B. How will the workforce be trained to efficiently utilize the automation?
	Key performance indicators (KPI)	A. Return on investment B. Productivity C. Error reduction
Perspective	Strategic objective/element on strategic map	Create a culture of high performance and teamwork
Learning and growth perspective	Definition of element	Create a culture of high performance and teamwork in the company
	Key performance questions (KPQ)	How to guide high performance and teamwork to aid the organizational vision, mission and goals?
	Key performance indicators (KPI)	A. % employees rated as high performers B. % of employees in active teams

(continued)

5.5 SWOT Analysis

Perspective	Strategic objective/element on strategic map	Enhance strategic skills/competencies
Learning and growth perspective	Definition of element	Enhance strategic skills/competencies of employees
	Key performance questions (KPQ)	What are the skills needed in present and future to drive the growth of the company?
	Key performance indicators (KPI)	% adherance to strategic training plan
Perspective	**Strategic objective/element on strategic map**	**Enhance employee well-being, motivation and satisfaction**
Learning and growth perspective	Definition of element	Enhance employee well-being, motivation and satisfaction through HR initiatives and safety practices
	Key performance questions (KPQ)	A. Are the safety standards at OPGC as per the industry best practices? B. How to improve the satisfaction and work/life balance of employees?
	Key performance indicators (KPI)	Employee satisfaction index

5.5.3 Benchmarking

Benchmarking is the continuous search for and adaptation of significantly better practices that leads to superior performance by investigating the performance and practices of other organizations (benchmark partners). In addition, it can create a crisis to facilitate the change process.

Benchmarking is not only intended at imitating the practices of superior competitors but exploring practices that validate the performance gaps. It is a means of achieving better process performance by looking at (and outside) the industry. It is possible to gain competitive advantage due to benchmarking rather being at par with the average industry standards.

The quest is always to ingrain the best practices. Benchmarking has a few constraints which need to be tackled. Not all best practices are applicable for an organization. Significant effort and attention to detail is required to ensure that problems are minimized.

5.5.3.1 Need for a Benchmark

- Provides realistic and achievable targets
- Prevents companies from being industry led
- Challenges operational complacency
- Creates an atmosphere conducive to continuous improvement

- Allows employees to visualize the improvement which can be a strong motivator for change
- Creates a sense of urgency for improvement
- Confirms the belief that there is a need for change
- Helps to identify weak areas and indicates what needs to be done to improve

5.5.3.2 Benchmarking Company: TATA Power

Apart from being the private largest power company in India it is also the leader in the power sector when it comes to technology. The following are a few technological initiatives taken by the company:

- Creation of an online knowledge management system (KMS)
- Business and process innovation (BPI) system
  - Web-portal for customers to enable easy information, spot billing and power trading facilities
- Integrated data warehouse
- Business Information Warehouse (BIW)
- Data Management System (DMS)
- Content Management System (CMS)
- KMS to support all information needs across the company

5.5.4 Critical Success Factors

- On time implementation of the system
- Implementation within the budgeted amount
- Are all the end users happy?
- Are all the users using the implemented system
- Improved relations with suppliers and vendors
- Increase in productivity and increased efficiency of the system
- MIS accuracy, efficiency and relevance

5.6 Business Process Modelling and Recommendations

The key to a successful implementation and usage of an IT system is the fit of planned processes in an organization with processes implemented in the solution. There is a difference between designing processes to fit end user organizations, and designing a business process model that will fit in the existing systems which when deployed will be aligned with the business processes. In an IT implementation, modules are implemented according to the organization need. These modules have their processes and flow already defined; however, there is room for customization and codification according to the organization needs. The implementation team is responsible to understand the existing processes of the organization and to achieve a fit between the two. However, it is not possible that all the processes can be accommodated in the new application. So an effective strategy in business process modelling should follow the following steps:

- First task is to define the already existing processes across all the departments in the organization
- These processes should be in great detail and should capture all the integrities of the process flow and the workflow of the operations
- Next step is to map the existing processes of the organization and the application modules. This will be done by the implementation team
- Now the areas where there is a mismatch, there the application module should be customized to achieve the mapping
- If customization is not able to map the processes fully then the only option is to change or tweak the organization process to achieve the fit between the application module and organization process

5.6.1 Customer Management

OPGC enjoys a huge advantage in comparison with other similar companies on this front, in the sense that it serves only one customer, GRIDCO. This deal is sealed by a long-term PPA, and hence, OPGC is assured of a steady income through an escrow account and a rotating bank guarantee. However, having one customer is not a sufficient reason to disregard customer management completely.

Previously, like any other typical thermal power plant, OPGC's plants too observed a reactive approach to solving customer problems. The methodologies in place were the following:

- Centralized control room nodes.
- Divisional control rooms.
- Direct allocation of fault-duty engineers on a long-term relationship basis.
- Written recording of complaints.

There is a scope for improvement in the following areas:

- **Perception of customer requirements**
  This aspect can be fortified through regular meetings with representatives of Gridco. Select employees of OPGC can also be trained in a few Gridco processes so that OPGC has a thorough understanding of the nature of Gridco's requirement.
- **Efficient complaint redressal**
  Given next is a suggested flow chart of the process for customer complaint management.

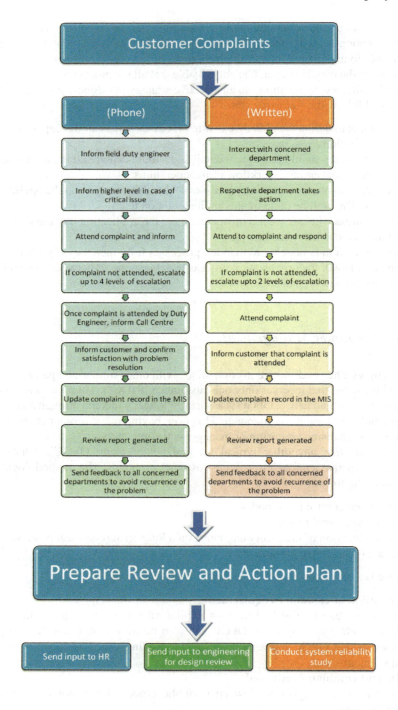

5.6 Business Process Modelling and Recommendations

- **Communication with client**
  Front line staff can be equipped with time-saving measures such as FAQ documents so that expert engineers do not need to be consulted for every problem and valuable customer time is saved.
- **Service level agreement**
  OPGC can agree upon certain predefined service levels for various activity support. This will ensure that OPGC remains accountable to its client for any problems faced.
- **Customer delight**
  OPGC should carry out customer satisfaction surveys in order to find the pain areas for the client at the current moment. The workers familiar with Gridco's processes also need to get together and brainstorm so that they can pre-empt any requirement from the client side due to the changing nature of the client's business. Also, along with the usual measurement of client satisfaction, client dissatisfaction can also be measured separately in order to pinpoint sore areas that need immediate attention. A customer information web page should be introduced as part of the web portal to serve the customers as two way sharing and addressing concerns. In the future the setting up of an integrated web portal dedicated for customer management should be created.
- A likely timeline for implementation of such measures is suggested next.

5.6.1.1 Roadmap for Implementation of Customer Management System

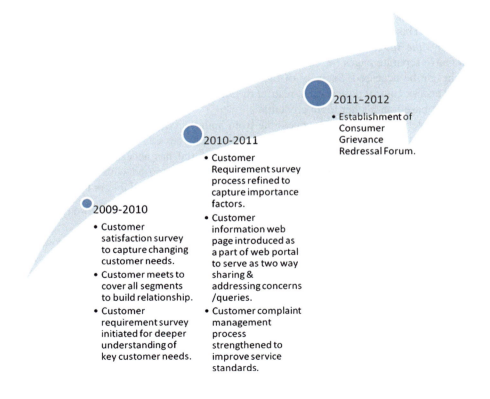

5.6.2 Knowledge Management

A thermal power plant invariably produces a large amount of data. This data can be very critical in the smooth operation of the plant, as sometimes, past knowhow can help solve minor glitches in a jiffy. Also, the workers in the plant gain practical expertise due to their prolonged exposure to the various processes in the plant. This knowledge needs to be captured in an efficient manner so that it can be easily accessed by a different set of workers of the plant at any point of time in the future.

Most of the times, such data is stored by a legacy MIS in a database that, more often than not, is extremely rudimentary. Such data is hardly ever checked for consistency and duplication. This results in quite a few problems as one can never be sure as to whether the data one is accessing is accurate or not! Also, over the years, a lot of data accumulates and starts occupying large amounts of virtual space. Data archived into storage in order to circumvent this problem suffers from lack of easy accessibility, as well as susceptibility to corruption due to various reasons, some of which could be improper storage or forces majeure. Retrieval of such data can also be a very tedious task and is most definitely not STP (Straight-through Processing)—it needs some level of human interference. This means unnecessary deployment of valuable labour for the task.

Most of these problems can be usually eliminated by use of an efficient ERP system that encompasses the processes in all the department of the organization manning the plant, from Material Management right down to Finance. However, ease of access still remains an issue, especially for employees who may at a remote location. This problem can be overcome with the *development of a web portal that employs the suggested ERP software as a backbone to its functioning*. The portal can have separate pages for each department where the data relevant to that department can be accessed. Security of the data can be ensured by implementation of strict access control policies that restrict the amount of data accessible to a particular user based on his/her login credentials.

This web portal should be accessible from both the company intranet as well as the Internet. This ensures that the company's employees can access required data from anywhere at any point of time. Since the portal has access to all the plant related data, cross departmental reports can also be composed without any problems. Following are the suggested menus that can be made available in the portal.

- Plant performance: This feature can generate reports about the day-to-day functioning of the plant at predefined intervals.
- Documentation: This section can house the various documents that provide information on previous best practices, anomalies, training, etc.
- Research: This section can contain the results of various surveys and other in-house research activities that may have been carried out by the organization, so that they can be used by the users as desired.
- Tools: In this section, links can be provided to various custom-made tools in order to simplify/automate oft used processes.

5.6 Business Process Modelling and Recommendations

- Training: This section can contain the various training presentations and other training documents which will help new inductees to familiarize themselves with the various relevant processes in the company. This section can also prove to be invaluable when a new technology is introduced, as it can help to disseminate information to the employees about the same.

A rigorous backup schedule can also be chalked out for the data contained on the web portal so that the contingency of loss of data is already hedged against.

Given below is an indicative tree diagram of the web page structure for a single department.

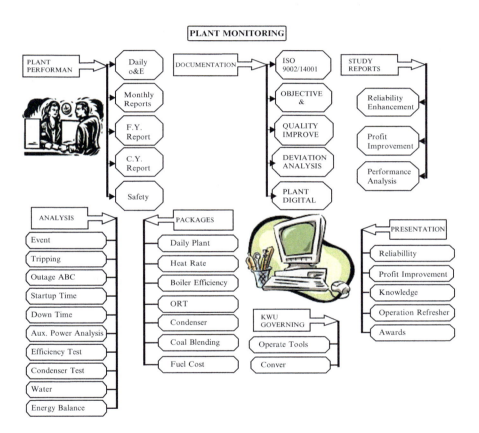

5.6.2.1 Critical Success Factors for the Web Portal

The critical success factors of such an implementation are given below.

- Availability of precise data for instant study and reference.
- Accessibility to multiple users from different locations, simultaneously.

- Prevention of loss or corruption of data.
- Reduction of cost due to availability of data in electronic format.

5.6.3 Energy Management System

For any modern power plant today, an energy management system is necessary for evaluating the continuous stream of data from the system and recognizing the potential for optimizing utilization of raw material by assessing the processes and components continuously.

Such a system is pre-programmed with benchmark values for optimal functioning of various components. The system analyses the data it receives from the other online systems and tries to assess whether the components are functioning close to their optimal best. If not, the system tries to come up with suggestions for reaching the said optimal level. The more advanced systems are even capable of making the tweaks to the systems on their own to reach these optimum levels. However, optimization also means finding the best middle path, as all systems cannot run at maximum efficiency simultaneously. This system tries to minimize the reduction in operational efficiency so that the plant can run at maximum possible efficiency overall.

This is achieved through a 3-tiered process which comprises the following levels.

- Analysis
- Optimization
- Forecast

The primary driver behind all these levels is cost which is, after all, the best indicator of the performance of a system from the business point of view. The critical success factors for the implementation of such a system would be

- Accuracy of computation of ratios and key figures such as efficiencies, electric energy from cogeneration, start-up cost, etc.
- Accuracy of component evaluation (steam generator, steam water cycle, condenser, pumps, flue gas circuit, etc.).
- Successful optimization (soot blowing, gas turbine compressor washing, etc.).
- Accuracy of forecast (unit efficiency, maximum unit output, etc.).

5.6.4 Plant Management System

A plant management system acts as an umbrella system for all sub-systems in a plant and hence is necessary to provide an efficient integration medium for all the sub-systems. It also helps the plant workers to identify lacunae in the existing systems and optimize various processes followed in the plant. It also provides accurate and timely information with details about the organizational, technical and commercial aspects.

Though the level of engagement may vary from plant to plant, a typical plant management system provides the following services.

- Significant reduction in effort directed towards plant management
- Job scheduling and control, supported by performance recording and documentation
- Integration of payroll data acquisition with shift planning, optimized for cost
- Management of supplies and optimization of use of the same
- Provision of daily indicative data such as cost status
- Compliance with existing processing and quality standards
- Access control based on credentials
- Provision of emergency processes with possibility of switch in warning

5.6.5 Performance Monitoring System

A performance monitoring system is generally set in place for continuous assessment of efficiency in operations for aspects. This system differs from other systems, say a KMS in the sense that it simply monitors and returns data to the users about the efficiency of the system's functioning. It is not capable of coming up with new processes or any tweaks to existing processes.

Take for example process quality. Now, process quality is defined as the ratio between current unit efficiency and optimum efficiency of operation under the current operating condition. The optimum efficiency is calculated using proven process calculation software based on reference data obtained during heat consumption tests with calibrated measuring equipment. Post this step, the system identifies those components which have shown maximum deviation from this optimal figure. This information aids the plant engineers to make changes to the working of the plant's components, if necessary.

In case of a thermal power plant, at least the following systems need to be monitored.

- Water steam cycle
- Cooling water cycle
- Air flue gas system
- Milling plant
- Boiler

A performance management system should be in place to monitor all the above parameters.

5.6.6 Energy Capital Management

Energy capital management is used to control the energy supply chain and sales and procurement processes through collection, management and use of energy-relevant data for:

- Forecasting and monitoring
- Customer service
- Operations
- Regulatory compliance

Energy capital management processes include modules for *energy portfolio management* (to fulfil demand at the lowest cost) and *smart metre data integration* (communicate with smart metres to develop of new products and services tailored to the customer's energy consumption behaviour). Energy capital management package is offered by many companies, notably, SAP.

5.6.7 Availability Based Tariff

Availability Based Tariff (ABT) regime for power trading and grid discipline is one of the high points of the electricity act of 2003. It is credited with as a successful scheme worldwide for bringing about grid discipline.

ABT frames the tariff structure for bulk power and intends to bring about more accountability and responsibility in power generation and consumption through a scheme of incentives and disincentives. Central electricity regulatory commission has placed its bet upon ABT to improve the quality of power.

ABT splits up the existing bulk energy charge structure into three components:

- Capacity charges (fixed)
- Energy charges (variable)
- UI (unscheduled interchange) charge

The UI charge component is expected to bring about the desired grid discipline. This splitting of the tariff into fixed and variable cost components is expected to incentivise power trading to culminate in a self-regulating power market regime along with the promotion of the concept of ELD (Economic Load Dispatch) among power generators.

5.6.8 Current ERP System: RAMCO

5.6.8.1 Benefits

- Single reference database and all information of equipment and its maintenance history available on-line.

- Point-of-performance corrective actions.
- Unscheduled breakdowns minimized through planned maintenance.
- Decreased mean-time-to-repair through optimal utilization of resources.
- Equipment history analysis for preventive/corrective action.
- Planning and monitoring shutdown activities efficiently.
- Maintenance budgets compare expenses against plan.
- Automatic routing work requests and work orders.
- Reduced inventory costs through enterprise wide visibility of inventory.
- Reserve and allocate critical items/spares for future use.
- Reduce inventory stocks through optimum inventory holding.
- Tracking inventory stocks through online stock-status check.
- Improve materials management by analysis of consumption pattern.
- Efficient and effective cost analysis of spares and consumables.
- Reduce tendering and order time through vendor database detailing products and terms for each vendor.
- Reduce procurement lead-time through electronic ordering and tracking of purchase orders.

5.6.8.2 Limitations

- Except the integration of maintenance management with purchase and inventory, all other domain activities are desperate and manual.
- The maintenance management has no link to finance software; hence, plant maintenance costs are not stored and analysed in detail.
- Detail cost accounting records are not available in the system, procurement process is not integrated with finance.
- Vendor invoices cannot be verified through the system with relevant PO.
- Assets accounting is not handled by any software application.
- HR activity is not automated and payroll system is not integrated to financial accounting.
- Capital investment costs are accounted and analysed manually.
- No project planning and document management solution to accommodate immediate business expansion needs.

5.6.9 Proposed ERP System: SAP

SAP has traditionally provided enterprise resource planning (ERP) solutions, with one of the largest installed customer bases among competing providers in this space. SAP's set of e-business solutions include Customer Relationship Management (CRM), Supplier Relationship Management (SRM), Product Life cycle Management (PLM), BIW. BW and Supply Chain Management (SCM).

Companies licence and use SAP applications either as separate modules or as part of the overall mySAP.com suite of e-business solutions. In the past, many companies invested in ERP solutions that bundled functionality for financial reporting and operations management. Recently, ERP providers, including SAP, have tried to diversify their offerings into more discrete offerings that meet specific business needs and challenges, such as product data management, SCM and corporate financials.

SAP ERP initiative will enable OPGC to meet the scalability and replicability requirements for its IT systems needed due to its growth plans; realize information value; extend enterprise boundaries; improve project management and execution skills.

5.6.9.1 SAP Implementation at TATA Power

SAP ERP has been implemented at TATA Power, which is the benchmarking company for our report. TATA Power decided to implement ERP in 2001–2002. SAP was the only company with an ERP solution for the power sector. SAP was also considered as SAP is implemented all across Tata Group of Companies and also got pricing benefits.

The ERP implementation began in early 2001 with the formation of a core team for each functional area and with a tie up with Tata Technologies for implementation. The system went live in 2002 and the entire process was completed by May 2003.

The following are the salient points in the implementation

- SAP R/3 implementation covered 28 locations.
- It had the following functionalities:
  - Complete supply chain
  - Centralized procurement
  - Vendor management
  - Complete cash cycle
  - Centralized accounting
  - Project management
  - Budgeting and monitoring
  - Plant defect notification and work order management
  - HR organizational and personnel administration
  - Customer management and bill-processing
- The first utility company in India to implement SAP.
- The HR module handled 3,300 employee master records and automated the organization management, personnel administration as well as training and event management.
- TATA Power connected all geographical locations—Mumbai and other states that we have presence in over a WAN backbone.
- Procured 570 SAP user licences across Tata Power.

- Implementing SAP R/3 reduced procurement cycle times from 41 to 17 days.
- Billing integrity index improved from 3.00 to 1.83%; billing complaints response index has improved from 90 to 99%.

Training

Training the people on the SAP modules was very critical to the success of the implementation process. A core team with 47 people both from IT department as well as various functional experts were trained in the first lot by our implementation partners, Tata Technologies. This team was trained in the software configuration, implementation as well as the testing of various modules. This team in turn trained the end users.

5.6.9.2 Advantages of SAP ERP Implementation at OPGC

- Implement a core enterprise-wide IT platform to enhance corporate management, improve asset management, reduce costs, and ultimately, enable higher profitability
- Make available shared, real-time information in project planning, execution, accounting, inventory and procurement management, and more
- Phasing out of outdated legacy systems which currently handle HR and Finance functionalities
- Consistency in transactions and lower manual involvement in dealing with vendors and customers
- Improved planning and forecasting taking into view cross functional inputs apart from materials and purchasing

5.6.10 Additional Systems

In addition to the above systems OPGC will also need to implement the following systems which are crucial to any large IT system.

- IT Policy development and implementation
  It strategy needs to be reviewed in a timely manner to make improvements and remove drawbacks from the system. This process should be undertaken periodically.
- IT Security Solution and Implementation
  Any large IT infrastructure needs a dedicated security system. It will consist of protecting information and information systems from unauthorized access, use, disclosure, disruption, modification or destruction.

- Information Technology and Information Library (ITIL) implementation
  ITIL gives a detailed description of a number of important IT practices with comprehensive checklists, tasks and procedures that any IT organization can tailor to its needs.
- e Procurement
  Electronic procurement is the business-to-business purchase and sale of supplies, Work and services through the Internet as well as other information and networking systems, such as Electronic Data Interchange and Enterprise Resource Planning. In case of OPGC we are looking at long-term implementation of e procurement routed through its SAP enabled web portal.

5.7 Approach for Implementation of IT Strategy

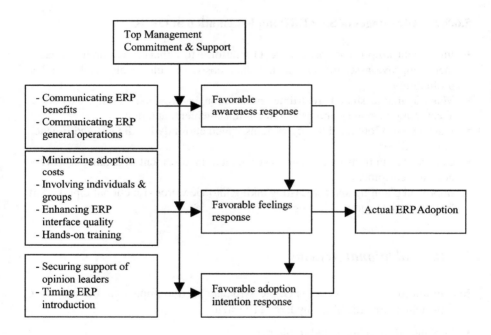

A model of successful ERP adoption

5.7.1 Implementation Plan

Major challenges to ERP implementation

5.7 Approach for Implementation of IT Strategy

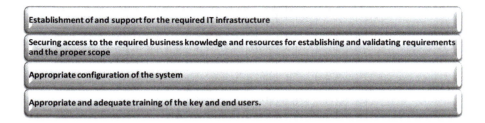

5.7.2 Road Map

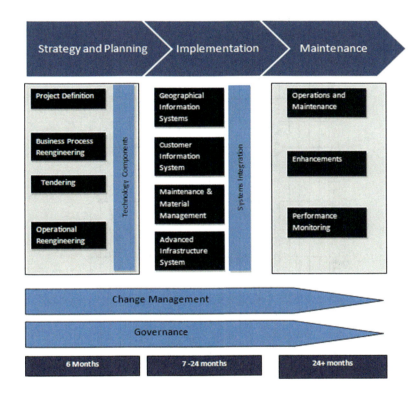

The following MS Excel file gives the detailed roadmap for the ITS implementation at OPGC. It not only details the SAP implementation but also all the other systems discussed in the previous sections. The roadmap has been divided into three phases as has been described.

Tasks	Short term						Medium term										
	Jan-10	Feb-10	Mar-10	Apr-10	May-10	Jun-10	Jul-10	Aug-10	Sep-10	Oct-10	Nov-10	Dec-10	Jan-11	Feb-11	Mar-11	Apr-11	May-11
IT Strategy Development																	
IT Organization Setup																	
IT Infrastructure (LAN,WAN,Data Center) set up																	
Communication (email, IPT, Blaackberry)																	
SAP Implementation Phase- 1																	
MM, PM,PS,FICO,QM,EHS,HCM,Payroll,DMS,ESS,BI,BW,SEM,KM)																	
Post Go Live Stabilisation																	
SAP Enabled Intranet Web Portal																	
Energy Management System																	
Knowledge Management System																	
Performance Management System																	
Availability Based Tariff																	
Energy Capital Management																	
Integration of Energy mgmt KM System with Web Portal																	
Portal Beta Testing and Stabilisation																	
SAP Implementation Phase- 2																	
IS-Utilities																	
Master Data Management																	
Post Go Live Stabilization																	
IT Strategic Review & Planning																	
IT Policy development & implementation																	
IT Security Soln Implementation																	
ITIL implementation																	
e Procurement																	

5.7 Approach for Implementation of IT Strategy

Tasks	Jun-11	Jul-11	Aug-11	Sep-11	Oct-11	Nov-11	Dec-11	Jan-12	Feb-12	Mar-12	Apr-12	May-12	Jun-12	Jul-12	Aug-12	Sep-12
								Long term								
IT Strategy Development																
IT Organization Setup																
IT Infrastructure (LAN,WAN,Data Center) set up																
Communication (email, IPT, Blaackberry)																
SAP Implementation Phase- 1	■	■	■	■	■	■	■	■								
MM, PM,PS,FICO,QM,EHS,HCM,Payroll,DMS,ESS,BI,BW,SEM,KM																
Post Go Live Stabilisation																
SAP Enabled Intranet Web Portal																
Energy Management System																
Knowledge Management System																
Performance Management System																
Availability Based Tariff																
Energy Capital Management																
Integration of Energy mgmt KM System with Web Portal																
Portal Beta Testing and Stabilisation																
SAP Implementation Phase- 2					■	■	■	■	■							
IS-Utilities																
Master Data Management	■															
Post Go Live Stabilization													■	■	■	
IT Strategic Review & Planning																
IT Policy development & implementation			■													
IT Security Soln Implementation																
ITIL implementation																
e Procurement																

The phases are Short Term (6 months), Medium Term (next 18 months) and Long Term.

However, from the implementation point of view, the IT strategy implementation will happen in three phases. The initial phase will consist of Strategic planning. The second phase will integrate the systems together. This phase will also consist of introduction of new systems Energy Management, Personnel Monitoring System, ABT systems and the internal web portal. This phase will occupy the largest time period so that all the systems can be tested in beta phase along with systematic phasing out of the older systems wherever applicable. This phase will see the implementation of SAP in two stages. The first stage will consist of all the major modules of SAP. The second level SAP implementation will consist of IS Utilities and Master Data Management modules. The next phase of ITS implementation will be maintenance of ERP and other systems. Some value added systems such as e Procurement will be implemented to improve profitability of the organization and business opportunities.

5.7.2.1 Phase I

- Information gathering for ITS
- Preparation of the ERP implementation plan and change strategy

5.7.2.2 Phase II

- Implementation of SAP
- Rolling out of all the functional modules
- Testing and customization
- Trainers training
- Users training
- Feedback and further customization
- Withdrawal of legacy systems

5.7.2.3 Phase III

- Maintenance of ERP and other systems
- Integration of newer systems with the ERP system
- Further customization of ERP system
- Performance measurement and improvement

5.7.3 Training

In implementation of any system, training is of critical importance because acceptance of any new system depends on the way users have been trained and accepted the system. In ERP implementation the caveat is the users of the system should know it extensively, in order to know about the shortcuts and various features of it. The training for the implementation is conducted in two phases. In the first phase vendor consultants should be employed to train the implementation and the technical team. The second phase is the training of users of the application by the technical team. The training should be hands-on training with following features:

- A facilitator should walk the entire class through the process.
- Each participant should follow the process and the training should be on the basic navigation course at first.

Hands-on training is important driver of ERP implementation success. It helps build positive attitudes toward the system and they appreciate the quality attributes of the system and its potential benefits. Formation of training teams among each functional group is also necessary. Each department should identify a core team of members who would drive the training in their department. They would themselves undertake trainings in *train the trainer* programmes and then conduct formal and informal training sessions in their department. This team is required since during the implementation phase users face innumerable difficulties in accessing the system. At such time trained members should be present in the team who can provide informal guidance and training. Apart from the formal teams there should be a helpdesk set-up to cater to the ad hoc needs of the users. Also *drop in labs* could be of great use where employees could just drop in and access the system real time. *Common FAQ's on notice boards* will also be of great help in making the users aware of the system. Apart from the training schedules user group conferences could be arranged where in the users can discuss their common problems and about the features of the system. Also all the employees should be communicated about the each phase of implementation and info sessions should be conducted. This would involve the employees in the process of implementation and will develop an affinity towards technology.

5.7.4 Change Management

When an organization is planning to undergo change on such a massive scale such as ERP implementation, change management becomes of pivotal importance. The biggest asset of an organization is its resources and such a change requires high level of responsiveness to internal customers to avoid the difficulties associated with this change. The biggest challenge to successful implementation of a technology-enabled operational and business transformation change management, according to researches and studies, are people and organizational issues. Technological factors take a backseat to such issues. Such transformations are as much cultural as technological. While technology is important to the success of the programme, it often consumes most of the programme's attention and leaves significant challenges in its wake, especially for the users of the new tools. In the OPGC environment, there are additional challenges represented by the unionized workforce towards the overall cultural shift.

5.7.4.1 Knowledge Formulation Phase

The first step in effectively managing change introduced by IT is to identify and evaluate the attitudes of individual users and influential groups.

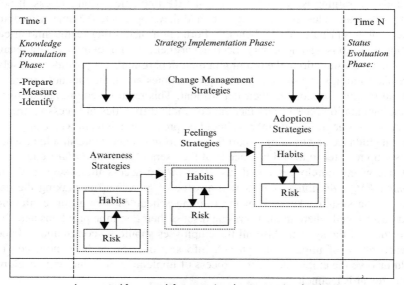

A suggested framework for managing change associated with ERP

This strategy tells us the way implementation of ERP should be approached. At first the awareness about the new system should be generated by studying the existing habits and objections of the employees if any. The next logical step is to create an environment where technology should be seen as enabler rather than an inhibitor to progress. The low exposure of personnel at OPGC to technology creates an additional challenge. For example, some users may raise issues about their computer illiteracy, or may say that they have spent many years doing an excellent job without help from an ERP system. Other users may develop beliefs that their jobs will be threatened by the new system, or that they will not know how to do the job within the scope of such a system. Yet another group of users may stress values such as the importance of existing power and authority structures, which may be jeopardized by the new ERP system. An effective change management program should place the end users at its core in order to succeed. The following provides a broad framework for Change management at OPGC.

Requirements for change management
Dimensions of change management programme

Requirements for Change Management

- Individuals throughout the organisation must clearly understand what is expected of them
- Individuals must have the tools, skills, and competencies to do what is expected of them
- Individuals must be held accountable for their performance of these expectations
- Leadership must be proactively engaged and active in the change process
- Linking change with individual performance, motivation, upward movement, and awards/incentives.

Dimensions of Change Management Programme

- Defining the drivers for change in organisation and individuals
- Defining specific changes to be instituted at various levels
- Communications and stakeholders participation in finalising the required change
- Mobilising commitment to change across the organisation
- Defining steps for implementing change
- Monitoring, feedback, and evaluation to measure the impact of change
- Integrating change into the HR policies and functions
- Linking change with individual performance, motivation, upward movement, and awards/incentives

5.7.4.2 Strategy Implementation Phase

The three-level adoption process (think-feel-do) provides a good framework for describing this phase. In an attempt to change the attitudes of potential users of ERP, management must first try to affect the cognitive component of users' attitudes. A major strategy and driver for achieving this goal is communication. One effective communication strategy is to inform potential users of the benefits of ERP. Top management should take interest in more effective awareness for the ERP system by communicating its benefits to the workers management. It should clarify the general inputs and outputs of the system, determine departments that will provide the data, and define the computer knowledge needed to operate the system. Involvement of all stakeholders is critical to implementation and commitment to the cause of implementation. Another important factor is to define the steps of implementation clearly and enough mechanisms should be put in place to monitor and evaluate the implementation strategy and improvements can be thought of. As the implementation picks up pace and the system becomes life of the organization, integrating change in the HR policies and linking individual performance with the usage and adoption of technology should be done. This is to ensure that the culture change and embracing the technology takes place at faster place.

5.7.4.3 Change Management Team

Team	Responsibilities	Representation from company	Representation from consultants
Implementation team	• Project management and decision-making • Prepare the overall rollout plan across the organization • Strategic direction to implementation • Tracks goals	• Managing director • Technical experts (3–5) • Top management	• Project managers (3–5) • Consultants (7–10)
Core group team	• Training the middle management • Define success criteria for completion	• Inter-department technical • Middle management	• Project managers (3) • Consultants (0–3)
User group team	• Supervising development of training materials and imparting training to end users • Reporting progress at defined milestones	• Junior management • Workers	• Nil

Source: OPGC-AES Implementation Team Member, 1999

5.7.5 Proposed IT Organization Structure Changes

5.7.5.1 Mission and Goal of IT

The IT department should have a mission and goal which is in alignment with the business goals of the organization. The following is the proposed mission and goal for OPGC.

The Mission and Goal of IT is to facilitate the availability of timely and accurate information needed by the operational units to manage the day-to-day business and strategic directions of the company in achieving its objective and becoming one of the leader in its industry segment by developing, implementing and maintaining a reliable IT system.

5.7.5.2 Appointment of CIO

The study recommends the appointment of a CIO in the company to guide the implementation of IT strategy. The benefits of having a CIO are numerous: from having an IT vision for the company to leveraging on cost competitiveness to offer great customer satisfaction. The CIO would also need a separate organization structure to accommodate the IT related workforce.

The following are the responsibilities of CIO in OPGC

- Provide strategic and tactical planning, development, evaluation, and coordination of the information and technology systems for the organization.
- Facilitate communication between staff, management, vendors, and other technology resources within the organization.
- Oversee the back office computer operations of the affiliate management information system, including local area networks and wide-area networks.
- Responsible for the management of multiple information and communications systems and projects, including voice, data, imaging, and office automation.
- Designs, implements, and evaluates the systems that support end users in the productive use of computer hardware and software.
- Develop and implement user-training programs.
- Oversees and evaluates system security and back up procedures. Supervises the Network Administrator.

5.7.5.3 Formation of Steering Committee

For successful implementation of the IT strategy there is a need to form a horizontal structure steering committee to involve the various organization levels of OPGC. The steering committee would be the most important group involved in the planning process and would be instrumental in the success of the plan and implementation and ongoing governance. The steering committee would provide OPGC with a voice from all areas of the business. This group will formulate recommendations regarding project priorities and resources and provide input regarding the strategic direction of IT systems implementation. The Key role of the steering committee would be to ensure that the project focuses on business objective and has the required resources.

Organizational structure for IT strategy implementation

Composition

This committee will typically consist of department heads and functional heads, or managers from the various business departments and functional areas of OPGC such as finance, maintenance, planning, inventory, etc. It will also have representation from different plants of OPGC spread across Orissa.

Although it is critical to have major business areas represented, it would be difficult to manage at group larger than 12 individuals. So the size of the size of the group would be kept to around 12–14 members which is small enough to efficiently conduct meetings and make decisions. In case the members of steering committee are in physically different geographical locations then the meetings would be held through video conferencing or teleconferencing.

5.7 Approach for Implementation of IT Strategy

The Steering Committee members would need to have executive level decision-making authority, a high level industry and business understanding, strategic level perspective and a fundamental understanding of the importance of communication, the role of leadership action and competence in creating the right psychological climate for change.

The reason that executive management of OPGC is involved in IT strategy planning is the straightforward. In the implementation process it they who will ultimately approve or reject the expenditure of funds. Executive Management's involvement in the steering committee will make the approval process significantly easier.

Specialized working groups can be formed by the steering committee to study various aspects of the IT systems implementation process, prepare the blue print, set time schedules and facilitate the implementation. Services of outside experts and consultants can be engaged to further professionalize the process.

Function

The steering committee will provide recommendations in the allocation of resources and monitor project progress against the approved plan. The group will monitor

- Whether estimated hours to complete the project exceeds the predetermined amount of hours
- Whether departmental boundaries are crossed during implementation of project and the resolution of such standoffs
- Whether capital expenditure and non-recurring costs exceed the predetermined budget
- Whether recurring costs are exceeding the yearly predetermined budget

This group would also be the vehicle for end users to propose and recommend changes in the IT systems. The group will prioritize these tasks and projects and determine hours and cost limit thresholds for each of these tasks.

It will also establish an approval level for each of the projects so that the committee is focussed on major projects rather than work orders and small requests from end users.

Following the 80/20 rule, 20% of the projects will use 80% of the resources, it is this 20% that will have to be managed by the steering committee.

The steering committee will also

- Provide communication to other members in the organization regarding the IT activities
- Sponsor and initiate business process reengineering projects
- Commit to deliver business benefits identified in the projects
- Communicate and discuss functional business issue arising from IT activities—for e.g. if the maintenance department wants to structure bill of material or product number one way and the engineering department wants it the other way
- Review IT standards and procedures which will have an impact on the other business functions
- Approve allocation of budget for IT implementation

5.7.5.4 Roles and Responsibilities

Chairperson

The Chairperson would schedule, organize, document and chair the steering committee meetings. The Chairperson would typically be the CIO or IT Department head in OPGC.

Vice Chairperson

The position shall provide support to the Chairperson. The Chairperson may also direct the Vice Chairperson to perform certain functions which the Chairperson is unable to carry out, such as preparation of the meeting's agenda, running regular meetings, and making formal presentations on the steering committee and its work to Executive Management and Board of Governors.

Managing Director or Executive Committee Member

Executive Management's involvement in the steering committee will make the approval process significantly easier. They will provide the necessary business vision and alignment to the committee.

Task Group Leaders

The departmental heads which are members of the steering committee would be acting as project or task leaders for different projects. These task group leaders will study various aspects of the IT systems implementation process, prepare the blue print, set time schedules and facilitate the implementation. At the discretion of the Chairperson of the committee each of the task group leaders may also perform other department related functions or oversee special task and duties as deemed necessary. For example, the departmental head of finance would overlook implementation of ERP modules in the Finance department of the organization.

Functional Experts/Consultant

The committee can also consist of ERP consultants and functional experts who would help the steering committee with understanding the technicalities of the technology and help in dealing with any issues with the vendor. This would also help in further professionalizing the committee. Additionally sometimes the vendor may themselves as a functional consultant on the steering committee.

The steering committee should document the meeting decisions, conversation and topics. Out of town members should be sent material and notes from the meetings whenever they are not able to attend critical meetings. Also steering committee should post these minutes and presentations on bulletin boards across the organization for all the employees to see. Getting as much visibility to the information as possible is critical.

Additional members from the IT department and implementation team can attend meetings as required to provide information or to give presentations. The business representatives should feel that they are giving direction to the committee which would not be the case if committee includes too many members from the IT department and implementation team.

5.8 Cost Benefit Analysis: ROI

Before starting any large implementation project, it needs to be examined if the implementation makes economic and social sense. The business requirement needs to exist before approving and starting any project. OPGC needs to have this culture of decision-making which is need driven before all technology investments. Proprietary solutions are available from many software vendors which can give OPGC the ability to create a strategic edge. Another option is the use of in house software but the problem with this approach is the significant development cost involved. But in some cases due to the peculiar nature of the industry proprietary solutions have significant limitations. The amounts of customization required in case of such industries typically outdo the cost that would have been involved in developing them in-house.

In our recommendations, we are not advocating the use of proprietary software only from the cost point of view but from other benefits as well. These are further elaborated below.

5.8 Cost Benefit Analysis: ROI

	Annual Increase	2010	2011	2012	2013	2014
IT Implemetation cost						
SAP Rollout	0.00%	12.00000	5.00000	1.00000	1.00000	1.00000
Additional Software	0.00%	2.00000	1.00000	1.00000	1.00000	1.00000
Training	0.00%	1.50000	0.05000	0.00050	0.00050	0.00050
Personnel	10.00%	3.00000	3.30000	3.63000	3.99300	4.39230
Hardware	−20.00%	8.00000	1.00000	1.00000	1.00000	1.00000
Performance Monitoring System	0.00%	2.00000	1.00000	1.00000	1.00000	1.00000
Plant Management System	0.00%	1.50000	1.00000	1.00000	1.00000	1.00000
Energy Mangement System	0.00%	3.00000	1.00000	1.00000	1.00000	1.00000
Website Enhancement	0.00%	0.50000	0.05000	0.05000	0.05000	0.05000
Consultancy Charges	−10.00%	5.00000	0.05000	0.05000	0.05000	0.05000
TOTAL (in Rs Crores)		38.50000	13.45000	9.73050	10.09350	10.49280
Operational and Maintenance costs						
Change Management	−10.00%	0.01000	0.00900	0.00909	0.00917	0.00926
Security Costs	10.00%	0.05000	0.05500	0.05775	0.06093	0.06444
ISO Certification Cost	0.00%	0.03000	0.00500	0.00500	0.00500	0.00500
Maintenace Charges	2.00%	0.00500	0.00510	0.00513	0.00515	0.00518
Miscellaneous IT cost	2.00%	0.03000	0.03060	0.03152	0.03248	0.03351
ICT Charges	5.00%	0.04000	0.04200	0.04368	0.04551	0.04750
TOTAL		0.16500	0.14670	0.15216	0.15825	0.16489
Total Costs (In Crores)		38.66500	13.59670	9.88266	10.25175	10.65769

Cost Reduction	Annual Increase	2010	2011	2012	2013	2014
Coal Inventory reduction	10.00%	5.0000	5.5000	6.0500	6.6550	7.3205
Reduction in warehouse Cost	10.00%	0.5000	0.5500	0.6050	0.6655	0.7321
Stock record accuracy	10.00%	0.2000	0.2200	0.2640	0.3221	0.4071
Lead time reduction	10.00%	1.0000	1.1000	1.2100	1.3310	1.4641
Bill of material accuracy	20.00%	0.0100	0.0120	0.0144	0.0173	0.0207
Dematerialisation of Physical goods(Paper less office)	10.00%	0.8000	0.8800	0.9680	1.0648	1.1713
Streamlining of Tender Process	20.00%	0.0100	0.0120	0.0121	0.0123	0.0124
Reduction in Manpower Cost	20.00%	0.0200	0.0240	0.0288	0.0346	0.0415
Quality Control	10.00%	1.0000	1.1000	1.2100	1.3310	1.4641
Reduction through ERP Finance & Control (FICO)	25.00%	0.5000	0.6250	0.7813	0.9766	1.2207
Reduction in project cycle time	20.00%	1.0000	1.2000	1.4400	1.7280	2.0736
Efficient Vendor Management						
Increase in Sales						
Increase in Capacity Utilisation	10%	5	5.5	6.05	6.655	7.3205
Meeting Delivery Schedule	5%	0.05	0.0525	0.055125	0.057881	0.060775313
Improved Worker Productivity	15%	1	1.15	1.3225	1.520875	1.74900625
Efficient Use of Equipments	5%	2.00	2.10	2.21	2.32	2.43
Improvement in Energy Efficiency	10%	2.00	2.20	2.42	2.66	2.93
Improved raw material forecasting	10%	0.50	0.55	0.61	0.67	0.73
Improved Demand forecasting	5%	0.50	0.53	0.55	0.58	0.61
Improved Grid Efficiency	5%	1.00	1.05	1.10	1.16	1.22
Brand Equity/Good Will						
Improved Employee morale	15%	1.00	1.15	1.32	1.52	1.75
Improved Vendor/Supplier Relations	20%	0.50	0.60	0.72	0.86	1.04
Reach out to New Customers	20%	1.00	1.20	1.44	1.73	2.07
Improved Quality	15%	0.50	0.58	0.66	0.76	0.87
Contribution to Environment	20%	0.50	0.60	0.72	0.86	1.04
Increase in Human Capital	10%	0.50	0.55	0.83	1.28	2.33
Total Benefits (In Crores)		26.0900	29.0255	32.5837	36.7671	42.0773

Current Financial Year	2010
Discount Rate	20%

	2010	2011	2012	2013	2014
Total Benefits (1)	26.09	29.03	32.58	36.77	42.08
Total costs (2)	38.67	13.60	9.88	10.25	10.66
Present value of Costs	38.67	11.33	6.86	5.93	5.14
NPV	67.93				
Free Cash Flows (3)=(1-2)	(12.58)	15.43	22.70	26.52	31.42
Present value of FCFs	(12.58)	12.86	15.76	15.34	15.15
NPV	46.54				
ROI	1.46				

For the calculation of the ROI of the IT strategy, we have assumed a 5-year horizon and a discount rate of 20%. The breakeven period for the investment was estimated to be 18 months.

To get a positive ROI OPGC has to minimize the investment and optimize the results from the investment. The cost of maintenance should be kept a bare minimum as the personnel cost can significantly add up to the overall cost. The following is a guideline for companies in order to have positive ROI from their IT investment.

Ensure that the software being licenced does not exceed the foreseeable business and functional needs of the organization.

- Develop a clear road map for the full exploitation of functionality to a wide breadth of users and departments within a reasonable period of time.
- Conduct a thorough review of reference users in similar industries to evaluate whether the promised benefits really apply to the industry and the user base in question.
- Avoid excessive customization of the solution and its interfaces, focusing instead on deploying a usable system that will deliver returns within a measurable time frame.
- Conduct a pre deployment ROI analysis that evaluates expected returns and costs, taking into account the probability of achieving those returns and the payback period for the investment.

5.9 Risk Analysis

Risk analysis consists of assessing the importance of threats and how to mitigate or eliminate them. We usually evaluate a threat in terms of how likely it is to materialize and how much damage or cost would result if it did materialize. Consequently, risk analysis can be thought of as having five basic steps:

1. Identifying the source of threats
2. Assessing the extent of potential
3. Damage or cost to the project
4. Assessing the likelihood of the threat materializing, and
5. Devising ways to reduce or eliminate the threat (i.e. mitigate the risk)

A risk management form is to be used to capture the details of a risk. A sample form is given below:

5.9.1 Probability Determination for Identified Risks

Magnitude	Capability factor	Cost factor	Schedule factor
0.1 Low	Minimal or no consequences, unimportant	Budget estimates not exceeded, some transfer of money	Negligible impact on other development schedules; changes compensated by available slack
0.3 Moderate	Small reduction in capability (10% requirements not met)	Cost estimates exceed budget by 1–5%	Minor slip in schedules (less than 1 month), small adjustments in milestones required
0.5 High	Some reduction in capability (25% requirements not met)	Cost estimates increased by 5–20%	Other schedules slip in excess of 3 months; a few projects are shelved
0.7 Significant	Significant reduction in capability (50% requirements not met)	Cost estimates increased by 20–50%	Other schedules slip up to 12 months; many projects are shelved
0.9 Catastrophic	Technical goals cannot be achieved	Cost estimates increased in excess of 50%	Other schedules slip more than 12 months; most projects are shelved

5.9.2 Risk Mitigation

Risk	Probability	Impact (scale 1–5)	Risk mitigation plan
Over-relying on automated systems might lead to shortcuts for decision-making	0.8	4	Design intelligent systems to take on the work when the operator is overloaded and pass it on to the operator, when he is under loaded
Maintaining database of all sensitive information leads to various security risks like			
Physical threats to the database	0.3	3	Back up database and infrastructure
Technical failure	0.4	4	-do-
Infrastructure failure	0.2	4	-do-
Potential cost and schedule impacts	0.7	2	Oversee contractors and delivery vendors
Obsolescence	0.7	2	Review and update regularly
Data security	0.5	4	Restricted access arrangements and audits
Regulatory and compliance risk	0.2	4	Periodic inspections to check regulatory compliance
Standards and certifications	0.3	2	Robust checks and constant updating

5.10 Practice Questions

1. What are the characteristics of utilities industry?
2. How is OPGC positioned in Indian Utilities sector?
3. What are the critical success factors that affect IT Strategy for OPGC?
4. What are the application integration strategies in IT Strategy?
5. How will you measure benefits of all stakeholders?
6. What are the components of IT strategy implementation?

5.11 Appendix

5.11.1 Appendix 1: OPGC Financial Credentials

Sl. No.	Description	FY 05-06	FY 06-07	FY 07-08
1.	Turnover in crores	439.82	477.07	484.69
2.	Profit in crores	161.91	170.22	168.70

5.11.2 Appendix 2: Questionnaire

- Vision and mission of the company.
- Business objectives to achieve the mission stated.
- Business processes followed. How it has evolved over the years?
- Shortcomings in the current business processes.
- Average life of business processes.
- Ongoing changes in the business process being implemented. Plans for implementation in the future.
- Current metrics for measurement of efficiency of the business processes.
- If documentation procedure is in place for the activities involved in your Business processes?
- What are the training and development procedures that you follow for your employees?
- What are the risk mitigation plans and procedures that you follow?
- Safety policy within the company.
- Presence of any safety management system in the company. If yes Processes in place to monitor and manage safety standards.
- Capability and proficiency to handle all the business requirements and safety procedure.
- Presence of a proper environmental policy.
- Procedures and practices in place to manage the environmental policy.
- Issues and concerns within the current framework and scope for improvement.

5.11.3 Appendix 3: Topology of the Earlier System (Source OPGC)

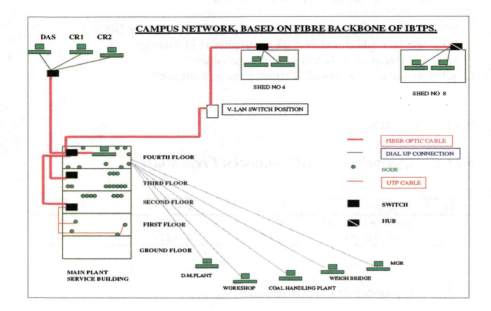

5.11.4 Appendix 4: Sample Risk Management Form

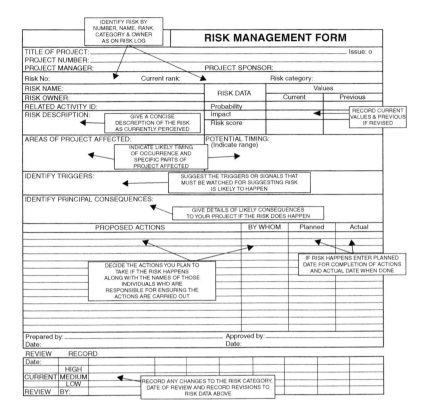

5.11.5 Appendix 5: OPGC Balance Sheet

ORISSA POWER GENERATION CORPORATION LTD. BHUBANESWAR
BALANCE SHEET AS AT 31ST MARCH, 2007

Amount in Rs.

Particulars	Schedules	As at 31.03.2007		As at 31.03.2006	
SOURCES OF FUND					
Shareholder's Fund :					
Share Capital	1	4,902,174,000		4,902,174,000	
Reserves & Surplus	2	3,068,526,246	7,970,700,246	1,422,560,207	6,324,734,207
Loan Funds	3				
Secured Loans		-			
Unsecured Loans		513,422,126	513,422,126	763,145,545	763,145,545
Deferred Tax Liabilities(Net)	4	384,986,543	384,986,453	239,762,221	239,762,221
TOTAL			**8,869,108,825**		**7,327,641,973**
APPLICATION OF FUNDS					
Fixed Assets	5				
Gross Block		11,374,799,818		11,356,099,843	
Less Depreciation		8,185,306,301		7,579,124,181	
Net Block		**3,189,493,517**		**3,776,975,662**	
Capital Work-in-progress					
including Construction		178,789,409		167,586,479	
Stores & Advances	6		3,368,282,926		3,944,562,141
Current Assets, Loans & Advances	7				
Inventories		296,225,373		297,904,970	
Sundry Debtors		960,442,921		1,105,744,568	
Cash & Bank Balances		3,990,489,824		2,616,989,180	
Other Current Assets		158,864,472		122,285,775	
Loans & Advances		486,742,689,		189,147,287	
		5,892,765,279		**4,332,071,780**	
Less Current Liabilities & Provisions	8				
Liabilities		244,679,632		291,846,575	
Provisions		171,276,704		681,288,571	
		415,956,336		973,135,146	
Net Current Assets / (liabilities)			5,476,808,943		3,358,936,634
Miscellaneous Expenditure	9				
(To the extent not written off or adjusted)		24,016,956	24,016,956	24,143,198	24,143,198
TOTAL			**8,869,108,825**		**7,327,641,973**

5.11 Appendix 227

5.11.6 Appendix 6: OPGC Internal Target Operating Model

References

http://www.NucleusResearch.com
Manual on best practices in Indian Thermal Power Generating Units, CII-Sohrabji Godrej Green Business Centre
http://web.njit.edu/~jerry/OM/OM-ERP-Papers/ERP-10-Success.pdf
http://www.ciol.com/ciol-techportal/content/erp/interviews/2006/2060804644.asp
http://www.ctg.albany.edu/publications/guides/roi
http://www.smthacker.co.uk/introduction_to_benchmarking.html
http://www.oracle.com/corporate/analystportal/insider/nucleus_real_ROI_SAP_2003.pdf
Kaplan & Norton (1992) The balanced scorecard – measures that drive performance. Harvard Business Review

Chapter 6
Case Study: IT Strategy for Mayfair

6.1 Learning Objectives

This case explains how information system is used as a comprehensive, integrated strategic tool in Mayfair which helps to manage the administrative, financial, and customer delight aspects of a chain of hotels. The case also illustrates how the information system ensures smooth flow of information between different departments which reduces costs and improves the accuracy and timeliness of customer care, new business strategy implementation, and management reporting. The case has been developed through visits to the hotel and secondary sources of information. This case can be taught in Information System Strategy course, hospitality certification programs, postgraduate diploma courses, executive MBA programs, MCA and MSc (Computer Science) courses. The case can be used to illustrate the following themes:

– Characteristics of hospitality industry.
– How information system will help in achieving its business objectives?
– How to calculate ROI for technological investment?
– What are the factors to be considered for implementing information systems?

6.2 Executive Summary

Mayfair is a fast-growing hotel chain in India. It has a strong presence in Eastern part of the country with presence in popular commercial and business locations such as Bhubaneswar, Puri, Rourkela, etc. This project was aimed at preparing an IT strategy for the company.

As for any strategic framework, an understanding of the industry trends is very important. The same has been provided along with the description of the major players in the industry. With increasing IT and business interdependence, IT has become a strategic arm for most organizations. With this view, the vision and mission of the company have been prepared for the organization. Next, a set of business objectives were prepared which shall help the hotel in achieving its long-term objectives. The corporate strategy which gives the direction to all business decisions was arrived at using two techniques—Balance Score Card and SWOT analysis.

To understand better the performance of Mayfair relative to other leading hotels in this range and at a level above this, Benchmarking technique was used. Benchmarking was done against 8 hotels including international hotels against 20 parameters. This helped in doing the gap-analysis. There are several interlinked business processes in the hotel industry which need to be identified. Our of the several business processes, the key ones which influence the performance of operations the most, were identified. The IT strategy will primarily focus on making these selected processes more efficient.

There are several stakeholders in the strategy formulation which get affected in the implementation. These stakeholders have been identified to address their respective concerns through the strategy. In addition to the stakeholders, there are factors that affect the IT strategy such as the industry characteristics, the organization, etc. which have been kept in mind while forming the strategy. The need for a CIO was identified, and the responsibilities for the same have been provided.

An IT-business process mapping has been provided for efficient solution design. Additionally, a technology framework has been provided for implementation. The organization structure for the implementation including the steering committee has been suggested. The roles and responsibilities for the implementation have been described in detail. The roadmap for implementation and an elaborate implementation plan have been provided.

Training and change management are critical aspects of IT strategy to tackle resistance and ensuring project success. The strategies for the same have been described. The communication strategy helps in keeping the employees aware of the changes in the organization and keeps them motivated. Another complementary approach in motivating employees is reward and recognition.

Since IT projects involve high investments, a thorough analysis of the return on investment is a must for the management to decide on the implementation feasibility. Also, the major benefits of the IT strategy implementation such as reporting, business integration have been highlighted. Finally, the system risks and the subsequent risk mitigation plan have been covered too in the IT strategy framework.

6.3 Hospitality Industry

6.3.1 Introduction

Hospitality is about serving the guests to provide them with a *feel-good effect*. It refers to the process of receiving and entertaining a guest with goodwill. India with its centuries old civilization is perhaps one of the few nations, which has a cultural heritage that is rich, diverse, and unique. In India, guests are treated with utmost warmth and respect (Atithi Devo Bhavo—Guest is God). They are served with the best services. Hospitality is deep rooted in our traditions and comes as an integral part of our heritage.

The hospitality industry is a major service sector in the world economy. Today, hospitality has evolved from the basic food and accommodation industry and taken a very important position in almost all businesses. In fact, it has become a huge industry and drives economies across the globe. The scope of hospitality/service industry today is far more than one could have ever imagined a few years back. The hospitality industry is a 3.5 trillion dollar service sector within the global economy. It is very diverse and global. The industry is cyclical, dictated by the fluctuations that occur with an economy every year. Indian hospitality industry has gained a level of acceptance world over. It has yet to go miles for recognition as a world leader of hospitality.

6.3.2 Characteristics

It is one of the fastest growing sectors and is expected to grow at the rate of 8% between 2007 and 2016. Tourism contributes around 5.9% of India's GDP. It has a cascading effect on the hotel industry. Below is the customer profile in FY 2004:

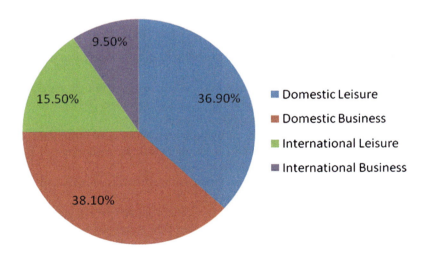

Many international hotels such as Sheraton, Hyatt, Radisson, etc. are well established and expanding. Top players in India are the following:

- ITC Hotels
- The Taj Hotels, Resorts, and Palaces
- Oberoi Hotels
- Hotel Leela Venture

Hospitality Industry includes the following:

- Accommodation
- Food and beverage
- Travel and tourism
- Recreation and entertainment

Industry is very dependent on Metropolitan cities (75–80% revenue comes from Metros).

Critical factors determining profitability:

- Average room rate (ARR) Increase in room rates over the last year has been 22–25%.
- Occupancy rate (OC)—currently, it is around 80–85% (Up nearly 10% in last 3 years).

The hotels in India can be classified as follows:

- Five Star and Five-Star Deluxe
- Heritage Hotels
- Budget Hotels
- Unclassified

6.3.3 Issues and Challenges

- *Shortage of skilled employees*—Unavailability of quality workforce at different skill levels.
- *Retaining quality workforce*—Retention of employees through training and development in the hospitality industry is a big challenge. Though there is a boom in the sector, the wages are still highly unattractive.
- *Shortage of rooms*—In India, the current requirement is 1, 50,000 rooms. Even after government's new investment plans, there will be a shortage of rooms. Supply is not able to cater to the demands.
- *Intense competition*—The industry is facing competitions from arrival of foreign players.
- *Image of India*—Negative perceptions about India due to terrorist attacks, political instability have led to an unhealthy image of the country.
- *Manual back-end*—In most of the hotels, data is manually entered in log books and is simply not tracked.
- *Human resource development*—Some of the services required in the tourism and the hotel industry are highly personalized, and no amount of automation can substitute for personal service providers. The shortage of blue-collar employees is an issue.

6.3.4 Major players

The Hotel Industry mainly has following major players:

6.3.4.1 Hotel Chains

The major hotel chains in India include The Taj Group, The Oberoi Group, and ITC Welcome Hotels. Most of these hotel chains were well established in one or more of the metro cities before the tourist boom began in the 80s. Subsequent to the tourism boom, these chains aggressively expanded their presence in other locations. The private players among the hotel chains are industry leaders and have well-established brand identities across the different industry segments.

6.3.4.2 Small Chains

Several small hotel chains have mushroomed in the country since the tourism boom of the 1980s and 1990s. As a strategic decision, these players have preferred to opt for operating and management arrangements with international players of high standards, due to their lack of prior experience in the hotel industry. Some of the companies in this category are Bharat Hotels (formerly with Holiday Inn and Hilton and now with Intercontinental), Hotel Leela Venture (with Kempinski), and Asian Hotels (Hyatt International Corporation). As late entrants, most of these hotel companies have fewer properties, compared with the big chains. However, these players are coming up in a big way, and most of these players have initiated expansion plans during the late 1990s.

6.3.4.3 Public Sector Hotel Chains

The major advantage that government run hotel chains enjoy is that they have hotels in the best locations in most cities of the country. For example, ITDC and HCI, though underperformers, boast of some of the best locations in major cities, as compared to the locations of the hotels by their private sector counterparts.

6.3.4.4 International Hotel Chains

Recognizing the boom in tourists visiting the country from abroad, several foreign hotel chains have set up hotels in Indian cities. These chains target the Indian market by either entering into joint ventures with established Indian partners or by entering into management or franchisee contracts. Some of the leading hotel chains that come under this category are Marriott, Emaar MGF, and Starwood. Most of these chains have high expansion plans and focus toward entering the budget hotel segment in the tier II cities.

6.3.4.5 Regional Hotel Companies

There are a good number of hotels which are well known but have a regional presence only. For instance, LMB at Jaipur, Swosti in Bhubaneswar, etc. These hotels have a loyal customer base and have limited plans of expansion and focus only on a steady organic growth.

6.4 Mayfair

6.4.1 About Mayfair

Mayfair lagoon is the only five-star Hotel in eastern India besides Trident. It is a low rise hotel spread across 10 acres of land of which 1.5 acres is a lagoon. It has 102 rooms with 56 standard cottages, 6 deluxe cottages and 2 Villas. The average occupancy of hotel is about 55–60% which varies according to season. The number of repeat customers is high which is a proof of customer satisfaction. Corporate clients form the majority of the customers. Some FIT (Free Independent Travelers) also visit the hotel. They are not given any discount. The price of hotel rooms varies according to seasonality. There are group and corporate discount schemes also. There are different types of packages available most of the time depending on the time of visit such as monsoon package, festival package, etc. The information about these packages is given whenever a customer enquires about the availability. The normal prices of Mayfair lagoon are given below. The prices of various amenities and room rent are revised annually.

6.4.1.1 Price list

	Single Occupancy	Double Occupancy	Size
Executive Cottage	9000	9000	750 sqft
Deluxe Cottage	16000	16000	1750 sqft
Executive Room	9000	9000	750 sqft
Deluxe Suite	16000	16000	1200 sqft
Villa	30000	30000	3000 sqft

6.4.2 Services offered

Deluxe cottages

- Personal fax machines
- Two dedicated telephone lines
- A personal computer with 24 hr Internet connection
- 2 television sets
- DVDs
- Private car park
- Minibar

Suites/Villas

- Regent & Royal
- Round-the-clock butler service

- Three dedicated Phone lines
- Private study with library

  Business services

- Banking
- Banquet hall
- Conference hall

  Leisure and other services

- Swimming pool
- Travel desk
- Doctor on call

  Recreation

- Fitness center
- Spa facility

6.4.2.1 Allied Business Activities

- 10 Downing Street
- Banquet
- Baron and Baroness (Pub)
- Kanika (Oriya Restaurant)
- Lemon Grass
- Mayfair Breads and Cookies
- Minibar
- Nakli Dhaba
- Outdoor Catering
- Orissa Restaurant
- Room service
- Super snax
- Mayfair Spa
- Tea Pot

6.4.2.2 Feedback Mechanism

The hotel has an excellent feedback mechanism. When a customer is checking out he is requested to fill the feedback form. In case he is not able to fill due to lack of time, Guest relation Executive talks to them and takes down the main points. There are different feedback forms for different departments. The feedback forms once collected is then studied and main point is taken down which is then checked if that service can be improved in any way.

6.4.3 Future Plans

- Just launched Mayfair Gangtok Spa Resort & Casino in Gangtok which has bamboo and forest retreats as well as conference room with 200 people capacity.
- The group will also launch its convention center in Bhubaneswar, which post launch will be the biggest in the city with a total capacity of 1,200 people.
- The group plans foray into western part of the country with Mayfair Goa
- The group will also plan to set up properties and acquire land in Cuttack, Chilika Lake, Kalimpong, and Siliguri by 2010.
- The company plans to hit the capital market with an initial public offer (IPO) in about 24 to 36 months after utilization of the proceeds of the 19.7 percent equity issued to SBI in an Private equity deal

6.5 Vision

To achieve 1000 room inventory in major tourist circuits, industrial and commercial hubs of the country by 2012

6.6 Mission

To be the first choice in providing hospitality at each location of our presence through continuous innovation, service excellence and perfection.

6.7 Business Objectives

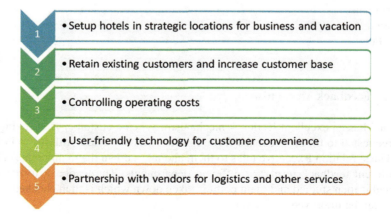

6.8 Corporate Strategy

The corporate strategy for Mayfair has been prepared based on the following strategic tools—Balance Score Card and SWOT Analysis.

6.8.1 Balance Score Card

The BSC helps us prioritize the various parameters and issues that need to be addressed in formulating the IT strategy. This is done by grouping the various parameters into relevant heads and then assigning weights to them.

BSC—Mayfair				
Areas	Weights	Performance Measure	Measure	Weights
Customer Perspective	0.35	Customer Satisfaction Index (CSI)	Customer feedback ? database	0.3
		Customer Escalations/ Complaints	Number of customer escalations	0.1
		Value-added services	Additional services to customers such as on-demand entertainment	0.2
		User-friendly technology	Making services and information more accessible	0.2
		Customer References	New customers referred by existing customers	0.2
Financial	0.3	Gross Profit Margin (%)	Effectiveness of a company at cost control	0.15
		% increase in revenues	Increase in sales of company over a period of time	0.1
		Operating margin	Pricing strategy and operating efficiency	0.2
		Net income	Profitability of the company over a period of time	0.1
		Operating cash flow	How well current liabilities are covered by the cash flow generated from a company's operations?	0.2
		Net Interest Margin	How successful a firm's investment decisions are compared to its debt situations?	0.1
		Current Ratio	Measures a company's ability to pay short-term obligations	0.15

(continued)

BSC—Mayfair				
Areas	Weights	Performance Measure	Measure	Weights
Internal Processes	0.25	Employee Satisfaction Index	Employee Satisfaction Index	0.2
		Training and Development	Mandatory training hours	0.3
		Skill upgradation	Multiskill attributes	0.2
		Operational efficiency	Reduced operational and logistics costs	0.2
		Performance Measure	Client feedback on performance	0.1
Community initiatives	0.1	Green technologies	Reduction in energy consumption and resources	0.3
		Environment friendly operations	Waste control and campus greenery	0.3
		Corporate Social Responsibility	Local community employment and social initiatives	0.4

Customer Perspective is assigned maximum weightage because of the nature of the industry.

6.8.2 SWOT Analysis

The SWOT analysis provides a 360 degree analysis of the firm with respect to its internal as well as external environment. The strengths and weaknesses are internal to Mayfair, in the sense that these can be controlled by Mayfair. However, the opportunities and threats are external to the system and beyond the organization's control. Though beyond the control, an analysis of the opportunities and threats helps the organization in being prepared for future.

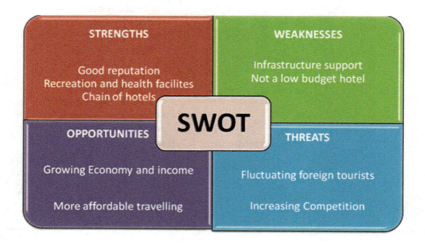

6.8 Corporate Strategy

Having analysed the two approaches, we can now arrive at the corporate strategy for Mayfair. These strategies have been grouped into relevant heads for better understanding.

Customer Centricity
- Technology investment
- Innovation

Internal Focus
- Develop multi-skilled workforce
- Employee retention
- Operational efficiency

Community Responsibility
- Environment friendly operations
- Corporate Social Initiatives

6.8.3 Business Problem Statement

6.8.4 What Is the Problem/Issue at Hand?

- To expand room inventory to 1000 by 2012 and be the first choice in providing hospitality to the customers.

6.8.4.1 Key Concepts on which the Problem Rests

- *Service efficiency*
  The company is striving to offer top-of-class service to existing and new customers. This involves process improvements and optimizations at various operational levels.
- *Customer centricity*
  Increasingly, almost all organizations across industries have started realizing that the need of the hour is customer focus. It is all the more pertinent in service industries particularly the hospitality industry. Offering customized services to the clients is a step in this direction.
- *Employee engagement*
  Employee retention is an important concern for most organizations and Mayfair is no exception to it. Organizations invest a lot of money in hiring and training employees, hence, retention is critical. Higher employee morale shall get reflected in better client service.

6.8.4.2 Constructs

6.8.5 Interrelationship of These Concepts: "Constructs"

- Better quality service to the consumers can be provided by focusing on customer's needs and wants
- The industry is seeing a trend of acquisitions for inorganic growth; thus, process standardization in diverse acquired hotels is desirable
- The competition for the hotel group may come from not only traditional hotels but also upcoming service apartments.
- The overall brand image of the hotel group has to be very strong in the customers mind for top-of-mind recall and to become the preferred choice of hotel
- Human resource practices should be employee friendly for higher morale and productivity

6.8.5.1 Fundamental Constructs

6.8.6 What Is/Are Fundamental in this Construct W.R.T. the Issue?

- Customer centricity is the key for success in hospitality industry and hence continuous improvement in operational processes and services offered is necessary

6.8.6.1 Research Question

- How should Information Technology, as a strategic business partner, be leveraged to achieve the overall business goals for sustainable growth in hospitality sector?

6.8.6.2 Key Variables

The three core concepts (Service efficiency, Customer centricity and Employee engagement) can be further subdivided to arrive at several variables. These variables shall form the foundation of the subsequent questionnaire. The variables have been grouped into relevant categories.

Dependent Variables

- Repeat customers
- Customer delight
- Turnover
- Employee retention
- Safety
- Room inventory
- Customer database
- Turnaround time

Independent Variables

- Customer profiling
- Competitor's tactics
- Incentive schemes
- Process integration
- Room design
- On-demand entertainment

Moderating Variables (other independent variable):

- Online reservation
- Value added services
- Emergency services

Intervening Variable

- New hotel facilities (expansion)
- Acquisitions
- Standardization

Extraneous

- Resource crunch (shortage of skilled employees in the organization)
- Economic and business environment

6.9 Benchmarking

6.9.1 Scope of Benchmarking

1. To identify the IT implementation in other organizations in hospitality industry
2. Understand standards that are followed
3. Technology implementations used
4. Overall return on investment in IT
5. Process improvement recommendations

The following is an overview on the benchmarking process:

6.9.2 Benchmarking with Similar Hotels

Below are benchmarking done with a few hotels:

6.9 Benchmarking

	Mayfair Lagoon	Bayview Hotel (Malaysia)	Ginger Hotel	Taj Palace Hotel	Marriott Hotel	Grand Hyatt	Hotel Oberoi	Sonar Bangla Sheraton	Hotel Leela Palace
Wi-Fi	✓		✓	✓	✓	✓	✓	✓	
Gymnasium	✓	✓	✓	✓	✓	✓	✓	✓	✓
Restaurant	✓	✓	✓	✓	✓	✓	✓	✓	✓
Safe Zone	✓	✓	✓	✓	✓	✓	✓	✓	✓
Meeting Room	✓	✓	✓	✓	✓	✓	✓	✓	
Conference Room	✓	✓	✓	✓	✓	✓	✓		
Self-Check-in			✓						
Golfing	✓	✓		✓	✓				
Tennis Courts	✓			✓					
Swimming Pool	✓	✓		✓			✓	✓	✓
Spa Facility	✓	✓		✓	✓		✓	✓	
Casino					✓	✓			
Ski/Snowboard						✓			
Yoga					✓	✓			
Beach Volleyball					✓				
Kids Play Area				✓					
Beauty Saloon	✓	✓							
Shopping Arcade	✓				✓	✓	✓		✓
Tea and Coffee Making Machines in rooms	✓	✓	✓		✓				
IDD Telephones		✓			✓			✓	
Banking Facility	✓	✓		✓		✓	✓	✓	✓

6.10 Hotel Business Processes

- Front-Desk
  - Registration and reservation
  - Guest History
  - Housekeeping
  - Reports Front-Desk
  - Point-of-sale
  - Billing
  - In-house rates
  - Competitor sales analysis
  - Foreigners in house
  - Reports
  - Look-up
- Banquets and conferences
- HR & Payroll
- Material Management
- Food & Beverage center
- Financial Management
- Accounts Receivables
- Account Payables
- Sales and Marketing
- Telephones

6.10.1 Key Business Processes to be Targeted

- On-line reservation
- Integrated finance and accounting management
- Customer relationship management
- Vendor collaboration
- Portal for employee engagement resources
- Business solution to integrate the hotel chain

6.11 Evolution of IT Infrastructure at Mayfair

6.11.1 Growth of IT

In 2001, the Mayfair hotel had 8 Desktops but no server. Today, they have 83 desktops and 4 servers. They are using IDS software for their hotel management purpose which is a leading software provider in hospitality industry. The different departments of Mayfair use software specific to their need and use; for example, Tally is used by accounting department.

6.11.2 Current IT Architecture

In the hotel industry customers come to a hotel on word of mouth recommendation, the hotels have their complete data, video footage from security cameras which are important to a person. So data security is of immense importance in places such as Mayfair. The data available to different departments is integrated in the database which serves as backbone for all information requirements. The access to data is controlled by using authority based access to data. The below picture shows the IT architecture of Hotel

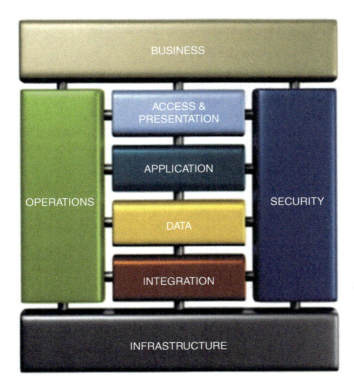

6.11.3 Benefits of Current IT System

- *Wi-Fi*—The whole hotel is Wi-Fi enabled which can be accessed by subscribing to the service. This helps the customer to access Internet from anywhere in the hotel.
- Card reader—The doors are magnetic card reader based which reduces work for employees and customers, but it causes trouble when kept with mobile which is a minor hiccup compared to benefits given.
- *Online reservation system*—At the official Web site of the hotel http://www.mayfairhotels.com/, one can reserve room for oneself. The room rent and availability are shown online. One fills up the form there and after submission the sales team of the hotel contacts the person to complete the formalities
- Self-help Kiosk—There is a self-help kiosk in the hotel where one can go and check the availability of different services at different times. So, for booking Spa one needs no assistance just check in the self-service kiosk and book it then and there

6.11.3.1 Stakeholders

- Customers—They are the biggest shareholders Mayfair as in the case of hospitality industry which is a very customer centric industry.
- Promoters/Owners—They are stakeholders as they are the ones who earn profit.
- Vendors and Third Party Suppliers—They may include:
  - Travel and Transport Service Providers.
  - Laundry Services.
  - Facilities such as Spa, Health care, etc.
  - Software Provider for IT Implementation—In case of Mayfair it is Fortune Enterprises based in Kolkata. Below is the snapshot of the comment of Mr. Dilip Ray, Chairman and MD, Mayfair Hotels & Resorts for IDS software: In eastern India, we just know one reliable hotel technology company—IDS. We have bestowed my complete faith in them for smooth flow of Mayfair's operations.
- Employees—The hotel employees are also a very important stakeholder.

6.12 Factors Affecting IT Strategy

Broadly there are four factors affecting IT Strategy and they are:
- Industry Characteristics
- Organization
- Process Flow
- Issues and Challenges

Let us take each of the factors and elaborate upon with respect to our case.

6.12 Factors Affecting IT Strategy 247

6.12.1 *Industry Characteristics*

We have covered this part in detail in the first section. Included in introduction section is industry brief with a few facts such as growth, contribution to GDP, critical factors determining profitability. Also, we have presented the SWOT analysis of the industry.

6.12.2 *Organization*

As Mayfair is not a publicly listed company, not much information such as annual report, financial analysis is available from secondary sources. In fact, promoters have 80% share. Anyway, from the secondary sources we have already listed a few financial parameters.

But in one of the speeches by Mr. Dilip Ray, Chairman and MD, he commented "Nowhere the slowdown has impacted our business. We have 100 per cent occupancy in our Bhubaneswar, Puri and Rourkela property". This clearly indicates that Mayfair hotels are very confident on their operational capacity and can plan for future without worrying about recession.

Also from industry perspective, hospitality industry on an average shows healthy growth trends in developing economies such as India. Thus, combining two important factors (strong top line of Mayfair and growing sector), we can infer that Mayfair is relatively best positioned to increase its revenues as well as profit.

6.12.3 *Process Flow*

Mayfair business model is to provide best of hospitality services and is continuously looking to increase its number of offerings. They started with services in hotel industry and steadily have expanded their services offerings to resorts, tour packages, banquet and board, spa and fitness center, etc. and looking to expand to other hospitality services such as casino.

Process flow

The focus of process flow in hospitality industry (and thus Mayfair) is customer centricity unlike manufacturing sector where the focus is on the product. Thus, all the processes are designed by keeping customer as focus and emphasis is to reduce the pain points to customers.

The different processes in Mayfair can be: advance booking, on demand service, loyalty programs, etc. Below is the process flow of three generic processes.

- *Advance booking*
  Customer checks for availability (either online or telephonic) ->corresponding system checks the availability, if available as per customer preferences booking

else give options ->when booking done—payment made by customer and receipt confirmed by hotel

- *On demand service*
  Customer while in hotel, orders for a new service ->check whether service can be accomplished ->if yes, then serve customer; if no then tender apologies and give option (if customer avails option then start from beginning) ->if order served then add price of service to the total bill

- *Loyalty program*
  Customer is either making online booking or availing service ->check whether customer can take any benefit of loyalty program such as repeat customer or corporate discount ->if yes, then give benefits and adjust amount in final bill; if not then check can customer be associated with loyalty program ->change customer status in database for future reference.

6.13 Alternatives

To further the IT Strategy, Mayfair Lagoon and Resorts should implement ERP (Enterprise resource Planning). ERP is a system that organizes functions of an institution; supporting, for example, accounting, finance, human resources and e-commerce applications through the creation of relational databases and graphical user interfaces that unify the tasks of institutions such as corporations, government agencies, nonprofit organizations, powerful institutions and industries, and business establishments. ERP is a way to integrate the data and processes of an organization into one single system. Following are the software packages which help us achieve ERP:

- *Oracle applications*: Oracle unites the world's best enterprise applications. The Product Lines available are as follows:
  - Oracle E-Business Suite
  - PeopleSoft Enterprise
  - JD Edwards EnterpriseOne
  - Oracle Fusion Applications

- *SAP*: It is the world's leading provider of business software. It delivers products and services that help accelerate business innovation for customers.
  - SAP BusinessOne: It is a single integrated management application for small businesses. Benefits that SAP Business One Solution gives are:

    Improves efficiency for stronger bottom line.
    Focuses on growing the business.
    Aids in faster and smarter decisions.
    Supports changing needs.

- *OPERA OES*: The OPERA Enterprise Solution is a fully integrated suite of products that can be easily combined for deployment at any size organization—from the single-property hotel to global, multibranded hotel chain environments. The OES is modular and scalable.

6.14 Need for a CIO

To choose between the above alternatives and successfully implement them, Mayfair Lagoon and Resorts needs a CIO. Apart from successfully implementing IT Strategies, he would also need to coordinate the maintenance and required upgradations of the software and technologies. For fulfilling these roles, the basic recommended responsibilities of the CIO would be the following:

- Establish credibility of the IT department.
- Develop competent IS Staff and IT-Savvy employees.
- Create a vision for the future and sell it.
- Implement IT Architecture.
- Ensure that electronic infrastructure for e-commerce is in place.
- Rapidly develop new IT uses.
- Nurture relationships with senior management.

To carry out his roles and responsibilities in an efficient manner, the CIO is required to understand the business (products and services). He should have a balance of IT and Business Knowledge. Also, he should wisely choose between "Value Addition" features and its "Cost Impacts". The following diagram illustrates the need for a dynamic CIO.

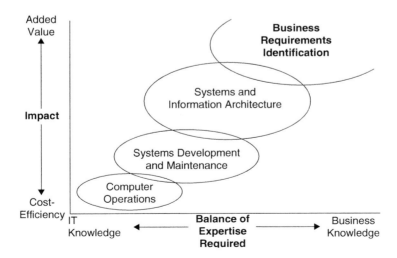

Detailing the above requirements, Mayfair Lagoon and Resorts needs to publish a job advertisement. The details of Job Advertisement are given below:

6.14.1 Job Advertisement

6.14.1.1 Position

Chief Information Officer of MAYFAIR Group

6.14.1.2 Job Description

The MAYFAIR Group is a leading hospitality player in Eastern India. With a high recall of its brand "MAYFAIR" among discerning clientele and industry fraternity, the group has over the years built its reputation as a high end niche player. MAYFAIR Group is looking for a CIO, who as a member of the Executive Committee would be responsible for giving the direction for the overall strategy with respect to technology excellence.

This person must direct and manage computing and information technology, strategic planning, policies, programs, and schedules for business and finance data processing. He is also responsible for computer servers, network communications, and management information services to accomplish corporate goals and objectives.

6.14.1.3 Qualifications

Mandatory

- Masters degree in information technology or computer science or MBA from reputed institute and 10+ years of experience in a senior-level IT position is required.
- Proven success in designing, implementing, and delivering products.
- Willingness to work a flexible schedule and travel as needed.
- Ability to communicate highly technical information in a comprehensive manner to all levels of the company.
- Must have professional written and verbal communication and interpersonal skills.
- Ability to motivate teams to produce quality materials within tight time frames and simultaneously manage several projects.

Experience
Mandatory

- 3+ years of experience working in a management role looking after software implementation and development, operations, and technology infrastructure in hospitality sector.

- Proven success in cost control and delivering ROI.
- Experience in managing multiple projects
- Proficient in MS Office suite software, ERP systems, database operations, project management software and tools.
- Thorough understanding of Internet marketing, technology, and philosophical concepts including e-commerce, advertising/sponsorship, promotion, online community, content delivery, user interaction, database storage/security/operations, and project management.

Good to have

- Good to have experience in integrating systems resulting from mergers and acquisition
- Good to have knowledge of administrative procedures, such as budgeting, hiring, and supervision
- Good to have knowledge of specific software such as Lead PeopleSoft 9.0

Benefits/salary
MAYFAIR group offers a competitive salary, bonus, and benefit program. The compensation would not be a constraint for the right candidate.

6.15 Architecture

6.15.1 Business Process Modelling

When applied in the hotel quality management system, this process approach underlines the importance of the following:

- Understanding and meeting of guest's requests
- Need of supervision of business processes in value added conditions
- Achieving results of business processes and their efficiency
- Permanent improvement of business processes, based on impartial estimation

Regardless of many possible types of business processes, and much diversity of process structures, all business processes in hotel can be divided into three types:

- Management processes
- Core processes
- Support processes

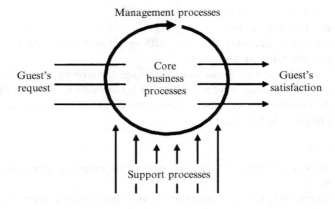

Management business processes
Management business processes are important for progress of core business processes, as well as of support process. These are business processes of development, planning, quality management and management of hotel organization. Because of entirety and directions of their influence onto core business processes—Management business processes are called—vertical processes.

Core business processes
Core business processes are focused on the achievement of satisfaction of customers, (buyers/users), i.e., hotel guests. They directly add new value to the product, meaning service. They meet requests of hotel guests and are generator of their contentment. Core business processes, processes of fulfillment or realization, are business processes whose result—in the form of product or service—has direct value confirmation on the market. The plan and the product of their creation in core business processes are strongly integrated. Core business processes are called horizontal processes.

Support processes
Support processes which are also called logistical or resourceful business processes, are directed toward producing satisfaction of internal users within hotel organizational structure. They are able to create added value for the guest. However, this influence on making added value is indirect and is fulfilled through support of core business processes. Support processes are auxiliary business processes and represent a support to core business processes. With regard to direction of activities onto core business processes, they are also called vertical processes.

6.15 Architecture

Interactivities of different types of business process

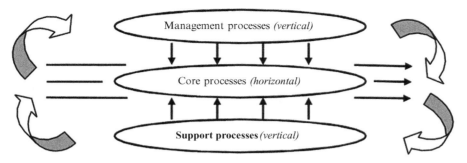

Source: http://kvaliteta.inet.hr/t_Rad%20Opatija.pdf

Business Processes in a Hotel
The whole spectrum of work processes of a hotel consists of production activities and service activities. Purpose of production activities is rendering of services which have product characteristics. Purpose of service activities is providing guests with: accommodation, serving of meals and beverages, entertainment, laundry washing, ironing, etc. Process contains all activities linked into a chain. It starts with defining of all possible needs a guest may have during the trip.

6.15.1.1 Types of Business Processes in a Hotel

Management business processes in a hotel

1. Process of hotel management
2. Process of planning
3. Process of development
4. Process of marketing
5. Process of quality management
6. Process of environment management
7. Process of social responsibility management
8. Process of security/safety at work management

Core business processes in a hotel

1. Process of producing food and beverages which are specifically prepared
2. Process of serving meals and beverages
3. Process of reception and accommodation of guests

Support business processes in a hotel

1. Process of human resources management
2. Process of financial management
3. Process of infrastructure maintenance
4. Process of information management

5. Process of purchase
6. Process of sale

6.15.1.2 Methodology

Basic task of hotel management during of business processes development is in fact establishing, directing and describing of events during transformation process of input into output.

Static Vs Dynamic Process model
Static model of business process presents logical sequence of process steps development as consisting parts of the business process. This phase of business process development identifies structural units where individual process step develops, and locates control points at which measurements will be performed—and thus manage the business process.

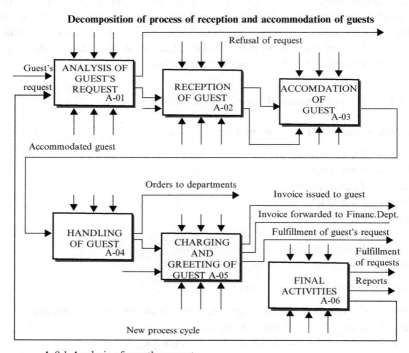

A-0.1 Analysis of guest's request
A-0.2 Reception of guest
A-0.3 Accommodation of guest
A-0.4 Handling of guest
A-0.5 Charging of services and greeting of guest
A-0.6 Final activities

Source: http://kvaliteta.inet.hr/t_Rad%20Opatija.pdf

6.15 Architecture

Dynamic model of the process is plan of implementation of developed business process into functional structure of organization of the hotel. The plan shows that in which structural hotel unit develops activities of each process step, and which unit of organization is responsible for their execution.

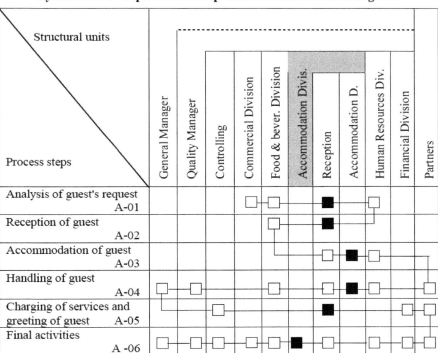

Dynamic model of process of reception and accommodation of guests

Source: http://kvaliteta.inet.hr/t_Rad%20Opatija.pdf

6.15.1.3 Standardization Vs Customization

The traditional view as reflected in the service management literature is that service should be customized in order to satisfy customers. It seems paradoxical to strive for standardization and customization at the same time and the findings show that customized service is seldom found in practice. Control, predictability, and risk minimization are just as important to hotel operations as customized service.

Here are a few challenges that hotel saw due to growing invasion of technology in our lives:

1. The arrival of the Internet has transformed the travel industry, presenting hotel chains with enormous opportunities and challenges. Where travelers would once book hotels through an agent, many now rely on Internet travel portals, hotels' own Web sites and online travel agents. If hotel chains do not adapt to this new market, they run the risk of losing an enormous proportion of their business to Web-enabled competitors.
2. To transform this luxury hotel by combining its traditional, elegant styling with state-of-the-art communications solutions.
3. Going Green—leveraging IT for it.
4. The implementation of wireless LAN as a critical business decision to further the Hotel's positioning as a preferred business destination. The wireless LAN network can be a key competitive differentiator, and be a potential revenue generating service.
5. They not only need to keep pace with customer demand but also embrace new channels for selling its services.
6. Allow centralized hotel administration and improved customer relationship management capabilities.
7. Revolutionize customer relationships by taking advantage of technology to provide a wider array of faster, more cost-effective services.
8. Mayfair's situation was that they would not lose a lot of business because they did not have Internet access, but they would very probably gain substantially more if they had it.

6.16 Technology

The stage has been set with the inclusion of CIO in the top management, to go tech savvy, and not just for the sake of modernization, but to gain miles by cutting costs, increasing efficiency, going Green, and finally transforming all this into customer delight and thus better profit margins.

As has already been discussed in earlier sections about the various alternatives available with the management to implement the It infrastructure, we would advise to go for *SAP Business One* solution. The SAP Business One application is an affordable, integrated business management solution designed specifically for small and midsize businesses. SAP Business One can help by providing a single software system that automates business processes and delivers a true and unified picture of critical, up-to-the-minute business information across customer relationship management (CRM), manufacturing, and finance.

6.16.1 Modules Provided by SAP Business One

6.16.2 Architecture of SAP Business One

SAP Business One as said earlier is based on client/server architecture, howbeit a "2 tier": strictly, clients and server. This technology is often referred to as a fat client. This is because all processing and business logic are carried out on the client. The result therefore is a system where logon and load balancing is a mirage (Figs. 6.1 and 6.2).

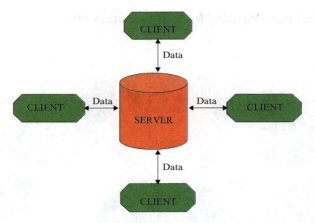

Fig. 6.1 Fat clients drawing data for manipulation and feeding it back into the server *Source*: http://www.maringo-usa.com/projectmanagement/US/SBO_Solution_Detail_UK.pdf

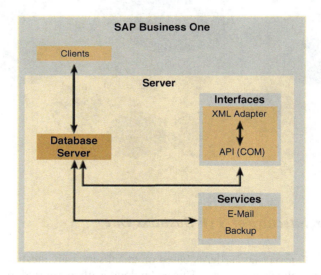

Fig. 6.2 Single-Server Environment That Makes SAP® Business One Easy to Administer Maintain, and Integrate with Other Solutions *Source*: http://it.toolbox.com/blogs/sap-library/challenges-of-the-fat-client-technology-11276

Advantages of SAP Business One

1. It is software that can evolve as the business needs change: It's easy to adapt SAP Business One to changing business conditions and new requirements—without burdening the IT staff.

2. It gives immediate notification about and automatic response to important business events:
  With SAP Business One, business owners can manage by exception—monitoring, notifying, and taking action when specific events occur. Any breach of preset business policies triggers an immediate notification to a preselected person and initiates a workflow process to manage the event.
3. Software that works the way you do and not compels business to adapt as per the software: SAP Business One gives users powerful tools to tailor the solution to meet specific working needs. With SAP Business One, users can specify their preferences for forms, policies, queries, reports, etc, can use powerful customization functionality to easily define most changes to the application—without technical training, and implement changes to the software almost instantly.

What's Different about SAP Business One?
We just elaborated about the business advantages of SAP Business One. Here are some of the outstanding features that make it stand tall among all other ERP packages:

1. *Integration*—SAP Business One is the only integrated business management solution for small businesses that can automate CRM, manufacturing, financial management—through a single software system.
2. *Embedded CRM*—Only SAP Business One is built with CRM embedded into the application. Sales, support, and customer facing processes are seamlessly integrated into all relevant functions across the company.
3. *Drag and Relate*—Only SAP Business One uses Drag & Relate to provide users at all levels with end-to-end visibility of all operations—and the ability to understand key relationships and transactions within the business instantly.
4. *Workflow-based alerts*—Only SAP Business One offers workflow-based alerts that let users monitor, notify others, and take action based on specific events.
5. *Adaptability*—SAP Business One is the only solution that provides users with the freedom to easily add fields, change forms, and personalize queries and reports.

6.17 Organization Structure for Implementation

6.17.1 *Current Organization Structure*

Currently, MayFair has three divisions, and they are Operations division, Business Planning & Development division, and Finance & Systems division. Further Systems department structure is shown below:

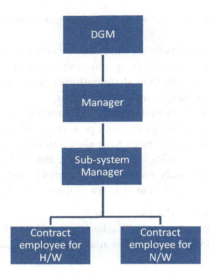

The s/w part is looked upon by DGM and Manager. Any upgradation in s/w is decided by senior management and carried out by software service provider with support from Mayfair IT staff.

6.17.2 *Proposed Organization Structure*

From IT implementation point of view, Systems division need to be distinct and suggestions regarding IT implementation should come from steering committee. The structure of steering committee is proposed below:

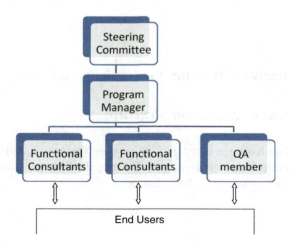

6.17.2.1 Roles and Responsibilities

Below are Roles and Responsibilities of Systems division:

- Identification of new technologies available in market so that there is clear gain over competitors
- Measure and improve upon gains from IT implementation.
- Increase awareness of IT within organization
- To train employees for use of IT
- Need a small group taking care of any day-to-day operations issues with respect to IT, as users of IT systems in MayFair might not be proficient in its use.

6.18 Approach for Implementation

6.18.1 Roadmap

We suggest roadmap with respect to IT implementation as well implementation of facilities

6.18.1.1 IT Implementation Timeline

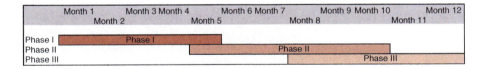

6.18.1.2 Implementation Timeline for Facilities

In this we have considered a few facilities present in similar other hotels but not in Mayfair. Below is roadmap for those facilities:

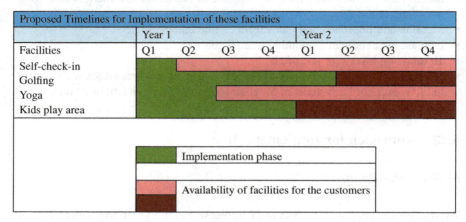

6.18.2 Implementation Plan

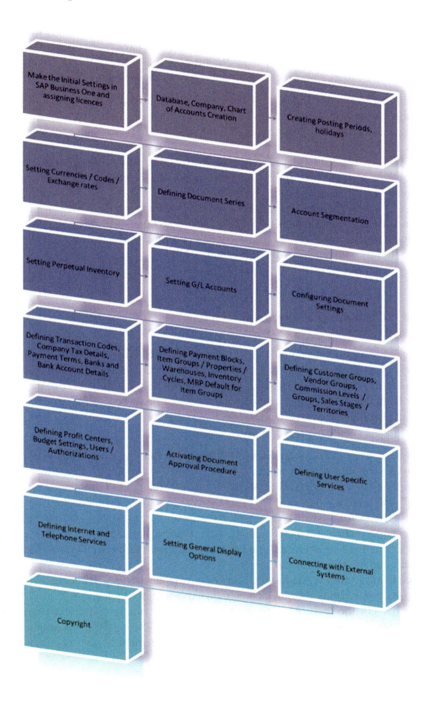

6.18.3 Training

There are regular trainings for different services or departments except for training related to IT services. Like for employees at reception, there are trainings related to soft skills, interacting with guests, etc. We propose that training for IT employees also needs to be there. It needs to be implemented in the following ways:

- Right employees for training on IT need to be identified; otherwise, IT implementation would be disaster.
- Expected deliverables from training need to be identified in advance so that progress can be measured.
- For IT employees, there need to be a few external certifications. This will make sure that Mayfair IT employees are technically equipped with changing technology.
- Once IT employees are comfortable with the current technology, they need to be trained on emerging technologies such as Virtualization, etc. as these emerging technologies would be deciding on savings in future. For the same, Mayfair can have tie-ups with teaching institutes such as NIIT.

6.18.4 Change Management

In today's business environment everything is changing. With respect to hospitality industry, the ever changing parameters include customers taste & preference, competition, prices, government policies, people, employees, and products. So the ability to effectively manage and embrace change is of great benefit for an emerging player in hospitality industry such as Mayfair groups.

The change can be managed in following ways:

- Identifying Critical Success Factors (CSF's) and planning a roadmap for change management with respect to CSF's
- Adopt right technologies for online booking, integration of IT architecture resulting from mergers, collaboration with other vendors for value added services, etc. as it will determine the advantage over competitors. Further for any technological change, a change management plan needs to be in place.
- Proper communication from senior management such as by Mr. Puri on the need for having any technological change.
- Need to have rewards and recognition system in place. This will encourage those who are contributing for quick change management in Mayfair.
- Last but not the least, Mayfair would be required to overcome resistance for change from employees those who are not using IT or from those who might lose job due to IT implementation. Thus, change management needs to be managed proactively and not reactively.

6.19 Budget and ROI

For the hospitality industry, occupancy rate is the single most significant source of revenue over the allied business activities such as restaurants, spas, pubs, etc. Therefore, the IT Strategy implementation for Mayfair is a long term investment which seeks to increase the business efficiency, improve the internal processes, and reduce internal transactions' costs. Apart from that, a 10 percentage point increase in occupancy level is targeted through customer centric IT solutions and offering better services to loyalists, thus creating repeat customers. The IT Strategy implementation will help the management in decision-making through better reports and data through different phases of the year.

6.19.1 IT Strategy for Mayfair

6.19.1.1 Budget

Mayfair Hotels and Resorts reported a profit of Rs. 9.27 crores for the year 2007–08. The ITS implementation budget has been estimated to be 13.30 % of the reported profit. The ITS implementation is proposed to be in three phases.

Phase I
Tie-ups with travel portals such as Cleartrip.com, Travelguru.com, etc. for online booking

Phase II
Integration of the existing IT infrastructure

Phase III
ERP implementation and database centralization

The phased approach will take an estimated 1 year to implement, and therefore, the budget allocation would also be distributed through the first year of implementation.

Points under consideration/Assumptions
The current occupancy of Mayfair Hotels and Resorts is around 60%. As per the corporate vision, Mayfair group intends to achieve 1000 rooms by 2012 and currently has 450 rooms including villas.

The reported profits data, for the year 2007–08, at room strength of 102, per room profit has been calculated.

No. of rooms	Days	Occupancy	Net profit
102	365	0.6	83000000
Per room profit	3715.642		

Per Room Profit per day of occupancy = Rs 3715.

Current Scenario
Assumption: Per room profit per day of occupancy increasing at 10% Y-o-Y

No. of rooms	350
Per room profit per day of occupancy	4495.926

Extrapolating the above calculation, an increase in occupancy under different scenarios has been represented as below:

No. of rooms	Per room profit per day of occupancy			Profit	Increase in profit
350	4495.926	365	0.7	402048203	57435458
350	4495.926	365	0.63	361843382	17230637
350	4495.926	365	0.6	344612745	

6.19.1.2 ITS Plan Expenditure Outlay

Phase I	INR
IT team	
Remuneration expenses	4000000
Vendor short-listing	100000
Corporate tie-ups	500000
Online booking	
Web development	80000
	(continued)

Payment gateway	75000
Database management	75000
Outsourcing	500000
	5330000
Phase II	
Server integration	500000
Centralized database and data migration	600000
Training and development	400000
	1500000
Phase III	
ERP implementation (SAP Business One)	5000000
Training and development	500000
	5500000
Total ITS plan outlay	12330000

6.19.1.3 Investment Vs. Returns

Expenses	INR		
Total plan outlay	12330000		
Saving in corporate tax	4110000		
Net cost to the company	8220000		
Break even		Increase in occupancy in %	
	Tax scenarios	1	2
Increase in annual profit		5743545.752	11487091.5
Years to break even	Considering tax saving	4.658116073	
	Without considering tax saving	9.926562317	0.920093975
		Years	
Assumption	IRR = 8 %		

6.20 Benefits of IT Implementation at Mayfair

1. As of today, there is no IT alignment for the organization. IT is in a very primal stage and not aligned to the business goals. The first and the foremost benefit the ITS implementation will have for Mayfair is to make the process aligned to the business objectives.
2. Better reports and decision-making assistance: Centralization of the database and the IT systems will ensure better data management which will ensure better decision-making process. A central database will enable the management to monitor the process within different departments of the organization.
3. As the Mayfair group is in expansion phase, after the ERP implementation in Phase III, all the hotels and resorts under the umbrella would be integrated on the same SAP system.

4. Reduction in accounting support staff per hotel will lead to increase in productivity as compared to what is at present. Many accounting activities can be handled centrally with the SAP implementation.
5. Alignment of the business and the IT goals
6. Faster execution of key processes: Monthly and quarterly consolidation of reports, accounts, with higher accuracy. Automatic reconciliation of the reports.
7. MIS reports: Regular MIS reports and exception reporting
8. Online booking system with payment gateway: The online reservation system can be integrated with the SAP backend and will certainly increase customer convenience and thus result in higher occupancy.
9. Better customer service: It is imperative for a five-star hotel to provide high level of customization yet to achieve efficiency; the processes need to be standardized. IT strategy implementation is a step in this direction wherein the processes followed in the organization would be standardized and customer satisfaction given priority.
10. Customer satisfaction and feedback database: As of today, the feedback is taken in a paper form from the customers. With the IT implementation online feedback facility can be introduced which will ensure better service levels resulting in higher customer satisfaction.
11. With SAP implementation, vendor/ supplier management can be improved
12. Reduction in accounting and billing expenses on routine purchases

6.21 Risks and Mitigation

An integrated IT implementation in the organization has a lot of advantages, yet there would be pain points which need to be considered to keep the systems running.

The following are the risks involved with the entirely new IT system:

- High initial costs of implementation is a hindrance in the decision-making by the management toward carrying out a new IT implementation
- Lack of adequate training of the employees will result in initial hiccups
- Server maintenance: With a central server client model, with integration of the IT systems of all the Mayfair hotels, server maintenance becomes critical. Therefore, an additional backup server should be deployed to be used in case of failure.
- Network connectivity: Although it is a trivial issue, it can lead to a lot of business getting lost in case the server gets disconnected due to a network disconnectivity
- Security of the payment gateway is highly important and a critical issue with online booking
- Server consolidation has the benefits of single point of maintenance, yet a backup is important to retrieve data in case of a system crash

6.22 Practice Questions

1. What are the characteristics of hospitality industry? What are the issues and challenges faced by the industry?
2. What is the need for IT strategy in Mayfair?
3. How do you calculate ROI for IT implementation?
4. What are components of risk management plan?
5. How do you design an IT implementation plan?

References

"Taj Palace Hotel" http://www.fivestaralliance.com/luxury-hotels/delhi/taj-palace-hotel. Retrieved on 29 Aug 2009
"Facilities at Ginger" http://www.gingerhotels.com/facilities/index.aspx Retrieved on 29 Aug 2009
"Hotel Overview" http://mumbai.grand.hyatt.com/hyatt/hotels/index.jsp?src=tc_googlelocal_mumgh_lk_1108 Retrieved on 29 Aug 2009
"Marriott" http://www.marriott.com/default.mi. Retrieved on 29 Aug 2009
"Oberoi Hotels and Resorts" http://oberoi-hotel-mumbai.blogspot.com/ Retrieved on 29 Aug 2009
"Sonar Bangla Sheraton Hotel Kolkata" http://www.indiaprofile.com/kolkata-hotels/sonar-bangla-sheraton-hotel.html. Retrieved on 29 Aug 2009
"The Leela Palace Hotel" http://www.hotelsbangaloreindia.com/leela-palace.html. Retrieved on 29 Aug 2009
"Bayview Hotel Langkawi" http://www.langkawi-resorts.com/citybayview/ Retrieved on 29 Aug 2009
"Mayfair Lagoon Bhubaneswar" http://www.nivalink.com/mayfairlagoon/index.html. Retrieved on 29 Aug 2009
"Oracle Applications" http://www.oracle.com/us/products/applications/index.htm. Retrieved on 29 Aug 2009
"SAP: Delivering IT-powered business innovation" http://www.sap.com/about/index.epx. Retrieved on 29 Aug 2009
"SAP Business One" http://www.sap.com/sme/solutions/businessone/index.epx. Retrieved on 29 Aug 2009
"Hotel Management Software" http://www.micros.com/Industries/HotelsAndResorts/HotelManagement/hotel-management-software.htm. Retrieved on 29 Aug 2009
http://www.4hoteliers.com/4hots_fshw.php?mwi=1159
http://www.expresshospitality.com/20090215/market12.shtml
http://www.naukrihub.com/india/hospitality/overview/
http://www.naukrihub.com/india/hospitality/overview/swot/
http://www.naukrihub.com/india/hospitality/overview/challenges/
http://www.economywatch.com/world-industries/hospitality/
http://www.zibb.com/article/5353198/LodgeNet+Announces+First+Implementation+of+Intel+Based+Mobile+Internet+Devices+For+the+Hospitality+Industry
http://www.mayfairhotels.com/
http://www.business-standard.com/india/storypage.php?autono=345232
http://www.cci.in/pdf/surveys_reports/tourism-hotel-industry.pdf
http://www.business-standard.com/india/storypage.php?autono=345232

Chapter 7
IT Strategy for iSOFT Plc

7.1 Learning Objectives

This case explains how an organization engaged in developing software products uses information strategy to manage its resources, customer requirements and support its marketing strategy. The case also illustrates how the information system ensures smooth flow of information among project team members and other stakeholders such as management and customers, which makes the entire development process a transparent one. This case can be taught in the information strategy, system analysis and design course, healthcare certification programmes, postgraduate diploma courses, executive MBA programmes, MCA and MSc (Computer Science) courses. The case can be used to illustrate the following themes:

- Evaluation of strategy to implement technology for automation of software product development process
- To explain how productivity increases with automation
- To explain how information system helps in meeting expectations of all stakeholders
- To explain how IS can be used for innovations in product design
- Implementation strategy that can be adopted as a long-term solution

The data has been collected by visiting the product development department of the organization and interviewing project managers, delivery managers and team members of different project. Also, secondary sources related to healthcare industry in India and the UK have been used for providing recommendations for possible future technological investments.

7.2 Executive Summary

This chapter focuses on developing the automation strategy for development of Lorenzo, the unique healthcare solution from iSOFT Plc, which has the promise of revolutionizing the healthcare industry by providing single point patient information. The automation strategy is developed by carefully analysing the requirements of the UK healthcare industry and its expectations, the corporate strategy, competitors and various constraints. The paper further elaborates on the implementation of IT strategy, the risks associated with it, the audit of IT strategy and the road map from the view point of iSOFT. The paper also focuses on the subtle aspects of the IT strategy at iSOFT, the change management and the benchmarking processes. In addition it throws light on the importance of data security and integrity for iSOFT in implementing this project.

7.3 Introduction

> A strategy is the pattern or plan that integrates an organization's major goals, policies, and action sequences into a cohesive whole. A well-formulated strategy helps to marshal and allocate an organization's resources into a unique and viable posture based on its relative internal competencies and shortcomings, anticipated changes in the environment, and contingent moves by intelligent opponents.
>
> James Brian Quinn

As per the quotation, a good business strategy is an imperative for the success of any organization. Most of the organizations that fail do not have a clearly defined strategy. The overall Corporate Strategy is achieved through the implementation of strategies in different functional areas. Information Technology Strategy (ITS), is something that binds all of these strategies together. It is defined as the science or art of effective use of information technology, allied technologies and IT resources of the organization to execute strategic plans optimally or as effectively as possible to achieve business objectives.

In this report, we look to develop an IT Strategy for iSOFT's product *Lorenzo*, which is used by major healthcare organizations in the UK.

7.4 Overview of Healthcare Industry in the UK

The UK healthcare industry serves the needs of an increasingly health-aware population. It is a very diverse sector covering a very wide range of product types and healthcare uses. The healthcare industry in the UK is in the *maturity* stage of its growth.

7.4 Overview of Healthcare Industry in the UK

7.4.1 Value of the Market

The term "Healthcare Industry" is not clearly defined and may be used to encompass medical devices, systems and technologies, laboratory equipment and associated support services e.g. planning, design, management, training and education. Most of the large companies operating in the UK are foreign-owned, notably American. The healthcare sector exports around £4 billion worth of goods and services annually into a global market that is growing rapidly, as individual expectations rise, and political pressure grows in many countries to improve services and facilities. The sector employs about 50,000 staff.

The number of significant UK medical device companies is small and vary from those with less than £1 million per year turnover (about 1,800 companies or 85%) to those with £500 million–£1 billion sales. It has been estimated that about 38 million people in the UK per day have contact with a medical device. Patients on whom medical devices are used include those visiting hospitals, GPs, dentists, opticians, chiropodists as well as those who daily use glasses, contact lenses, dentures, etc.

7.4.2 Factors Affecting the Industry

Overall the sector's export is growing rapidly as individual expectations rise, and political pressure grows in many countries to improve services and facilities. The UK's increasing presence in the global market has been attributed to three main factors:

1. Complementary relationships between the industry, the Government, the NHS, the private sector and voluntary organizations
2. A highly developed healthcare infrastructure
3. An outstanding and well-supported research base

7.4.3 Recent Developments

Spending on health in the UK is rising at a much faster rate than spending on the other public services, says the Office of Health Economics, an organization largely funded by the UK drug industry to provide independent research on healthcare. In the 2008 financial year the NHS, after several years of growth, received $102.2 billion of total central public spending. The details of the spending are given in Appendix 1.

In 2003, the British government launched a massive 10-year project to modernize IT support for the key administrative and patient care processes of the National Health Service (NHS). Known as the National Programme for IT, this IT software and services contract is valued at £6.2 billion, (US $10.7 billion), according to the NHS National Programme for IT web site.

The goal of the project is to improve the quality and reduce the cost of healthcare in the UK through an integrated patient health record on a national scale. To achieve this goal, the NHS has begun a process to install a comprehensive, integrated, and standardized portfolio of clinical and administrative IT systems for the NHS-affiliated healthcare providers (hospitals, clinics, primary care practices, and other allied healthcare delivery organizations) in each of five health regions (or "clusters") into which the NHS divides its services.

7.4.4 Challenges

Healthcare industry is faced with challenges such as increased government regulations, E-Business challenges, rising patient expectations and demand for lower healthcare costs. All of these factors must be taken into account while developing the IT Strategy.

7.5 iSOFT: The Company, an Overview

7.5.1 About the Company

iSOFT, now an IBA Health Group Company, is one of the world's largest providers of healthcare IT solutions. They design, build and deliver industry-leading software systems and deliver healthcare IT platforms and applications that address the administrative, clinical and connectivity requirements of healthcare organizations around the world, optimizing patient and financial outcomes that serve the entire health sector. Their capacity to embrace change and keep abreast of emerging new directions in healthcare allows their customers to explore the exciting potential of new technologies while securing their existing investments. Through significant investment in research and development and continuous process improvement, they have built up the capacity necessary to play a significant role in the use of information technology to enhance the quality of health services in all care settings.

iSOFT has an extensive international experience and wide reach, with a strong presence in Europe and the Asia Pacific region. Over 13,000 provider organizations in 35 countries across five continents use iSOFT's solutions to manage patient information and drive improvements in their core processes. As a catalyst for change, their solutions increase efficiencies and provide direct benefits to all stakeholders across the whole spectrum of care.

iSOFT is the leading provider in the UK and Ireland, where its current market share is more than 40%, following the award of contracts under the NPfIT national programme now underway in England. iSOFT now has a greatly expanded market presence in places such as Australia, New Zealand, South East Asia and China, Africa and the Middle East also.

The company's supporting service portfolio complements its advanced technology products by concentrating on installation, system configuration, training, on- and off-site managed services and customer support.

7.5.2 Timeline

iSOFT has grown mostly inorganically through mergers and acquisitions throughout its lifecycle. The detailed timeline is shown in Appendix 2.

One significant development for iSOFT was that on 30 October 2007; iSOFT became part of *IBA Health Group Limited*, a healthcare IT company listed on the Australian Securities Exchange (ASX), creating one of the world's largest healthcare IT companies with offices in 17 countries. The combined Group had the financial strength, international scope and enhanced skills to deliver major growth opportunities and value to shareholders, customers and employees after the acquisition. This has paved the way for the enlarged group to move into new markets and to offer a wider range of products and services to a greater number of customers, while simultaneously continuing to deliver world-class products, services and support to customers at local level.

7.5.3 Vision

"To put the individual at the centre of healthcare provision by extending the reach of healthcare information".

7.5.4 Mission

- To be the Pan-European healthcare systems vendor based on a truly portable single technology and application platform
- To use Europe as a strong base from which to establish distributorships to reach the rest of the world

7.6 LORENZO: Delivering the Future of Healthcare

7.6.1 About the Product

iSOFT's products are recognized as the best in the market and are designed for a wide range of healthcare activities in all areas, including patient administration, clinical information and medical practice management and laboratory, radiology and pharmacy management. LORENZO, their next-generation core application offering, is an integrated healthcare information management suite, currently being installed at hospitals in England under the UK National Health Service (NHS) National Programme for IT (NPfIT).

LORENZO is a comprehensive solution that addresses the needs of patients and all other participants in the healthcare supply chain, enabling them to access critical information whenever and wherever they need it.

iSOFT's overall strategy has been to bring the benefits of the supply chain approach to healthcare. This radical new way of doing business is enabled by innovative technologies, which support the exchange of information across global networks. Their revolutionary solution, LORENZO, is the key to this approach.

7.6.2 Uses

LORENZO is highly flexible. It can be used to assemble solutions that support every major activity in healthcare. These solutions do not simply automate, but make it possible to transform traditional roles and responsibilities, furthering collaboration and increasing efficiency across the entire healthcare supply chain.

For healthcare professionals, administrators and governments LORENZO provides accurate, on-demand information which supports the delivery of more timely, effective and convenient care. In addition, LORENZO supports the appropriate redistribution of workloads from acute services into more efficient local settings, such as community care.

LORENZO also supports healthcare provider organizations as they strive to extend the lifespan and value of existing system investments. Based on international standards and highly interoperable, open technologies, LORENZO can be introduced incrementally as part of a carefully planned process that enables the retirement of legacy systems in an evolutionary fashion.

7.6.3 Other Benefits of LORENZO

Apart from the primary features, LORENZO provides support for complete patient management, Shared patient records, improved communication and interactions, Intelligent prescribing, Intuitive consultation recording, Advanced decision support and rapid access to online resources, etc.

The detailed solutions of Lorenzo are given in Appendix 3.

7.6.4 Stakeholders

Already more than 8,000 healthcare provider organizations in 27 countries rely on iSOFT applications to manage patient information and drive improvements in their core processes.

Many of the world's leading hospitals in the UK, Ireland, the Netherlands, Germany, Switzerland, Scandinavia, Spain, Singapore, Canada, Australia and New Zealand have invested in iSOFT applications to meet their strategic and operational information requirements. Among other stakeholders are doctors, patients, pharmaceutical companies, vendors of computers and cell phones.

7.7 Corporate Strategy

7.7.1 Brainstorming

As the UK healthcare sector is already at a maturity stage, brainstorming will be a better approach to generate new ideas for forming corporate strategy.

For forcing various perspectives and facilitating detailed idea generation we will go for the "Six Thinking Hats" technique, invented by Dr. Edward De Bono for brainstorming. It will help making better decisions by pushing participants to move outside their habitual ways of thinking. The problems are revisited and ideas on probable solutions thought of wearing each of the thinking hats in turn. The sequence of thinking process o be adopted will be Blue, yellow, Black, White, Blue, Green, Blue as adopted in many strategic thinking exercises.

The details about the significance of the different hats have been described below:

- White Hat: facts and information
  This is the neutral hat. With this thinking hat, participants focus on the data available. Look at the information they have, and see what they can learn from it. Look for gaps in knowledge and either try to fill them or take account of them. The key information that represents the input to the session are presented and discussed. This is where they analyze past trends and try to extrapolate from historical data.
- Red Hat: feelings and emotions
  Wearing the red hat, participants look at the decision using intuition, gut reaction, and emotion. It is a method for harvesting ideas: everyone lists his top two or three choices from a list of ideas or items generated under another hat. Also participants try to think how other people will react emotionally, and try to understand the intuitive responses of people who do not fully know their reasoning.
- Black Hat: critical judgment
  When using black hat thinking, participants look at things pessimistically, cautiously and defensively by identifying barriers, hazards and risks. They try to see why ideas and approaches might not work. This is important because it highlights the weak points in a plan or course of action. It allows you to eliminate them, alter your approach or prepare contingency plans to counter problems that arise.
- Black Hat thinking helps to make the plan tougher and more resilient. It can also help one to spot fatal flaws and risks before you embark on a course of action. Black Hat thinking is one of the real benefits of this technique, as many successful

people get so used to thinking positively that often they cannot see problems in advance, leaving them under-prepared for difficulties.
- Yellow Hat: positive judgment
The yellow hat helps the participants to think positively. It is the optimistic viewpoint that helps in seeing all the benefits of the decision and the value in it, and spot the opportunities that arise from it. Yellow Hat thinking helps to keep going when everything looks gloomy and difficult.
- Green Hat: alternatives and creativity
The Green Hat stands for creativity. This is where one can develop creative solutions to a problem. It is a freewheeling way of thinking, in which there is little criticism of ideas. A whole range of creativity tools can be of help here.
- Blue Hat: the big picture
The Blue Hat stands for process control. This is the hat worn by people chairing meetings. When running into difficulties because ideas are running dry, they may direct activity into Green Hat thinking. When contingency plans are needed, they will ask for Black Hat thinking, and so on. Members of the team put it from time to time to direct their works together.

7.7.2 Corporate Strategy

The corporate strategy arrived at after a thorough brain storming session and in line with the vision and mission of the organization is detailed below:
- Development of world-class software application systems which address fully the administrative and clinical information management requirements of healthcare provider organizations.
- Supporting reform in healthcare industry.
- Create a sense of innovativeness within the organization to keep abreast with constant technological changes and customer requirements.
- Improve the Brand image of iSOFT to increase customer base.
- Create long-term relationships with partners and taking continuous feedback.
- Provide appropriate knowledge transfer inside the organization.

7.8 Factors Affecting IT Strategy

- Business goals
The decision on setting priorities for automation will be guided by the ultimate business objective of development of a world class software application system for the healthcare sector. This will lead to possible process automations to facilitate R&D, compatibility, etc.
- IT capability—current IT infrastructure and expansion capability (As-Is and To-Be)

With a full gamut of IT application products covering the breadth of healthcare industry, iSOFT has well-trained software and domain professionals to handle the automation needs.

- People and process capability

  The strong focus on IT and domain expertise as demanded by most of its technology driven products has resulted in qualified, experienced and enthusiastic professionals at the helm of iSOFT. The current processes have evolved over the time to become standards and are foolproof in carrying out automation needs.

- External factors

  The constant government support in bringing about healthcare reforms in the UK and the threat from possible competitors necessitates automation in R&D, customer support, knowledge management and training to be taken on priority basis to leverage the first mover advantage.

- Collaboration capability

  With government and healthcare organizations pushing healthcare reforms in the UK and worldwide, the service expectations will gradually increase and will demand automation in innovation and customer service to maintain the SLAs.

- Time and investment

  The current investment limits permits taking up automation with regard to R&D, compatibility, knowledge management, client support services and training.

7.9 Risks for LORENZO

Risk can be considered as a factor for developing IT strategy. Risks to Lorenzo can be viewed from both IT risks and Non-IT risks.

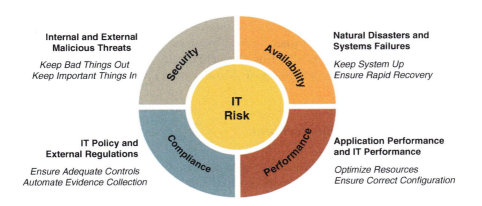

(*Source:* Symantec IT Risk Management Report: Myths and Realities - Volume 2)

7.9.1 IT Risks

IT risk can be composed of the following four types of risks:

i. Security risk
Security risk is the internal and external malicious threats for a system. The main purpose of this kind of security system is to keep the bad things out of the database and the important things in to the database.
ii. Availability risk
Availability risk mainly deals with the natural disasters and system failures. It keeps the system up and ensures rapid recovery of data.
iii. Performance risk
Performance risk takes care of the application performance and IT performance. It mainly helps in optimizing the resources required and also ensuring correct configuration.
iv. Compliance risk
Compliance risk takes care of the development of the IT policies and the external regulations. It helps in ensuring adequate controls and keeps automating the evidence collection.

7.9.2 Non-IT Risks

Non-IT risks are the risks which take care of the risks associated with competitiveness, technology obsolescence, intellectual property rights and the approval from the healthcare industry on international standards.

Firstly, there is always a chance that other companies can easily develop similar products by duplicating its features. This is known as the risk of competitiveness. Then there exists a certain risk of obsolescence of technology which will result in Lorenzo not being supported by new operating systems and electronic devices.

Apart from that there are risks of Intellectual Property Rights related issues and risks of not gaining approval from the Healthcare industry in various countries.

7.9.3 Risk Mitigation Techniques

The following are some of the risk mitigation techniques which will help in slowing down the various IT and non-IT risks involved in the IT security of the healthcare industry.

It is better to keep abreast with the recent technological developments in both the use of hardware and software. This will help in keeping the system updated and upgraded to take care of the recent threats of IT. Continuous training and learning processes will help the user to leverage the IT infrastructure implemented in the organization to take care of the security reasons.

Knowledge Management processes and use of the tools will help in integrating the whole organization at all levels so that everybody should be aware of the security reasons which will subsequently help the organization to incline towards more security of the system. Benchmarking of processes and products will help in setting the industry standards for IT security.

Continuous feedback from all stakeholders will help in knowing the root cause of each problems and keeping the system updated for the welfare of the organization.

After implementation of the security services it is important to have the up gradations for customers to keep them abreast of the current system.

IT Security in an organization can be more enhanced by focusing more on Encryption, Digital Certificates and firewalls. IT Security is described in detail in the following section.

7.10 IT Security

It has been found that many companies in the UK have no single point of responsibility for their information security, and purchasing is often split across several departments. Information Security still tends to be viewed as a technical matter rather than a mainstream business issue.

It is because of this reason that the Department of Health has published *Information Security Management: NHS Code of Practice* as a guide to the methods and required standards of practice in management of information security for those who work within, under contract to, or in business partnership with NHS organizations in England. Its purpose is to identify and address security management in the processing and use of NHS information and is based on current legal requirements, relevant standards and professional best practice.

This Code provides a key component of Information Governance arrangements for the NHS. The guidance within the Code of Practice is generally applicable to all organizations including, but not limited to, NHS organizations, third party IT/information service providers and private sector care providers providing care services under NHS contracts. The various techniques through which iSOFT can align with the NHS Code of Practice are described below.

7.10.1 Firewall

A firewall is defined as an integrated collection of security measures designed to prevent unauthorized electronic access to a networked computer system. It can also refer to a device or set of devices configured to permit, deny, encrypt, decrypt, or proxy all computer traffic between different security domains based upon a set of rules and other criteria. A firewall is a dedicated application, or software running on another computer, which inspects network traffic passing through it, and denies or permits passage based on a given set of rules. A firewall's basic task is to regulate some of the flow of traffic between computer networks of different trust levels.

Setting up Firewalls with zonal access can go a long way in improving IT security. For example, the Internet is a zone with no trust and an internal network which is a zone of higher trust. A zone with an intermediate trust level, situated between the Internet and a trusted internal network, is often referred to as a "perimeter network" or Demilitarized zone (DMZ).

Setting up a firewall will protect the servers against many hazards including, but not limited to Remote login, Application backdoors, SMTP session, Operating system bugs, Denial of service, email bombs, Macros, Redirect bombs, Source routing, etc.

7.10.2 Data Encryption

Encryption is the process of transforming information using an algorithm to make it unreadable to anyone except those possessing special knowledge, usually referred to as a key. Encryption method, by itself, can protect the confidentiality of messages, but other techniques are still needed to protect the integrity and authenticity of a message. Standards, software and hardware to perform encryption are widely available, but successfully using encryption to ensure security may be a challenging problem. Sometimes an attacker can obtain unencrypted information without directly undoing the encryption, for example traffic analysis, TEMPEST, or Trojan horse. Still, encryption may be used along with other security measures to enhance the overall risk mitigation process.

7.10.3 Information Security Management System (ISMS)

Compliance with information security standards are measured through an organization's Information Security Management System (ISMS) or equivalent. It is a documented model for establishing, implementing, operating, monitoring and improving the effectiveness of information security management within the organization. For the NHS, the NHS IGT provides the basis of an ISMS that supports a basic but acceptable level of information security.

For organizations such as iSOFT, which have special or advanced information security needs, the ISMS ensures a flexible approach that may be expanded in scope and content over time.

Effective IT security involves more than simply installing a security product, implementing anti-malware software, providing a security policy or signing a contract with a support service provider. The ISMS in this regard, provides means to identify and coordinate the approach to the management of information security by the organization in order to protect it and its business partners.

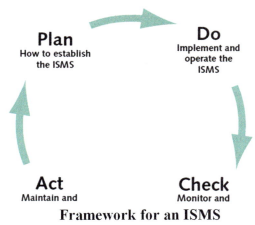

Framework for an ISMS

(Source: **Information Security Management:** *NHS Code of Practice*)

7.11 IT Strategy for Innovation

Lorenzo is a product that thrives on getting constant feedback from its customers and continuously evolving to incorporate changes and additional features. In a dynamic industry such as healthcare, where R&D plays a major role, keeping IT up-to-date with the latest medical advancements is very important. It is because of this reason that we suggest an "Innovation Approach" for implementation of the IT Strategy. This framework is described below.

(a) *Market innovation*: It involves conducting research and determining market requirements of the current requirements for a product.

IT can be used in this regard by creating online questionnaires and sending them to various healthcare organizations to know about what they really require from a healthcare IT solution.

Data Mining may be used to store the data on annual disease rates location wise etc. and analyze them to forecast how many patients will result for which diseases in the upcoming future and develop the products such that it has the ability to handle the performance and data requirements.

Furthermore, market trends of new entrants can be studied and potential customers identified who are not currently using packaged healthcare products through data analysis.

(b) *Product innovation*: Product innovation refers to change in technology used for products and changing the features of a product.

Online feedback from doctors, medical staff, etc. can be collected about the ease of use, features of the product and store them for incorporation in future versions. Newsletters and emails to healthcare organizations to inform them about the new products, its features, quality, etc.

Features such as Targeted Online Advertising (e.g. http://www.e-healthcaresolutions.com/) can be incorporated which will allow the users of Lorenzo to post their own ads online.

(c) *Process innovation*: Process innovation refers to changing the business processes in order to bring improvement in the end product.

iSOFT needs to create a dedicated R&D facility for delivering quality healthcare solutions. IT can be used to perform scenario analysis which will enable researchers to save time and money. Apart from that, processes in production such as error validation etc. which can be done without human support can be identified and automated.

(d) *Knowledge*: iSOFT can use Knowledge Sharing and Knowledge Management tools to share best practices and process differentiators inside the organization. There should be brainstorming sessions conducted and facilitated through use of IT (e.g. video conferencing) which aid in innovation.

Employees should be trained in latest technologies used in PCs as well as handheld devices that support Service Oriented Architecture concept. A pool of technical and domain experts should be kept for providing training and aiding in development.

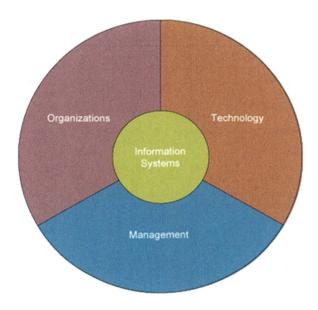

7.12 MIS

To improve the efficiency and effectiveness of the IT strategy through the provision of high quality information systems and services and to be the catalyst for change through improved business solutions is the prime aim of developing the MIS for the organization. The MIS is just an automated tool which enables the management to implement various strategies while keeping an eye on the performances and returns. In a period of significant and sustained change and in a climate of declining Healthcare business the management must have access to the information necessary to support the decisions needed to make change. The organization requires system to supply information so that it can improve its efficiency and effectiveness. That information must be supplied in a way that is accepted as "value for money", and must have the attributes of being: Complete, Accurate, Relevant and Timely.

The MIS we proposed for iSOFT is as follows:

Metrics'	Numerator	Denominator	Data collection tool	Publisher	Periodicity
Revenue increase	% Change in revenue	Average revenue	Sales management system	Sales manager	Quarterly
Cost reduction	% Decrease in costs	TCO	Accounting system	Accounts manager	Monthly
Increase asset utilization	% Increase in function points	Man hours	Project management system	Project manager	Weekly
Increase in ROTA	% Increase in ROTA	Total assets	Accounting system	Accounts manager	Monthly

(continued)

Metrics'	Numerator	Denominator	Data collection tool	Publisher	Periodicity
Quality of service	Number of projects meeting quality standards	Total number of projects	QA system	Quality inspector	Monthly
Timeliness of service	Change in average time taken	Avg. time taken to address a service failure	Surveys	Customer relationship manager	Semi-annually
Customer Satisfaction Index	% Reduction in no. of complaints	Avg. response rate	No. of participants in the survey	Customer relationship manager	Semi-annually
Innovation	No. of new products per year	Total no. of products	R&D Product database	R&D manager	Yearly
Data Integrity	% Reduction in no. of data entries	Avg. no. of data entries	Internal healthcare system	IT head	Monthly/weekly
Increase in new partnerships	% Increase in new partnerships	Avg. no. of new partnerships	Internal Tracking System	PR Department	Annually
Employee satisfaction	% Increase in Employee Satisfaction Index		Surveys, employee self-service system	HR department	Annually
Training and development	Increase in no. of training hours	Total no. of training hours	Training system	HR department	Semi-annually
Knowledge management	No. of projects using past data	Total number of projects	Shared services system	HR department	Annually

7.13 Architecture

iSOFT Healthcare creates solutions to help providers deliver administrative, clinical and diagnostic care across all scenarios and settings. LORENZO is the next-generation healthcare solution, built around the needs of patients. Based on a Service Oriented Architecture (SOA), it will help public and private healthcare organizations manage the future of distributed healthcare systems. LORENZO forms the backbone of information transfer in any healthcare environment, helping to form connections between patients, medical practitioners, healthcare workers and the funders of care. Uniquely, the solution also protects healthcare organizations' previous investments by integrating seamlessly with legacy systems. LORENZO is using SOA which is a relatively recent approach to designing software solutions that is inherently modular, highly flexible and highly interchangeable.

7.13 Architecture

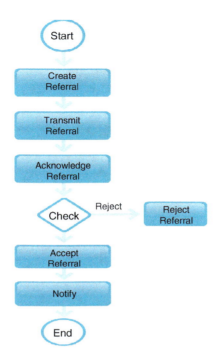

Within a SOA based approach individual tasks and functions are first broken down into their simplest generic components, described individually as *Services*. These services comprise intrinsically unassociated units of functionality that have no calls to each other embedded in them. Instead of services embedding calls to one another in source code, they use defined protocols that describe how one or more services can talk to each other. This architecture then relies on a business process expert to link, sequence services, and assemble them into groups in a process known as orchestration, to meet a new or existing business system requirement. They can then provide the clinical and business processes necessary to support the different functional activities undertaken by each individual participant, department or care setting within the healthcare environment.

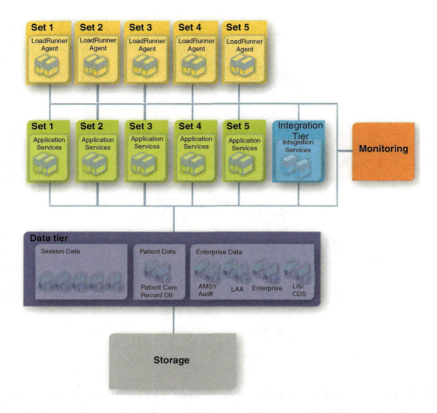

The five key Characteristics of the SOA approach are:

1. Modularity
2. Distributable capability
3. Clearly defined
4. Swappable
5. Sharable

Benefits
The benefits of using SOA are many fold. SOA has the features of distributable modular components, massive reduction in developmental cost, secure exchange of information, sharable and modular design for easy integration, process modelling capabilities, complementing existing system, etc.

7.14 Benchmarking

Benchmarking is the process of comparing the cost, time or quality of what one organization does against what another organization does. What results is often a business case for making changes in order to make improvements. Benchmarking is

7.14 Benchmarking

a process used particularly in strategic management in which organizations evaluate various aspects of their processes in relation to best practice, usually within their own sector. This then allows organizations to develop plans on how to make improvements or adopt best practice, usually with the aim of increasing some aspect of performance. Benchmarking may be a one-off event, but is often treated as a continuous process in which organizations continually seek to challenge their practices.

Lorenzo is a product which can be easily replicated by other software product development firms. To stay competitive and be the market leader, it has to attain the well defined standards by other software products as well as start new trends and milestones in performance and services.

Lorenzo as a product can benchmark in the following aspects:

1. In quality of the software Product
2. In the documentation and process of software development
3. In the technology of the software
4. In the performance metrics
5. Functional Benchmarking (Healthcare)
6. Data Security and encryption

	Concurrent Users (The four tier architecture which supports LORENZO)					
	25	250	3,000	5,000	15,000	25,000
Average Transactions (per hour)	8,289	60,683	731,897	1,282,535	3,473,425	6,111,116
Average Response Times (%)						
Under 1s	99	98	94	94	93	95
Under 3s	99	99	99	97	99	99
CPU Utilization (%)						
App Server	4	12	45	43	32	40
DB Server	4	2	17	17	14*	50

Current Benchmarking for LORENZO

In global markets the scale and complexity of healthcare is demanding solutions that are able to support an increased number of users and transactional workload.

Centralized delivery enables healthcare providing organizations to deliver a unified solution to the complexity and pace of change in today's healthcare landscape. This benchmark provides evidence of LORENZO's ability to support from the largest to the smallest healthcare organization in a cost-effective manner.

It supports a regional health economy with representative transactions of 25,000 concurrent users operating from 1,000 Primary Care Practices and 27 Secondary Care units on a 4TB database, with appropriate response times of less than 3 s 99% of the times. It also supports a messaging throughput of 160 messages per second and demonstrates solution manageability as part of an enterprise system management solution.

7.15 Change Management

Change Management is a systematic, organized approach to application of knowledge, tools and resources of change that provides organizations with a key process to achieve business strategy. Change management for organizations takes place in three major steps:

1. Defining current position of the organization and where it wants to go
2. Finding out what needs to be done to get there
3. Programme and the use of IT to make those changes

We have completed steps 1 and 2 through analyzing the vision and mission and deriving the Corporate Strategy of the company already. Let us focus on the implementation of IT change management.

Change Management is essential for a company such as iSOFT for the following reasons. *First*, iSOFT, as already mentioned in the company overview, has grown primarily through mergers and acquisitions. In such a scenario, different cultures from different organizations need to be merged and barriers broken. *Second*, iSOFT focuses on constant innovation through products incorporating new features and the use of newer technologies. Employees should be encouraged to incorporate the new features and technologies. *Third,* change management will have to play a key role if Business Process Reengineering (BPR) activities have to be taken up.

IT, therefore needs to contribute significantly to managing change. IT can be used to conduct Change Management in the following areas.

(a) Community of practice and community of interest

 A Community of Practice consists of people engaged in similar tasks and are informally bound by what they do together. A *Community of Interest* is defined by knowledge and rather than by task, and exists because participation has value to members. Both of these concepts can be aided using IT by providing *services such as E-forums and E-groups for shared learning* to keep the community members together as well as adding to quality of professional as well as personal life of employees.

(b) Responsibility of CIO

 A CIO plays a very essential role in Change Management. The person needs to focus across functional areas such as marketing, finance, etc. and has to have good communication skills so that he can facilitate cohesion among team members working on a particular section of Lorenzo.

(c) Documentation and knowledge management

 Create an online repository and provide documentations of the change management programme, its purpose, responsibility allocations, impact analysis, etc. Documentations containing previously successful and unsuccessful change management programmes in other organizations should also be made available to the appropriate personnel for reference.

(d) Employee feedback service
There needs to be an online feedback / survey mechanism through which employees can anonymously post their problems, recommendations, etc, which can be addressed by senior HR personnel.

(e) Mission and vision workshops
Workshops need to be conducted for employees where the business goals and objectives and the company's core values need to be put across. The misconceptions need to be done away with and the strategic messages conveyed to the employees and cultural boundaries broken. IT can be used to facilitate these meetings by remote video conferencing and net meeting facilities, so that employees from all over the organization come together. A formal planning model needs to be developed if possible.

(f) Training
Developers need to be trained on the most widely used and latest technologies for product development. Employees' training needs can be collected through ESS and training calendars developed by aggregating the needs. Employee self-learning can also be encouraged through online programmes.

(g) Performance measurement
Finally, the effectiveness of the change management programme needs to be determined. That can be done by implementing a performance measurement system and defining KPIs which will continuously measure employee's performances. Those performances over a period of time need to be analysed and the change management programme needs to be modified accordingly if results are not satisfactory.

7.16 IT Audit

An Information Technology Audit is an examination of the controls within an organization's IT infrastructure. It is the process of collecting and evaluating evidence of an organization's information systems, practices, and operations. The audit will have six major steps given below.

(a) Establish the role of Auditor
In the first step, the role of the auditor is to be defined in terms of Responsibility, Authority and Accountability. Responsibility includes scope, independence and deliverables, Authority includes right of access to information and Accountability includes auditor rights and completion date, etc.

(b) Preliminary review
It includes gathering organizational information and identifying organization's strategy and responsibilities to manage applications. The accounting system is reviewed to identify which applications are financially significant from the organizational point of view.

(c) Establish materiality and assess risk
In this step, preliminary judgment about materiality and assessment of the client's business risks are to be made to set the scope of the audit. The business risks include the IT and non-IT risks identified in an earlier section of this report.
(d) Planning the audit
Proper planning is required for efficiently and effectively conducting the Audit. A detailed procedure for conducting the audit is to be put forth.
(e) Internal control mechanism
It provides assurance that operations in the organization are effectively and efficiently performed, that there is reliability of financial reporting and due compliance with laws and that regulation is maintained. The Auditor should consider previous reviews to gauge the complexity of organization's operations and systems.
(f) Performing audit and issuing audit report
In this step, audit procedures are to be developed based on the Auditor's understanding of the organization and its environment. After all procedures have been performed and report has been evaluated, a qualified or unqualified report is issued.

7.17 ROI Framework

7.17.1 Benefits of Lorenzo

1. Revenue enhancement
   As the product (Lorenzo) is an integrated healthcare solution having excellent compatibility with other solutions from iSOFT and products from different equipment manufacturers, it will be a source of revenue growth by being able to attract new customers.

   With a wide range of functionalities enabling single point access of relevant patient data, it will lead to high customer retention and in turn contribute to revenue growth.

   Will help in positioning the iSOFT in the entire gamut of healthcare solution market
2. Cost reduction
   The product being an integrated enterprise wide healthcare solution will significantly reduce the cost as compared o developing, marketing and maintaining isolated systems.
3. Other benefits
   Increased customer satisfaction and strong brand equity. Also reduction in Physician's time will generate high good will.

7.17.2 Investments

1. Development cost
   - Hardware cost
   - Software development cost
   - Manpower cost
   - Training cost

2. Marketing cost
   - Sales Manpower cost
   - Cost of establishing links with hospitals and surgeons
   - Cost of arranging seminars and presenting in trade shows

3. Distribution cost
   - Cost of establishing distribution networks

4. Maintenance cost
   - Cost of maintaining service personnel and required SLAs

7.18 The Road Ahead

After the success of LORENZO, the next plans for iSOFT Health as a part of IBA health group are:

Business continuity
The next plan of iSOFT is to partner with *Inchware* and provide the next level of healthcare service. Inchware markets and supports a suite of medical applications designed for use by healthcare professionals with small—"inch-scale"—handheld computers. The extremely small size of such devices permits essential mobility, but limits the device in other ways; for instance, memory capacity, screen size and data entry systems do not begin to approach the capabilities of a desktop PC. This approach will allow iSOFT to (i) access and update patient data and information while mobile and (ii) access patient records in case of server downtime. During this downtime patient records can be updated and full synchronization can be attained when server is available again. This will be the first step of next generation healthcare services.

The "Dorking" project
Dorking Healthcare Limited Liability Partnership is a new organization formed by local GPs to provide high quality, local and timely outpatient appointments for patients of the Dorking practices. It aims to increase the range of services provided at Dorking Hospital, make sure that Dorking patients are seen at Dorking Hospital rather than at East Surrey or Epsom Hospitals, reduce waiting times for appointments, ensure that almost all appointments are with a consultant, attract experienced and

dynamic consultants to work in Dorking, develop a close working arrangement between the Dorking GPs and the consultants, and make savings to re-invest to develop more services in Dorking.

iSOFT is working on this project and will provide six Synergy practices in Dorking, which will also include provision of out of hours service at local hospital, access to patient records out of hours, and updating patient records, medication and treatment, etc.

7.19 Practice Questions

1. What are the salient characteristics of healthcare industry? What are the challenges faced by the industry?
2. How does iSOFT plan to face these challenges?
3. How can IT strategy help to face this challenge? What are the risks in this approach?
4. How can role based security be integrated with IT strataegy?
5. How can investment in IT strategy be justified with both quantitative and qualitative benefits?

7.20 Appendix 1: UK Central Government Spending

The following illustrates the overall view of the total public spending by UK government.

United Kingdom Central Government and Local Authority Spending
Fiscal Year 2008
Amounts in £ billion
GDP: £1,405.0 billion

COFOG	Central	General Gov.	Local	Total clk
Pensions	99.8	0.0	0.0	99.8
Health Care	102.2	0.0	0.4	102.6
Education	26.8	0.0	49.8	76.7
Defence	38.4	0.0	0.1	38.5
Welfare	49.0	0.0	41.2	90.2
Protection	16.2	0.0	16.2	32.4
Transport	10.7	0.0	9.1	19.8
General Government	13.2	0.0	12.3	25.5
Other Spending	42.7	0.0	32.3	75.0
Interest	29.9	0.0	0.8	30.7
Balance	1.1	0.0	-6.4	-5.3
Total Spending	430.1	0.0	155.7	585.9

This gives the breakup of the spending in Healthcare system.

[-] Health Care	102.2	0.0	0.4	102.6
—[-] Medical service	99.6	0.0	0.0	99.6
— Medical services (CKHME)	99.6	0.0	0.0	99.6
— National health service (GKHNH)	0.0	0.0	0.0	0.0
—[-] Public health services	2.0	0.0	0.0	2.0
— Central and other health services (CKHHC)	2.0	0.0	0.0	2.0
— Public health services (GKHPH)	0.0	0.0	0.0	0.0
—[-] R&D Health	0.6	0.0	0.0	0.6
— Health research (CKHHR)	0.6	0.0	0.0	0.6
—[-] Health n.e.c.	0.0	0.0	0.4	0.4
— Health n.e.c (CKHNC)	0.0	0.0	0.0	0.0
— Health services (GKHEA)	0.0	0.0	0.0	0.0
— Health (capital) (LCHEA)	0.0	0.0	0.1	0.1
— Health (current) (LKHEA)	0.0	0.0	0.3	0.3
— Total Health (PCHEA)	0.0	0.0	0.0	0.0
— NHS Trusts (Scotland) (PCSHT)	0.0	0.0	0.0	0.0
— NHS Trusts (Wales) (PCWHT)	0.0	0.0	0.0	0.0

(Source: - http://www.ukgovernmentspending.com)

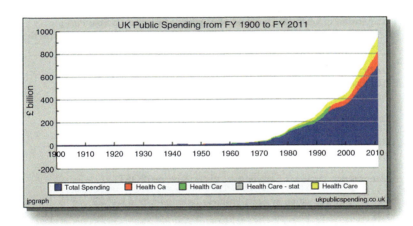

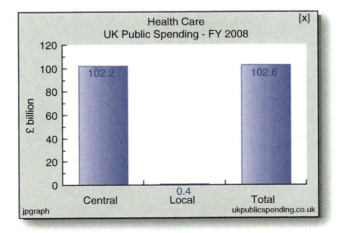

(Source:- http://www.ukpublicspending.co.uk)

7.21 Appendix 2: Timeline of iSOFT

- 2007
  - IBA Health Group merger
- 2006
  - Disposal of Swiss operations
- 2005
  - Acquisition of Novasoft Sanidad S.A.
- 2004
  - World-wide strategic alliance with Microsoft
  - Two principal contracts entered into to deliver software and services as part of the National Programme for IT (NPfIT) in England
- 2003
  - Merger with Torex plc
- 2002
  - Acquisition of Revive Group Limited
  - Acquisition of Paramedical Pty Limited
  - Acquisition of healthcare business of Northgate Information Solutions plc
  - Microsoft global launch partner, and the only European software partner for the Windows XP Tablet PC launch
- 2001
  - Dedicated offshore development business established in Chennai, India
  - Acquisition of ACT Medisys Limited
  - Acquisition of Eclipsys Limited and Eclipsys Pty Limited
- 2000
  - Full listing on London Stock Exchange
- 1999
  - Only Microsoft SQL Server 7.0 launch partner in UK health
  - Acquisition of CSC's Australian healthcare systems business
- 1998
  - Management buy-out by senior executives to create iSOFT
- 1994
  - Healthcare information systems business founded within KPMG

7.22 Appendix 3: Applications of LORENZO

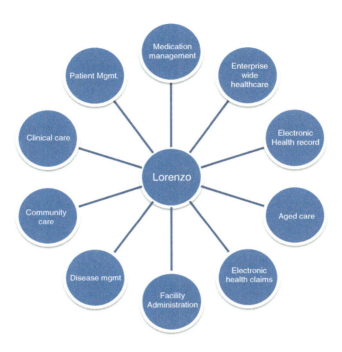

References

www.hospitaliteurope.com
www.ukaachen.de
Mark Holland (2006) Coming of age: a report on a performance benchmark test of iSoft's Lorenzo clinical information system. Health Industry Insights
www.isoftplc.com
http://www.computing.co.uk/computing/analysis/2196243/lorenzo-software-vital-isoft
http://www.ehealthinsider.com/News/2080/'no_believable_plan'_for_completion_of_isoft_lorenzo

Chapter 8
IT Strategy for McDonald's

8.1 Learning Objectives

The case deals with integration of business model and information strategy for a multi-national organization across different continents. The case also explains how IS is strategically used in ensuring that internal production processes and quality of deliverables remain consistent in a service-oriented fast food chain. By implementing IS, compliances to defined processes are ensured which helps in seeking formal or organized information before taking decisions. The case can be discussed in Information Strategy course as well as in Marketing Management courses. Also, the case can be used in MIS classes in MBA to explain monitoring processes being supported by IS. The data for the case have been compiled from field visits to different outlets of McDonald's and holding discussions with executives working with McDonald's and their customers as well as vendors. The objectives of the case are

- To learn about the business model of a multi-national organization engaged in fast food marketing.
- To understand how consistencies in quality of products and services can be maintained in a service organization.
- How to justify investment in technology for McDonald's.
- To get an idea about how ROI calculation should be done for finding feasibility of technology investment.

8.2 Executive Summary

McDonald's corporation is the world's largest chain of fast food restaurants and serves nearly 47 million customers daily. The company claims that it has served over 1 billion orders till date and primarily sells hamburgers, cheeseburgers, chicken products, French fries, breakfast items, soft drinks, milkshakes, and desserts.

In this chapter, we have attempted to understand how a company like McDonald's can leverage on an IT strategy to achieve operational efficiency and improve its service to customers.

Management of the operations of a company of the McDonald's is a mammoth task. Efficiency, timeliness, and low cost are the three most important aspects of its operations.

8.3 Company Background

The company began its business in 1940, with a restaurant that was opened by Dick and Mc Donald in San Bernardino, California.

Their introduction of the "Speedee Service System" in 1948 established the principles of the modern fast food restaurant.

McDonald's restaurants are found in 119 countries and territories around the world and serve nearly 47 million customers each day.

McDonald's operates over 31,000 restaurants worldwide, employing more than 1.5 million people. The company also operates other restaurant brands, such as Piles Café, and has a minority stake in Pret a Manger. The company owned a majority stake in Chipotle Mexican Grill until completing its divestment in October 2006.

	McDonald's corporation
Locations	31000+
Revenue	$22 .79 Billion (2007)
Employees	390,000 (2008)
Industry	Restaurants

Most standalone McDonald's restaurants offer both counter service and drive-through service, with indoor and sometimes outdoor seating; Drive-Thru, Auto-Mac, Pay and Drive, or "McDrive" as it is known in many countries.

8.3.1 McCafés

To accommodate the current trend for high-quality coffee and the popularity of coffee shops in general, McDonald's introduced McCafés.

The McCafé concept is a café-style accompaniment to McDonald's restaurants. McCafé is a concept of McDonald's Australia, starting with Melbourne in 1993. Today, most McDonald's in Australia have McCafés located within the existing McDonald's restaurant. In Tasmania, there are McCafés in every store, with the rest of the states quickly following suit. After upgrading to the new McCafe look and feel, some Australian stores have noticed up to a 60% increase in sales. As of the end of 2003, there were over 600 McCafés worldwide.

Some locations are connected to gas stations/convenience stores, while others called McDonald's Express have limited seating and/or menu or may be located in a shopping mall. Other McDonald's are located in Wal-Mart stores. McStop is a location targeted at truckers and travellers which may have services found at truck stops.

8.3.2 Business Model

McDonald's Corporation earns revenue as an investor in properties, a franchiser of restaurants, and an operator of restaurants. Approximately 15% of McDonald's restaurants are owned and operated by McDonald's Corporation directly. The remainders are operated by others through a variety of franchise agreements and joint ventures.

The McDonald's Corporation's business model is slightly different from that of most other fast food chains. In addition to ordinary franchise fees and marketing fees, which are calculated as a percentage of sales, McDonald's may also collect rent, which may also be calculated on the basis of sales. As a condition of many franchise agreements, which vary by contract age, country, and location, the Corporation may own or lease the properties on which McDonald's franchises are located. In most, if not all cases, the franchisee does not own the location of its restaurants.

As a matter of policy, McDonald's does not make direct sales of food or materials to franchisees, instead organize the supply of food and materials to restaurants through approved third-party logistics operators.

8.3.3 Scale of Operations

McDonald's has become emblematic of globalization, sometimes referred as the "McDonaldization" of society. The Economist magazine uses the "Big Mac Index": the comparison of a Big Mac's cost in various world currencies can be used to informally judge these currencies' purchasing power parity.

The company operates over 31,000 stores in over 100 countries across the globe.

- Global business.
- Operates in a highly competitive market where local players can have a major influence on the customer's preferences.
- Service efficiency and customer experience are given special emphasis at McDonald's.
- Company aims to improve on service, speed, and looks for avenues to standardize its processes across its restaurants.

8.4 Industry Scenario (Fast Food and Quick-Service Restaurants)

8.4.1 Industry Overview

The fast food and quick-service (fast food) restaurant industry includes about 200,000 restaurants with combined annual revenue of about $120 billion. Major companies include McDonald's, Burger King, Taco Bell, Subway, and Panera Bread.

The industry is *highly fragmented*: the top 50 companies hold about 25% of industry sales.

8.4.1.1 Competitive Landscape

- *Demographics* and *personal income* drive demand.
- The profitability of individual companies depends on efficient operations, effective marketing, and the ability to provide fast service.

- Large companies have advantages in purchasing, financing, and marketing. Small companies can compete by offering unique products or serving a local market.
- The industry is *highly labour intensive*: average annual revenue per worker is just under $40,000.
- Fast food restaurants differ from full service restaurants in that customers generally order and pay before eating. The category includes *fast-casual restaurants*, which offer higher quality, more expensive food without waitstaff.
- Fast food restaurants compete with companies that offer meals or prepared foods, including full-service restaurants; supermarkets; delis; convenience stores; snack shops (donut or bagel shops); and cafeterias.

8.4.1.2 Products, Operations, and Technology

Most restaurants specialize in *main dish* categories, including hamburgers, sandwiches, chicken, pizza/pasta, Mexican food, Asian food, or snacks.

- Among the major fast food chains, *hamburger restaurants* are 50% of the market; *sandwich, pizza, chicken, and snack shops* are each 10%; and *Mexican food* is about 5%, according to *QSR* magazine.
- *Side dishes* include French fries, baked potatoes, soup, chilli, onion rings, salads, and desserts.
- *Beverages* include soft drinks, bottled water, coffee, tea, juice, beer, and milkshakes. Restaurants may also offer breakfast items, children's meals, or meal packages.
- Customers consume about 60% of food *off-premise*.

Fast food restaurants include *national* and *regional chains, franchises*, and *independent operators*. The majority of companies are single restaurant operations. Franchises allow independent owners to leverage a well-known brand name and benefit from the purchasing efficiencies and operational expertise of the franchiser. Large companies may have both corporate and franchise-owned stores. Companies may issue franchises for an individual store or a geographical market. Franchisees must adhere to quality and operational guidelines dictated by franchisers and may have limited control over menu offerings, hours of operation, pricing, and store design.

8.4.1.3 Additional Features

Most fast food restaurants have a *food preparation area, dining area*, and *parking lot*, and many have a *drive-thru* section.

Drive-thru sales can be important and *double windows* help speed transaction times. Some restaurants have *children's play areas*.

8.4.1.4 Location/Site

Since *customer convenience* is critical, most fast food restaurants are located in *high traffic* areas. Companies carefully evaluate potential restaurant sites, considering *population*, *traffic flow*, and *walking patterns*.

Restaurants may be freestanding or located inside another building. Companies may place *kiosks*, with limited or no seating, in tight spaces like airports or train stations.

The average size of a fast food restaurant varies, depending on seating and equipment requirements. A Subway averages 1,200 square feet and typically seats about 30; a Wendy's ranges between 2,000 and 3,000 square feet and seats 60–90.

8.4.1.5 Profit

A typical fast food restaurant generates $670,000 annually, according to the National Restaurant Association (NRA). A franchised fast food restaurant can generate $1–$2 million annually.

8.5 Key Points About Fast Food Industry

- Fast food is a *volume-driven* business, and *transaction speed* is extremely important.
- *Process improvement* in every part of operations, including customer ordering, food preparation, packaging, and final order assembly, can help companies serve more customers and drive sales.
- *Limited menus* also help, since fewer ingredients reduce costs and make food assembly easier. Simplifying food preparation helps control *quality* by minimizing worker error.
- *Lunch* is the most important time of day, and most restaurants increase staff and food production to meet demand.
- *Cleanliness* is important, not just for customers, but also to ensure compliance with local health and sanitation codes. Most franchises have cleaning schedules for facilities and equipment.
- *Supplies* vary, depending on the menu, but include beef, poultry, pork, cheese, produce, buns/bread, cooking oil, paper and packaging material, and beverages.
- *Inventory management* is important because fast food restaurants use *perishable items*.
- Companies often have *long-term contracts* with *soft drink suppliers*.
- Most franchisees must buy food, packaging, and equipment from approved distributors.
- *Equipment* typically includes commercial ovens, broilers, grills, toasters, deep fryers, warming devices, refrigerators, coolers, freezers, and beverage dispensing systems.

- Fast food restaurants typically deal with limited room and may use *space-saving* or *ventless equipment*.
- New technology in ovens that combines *convection heat*, *air impingement* (high velocity jets of hot air), and *microwave energy* helps food cook faster.
- POS: Fast food restaurants may use *computerized point-of-sale* (*POS*) *systems* that link to the kitchen, and possibly the drive-thru, to reduce ordering errors. Most franchises have proprietary POS systems that link to corporate headquarters so that management can monitor sales.
- Some large companies have integrated *inventory management* systems that communicate with suppliers via the Internet, allowing for *automated replenishment*.
- A few companies allow *online orders* for customer pick-up or delivery.
- By using American Express' radio frequency identification-based (RFID) *Express Pay*, fast food restaurants can eliminate the need for a credit card payment signature and shave up to 30 s off transaction time.

8.6 McDonald's Vision Statement

The vision for an organization defines the desired or intended future state of a specific organization or enterprise in terms of its fundamental objective and/or strategic direction. McDonald's vision statement states that "McDonald's vision is to be the world's best quick service restaurant experience. Being the best means providing outstanding quality, service, cleanliness, and value, so that we make every customer in every restaurant smile". The important point to be looked at in the vision statement is the emphasis on four factors:

- Quality
    - McDonald's sees itself as a provider of the good and reliable quality of products to all its consumers all across the globe.
- Service
    - It looks to differentiate itself through the level of service it provides to all its customers globally. It also ensures that across the globe the level of service is maintained at the superior level that McDonald's promises.
- Cleanliness
    - McDonald's respects the fact that food provide in a safe, hygienic, and clean environment is a duty and also something that is desired by consumers worldwide. Hence, this is one of the core factors that is stressed upon in the vision statement.
- Value
    - Through all its endeavours, McDonald's looks to provide superior value to all consumers and a value for the money that they pay for the service.

8.7 Mission Statement

A mission statement defines the fundamental purpose of an organization or an enterprise, basically describing why it exists. McDonald's mission statements' are encapsulated below:

- Be the best employer for our people in each community around the world.
- Deliver operational excellence to our customers in each of our restaurants.
- Achieve enduring profitable growth by expanding the brand and leveraging the strengths of the McDonald's system through innovation and technology.

The mission statements ensure a goal to be kept in focus while playing to reach the final vision for the organization. Hence, these are measures to be kept in perspective while achieving the vision that has been mentioned above.

8.8 Corporate Strategy and IT Strategy

8.8.1 Corporate Strategy and IT Strategy

The corporate strategy is an organization's wide focus to achieve the objectives that have been planned for an organization to reach certain planned and strategized goals. Based on the balanced score card and SWOT analysis, the core areas of focus are decided and a corporate strategy was decided for the same. Based on the corporate strategy, an IT strategy was designed to ensure the achievement of the set objectives. The IT strategy is sub-part of the complete corporate strategy and it facilitates the same, and hence, is of utmost importance for any organization. The corporate strategy has been listed below, with the IT strategy that has been planned for the same written below the same. Hence, the IT strategy has been mapped to achieve the corporate strategy.

8.8.2 Corporate Strategy Focus Area I

Focus on continually improving customer experience to harness Quality and Service as differentiators to complement price competitiveness.

8.8.2.1 IT Strategy

- Improving customer feedback mechanisms and implementing advanced data mining solutions to notice trends and consumer needs
  - This is a key in understanding the markets they are presently in, and also prospective markets. Such a move would drive home an advantage of providing

the consumers exactly what they need, hence developing a competency in quality and serving the customers' changing needs. Hence, adding to the price competency with the competency of a value provider.

- Providing features such as Wi-Fi services to improve customer experience
- Enriching customer experience by providing technology to suit new consumer needs (Digital Jukebox's, Ringtone downloads, Digital printing services)
    – Providing services that can provide more service to the new youth and growing tech-savvy consumers.
- Implementing efficient and up-to-date knowledge management to enhance customer convenience
    – This can be ensured by keeping all the data across the media consistent and up-to-date. This includes keeping the website updated with all the latest information, such as new menus, food, and calorie information
    – Providing services such as online ordering system, calorie count metre, and nutrition guide for health-savvy consumers.
- Implement contactless payment services
    – This will ensure quick customer turn around in drive-in and drive-through counters, and hence, ensure better customer service.
    – This can be achieved using technologies such as RFID and bar code readers that can aid customers to pay directly via linked bank accounts or using a credit balance scheme. Hence, customers do not have to wait to be billed and the same can be done using remotely accessing such cards.
- Integrating complete retail network to bring about standardization of services
    – This will ensure that all the retail outlets get the exact same information regarding menus and other details related to the enterprise and provide the exact service globally.

8.8.3 Corporate Strategy Focus Area II

Using IT as an enabler to improve operational process efficiencies and increase cost-effectiveness of existing processes.

8.8.3.1 IT Strategy

- Integrating all existing processes into currently installed applications such as ERP solutions.
    – This will ensure that all processes follow best practices in the industry, and hence, can improve efficiencies of all the internal processes. This is a key

objective as it would lead to direct cost savings. An application such as ERP can improve productivity of all processes while increasing efficiency of the same.
- Enhance cost savings by integrating value chain by including channel partners who can maximize potential savings and returns from integrated partnerships.
  - This reduces wastages and redundancies in the value chain. Vertical integration also yields better results because the technology synergies achieved help in making the systems much more efficient.
- Using technology such as RFID to reduce resource requirement and improve cost-effective operations.
  - Reduction in human capital required for warehouse work, as technology can make it much more efficient.
- Looking at solutions such as outsourcing to improve operational costs.
- Implementing models such as Hub n Spoke to integrate branches to HQ's for increased data usage.
  - Such a model with integration of proper IT services and integration of applications such as ERP can lead to better inventory management, forecasting, and better management of all processes.
- Using Green IT as a tool of the future.
  - Green IT is a tool of the future and is the application of IT for environmental friendly practices in business. This could include reduction in usage of paper by increasing usage of e-services and reduction in power consumption by monitoring and conserving power using IT to monitor the same. Such activities lately have lead to huge cost savings as IT provides extremely minute and continuous monitoring of the same. In this way, Green IT could lead to a huge bonus going ahead.
- Centralized advertising control.

8.8.4 Corporate Strategy Focus Area III

Using IT as driver to implement standardization of global services.

8.8.4.1 IT Strategy

- Using knowledge management solution to ensure standardization of employee performance and customer service

- Knowledge management and distribution of knowledge can be done using IT as a tool, and this can ensure standardization of processes. The training exercises can also be run remotely leading to huge cost savings.
- Using extensive global data recovered with Data warehousing and Mining applications for finding new business opportunities
  - Storing all the relevant data from global operations and then using the same by applying data mining and business intelligence solutions. This can help in dynamic offer creation and also for deciding the menus and other activities such as these.
- Using IT as a tool for training and personnel management services
  - Remote training activities can be conducted using technology and this can help in standardization of the same and also in cost savings. This can also lead to reduction in training personnel required.
- Improve change management by using IT for increased reach and key driver to implement organizational change.
  - Change management can be spearheaded by using IT purely on the strength of its reach and the way it can be harnessed for managing change management. Using it for application such as getting organization wide awareness, participation from employees using the website and intranet, etc.

8.8.5 Corporate Strategy Focus Area IV

Continuing CSR activities concordant with the vision of the firm.

8.8.5.1 IT Strategy

- Increasing ventures such as Green IT.
  - Since McDonald's looks to build a reputation of being one of the global leaders and providers to society, ventures such as Green IT implementation in the processes will go a long way in ensuring success socially and developing the McDonald's brand globally.

8.9 Factors to Consider When Designing the IT Strategy

While designing the IT strategy for a firm, a list of important factors should be considered before deciding the IT strategy. These factors are:

- Stakeholders: Any firm will have a list of stakeholders such as customers, shareholders, society, employees, technology partners, business partners, suppliers,

and government. The effect of any strategy on these stakeholders should be discussed first before arriving to the IT strategy.
- Lifecycle of the industry: McDonald's started in 1955 and since then the fast food industry has undergone widespread changes. Currently, the industry is in its maturing stage. The industry is being consolidated with price acting as a major competitive advantage point for gaining market share. The diminishing market share of major players in the industry is forcing them to diversify their offerings.
- Existing Ventures of McDonald's: McDonald's owns chains such as Pre-A-Manager and Boston Grill. The new IT strategy should take into consideration this diversification.
- Additional Factors: Factors such as the division of McDonald's into various business units and the presence of their Global Business Model which is known as McDonaldization should also be looked into.

8.10 SWOT Analysis

The SWOT analysis allows us to gauge the strengths, weaknesses, opportunities, and threats existing for a firm. This analysis gives us a clearer understanding of the current position of McDonald's in its immediate environment.

8.10.1 Strengths

- Competency and experience in Quick service industry
- High TOMA
- Extremely high brand value
- Distribution reach
- Industry leadership

8.10.2 Weakness

- Decreasing market share
- Changing consumer preferences in Fast food category
- High inertia to change

8.10.3 Opportunities

- Diversification of fast food industry segments
- Existing ventures in other Quick Servicing Industries

8.10.4 Threats

- Close competition in market share and revenues
- Category pressures from other Fast Food categories
- Environmental and Societal forces
- Consumer defection from core product category

8.11 McDonald's Operations and Where It Could Be Used

A company of the size of McDonald's cannot run its operations without relying heavily on technology. Given the intense competition and the dynamic nature of the industry, the company has to ensure that it must correctly serve every customer and should also understand everything about a customer taste preferences and his choices in food.

McDonald's Corp. has helped revolutionize the way restaurants use technology, dating back to founder Ray Kroc's fascination with serving burgers and fries in a matter of minutes.

Throughout the years, the company has continued its efforts to advance technology. In the 1970s, for example, the burger chain spearheaded the industry's transition from old-fashioned cash registers to computerized POS systems that could track massive amounts of data in seconds. In the early 1990s, McDonald's was the first quick-service chain to instal touch-screen computers at the front counter and in the drive-thru, making it easier for servers to input orders.

"For us, it's all about providing our customers with a great experience and technology is key. Technology has great potential to improve our business—to render ourselves more efficient, simplify operations for our crew and offer the freshest possible food within a relevant customer experience," says Dave Weick, McDonald's senior vice president and chief information officer

In 2001, McDonald's began standardizing its technology by integrating its existing POS and back-office systems in more than 11,000 restaurants in the United States. The company now is investing in a common POS system for use around the world. NewPOS, a product developed by Savista, will help McDonald's improve restaurant productivity and enhance the customer experience. In addition, moving to NewPOS will create a common platform across the globe—a move that will better allow McDonald's to leverage future technology in the restaurants.

McDonald's emphasis on standardization has given the chain the ability to roll out new technology worldwide.

"It's relatively easy to deploy a solution in one restaurant, but we have 13,600 units in the U.S. and a total of about 30,000 worldwide, which is a true scaling challenge," Weick says, adding that in McDonald's view, "sticking with one [platform] minimizes the obstacles posed by large-scale deployment, such as the U.S. introduction of cashless payment systems with high-speed connectivity".

Areas where IT can be deployed at McDonald's:

- Order management
  - Self-Service Kiosks
  - Running Call centres to take orders in drive-thru's
  - Quality and safety checks
  - Cashless payments
  - Electronic payment systems
- Supply chain management
  - Inventory management
  - Procurement management
  - Vendor management
- Logistics and distribution
- Internal systems
  - Finance
  - HR
  - Payroll
- Analytics
  - CRM
  - Customer profiling
- Knowledge management

8.12 Balanced Scorecard

Perspectives	Performance measures	
1) Financial perspective	0.15	
Increase market share and revenues	Increased market share across categories	0.2
Improved margins	Improved selling margins	0.15
	Improved supplier margins	
Reduction in costs	Reduction in operational costs	0.5
	Reduction in logistics costs	
	Increase in savings on resources and personnel	
	Reduction in administration costs	
Increased synergies between business units	Reduction in transaction costs and transfer pricing	0.15
2) Internal business perspective	0.3	
Seamless integration between Business Units	Reduction in time redundancies across departments	0.2
	Reduction in response times across departments	
Improved forecasts and inventory reduction	Reduction in inventory costs	0.3
	Reduction in losses due to stock outs	
	Reduction in costs (supply and order) due to improved forecasting	

(continued)

Perspectives	Performance measures	
Improvement in process efficiency	Improvement in process times	0.2
Improved resource management	Reduction in requirement in nos. and costs of resources	0.1
Improved vendor relations and supply chain dynamics	Increased number of vendors integrated into IT systems	0.2
	Reduction in lead time	
	Reduction in ordering costs and savings	
3) Customer perspective	0.35	
Improved customer experience	Improved customer satisfaction index	0.2
	Reduction in customer complaints	
	Reduction in customer complaints response times	
Efficient customer feedback mechanism	Increased customer feedback responses	0.2
	Improved turnaround time to implement customer suggestions	
Improved customer interface and knowledge management	Increased completeness in customer data	0.2
Improved customer retention and additional feature usage	Reduction in customer defection and increase in customer base	0.1
Improved customer facing process performance	Reduction in customer billing times	0.2
	Improvement in customer servicing time	
	Increased customer churn ratio	
Internationalization	Reduction in complaints regarding internationalization	0.1
4) Learning and growth perspective	0.2	
Improved knowledge management	Increased number of educational courses	0.3
	Increased content for process and operational knowledge	
	Reduction in time for data retrieval for operational/ process data	
Process and knowledge standardization	Decrease in number of variances in process knowledge and practice	0.3
	Reduction in complaints regarding non-standardization	
Improved employee satisfaction	Increased employee satisfaction index	0.2
Enhanced employee motivation	Increased employee morale (qualitative)	0.2

8.13 Change Management

In an organization, changes in management system, operations, and other important activities are necessary particularly when the management has encountered problems with their current systems or they wanted to implement such change for enhancing and improving the overall performance of the organization. Internal or external drivers are the factors that force changes, innovations may be done at different level in the structure of any organization, and that reforms may be universal or limited in nature. Internal drivers for change could include evolving business requirements, organizational restructuring, or revision to corporate strategy/business objectives. External drivers could include developments in technology, economic trends that affect the profitability/value for money of the relationship, and the need for electronic or technical service.

Management of change can be considered as a primary activity in realizing the goals and objectives of any organization, even as implementation is the sensible or physical steps of employing an innovation. Individuals and their relationships are regarded as the major components to its successful execution, and sustainable mechanisms are needed to achieve the development and improvement in its procedures. The recognition of sections for improvement is the first level of the process of change, followed by the integration of plausible solutions to address conflicts and issues that are being identified. Actions in these sections are being held independent of position within the organization.

Thus, Mcdonald's should take into consideration:

- Importance of change management
  - Scale of operations
  - Brand value and risks due to bad implementation of change
- Standardization of services (website, customer service, outsourcing, etc.)
- Training exercises using IT as an interface to implement changes across enterprise
- Using IT to percolate change across enterprise, e.g. Menu additions, Value schemes
- Strategy will be common across the globe rather than localized change improving customer reach and experience

8.14 Management Information System

Management Information System (MIS) is basically concerned with processing data into information which is then communicated to the various Departments in an organization for appropriate decision making.

Data collection involves the use of Information Technology (IT) comprising: computers and telecommunications networks (E-Mail, Voice Mail, Internet, telephone, etc.).

8.14.1 Applications of MIS

Strategy support
While computers cannot create business strategies by themselves, they can assist management in understanding the effects of their strategies and help enable effective decision making.

MIS systems can be used to transform data into information useful for decision making. Computers can provide financial statements and performance reports to assist in the planning, monitoring, and implementation of strategy.

MIS systems provide a valuable function in that they can collate into coherent reports unmanageable volumes of data that would otherwise be broadly useless to decision-makers. By studying these reports decision-makers can identify patterns and trends that would have remained unseen if the raw data were consulted manually.

MIS systems can also use these raw data to run simulations—hypothetical scenarios that answer a range of "what if" questions regarding alterations in strategy. For instance, MIS systems can provide predictions about the effect on sales that an alteration in price would have on a product. These Decision Support Systems (DSS) enable more informed decision making within an enterprise than would be possible without MIS systems.

8.14.2 Data Processing

MIS not only allow for the collation of vast amounts of business data, but they also provide a valuable time-saving benefit to the workforce. Where in the past business information had to be manually processed for filing and analysis, it can now be entered quickly and easily onto a computer by a data processor, allowing for faster decision making and quicker reflexes for the enterprise as a whole.

8.14.3 Management by Objectives

While MIS systems are extremely useful in generating statistical reports and data analysis, they can also be of use as a Management by Objectives (MBO) tool.

MBO is a management process by which managers and subordinates agree upon a series of objectives for the subordinate to attempt to achieve within a set time frame. Objectives are set using the SMART ratio: that is, objectives should be Specific, Measurable, Agreed, Realistic, and Time-Specific.

The aim of these objectives is to provide a set of key performance indicators by which an enterprise can judge the performance of an employee or project. The success of any MBO objective depends upon the continuous tracking of progress.

In tracking this performance, it can be extremely useful to make use of an MIS system. Since all SMART objectives are by definition measurable, they can be tracked through the generation of management reports to be analysed by decision-makers.

8.14.4 Benefits of MIS

The field of MIS can deliver a great many benefits to enterprises in every industry. Expert organizations such as the Institute of MIS along with peer-reviewed journals such as MIS Quarterly continue to find and report new ways to use MIS to achieve business objectives.

8.14.5 Core Competencies

Every market-leading enterprise will have at least one core competency—that is, a function they perform better than their competitors. By building an exceptional management information system into the enterprise, it is possible to push out ahead of the competition. MIS systems provide the tools necessary to gain a better understanding of the market as well as a better understanding of the enterprise itself.

8.14.6 Enhance Supply Chain Management

Improved reporting of business processes leads inevitably to a more streamlined production process. With better information on the production process comes the ability to improve the management of the supply chain, including everything from the sourcing of materials to the manufacturing and distribution of the finished product.

8.14.7 Quick Reflexes

As a corollary to improved supply chain management comes an improved ability to react to changes in the market. Better MIS systems enable an enterprise to react more quickly to their environment, enabling them to push out ahead of the competition and produce a better service and a larger piece of the pie.

Further information about MIS can be found at the Bentley College Journal of MIS and the US Treasury's MIS handbook, and an example of an organizational MIS division can be found at the Department of Social Services for the state of Connecticut.

Metric	Data collection tool	Publisher	Periodicity
Revenues & Margins (±)	ERP system	Regional Heads of Depts.	Monthly
Operating costs (±)	ERP system	Regional Heads of Depts.	Monthly
PBIT (±)	ERP system	Regional Heads of Depts.	Monthly
% of revenues from new customers	ERP system	Regional Heads of Depts.	Monthly
Market share (±)	Market surveys	Chief/Regional marketing officer	Monthly
Response time towards customers	Tracking applications	Customer Relations/QA/IT	Weekly
Number of complaints (±)	Internal applications	Customer Relations/QA	Weekly
Customer satisfaction index	Surveys/Interviews	Customer Relations/QA	Monthly
Man hours required for maintenance	Internal applications	IS Department	Monthly
Number of high-performing employees	Performance appraisals	HR Department	Monthly
Reduction in lead times	ERP system	Area/Regional Heads	Weekly
Inventory	ERP system	Regional Heads of Depts.	Monthly
Stock outs	ERP system	Regional Heads of Depts.	Monthly
Process efficiency (time)	Internal applications	Branch Managers	Monthly
Avg. Customer servicing time	Internal applications	Branch Managers	Weekly
Cases of data discrepancy and integrity issues	Database	Information Tech Dept.	Monthly
Increase in certifications	HRIS	Human resources	Quarterly
Employee Turnover ratio	HRIS	Human resources	Quarterly
Employee satisfaction index	HRIS	Human resources	Quarterly

8.15 Return on Investment

- Computing incremental NPV using incremental cash flow method
    - Account for the cost of implementing the system
    - Compute annual or seasonal incremental cash flow coming from increased revenues and earnings
- Increase in revenues from existing customers
- Increase in customer base and additional revenue from the same
- Account for all the reduction in costs benefited accruing due to IT strategy
- Reduction in inventory costs
- Reduction in resource (labour, capital) costs
- Reduction in operational costs due to improved efficiencies
- Reduction in costs in cross-functional domains such as logistics, procurement, etc.
- Discount the same with appropriate discounting rate

8.16 Conclusion

McDonald's churns out an incredible volume and range of sophisticated propaganda. It often masquerades as factual information or as merely informing the public of "the McDonald's experience".

McDonald's strategy is to embrace multiple digital platforms, including web and mobile. The aim of the strategy is to build strong consumer relationships and ensure that consistent, compelling consumer experiences are delivered worldwide.

Its strategy signals an "elevated" commitment to digital by the global multi-national.

The commitment is being supported by a marked increase in online marketing spend. McDonald's has already increased its online investment "quite a bit" and will continue to do so in the coming year.

BASELINE GOALS in coming years for McDonald's would be

- Increase sales by at least 3–5%.
- Improve operating income by 5%.
- Cut capital expenditures.
- Cut the length of time needed for managers to collect and analyze individual restaurant sales and inventory from more than 1 week to a little as a minute.

8.17 Practice Questions

1. How does IT strategy help maintain consistency in following processes across continents?
2. How do you ensure that business goals are well integrated with information strategy?
3. How can ROI be calculated for such a massive investment in technology?
4. How does MIS help monitor different metrics?

Web Site

www.mcdonalds.com

Chapter 9
Devising IT Strategy for a Non-Government Organization: CTRAN Consulting

9.1 Learning Objectives

The case shows how information system can be used as a strategic tool in making a non-government organization (NGO) more efficient and effective. The case also focuses on using information system to reduce cost of operation and thereby passing on the benefit to the poor and needy people in the form of reduced lending rate. As a result, the case also discusses how effective implementation of IS can help NGOs to use inclusive technology at reduced cost to reach more people in economic way. Apart from Information Strategy course, the case can be taught in Financial Management, MIS courses as well as in Management Development Programmes (where senior executives from microfinance would be the target audience), workshops held for executives in NGOs, and in training sessions for capacity building in development areas. The case has been compiled from several secondary sources of data and field visits. The learning objectives of the case are:

- How NGOs operate at grass root levels.
- How measurements techniques are used in NGOs and how IS helps them in monitoring the progress.
- How investment in technology for NGOs are justified (ROI) calculations.

9.2 Executive Summary

CTRAN Consulting Pvt. Ltd. is an organization which offers consultancy services in the domains of energy and environment sector and climate change consultancy services with special emphasis on clean development mechanism, besides being a pioneer in rural infrastructure consultancy and livelihood enhancement.

It is a company with a countrywide network of 20 consultants and 50 employees in total. The major areas of service are—Energy Infrastructure, Climate Change and CDM, Environment, and Social Infrastructure Advisory services.

In trying to devise an IT Strategy for CTRAN, we have defined the business objectives of the firm in sync with its mission. While doing so, we understood who the stakeholders are and the possible competition. A Business model to meet the objectives was formulated with the appropriate process flows applied. The Pricing Strategy followed depends on prior experience of the CEO and previous client exposure and project engagements.

The issues and challenges that the organization will face given its size and its stage in the organization lifecycle in implementing an IT strategy have been identified and elaborated upon. We have devised a Balanced Scorecard and come up with an MIS implementation plan as strategic management tools to focus on various performance indicators.

The costs involved and the ROI when implementing an IT strategy were also calculated. Besides, the "critical success factors' for CTRAN were determined which included factors such as increase of customer count, high quality deliverable, and raising employee morale and productivity etc. Yet another aspect of an IT strategy which is the Change Management strategy was also included. In addition, a rewards and recognition scheme was also devised to take care of the employees" morale which is an important consideration when implementing a change management policy.

To sum it up, we have tried to define an IT strategy for CTRAN based on the various parameters that need to be looked into, e.g. architecture, technology, and organization structure. We have also defined an approach for implementation which includes training, change management, and ROI for the approach. It will be essential for CTRAN to embrace IT as an asset to create and sustain competitive advantage.

9.3 Introduction

CTRAN stands for Complete Transformation of value to its stakeholders, through in-depth study and careful analysis, into products and services designed to meet the growing requirements of its discerning clients. The organization offers consultancy services in the domains of energy and environment sector, climate change, rural infrastructure, and livelihood enhancement.

9.4 Mission

"Mission of CTRAN is to develop energy and infrastructure that enhance shareholder's value through a sustainable transaction based model using process and financial innovations contributing to inclusive growth and accountable development by managing climate change and reducing vulnerability through adaptation".

9.5 Industry Background

CTRAN has, as mentioned before, major streams of business which can be classified primarily under the industries Energy and Environmental Consulting, but the key differentiator here is their foray into livelihood and sustainability consulting. The energy and environmental consulting industry is dominated globally by the giants like Ernst & Young, PwC, KPMG, Accenture, etc. The same is true for the Indian market as well. But the industry situation is unique, since the industry is primarily knowledge-driven and hardly standardized. Hence, no one player can be said to have a stranglehold, nor can one player easily move across geographies and markets.

This, in turn, means that there exists a huge need for localized, regional, and niche consulting players in the energy and environmental space, whose execution and institutional knowledge in the region where they execute is unparalleled. These regional centres of excellence are eagerly sought out by the global players, for their local expertise and contacts in regional implementation projects. Thus, the industry situation is such that both large and small players co-exist and have a share of the entire consulting pie. Typically, the energy and environment consulting companies look at offering their customers services related to how to improve energy efficiency, adopting greener technologies, learning how to save using carbon credits trading mechanism, identification and selection of vendors for implementing the energy savings identified, etc.

9.6 Company Background

CTRAN Consulting Pvt. Ltd. is a part of the INR 5,000 million BASIX Group, a premier corporate house held in high regard in the field of micro-credit and livelihood promotion in India. The group has had over a decade of operation in over ten states in India with over 2,500 employees.

The company works with a countrywide network of twenty associates specialized in various core business areas of CTRAN Consulting. It has core strength of 50 employees in total.

The major areas of service are:

- Energy Infrastructure
- Climate Change and CDM
- Environment
- Social Infrastructure advisory services

9.6.1 Partners

- CTRAN, being a group company of BASIX, has the access and network of the parent company. It also has the advantage of being in various partnerships and

consortiums which give it the access and reach to a wide range of professional expertise for a wide range of activities. Consultancy firms like KPMG, Deloitte, and E&Y partner with CTRAN on certain key projects that require local expertise.
- The partnerships with the "Big Three" of consulting in turn ensure that CTRAN continually strives to match its processes, delivery quality, etc. with that of its partners.

9.6.2 The Competition

- Energy consulting is one of the most rapidly changing sectors, as energy costs soar and business and government leaders look for alternative ways of powering their organizations. Energy management consultants vary in the level of service that they provide. While many energy consulting firms represent manufacturers and push their products on their clients, CTRAN falls in that category of energy consulting services that stay independent and help one find the best solutions.
- CTRAN's competitors in this industry are "established" consulting bigwigs like KPMG, Deloitte, and E&Y. The advantage that these companies have is that their clients get reliable, cost-effective, and quality advice based on proven methodologies, efficient tools, and stable architectures, thus helping them achieve high performance in a number of ways. The insights gained across industries coupled with their expertise in implementing a number of associated technologies help these consulting firms in identifying opportunities better as well as structure project concepts in a more organized fashion.

9.7 Pricing Strategy

The pricing strategy of the company is derived from two fronts:

1. Previous project experience/client engagement
2. From the experience of the CEO

It is possible that Ashok Singha is able to understand from various inputs that he receives about the optimum price to quote for a tender, which is quite an ad hoc process.

Now the price quoted by the company to a client could have two components:

1. A flat fee: One that the company receives irrespective of the success/failure of the project and that the client is bound to foot.
2. A success fee: A percentage of the savings/carbon credit sales revenue that the customer receives with CTRAN's help.
3. Or a combination of the two.

It depends upon the negotiation with the clients as to what kind of fee structure is relevant for a particular project. There might be some projects where the success fee component is large and hence the stake that CTRAN has in its success is equally huge and other projects where the flat fee component is higher.

9.8 Business Objectives

1. To attract and retain clients through demonstration of capability and achievements.
2. Automate business processes to achieve greater efficiency.
3. Develop innovative process for undertaking challenging problems.
4. Knowledge management.

9.9 Stakeholders

1. Clients
2. End user
3. Shareholders
4. Government
5. NGOs and pressure groups

9.10 Process Flow

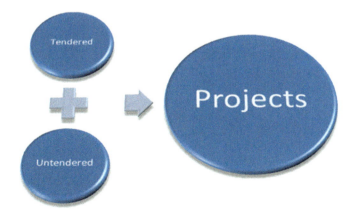

There are two types of projects which CTRAN is normally into. As shown in the diagram above, these can be classified into

1. Tendered
2. Untendered projects

Tendered projects are mainly government projects which are advertised in newspapers and are open for application to all interested parties. The process of application normally starts off with a Request For Proposal (RFP).

The normal flow for a tendered project is as follows: The RFP is applied by CTRAN through Expression of Interest (EoI). This is then shortlisted by the issuing authority and then the company is asked to present a detailed proposal including financials.

For the second type of untendered projects, CTRAN normally receives these projects through references and through pro-active pitching among clients, using existing client references to win a greater number of projects.

The existing process flow within the company can be described as follows:

The Pre-Award section of the process flow can be divided as mentioned into the activities given above. We see that a fledgling company like CTRAN must engage in multiple levels of marketing, including extensive participation in workshops and white paper presentations, so as to enhance their reputation among clients. A lot of research is inevitably involved, not only of the market and the client but also of the latest technologies in the domain, so that all the employees are constantly updated and can offer the latest advice to their clients.

9.11 Balance Score Card

The post-award process flow includes tollgates, so as to measure the time taken to complete the activities. This is important for CTRAN, since there is always a time pressure from clients to ensure timely delivery. This process also involves getting into tie-ups with different agencies since the implementation capabilities of CTRAN are quite limited and these partnerships are quite useful in the long term.

9.11 Balance Score Card

Balanced Score Card for CTRAN Consulting						
Overall weight	Sr.	Strategic Objective	Objective Weightage	Performance measures	Metric weightage	Overall Score
	A			Financial Perspective		
10%	F1	Improve profitabilty	30%	1. Profit Margins	30%	0.00900
				2. Cost per proposal	35%	0.01050
				3. Return on Investment	35%	0.01050
	F2	Increase Turnover	70%	1. % increase in revenue	60%	0.04200
				2. ROCE	40%	0.02800
	B			Customer Perspective		
25%	C1	Create a Powerful Name in Energy Consulting	33%	1. % age increase in number of bids asked for	50%	0.04125
				2. Increase in ratio of Contracts won to contracts applied for	50%	0.04125
	C2	Increase market share	33%	1. % increase in new customers	55%	0.04538
				2. % of old customers retained	45%	0.03713
	C3	Enhance Customer Satisfaction	34%	1. % retention of existing customer	50%	0.04250
				2. % reduction in SLA non-compliance and schedule slippage	50%	0.04250
	C			Process		
30%	P1	Standardize processes	45%	1. Reduction in time for proposal presentation	40%	0.05400
				2. % in delivery time	35%	0.04725
				3. % decrease in (Cost of Transaction/Value of Transaction)	25%	0.03375
	P2	Properly Track Activities	55%	1. % reduction in delivery time	60%	0.09900
				2. % increase in revenue / employee	40%	0.06600
	D			Learning and Development		
35%	L1	To retain a great team	80%	2. % increase in Average productivity of an employee	15%	0.04200
				4. % of employees retained	85%	0.23800
	L2	Attract good employees	20%	1. % decrease in employee search cost	40%	0.02800
				2. % rise in number of applicants	30%	0.02100
				3. % increase in recruitment budget	30%	0.02100

9.12 Current Issues and Challenges

The company is right now in the lower half of the growth stage where the processes are not well-defined. The company is right now looking at major business opportunities through partnership with the Big three who have bagged projects in Orissa and are looking for consulting partners like CTRAN who has local presence and expertise. Further with major projects coming through the UNDP and NREG schemes, it foresees further growth in areas of Social and Environmental sectors.

But right now at this juncture, the company needs to brace itself to such huge opportunities and formalize its processes to deliver quality services which are repeatable as well timely. Right now, many of the activities related to project are on ad hoc basis and as per the comfort of individual consultant. Thus, the company incurs a heavy cost in order to provide quality deliverables to its clients on a consistent basis. The project activities are tracked in excels and the templates are maintained separately by each consultant. There has been no centralized database for the external agents and prior projects which results in repetition of the effort. The activities are not tracked on regular basis and the CEO finds it difficult to monitor the progress. Further as the processes are decentralized, it is difficult to frame a decision support system.

The company now needs a system to manage the processes and standardize it as per industry standards. The company also has to ensure that there should be some flexibility in this system to ensure there are no bottlenecks. The new system should integrate different processes across departments. Finally, it should have a centralized database and MIS with different role and restrictions. The system should be scalable to keep abreast of the growth of the companies.

9.13 IT Strategy

Based on the Issues and Challenges, lists of applications required by CTRAN are identified as

1. Expression of Interest tracker
2. Project status tracker
3. HR system, Grievance system
4. PM system
5. Agency tracker
6. Resume container—Each agency has a different format
7. Resource centre—Knowledge repository
8. Time sheet, Leave sheet
9. Expense sheet—TA expenses, local conveyance, other expenses

Some of these applications need to be integrated while some others are standalone applications. One strategy that invariably comes into mind is the usage of an

ERP package. This option was analysed in the context of CTRAN and the team concluded that ERP is not a feasible solution for CTRAN. There are two key reasons for this:

1. Rigidity of systems
   ERP can be very rigid. CTRAN is in consulting business and hence there are no set patterns of completely standardized processes of working. Also being a very small organization, it cannot afford to be put into the rigidity of very strong procedures. A drawback of having robust process is that it can at times be cumbersome and time taking. CTRAN cannot afford to be such. For example, a big firm with large client bases like a E&Y can afford to keep customer waiting in case of a system failure. CTRAN may lose out the customer and with it a sizeable portion of its revenues if they keep a customer waiting. In such situations, they would have to revert to the manual systems to get work done. Also for CTRAN, not all systems need to be linked. The rigidity of ERP systems would put more pressure on timely delivery.
2. Cost and ROI
   CTRAN is a tiny company. Its turnover does not mandate a purchase of an ERP package worth a few lacs of Rupees. Also with such a tiny size, the benefits accrued will not add up for the costs incurred. ERP is not advisable for a small firm like CTRAN.

The given applications can be grouped into the following

1. Pre-award activity tracking systems (ATS)
   This includes those systems that track activities that happen before the award of the project. This includes

   (a) Expression of interest tracker
   (b) Costs tracker that tracks marketing; scouting costs-retrospective analysis of this can result in improvement of the processes
   (c) Proposal progress tracker
   (d) List of whitepapers, seminar presentations

   This is not a standalone application. It will be linked to the following

   (a) Client database which stores the details of prospective clients which can be used to profile clients. One of the key applications would be to distinguish firms which have had a history of awarding projects to CTRAN to those which have not. This would help tweak the proposal strategy to increase the conversion rate.
   (b) Knowledge Repository for scouting research, templates for proposal, etc.
   (c) HR Management Systems for appraisal purposes, performance-linked incentives, etc.
   (d) Personal management systems.

2. Post-award project tracking systems (PTS)
   This include those systems that track activities that happen after the award of the project

This include

(a) Project progress tracker—PM tools to track roles and responsibilities, deliverables, and tollgates.
(b) Cost tracker that tracks project costs and overheads—Retrospective analysis of this tracker can result in formulating better pricing strategies.

Although ATS and PTS systems are not linked, the PTS system is linked to the following:

(a) Knowledge Repository for research, templates, methodologies from past projects. Past learning can be incorporated and reused, and this, after a period of time, would reduce the time spent considerably, thereby reducing costs and increasing competitiveness.
(b) Personal management Systems—for business tours, travels details, attendance systems, leave management system, expense sheets, time sheets, payslip details, IT details, etc.
(c) HR Management Systems for appraisal purposes, performance-linked incentives, and other rewards and recognitions.

3. Personal management systems
   The ATS and PTS systems are linked to the Personal Management systems. The Personal Management Systems include

   (a) Attendance system.
   (b) Leave management system.
   (c) Time sheets.
   (d) Pre-award, post-awards overhead expense sheets.
   (e) Travel, tour details—this can be used to forge relationships with travel agents and can be used to avail discounts.
   (f) Pay slip details.
   (g) IT details.
   (h) Performance evaluation system.

4. Knowledge centre
   This is one of the most necessary areas for a consultancy firm. This is linked to both ATS and PTS systems. It is linked to Personal Management to get details of time spent per project by accessing the time sheets. It contains the following:

   (a) Research repository—including Gartner reports, whitepapers.
   (b) Past project details with learning.
   (c) Template repository with proposal, deliverable, and other templates.
   (d) Best practices repository.
   (e) Compliance norms repository—which consists of compliance norms for different clients.
   (f) Report generation tools.
   (g) Client, Agency, Partner information databases.

5. Accounting systems
   This is used for the accounting purposes. It is the repository for all the expenses, invoices collected by the firm. It is linked to the ATS, PTS, Personal Management Systems, HRM system (payroll), etc.

9.14 Architecture Design

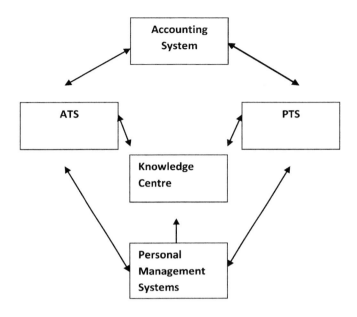

The architecture linkage can be explained using the matrix given below

To/From	ATS	PTS	Personal management systems	Knowledge centre	Accounting system
ATS	–	–	Travel details	Client information for first time clients, White papers, Seminars	Marketing costs, Scouting Costs
PTS	–	–	Travel details	Project learning	Project costs
Personal management system	Leave information	Leave information	–	Time sheet and other analytics data	Personal costs incurred during course of job
Knowledge centre	Required reports, research information	Required reports, Project information	No flow	–	No flow
Accounting system	Past cost data for benchmarking	Past cost data for benchmarking	No flow	Profit and Loss data	–

9.15 Access Rights

Three levels of access rights are needed for the system above

1. Basic user access—One who has entry rights. For example, applying for leaves. Here the access is restricted to the particular employee by login/password system.
2. Power user—This user can validate/approve the data entered. He can also generate reports from applications. For example, approval of leaves.
3. Administrator rights: He is the only one with delete/removal rights.

The rights for the various systems for different users are given on a discretionary basis.

9.16 Implementation Strategy

Any implementation strategy should have the following points kept in mind:

1. It should follow a module-wise implementation, starting from the least troublesome module, say the attendance registry module, to the most annoyance-causing module, like the project status tracker. A module-wise roll out with a gap of say 2–3 weeks between successive modules also get the employee accustomed to the fact that there is something else coming and give them the chance to understand the system better.
2. *Intervention from the administration*: This includes explicit and implicit support from the top management. The management also has to back up the system and ensure that any resistance to the new processes is smoothened out rather than allowing it to fester. Employees must be talked to about the importance of the system and how processes will in turn aid not only the organization but also themselves down the line.
3. *Communication strategy*: The correct communication strategy is essential to ensure that the change management is a success. The company already has a system of weekly team meetings with the various managers where Ashok Singha and the other managers constantly discuss about their experiences so far, the learnings that Ashok has picked up from his travels during the week/the people he has spoken to. Also, client feedback is also stressed. These meetings will continue and will serve as a important bridge between the top management and the team leads. Also, monthly town hall meetings are held to ensure that all the employees are on the right page with respect to the direction of the company.
4. *Freebies to be included*: The management can also toy with the idea of giving away certain freebies with the introduction of certain modules. Small applications

like an internal messenger or a to-do list for the employees will mean that employees see IT as an enhancer rather than a restrictor only, which can only be beneficial to the entire system roll-out.
5. *Training plan*: All employees are somewhat IT savvy, and as such with very uncomplicated application modules coming, the need for extensive training is not necessary, but a training of may be 1 or 2 h per week for a month is needed to familiarize with the critical modules of the applications like the project status tracker.
6. Implementation roadmap

    The implementation would be done in four phases

    - Phase 1 by end of quarter 1: This includes a sizeable portion of the Personal Management System along with Knowledge centre systems.
    - Phase 2 by end of quarter 2: This includes piloting smaller projects in PTS and starting to track tendered projects in ATS at a smaller scale. The Personal Management System is fully implemented along with Knowledge centre systems.
    - Phase 3 by end of quarter 3: The ATS and PTS systems are implemented and the Account system is piloted for smaller projects. The account systems are fully integrated with the Personal Management Systems.
    - Phase 4 by end of quarter 4: All the systems are fully functional and fully integrated by this phase.

7. Critical success factors

    Critical Success Factors are the essential areas of activity that must be performed well if you are to achieve the mission, objectives, or goals for your business or project. As a common point of reference, CSFs help everyone in the team to know exactly what's most important. And, this helps people perform their own work in the right context and so pull together towards the same overall aims.

    A critical success factor is not a key performance indicator (KPI). Critical success factors are elements that are vital for a strategy to be successful. KPIs are measures that quantify management objectives and enable the measurement of strategic performance. A critical success factor is what drives the company forward, it is what makes the company or breaks the company. As staff must ask themselves everyday "Why would customers choose us?" and they will find the answer is the critical success factors.

    There are four basic types of critical success factors. They are:

    1. Industry CSF's resulting from specific industry characteristics.
    2. Strategy CSF's resulting from the chosen competitive strategy of the business.
    3. Environmental CSF's resulting from economic or technological changes.
    4. Temporal CSF's resulting from internal organizational needs and changes.

CTRAN is a company working in Energy Consulting domain. It is a fledgling organization of about 25 people. It works in a domain dominated by government contracts. Hence, the critical success factors for CTRAN would be

Critical success factors for CTRAN		
Critical success factor	Source of CSF	Primary measures and targets
Increase of customer count	Environmental (CTRAN is moving from initiation to growth stage)	95% customer retention rate; 15% new customers per year
High quality deliverable	Industry (quality of work alone decides footprint in consulting domain)	Zero customer complaints
Acceptance of activity tracker by employees	Strategy (improve timeliness of deliverables)	100% Projects logged in activity tracker
Acceptance and use of expense sheet by employees	Strategy (track costs better to improve profitability of projects)	100% expenses accounted for in expense sheets
Raise employee morale and productivity	Temporal (cannot afford attrition as everyone is critical)	Not lose more than 2 person a year for the next 5 years

8. Change management strategy
   (a) Module-wise roll out with the least complicated application being rolled out first and so one would acclimatize the users to the new systems in a more subtle manner.
   (b) The rewards and recognition programme (given below) that incentivizes compliance is another change management strategy.

9.16.1 Rewards and Recognition

As a part of the BASIX group, there are group level recognition schemes that are instituted to reward excellent work throughout the entire group. These rewards, something on the lines of "Chairman's Award", can now be offered to CTRAN employees as well for outstanding contribution to setting up process flow and the implementation of systems. In addition to this, process adherence can also be mentioned as a part of the KRA of the individual, which would mean that it is captured during appraisal time and that the employees are aware that this issue could determine their final pay for the year.

9.17 Risks and Mitigation

The major risks associated with the project are as follows:

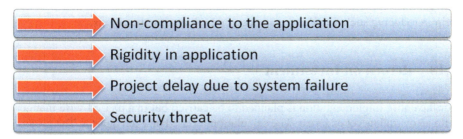

Non-compliance to the application
As the consultants have been working in their self-designed process with which they are comfortable, there is a lot of inertia to change. So there is a significant risk of having non-compliance among the consultants which would result in additional effort to track it back into the system.

Mitigation
The mitigation efforts would constitute the following initiatives

- Weekly monitoring systems: Weekly monitoring of the compliance code levels would help in mitigating the risk involved of data being channelled surpassing the system. The monitoring process would involve mails and reminder to the consultants about not updating the project progress and worksheet.
- Meeting with steering committee: Weekly or bi-weekly meetings with steering committee would help in enthusing the employees about the new systems.

Rigidity in the system
Even though the system should be flexible enough to accommodate some requests of user, there is a scope of having a bottleneck due to the system not allowing the consultants to move further. This would result in delays in the project.

Mitigation: the mitigation plans would incorporate more flexibility in the system, but there is a limit to which this flexibility can be given to the user.

Project delay due to system failure: The projects might get delayed due to system failure due to natural or unnatural causes. In that case the project might get delayed, which can be catastrophic for a small company like CTRAN, as it doesn't have bargaining power.

Mitigation: A parallel server which can serve as a back-up for the other server. They should be working on the same database and code instance which would result in seamless integration.

Security threats: As the company is dealing with lot of confidential data, any impact would result in serious loss of reputation and costs. The network should be well protected from viruses, spamwares, etc.; there needs to be proper security to check this.

Mitigation: Applying anti-virus and anti-spamwares with latest upgrades would help in reducing such a risk and enhance goodwill among the clients.

9.18 Return on Investment

For the entire implementation is planned to be carried out in a phased-wise manner with an overall target of 1 year. The calculation is based on each quarter. The project savings involved were divided into the following heads:

- Benefits
    - Direct labour savings
      One of the important components of direct labour savings are calculated on the pretext that for developing a proposal it takes on an average 3 days for a consultant in CTRAN which is 1.5 days as per industry standards. Taking the average cost per consultant at Rs. 2,000/day, we arrive at a figure of Rs. 4,50,000 savings per quarter.
      Similarly at many instances due to bad quality, there needs to be rework, apart from lowering of reputation. The time for rework is taken as 10 days with an average cost of Rs. 1,20,000 per quarter.
      Further in CTRAN, many project quotes to tendered projects are given based on prior experience of its CEO. But the growth plan it envisages will make constant monitoring by him untenable. So knowledge management of prior such project would immensely save the effort required and hence cause a direct savings of Rs. 60,000 per quarter.
      In all the direct savings, cost per project can be drastically reduced by a sizable amount of Rs. 1,15,000 per quarter.
    - Indirect labour savings
      The indirect labour savings contain many tangible as well as non-tangible aspects. Some of the more important cases where we can foresee a potential saving are in the following fields:
      Training a new joinee: Since CTRAN is a small company, there is no formal training system in place. The new joinee has to consult his senior colleague about the nuances of each sector. This would consume about 2 h of time of the senior consultant in a day, but also make the new joinee ready for industry earlier. Thus, it would be better with the new application installed as the effort required by senior consultant would be negligible and the time before the new joinee starts contributing to the company is increased. But on the whole the average cost reduction is around 5,000 per quarter

Performance and attendance management system: The absence of a Personnel management system makes it difficult for the HR manager as well as the reporting manager to collate data in order to analyse the data. A personnel management system would in that respect reduce the HR manager's effort from 5 to 1 man-day. Similarly, collating the data for attendance and leaves results in an extra effort of 5 days which can be minimized through this implementation.

Other expenses: Further the paper cost reduction and reduction in data storage requirements and data retrieval process result in a net benefit of Rs. 65,000 per quarter.

- Additional revenue
  In many cases like the government projects, it is necessary for the company to bid taking into consideration the past history with the dept. and the cost allocated by the centre or state govt. or the UNDP. This information if known to the consultants would increase the chances of winning the project by 0.15. Similarly, in case of untendered project it will increase the success rate by 0.1 providing additional revenue.

• Cost
The cost incurred in the project can be put under the following overheads.

- Change management cost
  The change management would be necessary to smoothly implement the project. The costs involved would be much higher in the initial phase, gradually decreasing as the level of comfort of the users would increase. The costs involved would consist of team presentations to explain the importance of such an initiative, rewards and recognitions (especially as this is a small company where monetary incentives are more appreciated), and the man-hours involved from the consultant's side.

- Application development cost
  The application on the whole is estimated to cost around Rs. 6,00,000 which has been amortized over the period of 1 year. This is because we can pay the vendors as and when part of the modules is delivered.

- Risk
  The risk associated with this project has been factored in as a cost. The risk has been allocated under four heads. Wherever the cost of its mitigation has been less, we have gone for the mitigation measures, while if the cost is less we factor in the cost.

  Non-compliance to the application: The non-compliance to the application would be a result in extra work to be done to bring the data into the application. The mitigation costs which involve weekly monitoring systems and pressures from upper management would cost less and hence the mitigation plans were taken into account.

Rigidity in application: As the company requires a lot of flexibility, there is a significant chance that the application might seem to be rigid. The mitigation plans would be much more costly as the overall system would not solve the purpose of streamlining the process flow which would result in serious damages in future. So we account for the risk only as we can later incorporate the data into the system for those instances where the rigidity delays the project.

Project delay due to system failure: The project delays to system failure can have a work around with certain manual processing which would save them from cost of damages due to loss of project. But the mitigation plan would involve setting up an additional server which would cost much more.

Security threat: As the company deals with highly confidential data of the client, it would be catastrophic for them if the data leak due to breaching of firewalls, spam wares, and viruses. Anti-viruses and firewalls are cheaper than the potential costs. Hence, we go for the mitigation plans.

Freebies: Freebies like messengers, to-do lists are non-value adding, but they enhance compliance to the system. The number of freebies required is more initially which can be reduced during the later half once the compliance levels are achieved.

From the overall estimation, we believe that the company would end up benefiting by a value of 30.42 lacs. This is a considerable benefit in comparison to the size of the company and is a necessity for the growth plans which the company envisions.

9.19 Conclusion

The system implementation would be of a great benefit for the company with a net benefit of over 30 lacs. The implementation road map would have to be in a controlled and phased-wise to ensure smooth implementation. There has to be a detailed planning regarding the change management process as employees are critical to its growth. The system, however, would have to be upgraded to incorporate changes required as and when the company grows. Critical to the success of its IT strategy is the extent of acceptance of the new process and systems by the employees of the company. Proper communication to address each and every apprehension of employees needs to take place. Only when employees accept the system and whole heartedly use it will IT strategy suggested bear fruits.

9.20 Practice Questions

1. What is Non-Government Organization (NGO)? What are its purposes?
2. What are metrics used by an NGO to measure its success?
3. How can investment in technology help an NGO to achieve its objectives?
4. How do you justify technology investment for an NGO?

References

http://www.ctranconsulting.com/, 2009
http://www.business.com/directory/energy_and_environment/consulting_and_engineeringservices/, 2009
http://www.ctranconsulting.com/, 2009
http://www.business.com/directory/energy_and_environment/consulting_and_engineeringservices/, 2009
http://rapidbi.com/created/criticalsuccessfactors.html, 2009
http://www.e-competitors.com/Strategy/SBUPlanning/SBUPositioning/SBU_Critical.htm, 2009

Index

A
Access management, 132
Agriculture, 19–22
All India Trade Union Congress (AITUC), 3
Amazon, 2, 3, 5, 29, 33
Application strategy, 88–94, 96, 97
Availability management, 128, 147

B
Backup, 102, 104, 107–109, 144, 197, 258, 268
Barrier for competition, 33, 39
BOOT, 141–142, 165
Budget formulation, 45
Business alignment, 56, 76, 78, 95, 111, 120, 150
Business external, 31–37
Business focused, 47
Business function distribution, 66, 67
Business innovation, 64, 65, 67, 69, 70, 248
Business internal, 31–32, 61, 104
Business lifecycle, 25, 40–43, 70
Business purpose, 11–12, 14, 27, 46, 61, 69, 77, 94, 150, 164, 170
Business strategy and drivers, 69–72
Business transformation, 29, 47–48, 62, 69, 83, 88, 152, 209

C
Capability maturity model integration (CMMi), 146–148, 165
Capacity management, 128
Carnegie Mellon University (CMU), 146
Change agent, 42, 47–48

Characteristics, 1, 4, 11, 49, 86, 126, 127, 162, 223, 229, 230–232, 246, 247, 253, 269, 288, 294, 331
Chuck, M., 1, 2
CIO, 8, 12, 14, 15, 25, 31, 35, 42, 44–54, 56, 57, 63–66, 70, 72–74, 77, 79, 85, 94, 97, 100, 107, 110, 115, 116, 120, 122–124, 136, 137, 143–146, 148, 150, 154, 156, 158, 161–165, 170, 172, 176, 213, 217, 249, 250, 256, 290
Citizen centric, 2, 3, 13, 45, 156
Cloud computing, 2, 99, 141, 142
Collaboration plan, 56
Collin, C., 2
Commercial off-the-shelf (COTS), 96, 100
Communication, 3, 4, 09, 10, 16, 85, 86, 97, 105, 108, 153, 155, 179, 181, 195, 211, 213, 215, 217, 230, 250, 264, 276, 290, 330, 336
Compliance, 5, 7, 12, 32, 42, 52, 57, 93, 95, 98, 104, 106, 113, 131, 140, 143, 145, 152, 153, 155, 162, 171, 199, 222, 280, 282, 292, 304, 328, 332, 333, 335, 336
Continual service improvement, 132
Control and governance, 31
Control and scalability, 4
Cost benefit, 5, 27, 28, 128, 137, 156, 159, 160, 218–220
Cost centre, 49, 133, 134, 156
Cost cutting, 27, 32, 33, 62
Cost of production, 2, 5
Culture of performance and value, 63–64
Customer management, 33, 90, 122, 193–195, 202

D

Data architecture, 77, 78, 94–96
Demand management, 126
Drivers, 27, 36, 42, 55, 61, 69, 70, 73, 76–78, 100, 110, 116, 161, 186, 313, 314

E

e-bay, 2
Economic value (EV), 156–161
E-government and IT implementation, 45
Emerging opportunities, 66
Evaluation, 30, 53, 106, 115, 131, 132, 152, 173, 198, 213, 271, 328
Event management, 113, 131, 202
Evolution of IT strategy, 3, 23, 25, 26–31, 71, 72
External stakeholders, 29, 66, 76

F

Financial management, 126, 140, 175, 244, 253, 259, 319
Functional grouping, 84–85
Futuristic needs, 65

G

Geographic Information System (GIS), 2, 19–21
Globalization, 18–19, 117, 176, 302
Governance, 2, 3, 7, 13, 15, 22, 31, 32, 38, 45, 52, 76, 90, 95, 99, 115, 125, 146, 161, 162, 165, 166, 213, 281
Green design, 17
Green disposal, 17
Green IT, 16–18, 23, 155, 308, 309
Green manufacturing, 17
Green use, 17

H

Heeks, R.B., 2, 3
High level and IT relationship, 1, 10, 74
Holistic approach, 9, 15, 31, 34, 62, 69

I

ILO, 3
Incident management, 113, 131
Information asset, 37, 48–51, 93
Information security management, 46, 52, 128, 146, 166, 281, 282
Information technology (IT), 1, 23, 25, 46, 58, 166, 204, 241, 250, 272, 274, 291, 314

alignment with business, 25, 37–40, 150, 165
and business, 15, 30, 44, 58, 64–69, 93, 156, 165, 229, 249
for efficiency, 31
infrastructure, 5, 11–16, 29, 31, 32, 36, 41, 43, 47, 51, 64, 71, 93, 102, 127, 132, 135, 137, 157, 158, 164, 166, 181, 203, 245–246, 256, 265, 278, 280, 291
for management effectiveness, 32
manager, 10, 14–16, 25, 27, 28, 34, 38, 41, 46, 47, 51–52, 78
organization, 17, 38, 43, 48, 53, 65, 87, 127, 128, 130, 134, 135, 137, 138, 144–148, 150, 152, 164, 179, 204, 212–218, 240, 248
for performance, 32
service continuity management, 128
service strategy, 111, 116, 124–149
strategy, 1–23, 25–58, 61–113, 115–120, 122, 123, 137, 138, 143, 144, 146, 148, 150–152, 155, 157, 158, 161, 162, 164, 169–170, 176, 180, 183, 184, 203, 204–217, 229–268, 271–294, 299–336
Infrastructure application, 15, 96–97, 135
Integration and collaboration, 6, 12
Integration strategy, 13, 87–89
INTUC, 3

K

Knowledge asset creator, 50
Knowledge management and learning, 7

L

Lean technique, 83, 84

M

Major components of IT strategy, 10–18
Metrics, 127, 132, 133, 149–155, 157, 159, 160, 163, 184, 223, 285, 286, 289
Mitigation strategy, 154, 155
Mixed approach, 89–94
Mohapatra, S., 2, 19
Multimedia and animation, 6, 103

N

Nasscom, 3
New business model, 1, 3, 19, 22, 28, 29, 33, 74, 83, 169

Index 341

New direction of IT strategy, 31–37
New role of CIO, 44–54

O
Open source, 101, 142–143
Opportunity search, 85–87
Optimization, 2, 32, 92, 107, 144, 151, 152, 154, 173, 198, 199, 240
Optimum services, 10, 32, 118, 180, 198, 199, 201, 322
Organization design, 26, 28, 77, 112, 118–121, 127
Outage, 1
Outsourcing, 15–18, 29, 52, 63, 110, 116, 117, 138–142, 146, 308, 314

P
Pending needs, 65
People enablement, 10, 16, 116, 117, 120–124, 158
People strategy, 111, 115–119, 121, 123, 137, 162, 164
Physical architecture, 108–110, 112
Planning for IT strategy, 54–57
Prepare management team, 55–56
Problem management, 132
Process models, 27, 77, 94, 111, 145–149, 192–204, 251–256, 288
Process re-engineering, 56–57, 92, 158
Process strategy, 78–87, 111
Profit centre, 47, 49, 133–135
Program management, 45

R
Record keeping and analysis, 5
Recovery strategy, 107–108
Regulatory compliance, 7, 144, 155, 200, 222
Release and deployment, 130, 131
Remote sensing, 2, 19–21
Request fulfilment, 131–132
Research and simulation, 6
Return on investment (ROI), 116, 151, 156–161, 175, 184, 218–221, 251, 265–267, 292, 299, 304, 319, 320, 327
Risk management, 83, 95, 116, 128, 151–155, 164, 221, 225, 279
Roles of IT, 4–8, 22

S
SaaS, 141–142
Sales channel, 2, 173
Security and privacy, 45–46
Security strategy, 103–107
Service catalogue Management (SCM), 127
Service design, 125, 127, 133
Service level management (SLM), 127–128
Service measurement, 132–133
Service operation, 125, 131, 147
Service oriented architecture (SOA), 41, 93, 94, 96, 166, 284, 286–288, 322
Service portfolio management (SPM), 126
Service reporting, 133
Service transition, 125, 129
Service validation, 130–131
Shelf stock, 1
Stakeholders, 29, 43, 45, 50, 61, 65, 66, 69, 71–79, 81, 84, 85, 87, 93, 94, 110, 119, 120–122, 124, 131, 133, 150, 153, 158, 159, 163, 164, 169, 170, 175, 212, 223, 230, 246, 271, 274, 276–277, 281, 309, 310, 320, 323
Standards, 14, 28, 31, 37, 45, 48, 51, 68, 69, 73, 74, 88, 91, 97, 100, 101, 107, 120, 125, 127, 136, 139, 141, 145–149, 155, 157, 160, 165, 183, 191, 199, 217, 222, 223, 233, 240, 241, 255–256, 268, 274, 276, 279–282, 286, 289, 302, 307–309, 311, 313, 314, 321, 326, 334
Strategic intent, 8–10, 22, 35, 41
Strategic mindset, 12–15
Strategic planning, 3, 8, 38, 44, 71, 208, 250
Strategy implementation, 49, 115–173, 208, 210–212, 229, 230, 265, 268
Supplier management, 92, 129, 268

T
Technique, 2, 7, 21, 26, 27, 34, 36, 41, 57, 58, 62, 77, 79, 80, 83, 84, 92, 95, 98, 105, 110, 119, 123, 124, 129, 152, 156, 159, 170, 230, 277, 280–282, 319
Technology focus, 88–89
Technology in agriculture, 19–22
Technology platform, 28, 41, 96, 100–103, 171
Technology strategy, 61, 65, 70, 99–111, 272
The Open Group Architecture Framework (TOGAF), 36, 77, 92, 94, 96, 100, 102, 162
Tool, 2, 6, 14, 18, 19, 21, 22, 41, 45, 47, 71, 98, 100, 106, 111, 117, 118, 120, 121, 129, 139, 143, 171–173, 196, 210, 229, 237, 251, 259, 278, 281, 285, 290, 308, 309, 315, 316, 319, 320, 322, 328
Transition planning, 130

V
Virtualization, 14, 41, 99, 101, 102, 264

W
Walmart, 1, 3, 4, 12, 28, 29, 33, 89, 91

Warehouse management system, 4
White, M.A., 2, 18

Y
Y2K, 28, 29, 42, 142